Australasia and Pacific Ombudsman Institutions

International Ombudsman Institute
Editor

Australasia and Pacific Ombudsman Institutions

Mandates, Competences and Good Practice

Written by Michael Frahm, Ludwig Boltzmann Institute of Human Rights

Springer

Editor
International Ombudsman Institute
Vienna, Austria

Written by Michael Frahm, Ludwig Boltzmann Institute of Human Rights, Vienna, Austria

ISBN 978-3-642-33895-3 ISBN 978-3-642-33896-0 (eBook)
DOI 10.1007/978-3-642-33896-0
Springer Heidelberg New York Dordrecht London

Library of Congress Control Number: 2012953095

Printed on acid-free paper

Springer is part of Springer Science+Business Media (www.springer.com)

Preface from the Editor

In 2008, a comprehensive study of European Ombudsman Institutions was published. The editor and main author, Professor Gabriele Kucsko-Stadlmayer, carried out a research project at the University of Vienna from 2005 to 2007, aiming at a comparative legal analysis of parliamentary Ombudsman Institutions in OSCE Europe. The project had been initiated by the present Secretary General of the International Ombudsman Institute (IOI), Dr. Peter Kostelka, then European Regional Vice-President of the IOI. The resulting work has proved to be a valuable resource for scholars and others interested in the development of the modern Ombudsman concept and how it was manifesting itself in the different jurisdictions in Europe.

The Institute determined that it should proceed to develop a full series of such publications to enhance understanding and facilitate dialogue among the Ombudsman community and to share learnings from a comparison of practice.

This volume covers institutions in Australia, New Zealand, Hong Kong, Taiwan and the Pacific. The Ombudsman model was adopted early in this region with New Zealand having the distinction of being the first English speaking country to appoint an Ombudsman in 1962. Other countries in the region quickly followed with only slight variations from place to place in how the legislation was framed.

There is no doubt that the institution of Ombudsman contributes to good governance and the enhancement of trust in government. This volume traverses the emergence and impact of the office throughout the region, its legal foundations, comparative strengths and the diversity of approaches in interpreting the Ombudsman concept. As such it will make a valuable addition to the growing body of publications about the role of the Ombudsman and specifically in relation to the role of the Ombudsman in the six regions of the IOI.

This study is based on the review and analysis of existing literature and relevant legislation. A comprehensive survey was carried out among the Ombudsman Institutions in the selected jurisdictions. This survey builds on the questionnaire developed by Professor Kucsko-Stadlmayer for the volume on the European Ombudsman Institutions and was undertaken with the aim to compare the institutions' activities, resources and competences in order to supply the reader with an overview of the institutions' similarities and special characteristics.

Special thanks are due to the author Michael Frahm and the Ludwig Boltzmann Institute of Human Rights for carrying out the study and the Austrian Ombudsman Board for financing the project. Thanks are also given to the 16 Ombudsman Institutions who participated in the study for their cooperation and everyone else who contributed to the success of this publication. Further acknowledgements go to the IOI General Secretariat, in particular Christine Stockhammer, Ulrike Grieshofer, Ursula Bachler and Victoria Schmid, who were in charge of the overall coordination and organization of the project.

The International Ombudsman Institute regards this publication as an important part of its work in facilitating the understanding of the role of the Ombudsman and the critical part it plays in a jurisdiction's constitutional arrangements.

Dame Beverley Wakem
President of the IOI
Peter Kostelka
Secretary General of the IOI

Table of Codes[1]

Australia[2]	AUS
Australian Capital Territory	AU-ACT
New South Wales	AU-NSW
Northern Territory	AU-NT
Queensland	AU-QLD
South Australia	AU-SA
Tasmania	AU-TAS
Victoria	AU-VIC
Western Australia	AU-WA
Cook Islands	COK
Hong Kong	HKG
New Zealand	NZL
Papua New Guinea	PNG
Samoa	WSM
Taiwan	TWN
Tonga	TON
Vanuatu	VUT

[1] The codes used are based on the ISO 3166 standard "codes for the representation of names of countries and their subdivisions", cf www.iso.org/iso/country_codes/updates_on_iso_3166.htm.

[2] To allow better distinction, when referring to the jurisdiction of the Commonwealth Ombudsman, occasionally AUS-CTH has been used instead of AUS.

Acknowledgements

I would like to thank the IOI General Secretariat, in particular Dr. Peter Kostelka, Secretary General of the IOI and Ombudsman of the Republic of Austria, Ms. Christine Stockhammer and Ms. Ursula Bachler who commissioned and facilitated this study and the contact and exchange with the institutions in the Australasia and Pacific (APOR) region. Particular thanks go to all Institutions in the APOR region which filled in the questionnaire that formed the basis of this work and provided feedback to the draft study. I am also grateful to Prof Dr. Gabriele Kucsko-Stadlmayer from the University of Vienna, who granted permission to base this study's questionnaire on the methodology developed by her in the book *European Ombudsman-Institutions*[3] and to adapt it to the new context.

I would like to express my appreciation to Prof Dr. Hannes Tretter (Scientific Director of the Ludwig Boltzmann Institute of Human Rights (BIM)) who accompanied the genesis of this study from the outset, to Ms. Barbara Liegl (BIM) who always offered me advice and support and provided feedback to the first draft of the publication and to Dr. Margit Ammer (BIM) and Dr. Joachim Stern (University of Vienna) who supported me with valuable comments and advice at an early stage of the publication. Further acknowledgement goes to Mr. Daniel Daroussis (volunteer with the BIM) who undertook the initial research at the project's early stages. Further, I am grateful to Mr. Matthias Schlögl for producing the graphic charts and to Ms. Eva Kuntschner for copyediting.

In addition, I would like to thank Ms. Nadja Gaus (visiting legal clerk with the BIM), Mr. Thomas Siebenbrunner (volunteer with the BIM) and Mr. Elio Dalpra (study assistant with Prof Dr. Tretter) for their assistance and support in editing and proofreading the draft.

Vienna, June 2012

Michael Frahm

[3] Kucsko-Stadlmayer, European Ombudsman-Institutions, 2008, Springer-Verlag Wien.

Contents

Part I Comparative Analysis of the Ombudsman Institutions

1 Introduction 3
1.1 History 3
1.1.1 Origins 3
1.1.2 Spreading of a Concept 4
1.1.3 New Developments 6
1.2 Scope of Research 10
1.2.1 Background and Objectives 10
1.2.2 Geographical Scope 11
1.2.3 Thematic Scope 12
1.2.4 Methodology 17
References 18

2 Legal Framework 21
2.1 Legal Basis 21
2.1.1 International Standards 21
2.1.2 Legal Basis of Ombudsman Institutions 22
2.1.3 Legal Basis for Additional Functions 22
2.2 Legal Status and Independence 23
2.2.1 International Standards 23
2.2.2 Independence and Connection to Parliament 24
2.2.3 Appointment Procedure 25
2.2.4 Monocratic or Collegial Body 26
2.2.5 Qualification Requirements 27
2.2.6 Term of Office 28
2.2.7 Removal and Suspension from Office 29
2.2.8 Incompatibilities 31
2.2.9 Immunity 32

2.2.10 Salary and Allowances 32
2.2.11 Functional Independence and Resources 33
2.3 Organisation 36
References 36

3 Mandate 39
3.1 Object of Control 39
3.1.1 International Standards 39
3.1.2 Public Administration 40
3.1.3 Judiciary 46
3.1.4 Legislator 48
3.2 Standard of Control 49
3.2.1 International Standards 49
3.2.2 General Overview 50
3.2.3 Violation of Law 51
3.2.4 Good Governance 51
3.2.5 Maladministration or Derelict of Duty 53
3.2.6 Human Rights 53
3.3 Access 57
3.3.1 International Standards 57
3.3.2 Accessibility of the Institution 58
3.3.3 Discretion to Accept and Investigate a Complaint 59
3.3.4 *Proprio Motu*-Proceedings 60
3.3.5 Proceedings Following Referrals 62
References 62

4 Powers 65
4.1 Administration 65
4.1.1 International Standards 65
4.1.2 Standard Functions 66
4.1.3 Additional Functions 74
4.1.4 Additional Roles and Functions under other Legislation 79
4.2 Judiciary 83
4.3 Legislator 84
References 85

5 Awareness and Outreach 87
5.1 International Standards 87
5.2 Publications 88
5.3 Training and Outreach Activities 88
5.4 Cooperation with other Institutions and Organisations 89
References 90

6 Good Practice Examples 91
6.1 General Overview 91
6.2 Legal Status and Independence 91
6.2.1 Appointment and Removal Procedure 91
6.2.2 Conflict of Interest 92
6.3 Mandate 92
6.3.1 Review of the Administration 92
6.3.2 Investigation of Human Rights Violations 93
6.3.3 Protection of the Term "Ombudsman" 94
6.3.4 Conciliation and Mediation 95
6.4 Powers 95
6.4.1 Protection against Victimisation 95
6.4.2 Injunction 96
6.4.3 Compensation 96
References 97

Part II Reports on Different Jurisdictions

7 Australia: Commonwealth Ombudsman 101
7.1 General Information 101
7.2 The Ombudsman Institution 103
7.2.1 Overview 104
7.2.2 Mandate 107
7.2.3 Powers 110
7.2.4 Other Characteristics 113
7.2.5 Workload 114
7.2.6 Publications 114
7.2.7 Annotations 115
References 115

8 Australia: Ombudsman New South Wales 117
8.1 General Information 117
8.2 The Ombudsman Institution 118
8.2.1 Overview 118
8.2.2 Mandate 121
8.2.3 Powers 123
8.2.4 Other Characteristics 127
8.2.5 Workload 128
8.2.6 Publications 128
8.2.7 Annotations 129
Reference 129

9 Australia: Northern Territory Ombudsman 131
9.1 General Information 131
9.2 The Ombudsman Institution 132

9.2.1 Overview . . . 132
9.2.2 Mandate . . . 134
9.2.3 Powers . . . 136
9.2.4 Other Characteristics . . . 139
9.2.5 Workload . . . 140
9.2.6 Publications . . . 140
9.2.7 Annotations . . . 141
Reference . . . 141

10 Australia: Queensland Ombudsman . . . 143
10.1 General Information . . . 143
10.2 The Ombudsman Institution . . . 144
10.2.1 Overview . . . 144
10.2.2 Mandate . . . 147
10.2.3 Powers . . . 149
10.2.4 Other Characteristics . . . 151
10.2.5 Workload . . . 152
10.2.6 Publications . . . 152
10.2.7 Annotations . . . 153
Reference . . . 153

11 Australia: South Australian Ombudsman . . . 155
11.1 General Information . . . 155
11.2 The Ombudsman Institution . . . 156
11.2.1 Overview . . . 156
11.2.2 Mandate . . . 158
11.2.3 Powers . . . 160
11.2.4 Other Characteristics . . . 163
11.2.5 Workload . . . 164
11.2.6 Publications . . . 164
11.2.7 Annotations . . . 164
Reference . . . 164

12 Australia: Tasmanian Ombudsman . . . 165
12.1 General Information . . . 165
12.2 The Ombudsman Institution . . . 166
12.2.1 Overview . . . 166
12.2.2 Mandate . . . 169
12.2.3 Powers . . . 170
12.2.4 Other Characteristics . . . 173
12.2.5 Workload . . . 174
12.2.6 Publications . . . 174
12.2.7 Annotations . . . 174
Reference . . . 175

13 Australia: Victorian Ombudsman . . . 177
13.1 General Information . . . 177
13.2 The Ombudsman Institution . . . 178
13.2.1 Overview . . . 178
13.2.2 Mandate . . . 180
13.2.3 Powers . . . 182
13.2.4 Other Characteristics . . . 184
13.2.5 Workload . . . 184
13.2.6 Publications . . . 185
13.2.7 Annotations . . . 185
References . . . 185

14 Australia: Western Australian Ombudsman . . . 187
14.1 General Information . . . 187
14.2 The Ombudsman Institution . . . 188
14.2.1 Overview . . . 188
14.2.2 Mandate . . . 191
14.2.3 Powers . . . 193
14.2.4 Other Characteristics . . . 196
14.2.5 Workload . . . 196
14.2.6 Publications . . . 197
14.2.7 Annotations . . . 197
Reference . . . 197

15 Hong Kong (Special Administrative Region of China): Ombudsman . . . 199
15.1 General Information . . . 199
15.2 The Ombudsman Institution . . . 200
15.2.1 Overview . . . 200
15.2.2 Mandate . . . 203
15.2.3 Powers . . . 205
15.2.4 Other Characteristics . . . 207
15.2.5 Workload . . . 208
15.2.6 Publications . . . 208
15.2.7 Annotations . . . 209
References . . . 209

16 Cook Islands: Ombudsman . . . 211
16.1 General Information . . . 211
16.2 The Ombudsman Institution . . . 212
16.2.1 Overview . . . 212
16.2.2 Mandate . . . 214
16.2.3 Powers . . . 216
16.2.4 Other Characteristics . . . 219

16.2.5 Workload . . . 219
16.2.6 Publications . . . 219
16.2.7 Annotations . . . 219
References . . . 220

17 New Zealand: Ombudsman . . . 221
17.1 General Information . . . 221
17.2 The Ombudsman Institution . . . 222
17.2.1 Overview . . . 222
17.2.2 Mandate . . . 226
17.2.3 Powers . . . 228
17.2.4 Other Characteristics . . . 232
17.2.5 Workload . . . 232
17.2.6 Publications . . . 233
17.2.7 Annotations . . . 233
References . . . 233

18 Papua New Guinea: Ombudsman Commission . . . 235
18.1 General Information . . . 235
18.2 The Ombudsman Institution . . . 236
18.2.1 Overview . . . 236
18.2.2 Mandate . . . 239
18.2.3 Powers . . . 241
18.2.4 Other Characteristics . . . 245
18.2.5 Workload . . . 246
18.2.6 Publications . . . 246
18.2.7 Annotations . . . 247

19 Samoa: Ombudsman . . . 249
19.1 General Information . . . 249
19.2 The Ombudsman Institution . . . 250
19.2.1 Overview . . . 250
19.2.2 Mandate . . . 252
19.2.3 Powers . . . 253
19.2.4 Other Characteristics . . . 255
19.2.5 Workload . . . 255
19.2.6 Publications . . . 256
19.2.7 Annotations . . . 256

20 Taiwan: Control Yuan . . . 257
20.1 General Information . . . 257
20.2 The Ombudsman Institution . . . 258
20.2.1 Overview . . . 258
20.2.2 Mandate . . . 262
20.2.3 Powers . . . 264
20.2.4 Other Characteristics . . . 268

20.2.5 Workload 269
20.2.6 Publications 270
20.2.7 Annotations 270
References 271

21 Tonga: Commissioner for Public Relations 273
21.1 General Information 273
21.2 The Ombudsman Institution 274
21.2.1 Overview 274
21.2.2 Mandate 276
21.2.3 Powers 278
21.2.4 Other Characteristics 280
21.2.5 Workload 280
21.2.6 Publications 280
21.2.7 Annotations 281
Reference 281

22 Vanuatu: Ombudsman 283
22.1 General Information 283
22.2 The Ombudsman Institution 284
22.2.1 Overview 284
22.2.2 Mandate 287
22.2.3 Powers 288
22.2.4 Other Characteristics 291
22.2.5 Workload 292
22.2.6 Publications 293
22.2.7 Annotations 293

***Annex*: Sample Questionnaire** 295

Bibliography 313

Part I
Comparative Analysis of the Ombudsman Institutions

Chapter 1
Introduction

Michael Frahm

1.1 History

1.1.1 Origins

The history of the Ombudsman, or *ombudsman*,[1] as it was originally called and is still called today by the overwhelming number of institutions and scholars, dates back to nineteenth century Sweden.[2] In 1809, the Swedish Parliament made the decision to appoint an Ombudsman to "supervise the King, his offices and courts for the *Riksdag*".[3] Nowadays, the typical Ombudsman has responsibilities which go far beyond these tasks. Much has been written about the history of the Ombudsman in recent years.[4] When looking at different categories of institutions, scholars define up to five different types which will be described in more detail later.[5]

However, the Swedish origin is only the root of the Ombudsman *strictu sensu*. Looking at the key idea behind the establishment of the Ombudsman, which is the delivery of justice to citizens by providing an easily accessible body authorised to supervise the public administration and investigate individual complaints,

[1] In Swedish, the term "Ombud" means "representative", cf Reif (2004b), p. 12 and is also used in English. Black's Law Dictionary dates the first use of the term in English for 1872.

[2] For a discussion of the terminology cf Sect. 1.2.3, p. 12 below. The term "Ombudsperson Institution" as official title is for example used by the Institution in Kosovo which was originally established by the United Nations (UN) Mission in Kosovo under UN Security Council Resolution 1244. Cf http://www.ombudspersonkosovo.org/new/?id=10,0,0,1,e,0.

[3] For more details cf Stern (Sweden) (2008), p. 411.

[4] For an overview on recent publications cf Buck and Thompson (2011), p. 12. For a short history cf also Reif (2004b), p. 4.

[5] Cf Sect. 1.2.3.2, p. 13 below.

M. Frahm (✉)
Ludwig Boltzmann Institute of Human Rights, Vienna, Austria
e-mail: michael.frahm@univie.ac.at

International Ombudsman Institute (ed.), *Australasia and Pacific Ombudsman Institutions*,
DOI 10.1007/978-3-642-33896-0_1, © Springer-Verlag Berlin Heidelberg 2013

references to the Chinese, Islamic, Roman and Spanish systems can also be made.[6] The basic idea that is embraced by today's Ombudsmen is also inherent in these bodies.[7]

There is no one universal definition of an Ombudsman. However, there is widespread understanding that an Ombudsman is an Institution that receives, investigates, and reports on complaints about actions (or lack thereof) by the public administration. While it often is a monocratic body led by one renowned person, there is usually an administrative entity with a number of staff. In practical terms, it are the staff or members of this Institution which, under the guidance of and derived from the authority of the head, fulfil the functions which the Ombudsman is entrusted with by law. At the least, this encompasses the power to receive complaints or act on his or her own motion, the power to investigate alleged maladministration and to recommend remedial actions.[8]

1.1.2 Spreading of a Concept

Despite the fact that the first Ombudsman Institution was established more than 200 years ago, the concept only started to experience a dynamic and global spread 50 years ago.[9] The oldest Institution covered by this publication was established in New Zealand in 1962, making the island the fourth country worldwide and the first Commonwealth country ever to install an Ombudsman. The New Zealand Ombudsmen became a role model for many Institutions in the region. Its establishing law largely follows the Danish model, adapting it to a Commonwealth context. The Danish model differs from the Swedish model in that it does not grant the Ombudsman prosecutorial powers and oversight over the judiciary.[10]

The concept of such an independent body which is accessible to all and has the power to control the public administration of a country is recognised nearly worldwide and has been incorporated into different national legal systems.[11] Today, the International Ombudsman Institute (IOI), a world-wide umbrella organisation, counts 147 public sector member organisations in 87 jurisdictions on all continents.[12]

---

[6] Cf Reif (2004b), p. 4, with further references, Yueh-chin (1995), p. 23 and Owen (1999), p. 52.

[7] Cf Reif (2004b), p.4.

[8] Cf Sect. 2.2, p. 23 for a short overview of the different functions.

[9] Cf Jacoby (1999), p. 15.

[10] The Finnish Institution is closely modelled on the Swedish original, whereas neither the Danish nor the Norwegian model include powers for the oversight over the judiciary and prosecution, cf Reif (2004b), p. 2 for more details.

[11] Cf Reif (2011), p. 270.

[12] Information provided by the General Secretariat of the IOI as of 26 April 2012.

The founders of the Swedish original did not place human rights at the core of the Institution's concern.[13] However, when the concept of the Ombudsman started spreading around the world, gradually, the idea that the Ombudsman Institution should be a watchdog and guardian of citizens' human rights began to take roots. As Keith rightly put it, "good administration is after all an essential human right".[14] The core task of the Ombudsman Institution as supervisor of administrative actions oftentimes has a human rights component due to the fact that maladministration can cause infringement of essential human rights.[15] This idea is reflected both in efforts at the international level to set up international standards as well as in the fact that in those years the first Institutions were explicitly vested with tasks concerning human rights. While those first steps were undertaken in the 1970s, this movement only gained ground with the establishment of new Ombudsman Institutions in Central and Eastern Europe after 1989/1990.[16] The final decade of the last century and the first decade of the new century saw a "human rights revolution",[17] as Koo and Ramirez put it, as during this time Ombudsman Institutions mushroomed worldwide. Many newly established Institutions in the post-communist states in Eastern Europe as well as in Central Asia were vested with an explicit mandate to protect human rights.[18] Reif establishes that in early 2004, about half of the 110 public sector Ombudsmen existing at the time worldwide had a human rights protection mandate.[19]

In 2009, at the ninth IOI World Conference in Stockholm,[20] Hammarberg, at the time the Commissioner for Human Rights of the Council of Europe, stated that the role of Ombudsmen has changed over the last decades and that many "have become active in protecting and promoting human rights". In recent years, some have even been labelled as "Human Rights Defenders".[21] In Hammarberg's opinion, three core principles should be upheld, namely independence, accessibility and effectiveness. At the same event Pillay, the UN High Commissioner for Human Rights, stressed the important role of Ombudsmen even if they are not mandated explicitly with the protection of human rights.[22] She made the nexus between the Ombudsmen's task to address "weak or dysfunctional institutions of governance" and the obligation of states to "alleviate human rights conditions".[23] This nexus clearly exists even in jurisdictions with the classical[24] mandate of an Ombudsman Institution.

---

[13] Cf Koo and Ramirez (2009), p. 1324.

[14] Cf Keith (2005), p.10.

[15] Cf Keith (2005), p. 9 et seq.

[16] Cf Reif (2011), p. 281 et seq. for details on these developments.

[17] Cf Koo and Ramirez (2009), p.1326.

[18] Cf Giddings et al. (2000), p. 443 et seqq. for further details.

[19] Cf Reif (2004b), p. 393.

[20] This conference also celebrated the Bicentennial of the Swedish Ombudsmen.

[21] Hammarberg (2009).

[22] Pillay (2009).

[23] Pillay (2009).

[24] Cf below Sect. 1.2.3.1, p. 12 for details on the definitions used.

1.1.3 New Developments

While the idea of the Ombudsman was spreading, international standards for the Institutions' structure and mandate began to emerge. They can be derived from different legal sources. Hierarchically, international treaties and covenants impose obligations on signatory states on the highest level. While there is no international treaty explicitly addressing the subject of Ombudsman Institutions, one of the most fundamental international human rights covenants, the International Covenant on Civil and Political Rights[25] (ICCPR) in its articles 2(3) and 14 stipulates the principles that guarantee effective, fair and timely access to redress, both judicial and non-judicial.[26] At UN level, other more specific standards[27] have been developed. There are no regional standard setting instruments in the APOR region.[28]

A term often used in the context of Ombudsman Institutions is that of a National Human Rights Institution (NHRI). The idea of NHRIs was first considered by the UN ECOSOC[29] in 1946. After this first consideration little progress has been seen over the decades. In 1978, a seminar organised by the UN Commission on Human Rights[30] resulted in draft guidelines on a proposed structure and function of NHRIs.[31] However, it was only after the fall of the Berlin Wall that in 1991 the "Paris Principles" were drafted. The Paris Principles, endorsed by the UN General

[25] Adopted by UN General Assembly Resolution 2200A (XXI) of 16 December 1966, cf http://www2.ohchr.org/english/law/ccpr.htm.

[26] The ICCPR and the International Covenant on Economic, Social and Cultural Rights (ICESCR) are the most important human rights covenants, signed and ratified by most jurisdictions in the world. They stipulate a comprehensive list of civil and political rights as well as of economic, social and cultural rights. Taiwan and Tonga have not ratified the covenants, however, cf report on Taiwan, Chap. 7, p. 259 for details on the covenants' legal effect in Taiwan. China has ratified the ICESCR and signed (but not yet ratified) the ICCPR. All other jurisdictions examined in this study are bound by the covenants.

[27] None of these standards is based on an enforceable legal instrument, they are all soft law.

[28] In Europe, for example, the Council of Europe and the Organisation for Security and Cooperation in Europe act as standard setters, cf Reif (2004b), p. 125 et seq. for more details.

[29] The United Nations Economic and Social Council established under Chapter X of the Charter of the United Nations.

[30] Replaced in 2006 by the UN Human Rights Council.

[31] The draft guidelines were endorsed by both the UN Commission on Human Rights and later by the UN General Assembly in Resolution 33/46 on national institutions for the promotion and protection of human rights, 1978. Cf Reif (2004b), p. 95 where she describes the "road to the Paris Principles" in detail.

Assembly in 1993,[32] list criteria for NHRIs that are widely accepted as standards.[33] These progressive criteria encourage states to establish NHRIs to strengthen and better implement their international obligations in the field of human rights according to the international treaties they have signed.[34] The Resolution calls for the development of "effective national institutions for the promotion and protection of human rights".[35] The Paris Principles, while not explicitly referring to Ombudsmen, set out standards for bodies with quasi-jurisdictional competence. They stress independence as an essential criterion, with three aspects relevant for Ombudsmen: institutional, functional and personal independence.[36]

The International Coordinating Committee of NHRIs (ICC) is responsible for the accreditation of NHRIs and, to that end, analyses the compliance of applicants with the Paris Principles.[37] Only national Institutions qualify for accreditation, regional Institutions (such as the seven Australian state/territory Ombudsmen) cannot be accredited. In the region examined in this study, the Australian and the New Zealand Human Rights Commissions have been accredited as "status A" NHRIs by the ICC and the New Zealand Human Rights Commission is a member of the ICC Bureau. The Asia Pacific Forum[38] functions as the regional coordination body. As a voluntary accreditation process, non-accreditation by the ICC does not signify non-compliance with the Paris Principles.

The UN General Assembly Resolution 63/169 on the role of the Ombudsman[39] refers to human rights standards, the rule of law and the principles of justice and equality as standards that should be reflected in forming the mandate of Ombudsmen in turn allowing them to adhere to these standards in their work. Part of these standards is the access to justice including effective remedy, access to court, fair trial, redress, judicial protection, due process, legal certainty, undue delay, reasonable time and non-discrimination. The Resolution underlines "the importance of the autonomy and independence of the Ombudsman" and "stresses that these institutions" can have a proactive role by advising "the Government with

---

[32] UN General Assembly Resolution 48/134 on national institutions for the promotion and protection of human rights, 1993.

[33] Cf Fundamental Rights Agency (2010) for more details.

[34] Cf Reif (2011), p. 290.

[35] UN General Assembly Resolution 48/134 on national institutions for the promotion and protection of human rights, 1993, paragraph 2.

[36] Cf Oosting (2002), p. 9 et seqq.

[37] Cf Reif (2011), p. 291. The Geneva-based ICC has been established with the aim to coordinate the emerging NHRI network. It is incorporated as a legal entity under Swiss law, cf www.ohchr.org/en/countries/nhri/pages/nhrimain.aspx.

[38] The Asia Pacific Forum is an association of ICC-accredited NHRIs in the Asia Pacific region, cf www.asiapacificforum.net/ for details.

[39] UN General Assembly Resolution 63/169 on the role of the Ombudsman, mediator and other national human rights institutions in the promotion and protection of human rights, 2008.

respect to bringing national legislation and national practices in line with their international human rights obligations".[40]

The UN General Assembly Resolution 63/172 on national human rights institutions[41] "reaffirms the importance of the development of effective, independent and pluralistic [NHRIs]" in line with the Paris Principles, and also encourages the seeking of "accreditation status through the International Coordinating Committee".[42]

The UN General Assembly Resolution 65/207 on the role of the Ombudsman[43] reiterates the statements made in Resolution 63/169, notes the work of the IOI with satisfaction, encourages states to "consider the [...] strengthening of independent and autonomous Ombudsm[e]n" and encourages Ombudsmen to "operate, as appropriate, in accordance with the [Paris Principles]".[44]

These Resolutions also refer to the role Ombudsmen can play "in promoting good governance in public administrations".[45] "Good governance" can be understood as a transparent, fair, all-inclusive and representative process of decision-making and how these decisions are implemented by the administration. Ombudsman Institutions are important for monitoring the implementation of these decisions.

The major characteristics of good governance are: *equal and representative participation* of men and women as well as of the most vulnerable groups in society; this does not only include the *right to vote* but also encompasses fundamental rights such as *freedom of expression and association*, which are essential in guaranteeing participation. The *rule of law* implies impartial enforcement of democratic legal frameworks, which require an independent judiciary, an impartial police and the full protection of human rights. The *enforcement of decisions* has to be *transparent*, which means it has to follow the existing rules and regulations. Those affected by the enforcement have to be informed well and comprehensively. *Institutions* have to be *responsive to their stakeholders* and *act in a timely manner*. Different social interests have to be balanced to achieve a broad consensus on the best interest of the community as a whole and how it can be achieved. *All groups*, especially those most vulnerable, *have to have a stake*. Institutions, structures and processes have to be *equitable and inclusive*. *Effectiveness and efficiency* imply that

---

[40] UN General Assembly Resolution 63/169 on the role of the Ombudsman, mediator and other human rights institutions in the promotion and protection of human rights, 2008.

[41] UN General Assembly Resolution 63/172 on national institutions for the promotion and protection of human rights, 2008.

[42] UN General Assembly Resolution 63/169 on the role of the Ombudsman, mediator and other national human rights institutions and protection of human rights, 2008.

[43] UN General Assembly Resolution 65/207 on the role of the Ombudsman, mediator and other national human rights institutions in the promotion and protection of human rights, 2010.

[44] UN General Assembly Resolution 65/207 on the role of the Ombudsman, mediator and other human rights institutions in the promotion and protection of human rights, 2010.

[45] Cf UN General Assembly Resolution 65/207, 2010, preamble and UN General Assembly Resolution 63/169, 2008, preamble.

Institutions deliver services which meet the needs of society while making the best use of resources. *Organisations or institutions are accountable* to those affected by its decisions or actions. Authorities should inform the public about their rights, should raise awareness regarding legal issues and remedies and should encourage and empower people to appeal if appropriate. In a jurisdiction where the government is committed to the idea of good governance and furthers it, the *Ombudsman Institution* can be a *valuable tool* for *promoting and improving good governance*, as its key function is to recommend changes in administrative practices and rules following the investigation of maladministration.

The international instruments and standards described lead to a number of principles applied to Ombudsman Institutions. They concern the Institutions in terms of structure, legal basis, statute, financing, general competences, inclusiveness and outreach, ethical standards and appointment procedure. The progressive implementation of these principles is crucial for the Ombudsman Institution's credibility, trustworthiness and responsibility.

In addition, Ombudsman Institutions also help to overcome the limits of traditional court systems: there is an inherent "power imbalance between the government and those it governs".[46] However, the traditional court system cannot fully address this structural problem. Going to a court or a tribunal is a question of affordability and, if several instances are required to achieve redress, the dimension of time is added on top of it. Even the best legal aid system cannot fully abolish these aspects. On the other hand, "the government always has deep pockets" and time is not an issue.[47] Furthermore, the Ombudsman is often more effective than a court in addressing administrative shortcomings because the Ombudsman has the power to point out systemic issues based on the number of complaints received over years, as Chen argues.[48] It is also a very flexible and "cost-effective means".[49] Lastly, an Ombudsman Institution has advantages over a traditional court system as it generally provides for a low-threshold access especially for vulnerable groups of the population and thus helps to "strengthen their capacity to seek a remedy".[50] However, if this *de facto* is the case, much depends on issues such as e.g. the existence of regional offices or other ways of allowing easy access, presence in media vulnerable groups have access to, the ways in which services are promoted, the language used when promoting services or a barrier-free access. These aspects are highlighted below in Sect. 3.3 and Chap. 5.

Wong and Yuen have established a list of criteria that are essential to "evaluat[e] the effectiveness of an" Ombudsman Institution[51]: independence, visibility,

[46] Cf Chen (2010), p. 726.

[47] Cf Chen (2010), p. 728.

[48] Cf Chen (2010), p. 729 and Keith (2005) Development of the role of the Ombudsman with reference to the Pacific. Speech held at the 22nd APOR Conference, p. 6.

[49] Cf Pearce (2000), p. 102.

[50] UNDP (2005), p. 111.

[51] Cf Wong and Yuen (2009), p. 123.

accessibility, jurisdiction, adequate power of investigation, remedial action and impact.[52] For a successful and credible fulfilment of its function, the Ombudsman Institution must be legitimate, independent, transparent, accessible, efficient and responsive. First and foremost, however, the Ombudsman him- or herself must be a highly reputable person due to the fact that the Institution as such possesses very few coercive powers and therefore the persuasive powers of its leader are decisive. The Ombudsman must show credibility, responsiveness and accountability.

1.2 Scope of Research

1.2.1 Background and Objectives

Between January 2011 and April 2012, the Ludwig Boltzmann Institute of Human Rights, a research institute based in Vienna, Austria, implemented the research project "Analysis of the Ombudsman Offices of the APOR region[53] of the IOI", which was commissioned by the International Ombudsman Institute (IOI). The IOI is an independent and impartial international association of Ombudsman Institutions and was established in 1978. It is "the only global organisation for the cooperation and information exchange of Ombudsman Institutions"[54] and currently represents more than 140 institutional members. Members include national, regional and local Institutions.[55]

The purpose of this project was to compile a comparative study on existing Ombudsman Institutions in the Australasia and Pacific region (APOR) of the IOI. It is one of the aims of the IOI to provide its members with well-processed information on the legal basis, the mandates and activities of Ombudsman Institutions from all over the world.[56] This research project — of limited size and extent — was the first step towards achieving this goal. The present report consists of two parts: first, an analysis of the various Institutions, and second, an overview of the data surveyed for each Institution. The project drew upon the methodology employed by Kucsko-Stadlmayer in her book "European Ombudsman-Institutions"[57] and adapted it to a non-European context.[58]

[52] Cf Wong and Yuen (2009), p. 123 for more details and definitions.

[53] Australasia and Pacific Ombudsman Region of the International Ombudsman Institute.

[54] Cf website of the IOI at www.theioi.org/.

[55] Cf website of the IOI at www.theioi.org/.

[56] Cf website of the IOI at www.theioi.org/.

[57] Kucsko-Stadlmayer (2008). In this book, Kucsko-Stadlmayer, Professor of Law at the University of Vienna, compares 88 Ombudsperson Institutions from 46 European countries, including the European Union (European Ombudsman).

[58] Cf Sect. 1.2.4, p. 17.

The project was implemented in three phases: first, based on an initial survey of data on the jurisdictions and Institutions concerned, a comprehensive, largely prepopulated questionnaire was submitted to each Ombudsman Institution in the region via the IOI General Secretariat. The second phase included several follow-up contacts with the Institutions to verify certain aspects of information received. The third phase consisted of the drafting of the report based on the data collected, the respective legal frameworks and the literature reviewed.

The study includes the description, analysis and comparison of different aspects of the Ombudsman Institutions examined, divided into the five following chapters: Legal Framework (Chap. 2), Mandate (Chap. 3), Powers (Chap. 4), Awareness and Outreach (Chap. 5) and Good Practice Examples (Chap. 6). These descriptions are followed by 16 reports on the different jurisdictions examined describing each Institution in more detail (Chap. 7). The last chapter depicts the legal bases and legal status of the various Ombudsman Institutions, their integration into the political system, questions of accountability, reporting obligations and rights, guarantees of independence and pluralism, the mandate in formal, procedural and substantive respect, including the right to initiate judicial review of legal provisions (e.g. before a Supreme Court), and the procedures, legal quality as well as impact of their decisions. The study will also look at cooperations with and links to other similar organisations within the respective jurisdiction, at accessibility for individuals and various, particularly vulnerable and disadvantaged social groups and at outreach activities and awareness raising. The study will also mention whether an Institution has been commissioned with the function of a National Preventive Mechanism according to the Optional Protocol to the Convention against Torture and other Cruel, Inhuman or Degrading Treatment or Punishment (OPCAT).[59]

Following the above-mentioned remarks on the historical development of the idea of the Ombudsman and the development of international standards which have influenced the Ombudsman Institutions in the last 50 years, the study looks at which implications international standards may have for Ombudsman Institutions with respect to the subject matter discussed in each of the sections. These standards are used to describe the state of the art and the variations among the various Institutions examined in this study.

1.2.2 Geographical Scope

Against the background of the IOI's aim to provide its member organisations with well-processed information on the legal foundations, functions and mandates of Institutions from all over the world, the IOI has commissioned this study. It has a regional focus on IOI member organisations in Australasia and the Pacific as one of

[59] Adopted on 18 December 2002 by UN General Assembly Resolution 57/199.

the six regions of the IOI (the others being Africa, Asia, Caribbean & Latin America, Europe and North America).[60] The regional focus was chosen to allow for an easy comparison of Institutions in one specific region that shares a common history and, for reasons of proximity, cooperates in many fields. This focus also allows the identification of regional trends, developments and best practices. The IOI has 17 member organisations in the geographical region selected,[61] 16 of which are covered in this study.[62] Due to the political situation in Fiji at the time of research, it was decided not to include the Fiji Ombudsman Institution.[63] The Institutions covered encompass national as well as regional organisations, all of which were objects of the study.

1.2.3 Thematic Scope

For a clarification of the thematic scope of this study, it is necessary to define the term Ombudsman and its use in this publication.

The type of bodies examined in this study is determined by the purposes pursued by the sponsor of the study.[64] The study thematically limits itself to an analysis of the work of the 16 IOI-members in the geographic region defined, which are all public-sector Ombudsmen. However, it is necessary to differentiate these 16 members from other bodies bearing the same name, yet with different functions.

1.2.3.1 Definitions

The term "Ombudsman" was first defined by the International Bar Association[65] in 1974:

---

[60] Europe has been covered by Kucsko-Stadlmayer (2008), the Caribbean has been examined by Ayeni et al. (2000).

[61] Australia (eight Ombudsperson Institutions), China/Hong Kong, Cook Islands, Fiji, New Zealand, Papua New Guinea, Samoa, Taiwan, Tonga and Vanuatu.

[62] In addition, there are Ombudsperson Institutions in the following countries in the region which are not IOI members: Kiribati, Marshall Islands, Micronesia, Nauru, Palau, Solomon Islands and Tuvalu. The Solomon Islands' Ombudsperson is connected to the region's IOI members via the Pacific Ombudsman Alliance, a regional organisation of Ombudsmen, cf www.pacificombudsman.org/.

[63] Cf www.bbc.co.uk/news/world-asia-pacific-14919067. According to Human Rights Watch, the present Ombudsperson was criticised for defending the 2006 coup d'état in her function as Chair of the Fiji Human Rights Commission. Some claim that she has been appointed as Ombudsperson in violation of the law, cf www.hrw.org/node/88450 for details.

[64] Cf Sect. 1.2.1, p. 10.

[65] Cf Reif (2004b) p. 3 and Kucsko-Stadlmayer (2008), p. 4. The IBA is an international association of lawyers and lawyers' associations, based in London and established in 1947.

"An office provided by the constitution or by action of the legislature or Parliament and headed by an independent high level public official who is responsible to the legislature or Parliament, who receives complaints from aggrieved persons against government agencies, officials and employers or who acts on his [sic] own motion, and has power to investigate, recommend corrective actions and issue reports."[66]

Pillay[67] defined the concept of the Ombudsman as follows:

"A public body entrusted with the task of supervising the conduct of public administration in order to ensure its fairness and accountability."[68]

Ayeni summarised what characterises an Ombudsman today:

"An independent and non-partisan officer (or committee of officers) often provided for in the Constitution, who supervises the administration. Traditionally, he/she deals with complaints from the public on administrative injustice and maladministration, but also increasingly with human rights and corruption-related matters. He/she has the power to investigate, report upon, and make recommendations about individual cases, administrative procedures and relevant system-wide changes. The [O]mbudsman, as an individual, is a person of prestige and influence who operates with objectivity, competence, efficiency and fairness. He/she is readily accessible to the public and does not ideally charge for the use of the service. He/she uses fast, inexpensive and informal procedures. In other words, the ombudsman is not a judge or tribunal, and has no power to make orders or to reverse administrative action. He/she seeks solutions to problems by processes of investigation and conciliation. The ombudsman's authority and influence derive from the fact that he/she is appointed by and reports to one of the principal organs of state, usually either Parliament or the chief executive. Generally, he/she can also publicize administrative actions."[69]

1.2.3.2 Categorisation

Ayeni differentiates four different types of Ombudsmen based on their mandate and competencies[70]: firstly, the classical Ombudsman is based on the Danish and New Zealand adaptations of the Swedish original. Also called "the traditional Ombudsman", this office has general jurisdiction over the administration but not over the judiciary. It may investigate maladministration following individual complaints, upon referral or on its own motion. Secondly, the "hybrid Ombudsman", while continuing to have a focus on the tasks inherent to the classical Ombudsman, has a broader focus that includes various human rights and anti-corruption activities. With regard to these two types, Ayeni however argues that this categorisation has become obsolete, as in practice these roles are merging increasingly. Thirdly, the agency-based Ombudsman, also called "in-house Ombudsman", addresses grievances within one institution. Fourthly, the single-purpose Ombudsman, also

[66] Cited in Caiden (1983), p. 44.

[67] Pillay N, a South-African jurist and the United Nations High Commissioner for Human Rights.

[68] Cf Pillay (2009), p. 2.

[69] Cf Ayeni (2009), p.4.

[70] Cf Ayeni (2009), p. 6.

called "speciality Ombudsman", addresses issues arising in one (or more than one, but typically similar) functional area that are usually brought up by clients using services in this area.[71]

Reif proposes a classification system which differentiates between the classical Ombudsman and the hybrid Ombudsman based on their different scope of mandate.[72] The classical Ombudsman is "appointed by but separate from the legislature"[73] and may supervise the "general administrative conduct of the executive"[74] based on complaints from the public, on own motion or upon referral. The hybrid Ombudsman, however, is vested with additional competencies in the field of human rights and/or other relevant functional areas such as anti-corruption or leadership code enforcement.[75] The hybrid human rights Ombudsman has a double role: on the one hand that of the classical Ombudsman and, on the other hand, that of a Human Rights Commission.[76]

Reif also differentiates further by categorising the following "variations" of the Ombudsman[77]: she identifies a "public sector legislative Ombudsman" and a "public sector executive Ombudsman". The former is appointed by the legislator and reports to it, the latter is appointed by the executive and reports either to the legislative or to the executive branch. Further, she also defines a "public sector hybrid Ombudsman" with competencies in the field of human rights, anti-corruption, leadership code enforcement etc. (established by and reporting to either the legislative or the executive branch) and a "public sector legislative or executive ombudsman" with "limited subject matter jurisdiction", also referred to as "single-sector, single purpose or speciality" Ombudsman.[78]

Kucsko-Stadlmayer proposes a slightly different classification system based on the powers they are endowed with, and differentiates three models: firstly, the "Basic Model" or "Classical Model" reflecting the classical Ombudsman described above; secondly the "Rule of Law Model", which deviates from the Classical Model in that the Ombudsman "is provided with additional measures of control exceeding his [*sic*] soft legal powers",[79] and thirdly, the "Human Rights Model".[80] The Institutions which Kucsko-Stadlmayer classifies as belonging to the Rule of

[71] Cf Ayeni (2009) Ombudsmen as Human Rights Institutions: The New Face of a Global Expansion. Speech held at the 9th IOI World Conference in Stockholm, p. 6.

[72] Cf Reif (2004b), p. 2 and pp. 7–11.

[73] Cf Reif (2004b), p. 2.

[74] Cf Reif (2004b), p. 2.

[75] Cf Reif (2004b), p. 8 et seq.

[76] Cf Reif (2011), p. 273 et seq. for more details on Human Rights Commissions and Ombudsmen.

[77] Cf Reif (2004b), p. 26.

[78] Cf Reif (2004b), p. 26 et seqq. Reif overall differentiates ten variations, which also include hybrid public–private Ombudsmen, industrial Ombudsmen and Ombudsmen established within or by international organisations or at a supranational level.

[79] Cf Kucsko-Stadlmayer (2008), p. 62.

[80] Cf Kucsko-Stadlmayer (2008), p. 64.

Law Model for example have the power to contest laws or regulations before constitutional courts, appeal to civil courts or administrative tribunals "without restriction to human rights" or apply "for the suspension of execution".[81] Those Institutions classified as belonging to the Human Rights Model have specific powers for "the observance of human rights and fundamental freedoms".[82]

As described above, the main function of an Ombudsman Institution traditionally is to receive, investigate and redress complaints of citizens related to maladministration of government agencies. Today, however, many Institutions have developed far beyond this classical function. Nevertheless, looking at the Ombudsman's original function remains important for two reasons: first, from a citizen's perspective, one could argue that this is what most directly concerns individuals. While all other functions also relate to and ensure the rights of individuals in different thematic fields (e.g. privacy rights or whistle-blower protection), the classical complaint function could be of relevance in any aspect of any person's interaction with the public administration. Second, from a human rights perspective, the classical function is of relevance when determining the international standards applicable to Ombudsman Institutions which can be seen as the minimum standards applicable to any Institution, irrespective of its concrete arrangement. In other words, whenever referring to Ombudsmen in the public discourse (without any further delineation in terms), it should be clear, what the minimum international standards are. Last but not least, the classical function is the most fundamental of all and essential in enabling other functions.

For the purpose of this study, the differentiation between the classical Ombudsman and the other "variations", as Reif put it, is essential since for the classical Ombudsman as a quasi-judicial Institution, human rights standards, including access to justice, are important. This type may not meet all requirements of the Paris Principles. However, the idea behind the Paris Principles is also that jurisdictions that reform an existing Institution, particularly if aiming at formal accreditation as an NHRI, have the Principles in mind and aim at progressing towards them. This type of Ombudsman can be found in its pure form only in Tonga. The variations of the Ombudsman that exist in the region studied include, *inter alia* Institutions with the classical mandate and a (partial) human rights mandate (ACT, New Zealand, Papua New Guinea, Taiwan and Victoria), an anti-corruption mandate (Papua New Guinea, Taiwan and Vanuatu), competences in the field of Freedom of Information, competences in the field of protection of whistle-blowers, and oversight and audit functions (see Fig. 3.2 for a comprehensive overview).[83] In these cases, the relevant human rights standards include access to justice and may include additional international standards. Despite small differences in regard to their functions and mandates, all Ombudsman Institutions

[81] Cf Kucsko-Stadlmayer (2008), p. 63 for a table of all powers described.

[82] Cf Kucsko-Stadlmayer (2008), p. 64.

[83] Cf Sect. 4.1.3, p. 74 and Sect. 4.1.4, p. 79 for more details on the different powers.

fulfil an important role in addressing grievances and helping the justice seeker to achieve appropriate redress.

Further down the study describes in detail the Ombudsmen's powers of the classical mandate (Sect. 4.1.2) and their different powers under the "variations" of the classical mandate (Sects. 4.1.3 and 4.1.4).

1.2.3.3 Terminology

Historically, the term "Ombudsman" has been the chosen name of many Institutions all over the world that have had the power to investigate and report on private persons' complaints about the public administration. However, while many states have adopted the Swedish word, others opted for a term that better describes what the Ombudsman does in the official language of their states; thus there are many more names used today.[84] Especially if the Ombudsman has a human rights mandate, also other terms are utilised.[85]

While some Institutions in the region label their bodies incorporating these powers differently and refer to them as the Parliamentary Commissioner (i.e. in Western Australia, but used in conjunction with the name "Ombudsman"), the Ombudsman Commission (in Papua New Guinea), a choice which highlights the collegial body type, or the Commissioner for Public Relations (in Tonga)[86] — the term "Ombudsman" is used for all other Institutions.

The term "Ombudsman" bears the connotation of a male office holder. This is true for the Swedish origin — where "man" means both "man" and "husband" — as well as for the similar English term. However, there are also more and more female office holders, deputies and assistants. Nevertheless, there seems to be some reluctance to deviate from the old and by now well-known specification. However, except for the fact that the term "Ombudsman" is a well-established brand, there are no reasons for not introducing a name that meets the requirements of gender-neutral language. In the meantime, some Institutions are simply called "Ombud(s)", thus avoiding any attribution to a specific gender.[87] In other cases, the more neutral term "Ombudsperson" is used, or the legislator, decides to change the official term

[84] Cf Reif (2004b), p.12 with an exemplary list of names in use. Cf e.g. Kucsko-Stadlmayer (2008), p. 6 for usage in Europe.

[85] Cf Reif (2004b), p. 12.

[86] However, this name is since long considered misleading and there is a proposal to rename the office to "Ombudsman of Tonga", cf in detail the report on Tonga, Sect. 2.1.2.2, p. 276.

[87] This is the way chosen *inter alia* by the Massachusetts Institute of Technology (MIT)/United States (US) (http://web.mit.edu/ombud/) and by the Stanford University/US (http://www.stanford.edu/dept/ombuds/). The term "Ombud" can also in the Swedish origin be used as a stand-alone term. Cf Sect. 1.1.1.

denoting the office from "Ombudsman" to "Ombudsperson" (e.g. in British Columbia).[88]

For the purpose of this study, it was decided to nevertheless use the term "Ombudsman" (respectively "Ombudsman Institution") in line with the title of the organisation that commissioned this publication—the International Ombudsman Institute — whenever referring to the office holder or the legal entity as such in general. The official (English) title of the Institution is utilised whenever a specific office holder or Institution in the jurisdictions examined is referred to. The latter is predominantly the case in Chaps. 6–22.

1.2.4 Methodology

Methodically, this study is based on the review of existing literature, relevant legislation and a comprehensive survey among the Ombudsman Institutions examined. The focus is on supplying the reader with an overview of the Institutions examined, their similarities and special characteristics. The review of literature and legislation covers the legal bases, mandates and activities of the various Ombudsman Institutions as well as their integration into the respective political systems. The desk research proved rather challenging in relation to smaller Island states in the Pacific, as there is little literature available and the legal foundation legislation as well as the Annual Reports are not always available online.

To get a comprehensive overview, a survey among the Ombudsman Institutions in the selected jurisdictions was undertaken. It mainly covered the Institutions' activities, resources and competences. To this end, the questionnaire developed by Kucsko-Stadlmayer for her book on "European Ombudsman-Institutions"[89] was adapted to the present context with her permission and formed the basis for the survey conducted. The IOI Regional Vice-President has been involved in adapting the questionnaire to the regional conditions and specificities. The adapted questionnaire then was pre-populated by the researchers, based both on information available on the Institutions' websites as well as on the study of the establishing legislations. The study profited from the continuous support of the IOI General Secretariat and the Regional Vice-President, who facilitated the submission of the pre-populated questionnaires and motivated the Ombudsman Institutions to revise and respond to them. Not all questions could be answered from the distance, therefore the study relied heavily on the revision and return of the questionnaires,

[88] Ombudsmen exist at the Yale University/US (http://medicine.yale.edu/ombuds/index.aspx) and the University of Bern/Switzerland (www.ombudsperson.unibe.ch/). In British Columbia/ Canada, the name of the office of the public sector Ombudsman was changed from Ombudsman to Ombudsperson by law in 2009, cf www.ombudsman.bc.ca/. In 2009, also the UN established an Office of the Ombudsperson by Security Council Resolution 1904 (to deal with requests to be removed from the UN Al-Qaida Sanctions List).

[89] Kucsko-Stadlmayer (2008).

which showed a varying degree of comprehensiveness. This survey data, enhanced with other information available, and the review of literature then formed the basis for the systematic analysis and comparison of the Ombudsman Institutions in the region.

There are certain limitations to the subject matter of the study. As the study compares jurisdictions of very different sizes both in terms of territory and of population and because the size of a country and the number of people living there require individual answers and adequate structures to face varying challenges, it would be overly simplifying to treat all Ombudsman Institutions covered in this study alike and apply one set of standards to all Institutions, disregarding their heterogeneity. The Institutions examined range from a classical Ombudsman Institution (e.g. Cook Islands, Samoa, Tonga and Vanuatu) over an Institution that constitutes one of five (instead of the traditional three) powers (i.e. Taiwan) to an Institution with far-reaching powers in the field of whistle-blowing or telecommunication surveillance (e.g. Australia and New Zealand). A thorough analysis therefore necessitates an approach which looks through "different lenses", depending on both the function and the mandate of the respective Institution.

References

Ayeni (2009) Ombudsmen as Human Rights Institutions: the new face of a global expansion. In: Speech held at the 9th IOI World Conference in Stockholm, p 4

Ayeni V, Hayden T, Reif LC (2000) Strengthening Ombudsman and Human Rights Institutions in Commonwealth Small and Island States. Commonwealth Secretariat, London

Buck T, Kirkham R, Thompson B (2011) The Ombudsman enterprise and administrative justice. Ashgate, Farnham

Caiden GE (ed) (1983) International handbook of the Ombudsman. Evolution and present function. Greenwood, Westport

Chen M (2010) New Zealand's Ombudsmen legislation: the need for amendments after almost 50 years. Victoria Univ Wellington Law Rev 41:723–760

Fundamental Rights Agency (2010) National Human Rights Institutions in the EU Member States. Strengthening the fundamental rights architecture in the EU. European Union, Luxembourg

Giddings P, Sladecek V, Bueso LA (2000) The Ombudsman and human rights. In: Gregory R, Giddings P (eds) Righting wrongs. The Ombudsman in six continents. IOS, Berlin, pp 441–457

Gregory R, Giddings P (eds) (2000) Righting wrongs. The Ombudsman in six continents. IOS, Berlin

Hammarberg T (2009) Ombudsmen need independence to speak out for human rights. In: Speech held at the 9th IOI world conference in Stockholm

Jacoby D (1999) The future of the Ombudsman. In: Reif LC (ed) The International Ombudsman Anthology. Selected writings from the International Ombudsman Institute. Kluwer Law International, Dordrecht

Keith KJ (2005) Development of the role of the Ombudsman with reference to the Pacific. In: Speech held at the 22nd APOR conference, p 2

Koo JW, Ramirez FO (2009) National Incorporation of Global Human Rights: Worldwide Expansion of National Human Rights Institutions, 1966–2004. Soc Forces 87:1321–1354

Kucsko-Stadlmayer G (ed) (2008) European Ombudsman-Institutions. Springer, Vienna

Oosting M (2002) Protecting the Integrity and Independence of the Ombudsman Institution: the global perspective. In: Reif LC (ed) The international Ombudsman yearbook, vol 5. Martinus Nijhoff, Leiden
Owen S (1999) The Ombudsman: essential elements and common challenges. In: Reif LC (ed) The international Ombudsman anthology: selected writings from the International Ombudsman Institute. Kluwer Law International, Dordrecht
Pearce D (2000) Ombudsman in Australia. In: Gregory R, Giddings P (eds) Righting wrongs. The Ombudsman in six continents. IOS, Berlin
Pillay N (2009) Current challenges to the protection and promotion of human rights. In: Speech held at the 9th IOI world conference in Stockholm
Reif LC (2004) The Ombudsman, good governance, and the International Human Rights System. Martinus Nijhoff, Leiden
Reif LC (2011) Transplantation and adaptation: the evolution of the human rights Ombudsman. Boston Coll Third World Law J 31(2):269–310
Stern J (2008) Sweden. In: Kucsko-Stadlmayer G (ed) European Ombudsman-Institutions. Springer, Vienna
UNDP (2005) Programming for justice: access for all a practitioner's guide to a human rights-based approach to access to justice. United Nations, Bangkok
Wong W, Yuen R (2009) The Ombudsman in Hong Kong: role and challenges under the transformation of governance in the post-1997 era. Asia Pac Law Rev 17(1):115–133
Yueh-chin H (1995) Role and responsibility of the control Yuan. In: Reif LC (ed) The Ombudsman concept. International Ombudsman Institute, Edmonton

Chapter 2
Legal Framework

Michael Frahm

2.1 Legal Basis

2.1.1 International Standards

The Paris Principles stipulate that an Institution should be given "as broad a mandate as possible, which shall be clearly set forth in a constitutional or legislative text, specifying its composition and its sphere of competence."[1] UN General Assembly Resolution 63/169 and UN General Assembly Resolution 65/207 both "underline the importance of the autonomy and independence of the Ombudsman" and encourage states to "consider the [...] strengthening of independent and autonomous Ombudsman"[2] Institutions, and UN General Assembly Resolution 65/207 recognises the "right of each state to choose the framework for [...] the Ombudsman which is best suited to its particular needs at the national level, in order to promote human rights in accordance with international human rights instruments."[3] There are no regional standard setting instruments in the APOR region.[4]

[1] Paris Principles, paragraph 2. The Paris Principles have been adopted by UN General Assembly Resolution 48/134, 1993 on national institutions for the promotion and protection of human rights to which they were annexed.

[2] UN General Assembly Resolution 63/169, 2008, preamble and paragraph 1 and UN General Assembly Resolution 65/207, 2010, preamble and paragraph 2.

[3] UN General Assembly Resolution 65/207, 2010, on the role of the Ombudsman, mediator and other national human rights institutions in the promotion and protection of human rights, paragraph 3.

[4] Cf Reif (2004), p. 215.

M. Frahm (✉)
Ludwig Boltzmann Institute of Human Rights, Vienna, Austria
e-mail: michael.frahm@univie.ac.at

International Ombudsman Institute (ed.), *Australasia and Pacific Ombudsman Institutions*, DOI 10.1007/978-3-642-33896-0_2, © Springer-Verlag Berlin Heidelberg 2013

2.1.2 *Legal Basis of Ombudsman Institutions*

Ideally, an Ombudsman Institution is enshrined in a jurisdiction's constitution. The reason for this is the fact that the threshold for the modification of constitutional provisions is always higher than for alterations or abrogation of an ordinary law. Such embedment thus guarantees a maximum of protection against any risk of modifications of the Institution's embodiment and therefore strengthens the Ombudsman's independence.[5] Where jurisdictions foresee organic laws,[6] the embedding of the Ombudsman Institution in such laws is an alternative which guarantees a maximum of stability for the Institution.

In the region examined, four Institutions are embedded either in constitutions (Victoria, Papua New Guinea, Vanuatu) or in organic laws respectively (Taiwan). In addition to the principal provisions in the constitution, there usually are additional ordinary laws which stipulate the functions and competences of the Institution in more detail. In case of Papua New Guinea, in addition to the embedding in the constitution, the implementing legislation itself has the status of an organic law. In all other cases the Institutions are enacted by ordinary laws.

2.1.3 *Legal Basis for Additional Functions*

The establishing law forms the legal basis of the Institution and also provides for the general framework which defines *inter alia* the Ombudsman's purpose, functions and powers. Over the years, the Ombudsman Institution appears to have proved its efficiency in addressing deficiencies in bureaucratic systems in the various jurisdictions and has developed a reputation as "peacemaker". In many cases (e.g. in all Australian jurisdictions and in New Zealand), the legislator has decided to expand the powers over the years and has endowed the Ombudsman with additional functions.[7] Partly, additional tasks were included in the legal basis (in case of ordinary laws); partly, new functions were assigned by way of additional laws which explicitly referred to the Ombudsman.[8] Furthermore, there are laws regulating a specific subject matter (e.g. anti-terrorism legislation) that task the Ombudsman with an oversight function related to specific aspects of that law such as privacy.

---

[5] Cf Buck et al. (2011), p. 27 and p. 155 et seq.

[6] Organic laws are a system of laws that define and establish a government; they are also called fundamental law. Usually, in connection with their higher status they again hold a higher threshold for modifications. Organic Laws cannot normally be abrogated by a simple Parliamentary majority. Cf Black's Law Dictionary.

[7] This approach, however, also leads to the risk that an Institution is overburdened with too many complaints and thus is not efficient anymore.

[8] Cf Creyke (2007), p. 707.

The Ombudsman Institutions examined in this study are endowed with many different functions. For a comprehensive picture, please refer to the more detailed descriptions in the reports on the different jurisdictions in Chaps. 7–22. At this point, only the main features will be highlighted. Many jurisdictions endow the Ombudsman with a function in the field of Freedom of Information (e.g. the Australian Commonwealth,[9] South Australia, Tasmania, Victoria, the Cook Islands, Hong Kong and New Zealand). Quite often, the Ombudsman is also given a role in the field of Public Interest Disclosures respectively Protection of Whistle-blowers (e.g. in New South Wales, South Australia, Tasmania, Victoria, Western Australia and New Zealand). In Australia, five Ombudsmen are entrusted with various aspects of auditing the implementation of Telecommunications Interception Legislation (the Australian Commonwealth, New South Wales, the Northern Territory, Tasmania and Western Australia). Far-reaching competences in the field of anti-corruption activities are given to three Institutions (Papua New Guinea and Vanuatu, based on the Leadership Code, and Taiwan based on the Sunshine Laws). Lastly, the New Zealand Institution has been designated as a National Preventive Mechanism (NPM), fulfilling the country's obligation under the UN Convention Against Torture (CAT).

2.2 Legal Status and Independence

2.2.1 International Standards

The Paris Principles stipulate that "the composition [. . .] and the appointment of [. . .] members [of NHRIs . . .] shall be established" ensuring "the pluralist representation of the social forces (of civilian society) involved in the promotion and protection of human rights".[10] Further, the office should have "infrastructure which is suited to the smooth conduct of its activities, in particular adequate funding."[11] The purpose of this is that the office should be "independent of the Government and not [. . .] subject to financial control which might affect its independence".[12]

To ensure a stable mandate, the "appointment shall be effected by an official act which shall establish the specific duration of the mandate. This mandate may be renewable, provided that the pluralism of the institution's membership is ensured."[13] UN General Assembly Resolution 63/169 and UN General Assembly Resolution 65/207 both "underline the importance of the autonomy and

---

[9] Cf McLeod (2001), p. 361 et seqq. for more details on the work of the Commonwealth Ombudsman on Freedom of Information matters. Cf also Paterson (2004), p. 13 et seq.

[10] Paris Principles, "Composition and guarantees of independence and pluralism", paragraph 2.

[11] Paris Principles, "Composition and guarantees of independence and pluralism", paragraph 2.

[12] Paris Principles, "Composition and guarantees of independence and pluralism", paragraph 2.

[13] Paris Principles, "Composition and guarantees of independence and pluralism", paragraph 3.

independence of the Ombudsman" and encourage states to "consider the [. . .] strengthening of independent and autonomous Ombudsman"[14] Institutions. Aspects to be assessed are thus the connection to Parliament, the way by which office holders are appointed, and the details of their appointment including qualification requirements, term of office, removal from office, incompatibilities and the avoidance of conflicts of interest, immunity, salary and allowances and the resources with which the office is equipped.

2.2.2 Independence and Connection to Parliament

To be able to fulfil the tasks it has been entrusted with, the Ombudsman Institution needs to be independent, especially from the executive power.[15] Otherwise there is always the risk of the executive not being able to resist intervening or exerting influence in case of an unwelcome investigation. Even if this never occurred in practice, the very possibility would undermine the Institution's credibility. Yet independence means much more than being placed outside the three powers (executive, legislative and judiciary).[16] The requirement for independence covers the appointment procedure of the Ombudsman and respective deputies as well as the financial independence, budget allocation and budgetary autonomy of the Institution. These further aspects are discussed in more detail in the following sub-sections (see also Fig. 2.5).

None of the Institutions examined in this study are bound by any order of any administrative body. None of the Institutions covered except for South Australia are affiliated to any other administrative entity. In case of South Australia the Ombudsman Institution is part of the portfolio of the Attorney-General for reasons of practicality. This inclusion is only relevant as far as internal administrative purposes are concerned and when it comes to presenting the budget in Parliament. A special case is the Control Yuan in Taiwan. As it is one of the five powers existing in this unique model of government, the Institution as such is on equal footing with the executive arm of government.

Connection to Parliament is seen as a valuable aspect in ensuring independence of the executive. In many cases, the close relation derives from the fact that the Ombudsman is considered an Officer of Parliament (in the Northern Territory, Queensland, Victoria, Western Australia, the Cook Islands, New Zealand and

[14] UN General Assembly Resolution 63/169, 2008, on the role of the Ombudsman, mediator and other national human rights institutions and protection of human rights, preamble and paragraph 1; UN General Assembly Resolution 65/207, 2010, on the role of the Ombudsman, mediator and other national human rights institutions in the promotion and protection of human rights, preamble and paragraph 2.

[15] Cf Buck et al. (2011), p. 156.

[16] Cf Buck et al. (2011), p. 24 et seq.

Samoa).[17] However, in all jurisdictions examined in this study, the Institutions have organisational links to Parliament. Mostly, these links are determined by reporting obligations (except in Taiwan),[18] sometimes by the appointment process,[19] and, in most cases, by the possibilities for dismissal or removal of the Ombudsman (except for Papua New Guinea and Tonga).[20] As a result of their work, Ombudsmen may often propose amendments to existing legislations to address systemic flaws.[21] These proposals are mostly directed to the body investigated in a specific case. However, many Ombudsman Institutions may also address this question directly to Parliament, be it as part of the Annual Report, be it as a special report. In most jurisdictions, the Ombudsman may *de facto* speak before Parliament or one of its committees. However, this has not been put into legislation as a statutory right in any of the jurisdictions examined.

2.2.3 Appointment Procedure

Despite the usually close link of the Ombudsman Institution to Parliament, the Ombudsman is not directly appointed by Parliament in any of the jurisdictions examined.[22] In the APOR region, as Fig. 2.1 shows, it is usually an administrator (Governor-General, Governor, Administrator, Chief Executive or Queens Representative),[23] or the President (Vanuatu, Taiwan), the Head of State (Samoa) or the King (Tonga) who appoints the Ombudsman. In half of the jurisdictions, the appointment authority acts on his or her own without any involvement of Parliament (the Australian Commonwealth, Hong Kong, Papua New Guinea, Tasmania, Tonga, Victoria, Western Australia and Vanuatu). However, in Vanuatu, certain senior officials are to be consulted and an Ombudsman Appointment Committee must be consulted in case of Papua New Guinea.[24]

In the other eight jurisdictions, Parliament is involved to varying degrees. In the Cook Islands, New Zealand, the Northern Territory, Samoa, South Australia and Taiwan, the appointment by the Governor or Administrator respectively is made

[17] There is no statutory definition of an Officer of Parliament. The term is used to refer to certain types of independent officers who have the statutory obligation to report directly to Parliament.

[18] Cf report on Taiwan, Chap. 20, p. 257 for more details.

[19] Cf directly below Sect. 2.2.3 for more details.

[20] Cf directly below Sect. 2.2.7, p. 29 for more details.

[21] Cf Sect. 4.1.3, p. 74 for more details.

[22] Cf Buck et al. (2011), p. 163. This differs significantly from Europe where 89 % of the investigated Ombudsmen are appointed by Parliament, cf Kucsko-Stadlmayer (2008), p.12 and p. 461. Cf also Buck et al. 2011, p. 163.

[23] This is mostly the case in countries of the Commonwealth of Nations.

[24] Cf report on Papua New Guinea, Chap. 18, p. 235 for more details.

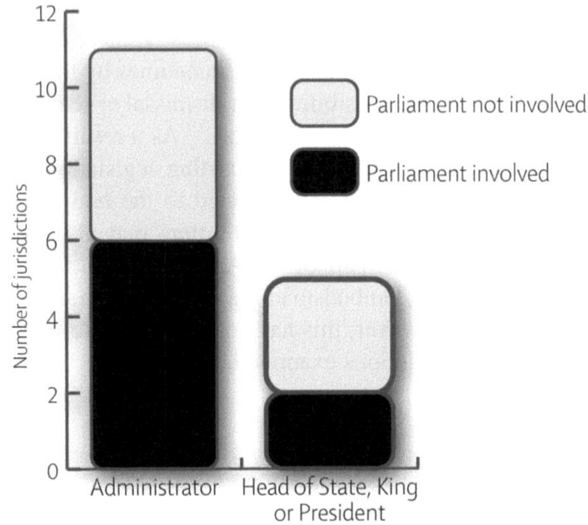

Fig. 2.1 Appointment of the Ombudsman

upon recommendation by Parliament.[25] In Queensland, the responsible Parliamentary Committee must be consulted beforehand, whereas in New South Wales the responsible Parliamentary Committee, while not involved beforehand by law, may veto an appointment.[26]

2.2.4 *Monocratic or Collegial Body*

Most Institutions are headed by one Ombudsman, who is appointed following the procedure described above. There are three exceptions: New Zealand, Papua New Guinea and Taiwan (see Fig. 2.2). In New Zealand, the law foresees that more than one Ombudsman may be appointed. Currently there are two Ombudsmen, a case in which the law stipulates that one is to be appointed "Chief Ombudsman". The Papua New Guinea model reflects the fact that there is more than one individual at work by naming the Institution "Ombudsman Commission". Here, the law prescribes that there shall be three Ombudsmen with one "Chief Ombudsman" as *primus inter pares* who is in charge of the administration. The Taiwan model differs somewhat more from the widespread monocratic shape of Ombudsman Institutions. The Taiwanese Control Yuan is considered one of the five powers of Taiwan (instead of the prevalent division into three powers — the legislative, executive

[25] Cf Buck et al. (2011), p. 164 who describes New Zealand as a model of good practice.

[26] Cf report on Queensland, Chap. 10, p. 143 and report on New South Wales, Chap. 8, p. 117 for more details.

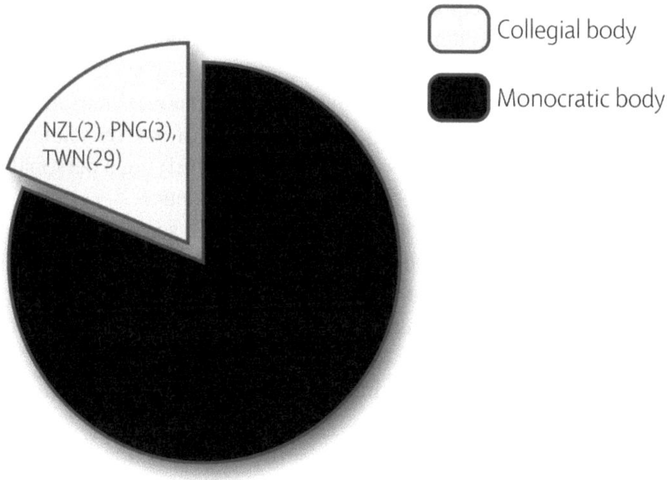

Fig. 2.2 Monocratic or collegial body. Number of members of the Ombudsman Institution in brackets

and judicial powers). It consists of a larger collegial body of 29 members which all have equal powers.[27]

As described, much of the leverage an Ombudsman Institution has does not derive from the formal powers prescribed by law, but from the reputation, standing and competence an Ombudsman has. This is reflected in the fact that many legislators have chosen to shape the Institution as a monocratic body.

However, there is a certain overlap between the organisation of a monocratic body and that of a collegial board: In many monocratic institutions, deputies with far reaching competencies are appointed, whereas in collegial boards it is not unusual for the Chief Ombudsman to stand out as the most prominent figure.[28] The Taiwanese model, however, differs from this once more, as in the Control Yuan always more than one of the 29 members are involved in the investigation; in case of impeachment, for example, a minimum of nine members shall formally approve such procedure.[29]

2.2.5 *Qualification Requirements*

Most jurisdictions in the APOR region do not foresee any statutory qualification requirements. The formal reason for this may partly be that the Swedish legislation

[27] Cf report on Taiwan, Chap. 20, p. 257 for more details.

[28] Cf Kucsko-Stadlmayer (2008), p.11.

[29] Cf report on Taiwan, Chap. 20, p. 257 for more details.

does not foresee any such requirements (however, the Danish model requires a law degree from the office holder).[30] Since the New Zealand legislation was the blueprint for many laws in the region, the absence of any such requirement in its law may also have influenced this development. The material reason is that such a requirement could be seen as a limitation of the choice of possible candidates, while the true focus in the selection process should be on identifying a personality with an excellent reputation in who the public will have confidence.[31]

Three out of the 16 jurisdictions examined specify some formal requirements (Papua New Guinea, Taiwan and Vanuatu). The law in Papua New Guinea for example foresees that the candidate shall be a "person of integrity, independence of mind, resolution and high standing in the community." The law further stipulates that one of the three Ombudsmen (other than the Chief Ombudsman) shall have "professional accountancy qualifications and experience", and the third shall have "administrative or legal qualifications and experience."[32] The law in Vanuatu requires "knowledge, understanding and appreciation of the culture, traditions and values of the Ni-Vanuatu-people" and, in addition, that the incumbent be "of high integrity and competence," politically independent, with appropriate qualifications and experience, capable of discharging the duties without fear or favour, and of high standing in the community.[33] The Organic Law of the Control Yuan (Taiwan) foresees a minimum age of 35 and requires at least ten years of work experience in various professions as listed (e.g. senior judge, prosecutor, senior public official, university professor).[34]

2.2.6 *Term of Office*

In most jurisdictions, the Ombudsman is appointed for a fixed term. Only in South Australia the law does not foresee such a fixed term of office. In the other jurisdictions the term of office ranges from three years (Cook Islands, Samoa) over five years (Queensland,[35] Tasmania, Western Australia, Hong Kong, New Zealand, Tonga and Vanuatu), six years (Papua New Guinea and Taiwan), seven years (Australian Commonwealth, New South Wales and the Northern Territory) to a maximum of ten years (Victoria) (see Fig. 2.3).

Usually, reappointment of the incumbent is possible — regularly without limitation other than age[36] — only the laws of the Northern Territory (term of office:

---

[30] Cf Kucsko-Stadlmayer (2008), p. 465 et seq.

[31] Cf Kucsko-Stadlmayer (2008), p. 11.

[32] Cf s4 OLOC (Papua New Guinea).

[33] Cf s3(3) OA (Vanuatu).

[34] Cf report on Taiwan, Chapter 20, p. 257 for more details.

[35] The exact provision is that the appointment shall be no more than 5 years.

[36] Cf Fig. 2.3, p. 29.

Fig. 2.3 Ombudsman's term of office. Ombudsman's term of office for . . . years

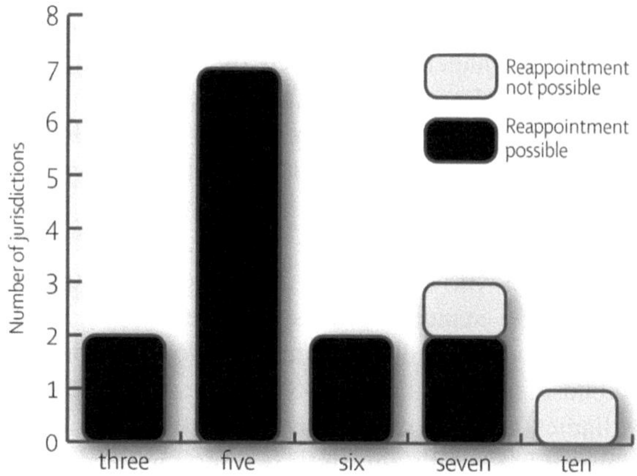

seven years) and Victoria (ten years) do not foresee this option. Tasmania and Queensland limit the number of possible reappointments by allowing for a total stay in office for ten years maximum.

The possibility of reappointment always carries the inherent risk of the incumbent, consciously or unconsciously, not always acting fully independently in view of his or her reappointment. Such risk should not be overestimated, but be kept in mind when considering modifications of existing legislation. It may be an alternative to resort to longer terms of office. However, for reasons of democratic hygiene, such a long, single period cannot be extended without limitation. With a view to the standard legislative period which lasts for four or five years, a period of eight–ten years for the incumbent appears to be the upper limit acceptable. The term of office should — in line with the democratic principle of the electorate's power to decide about its representation — be of limited duration. This is most evident in cases where the legislator is involved in the appointment thus ensuring active influence on the positions of certain senior office holders.[37]

Some jurisdictions foresee additionally a mandatory retirement age for office holders. This ranges from 55 years (Papua New Guinea) over 65 years (New South Wales and Southern Australia) to 72 years of age (Cook Islands, New Zealand and Tonga). The other jurisdictions do not foresee a concrete retirement age.

2.2.7 Removal and Suspension from Office

One aspect of independence is a stable tenure. Without it, there is always the risk of an office holder articulating only uncontested and conforming opinion to ensure

[37] In particular if the Ombudsman is an Officer of Parliament. Of note, in New Zealand, the term of office of the Ombudsman was originally for one legislative period only. A new appointment had to be made "in each Parliament's first or second session", cf Sawer (1968), p. 65.

continuation of his or her tenure.[38] In all jurisdictions examined, the Ombudsman may be (permanently) removed or (temporarily) suspended from office by the appointing authority.[39] It is often significantly more difficult to remove or suspend the Ombudsman than to appoint him or her. For example, while Parliament is involved in little more than half of the jurisdictions in case of the appointment of the Ombudsman, it is involved in the removal or suspension in almost all cases (special cases are Papua New Guinea, Taiwan, Tonga[40] and Vanuatu, see below).[41] Also, the law lists various reasons for removal or suspension (except for New South Wales). The standard process (all Australian Institutions, Cook Islands, Hong Kong, New Zealand and Samoa) is for the appointing authority to remove the Ombudsman from office upon advice or with approval of the Parliament.[42] If Parliament is not in session, the appointing authority may suspend the Ombudsman temporarily (usually for up to two months) and seek the Parliament's support for this decision, turning it into a permanent removal. If Parliament does not support this step, the Ombudsman is reinstated.[43]

The legislation differs only slightly when it comes to reasons for removal. Most jurisdictions refer to at least two of the following: disability, bankruptcy, neglect of duty, misconduct, misbehaviour, physical or mental incapacity, incompetence, conviction of a crime or offence or incapability to properly perform the duties of office.[44] What stands out is the very detailed and meticulous procedure in Queensland.[45]

The Institutions in Papua New Guinea and Vanuatu, whose officials have obligations under the Leadership Code,[46] follow a slightly different model. There, the Ombudsman may be dismissed for misconduct in office under the respective Leadership Code. In both countries, the Ombudsman can also be removed from office by the appointment authority on advice of a special tribunal (Papua New

[38] Cf Buck et al. (2011), p. 166.

[39] Cf for the respective appointing authority, Sect. 2.2.3, p. 25 above.

[40] In Tonga, the King acts on his own without any requirement to involve Parliament or other statutory bodies. Nevertheless, the law also contains an enumerative list of reasons for removal (disability, bankruptcy, neglect of duty or misconduct), which leaves a margin of appreciation. Obligatory involvement of another body would lead to a higher perceived degree of independence.

[41] In case of the Northern Territory, the Administrator may remove the Ombudsman permanently even without Parliament if the Ombudsman is found guilty of an indictable offence, becomes bankrupt or engages in remunerative employment outside the duties of office without the Chief Minister's approval, cf p. 133.

[42] In the case of the Cook Islands, the Queen's Representative acts on advice of the Prime Minster, who shall convey the recommendation of Parliament, cf p. 213.

[43] Cf for details of this process e.g. the report on Queensland, Chap. 10, p. 143.

[44] For some of these reasons, some jurisdictions foresee the position to automatically become vacant. For example in South Australia this goes for bankruptcy and conviction of an indictable offence.

[45] Cf report on Queensland, Chap. 10, p. 143 for more details.

[46] Cf Sect. 4.1.4.4, p. 81 below for more details.

Guinea),[47] respectively after consultation with those senior officials involved in the appointment procedure (Vanuatu). In Taiwan, members of the Control Yuan may be removed in an impeachment process by other members of the Institution if the former are found guilty of a violation of law or neglect of duty.[48] Lastly, the Ombudsman may also resign from office or be retired by the appointing authority for physical or mental incapacity in most jurisdictions at any time.

2.2.8 *Incompatibilities*

The legal basis of almost all Ombudsman Institutions stipulates rules on incompatibilities. Only the legislation of the Commonwealth of Australia does not foresee such a statutory incompatibility clause.[49] Incompatibility clauses differ from jurisdiction to jurisdiction (see Fig. 2.4). Oftentimes they bar the Ombudsman from holding a political position or from engaging in any other paid undertaking. Both situations could potentially undermine the Ombudsman's independence — the former due to the risk of political influence on or partisanship in the exercise of the position, while in the latter case, economical influence by third parties could jeopardise the Ombudsman's independence. Consequently, abstinence in both cases, supported by appropriate remuneration for the position strengthens the incumbent's independence.

All jurisdictions foresee that the position of Ombudsman be incompatible with being a Member of Parliament,[50] and often even running for election is considered incompatible (New South Wales, Tasmania, Western Australia). In the Northern Territory, Queensland and Western Australia even the direct change from a position in Parliament to that of Ombudsman is prohibited. Insofar the law foresees a cooling-off period of three years before a person becomes eligible for candidacy.

In most jurisdictions, the Ombudsman shall not simultaneously engage in any paid occupation outside the duties of his or her office (formulations vary). Often also the position of chairperson, mayor, president, councillor or member of a local government is considered incompatible.[51] Papua New Guinea, Taiwan and Vanuatu are three jurisdictions which explicitly stipulate that the Ombudsman position is incompatible with holding higher positions in political parties. The legislation in Queensland recognises the risk of potential conflicts of interest by requiring a new incumbent to lay open his or her interests and the interests of persons related to him or her within one month after taking office.[52]

---

[47] A tribunal responsible for certain senior officials (Constitutional Office Holders).

[48] Cf report on Taiwan, Chap. 20, p. 257 for more details.

[49] Like in the United Kingdom where legislation also does not contain an incompatibility clause, cf Kucsko-Stadlmayer (2008), p. 15.

[50] In Australia, it is often expressly stipulated that this refers to the House of the state or territory and any other Parliament in the Commonwealth, including at Commonwealth level.

[51] Cf the respective reports on the different jurisdictions in Chaps. 7–22 for more details.

[52] Relevant interests are those that (may) conflict with the discharge of the Ombudsman's responsibilities, cf report on Queensland, Chap. 10, p. 143 for more details.

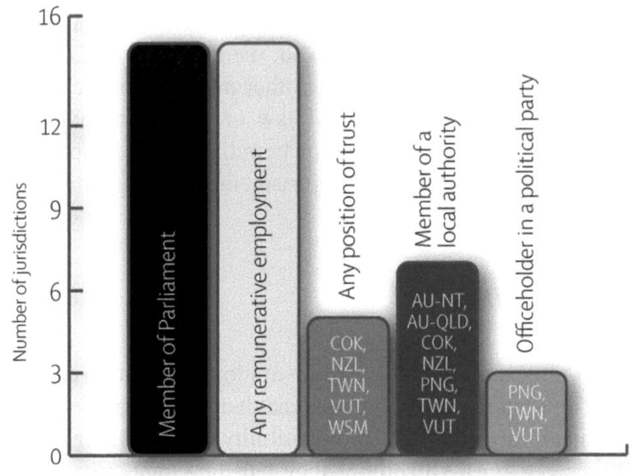

Fig. 2.4 Incompatibilities. The position of Ombudsman is incompatible with being a/having

2.2.9 *Immunity*

To effectively carry out the function of Ombudsman, it is important that the Ombudsman cannot be held liable for actions (or omissions) undertaken in the exercise of his or her duties. An additional general immunity clause is another safeguard to prevent arbitrary influence from outside. The latter is only granted to the members of the Control Yuan in Taiwan, where a constitutional provision stipulates that members enjoy immunity from arrest or detention unless they are caught *in flagrante delicto*.[53] In all jurisdictions examined, the Ombudsman is immune from any prosecution under civil law for any action undertaken or omitted to be undertaken in the exercise of his or her duties. In most jurisdictions, this is also true for criminal investigations (in Hong Kong, the privilege is limited to proceedings under the Defamation Law, in Queensland only civil liability is expressly excluded[54]).

2.2.10 *Salary and Allowances*

The salary and other allowances of the Ombudsman are usually regulated in broad terms only in the respective establishing legislations. In most jurisdictions, the

[53] Cf report on Taiwan, Chap. 20, p. 257 for more details.

[54] Cf Ombudsman Act (Queensland), s93.

details of the remuneration and other conditions are not established by law, but determined by the appointment authority (Governor-General, Governor, Administrator, Chief Executive or the Queen's Representative),[55] respectively by the King (Tonga), mostly implementing the rulings of (or having referred the matter in its entirety to) the respective remuneration tribunal.

In New Zealand and Samoa, the salary is determined by the country's remuneration authority, while in Vanuatu, the President determines the amount, acting on the advice of the Council of Ministers, which in turn receives a report from the Public Service Commission. In Taiwan, the law prescribes the salary of the members of the Control Yuan to be linked to the salary of the Presidents and Deputy Presidents of the other four Yuans (in case of the President), respectively to the salary of the Ministers of the executive (in case of the other members).[56] A constitutional provision only exists in Papua New Guinea, where salary and conditions of employment shall not be less than those of a judge other than the Chief Justice (for the Chief Ombudsman) and not less than those of a Prosecutor (for the two additional Ombudsmen).[57] In Tonga, the King decides about the conditions of the appointment.

To ensure independence, most legislations foresee the salary and other allowances not to be reduced or otherwise modified to the detriment of the office holder during his or her term of office.[58] This provision, together with other aspects (as already elaborated) guarantees, that the Ombudsman can act with the utmost independence and does not have to fear any act of indirect administrative "reprisal" for any action undertaken.

2.2.11 Functional Independence and Resources

Functional independence exists where the Ombudsman Institution is provided with the necessary resources to efficiently carry out its functions. This requires the appropriate infrastructure, including fully equipped premises, an appropriate number of personnel and an adequate budget. Yet the former is only the formal aspect; to ensure functional independence, these resources must – to the largest extent possible — be at the autonomous disposal of the Ombudsman.[59]

All Institutions examined reported that they were equipped with adequate infrastructure to carry out their functions. Usually, the Institution has one office. The Ombudsman of the Australian Commonwealth, however, has offices in each state and the two self-governing territories of Australia,[60] and the Institutions in

[55] This is mostly the case in countries of the Commonwealth of Nations, cf fn 23 above.

[56] Cf reports on the different jurisdictions in Chaps. 7–22 for more details.

[57] Cf report on Papua New Guinea, Chap. 18, p. 235 for more details.

[58] Cf Buck et al. (2011), p. 166.

[59] Cf Buck et al. (2011), p. 168.

[60] Cf report on the Commonwealth Ombudsman, Chap. 7, p. 101 for more details.

New Zealand, Papua New Guinea and Vanuatu also have at least one sub-office in each region (New Zealand: two sub-offices, Papua New Guinea: three, Vanuatu: one). All offices are equipped with standard office equipment such as computers, telephones, internet, etc. Most Institutions run their own website (except for Tonga and Vanuatu) to reach out to and inform the public and often also to make it possible to be contacted via the internet (sometimes with an online complaint form).

Appropriate financing is crucial for the Ombudsman's independence. Important aspects include budget autonomy,[61] i.e. the competence to autonomously decide how to spend the budget and the question of who drafts the budget proposal, respectively who submits it. In all jurisdictions, the Ombudsman Institutions' budget is appropriated by Parliament, and in each case, the Ombudsman has budget autonomy. The Ombudsman Institution must provide (annual) financial reports on its spending. Mostly, the Ombudsman Institutions submit their budget proposal for the following year in the course of the regular budget process (e.g. to the responsible Minister, the Attorney-General or the Treasurer).[62] The Ombudsman Act (Queensland) explicitly regulates the budget preparation process.[63] In New Zealand there is even a separate vote, the Vote Ombudsman, required in Parliament. Some Institutions with a broader mandate[64] have been vested with functions relating to other public entities such as the Police or private entities providing public services. These Institutions often receive part of their funding from those entities, as in the case of the Ombudsman of the Commonwealth of Australia, who is partially reimbursed by the ACT[65] and the Police.[66] The Institutions in Tasmania and Western Australia also receive funding from the energy entities under their jurisdictions with respect to their duties as Energy Ombudsman.[67]

The Ombudsmen may employ the staff required to successfully execute their functions — within the limit of the financial resources available to them. In recent years, there have been complaints that, while Institutions may receive new responsibilities, no adequate funding and staffing is provided by the lawmaker.[68]

---

[61] Cf Besselink (2000), p. 162.

[62] Cf the respective reports on different jurisdictions in Chaps. 7–22 for more details.

[63] Cf s88 Ombudsman Act (Queensland).

[64] Cf Sect. 2.1.3, p. 22 above for more details.

[65] For the provision of services done under the ACT Ombudsman Act, cf report on the Commonwealth Ombudsman, Chap. 7, p. 104 for details.

[66] For the provision of services in relation to the Australian Federal Police, cf report on the Commonwealth Ombudsman, Chap. 7, p. 107 for details.

[67] Cf report on Tasmania, Chap. 12, p. 165 and report on Western Australia, Chap. 14, p. 187 for more details.

[68] For example in the Cook Islands, the Cabinet appointed the Ombudsman to "be in charge of the Cook Islands Human Rights Office" in 2007, however due to budget constraints it was not possible to fund any additional position for this additional task. Cf report on the Cook Islands, Chap. 16, p. 211 for more details.

↑ above the average
↓ below the average
← on the average

	AUS Commonwealth	AUS New South Wales	AUS Northern Territory	AUS Queensland	AUS South Australia	AUS Tasmania	AUS Victoria	AUS Western Australia
Year of establishment	1976	1974	1978	1974	1972	1978	1973	1971
Appointment by: Administrator, Head of State/King, President	A	A[11]	A[12]	A[12]	A[12]	A	A	A
Term of office (Years)	↑7	↑7	↑7	↓5	-[4]	↓5	↑10	↓5
Age of retirement	-	65	-	-	65	-	-	-
Reappointment possible	Y	Y	N	Y[2]	-[4]	Y[3]	N	Y[5]
Number of staff	182[9]	185	21	54	14	23[6]	65[7]	60
Percentage of female staff	↑65	↑73	↑71	↑63	↑71	-	↑66	↑63
Budget (mio. US $)[10]	↑23.1	↑24.2	↓2.1	↓7.2	↓1.9	↓2.6	←9.5	↓7.9
Legal basis of Ombudsman[15]	L	L	L	L	L	L	C/L	L
Monocratic or collegial body	m	m	m	m	m	m	m	m
Qualification requirements	N	N	N	N	N	N	N	N

	Cook Islands	Hong Kong (China)	New Zealand	Papua New Guinea	Samoa	Taiwan	Tonga	Vanuatu
Year of establishment	1984	1989	1962	1975	1989	1948	2001	1994
Appointment by: Administrator, Head of State/King, President	A[12]	A	A[12]	H[13]	H[12]	P[12]	H	P[14]
Term of office (Years)	↓3	↓5	↓5	←6/3[1]	↓3	←6	↓5	↓5
Age of retirement	72	-	72	55	-	-	72	-
Reappointment possible	Y	Y	Y	Y	Y	Y	Y	Y
Number of staff	4	111	63[8]	107	5	465	5	13
Percentage of female staff	↓50	←60	↑65	↓43	↓40	↓48	-	↑69
Budget (mio. US $)[10]	-	↑12.3	↓6.8	-	↓0.5	↑26	↓0.08	↓0.6
Legal basis of Ombudsman[15]	L	L	L	C/O	L	O/L	L	C/L
Monocratic or collegial body	m	m	c(2)	c(3)	m	c(29)	m	m
Qualification requirements	N	N	N	N	Y	Y	N	Y

1: If candidate is non - PNG - citizen.
2: Up to ten years of total tenure.
3: For one term.
4: No fixed term of office.
5: No legal regulation, but in practice Ombudsmen have been reappointed.
6: 11 work part-time.
7: Including Ombudsman and casual staff.
8: FTE: 57.
9: FTE: 174.
10: 2010/11, if not available 09/10, rounded to one decimal figure.
11: Parliament may veto an appointment.
12: Parliament involved.
13: In accordance with the Ombudsman Appointments Committee.
14: In accordance with senior officials.
15: Organic, Constitutional or ordinary Law.

Fig. 2.5 Comparison of important data relating to autonomy and independence

Many Institutions report budgetary constraints.[69] Whether this is only due to the ongoing worldwide financial and economic crises since 2008 and will change in the future remains to be seen. Tight budgets appear to be a problem for many Institutions worldwide.[70] Differing staffing levels (reaching from six staff in Samoa and Tonga to 185.2 staff[71] in New South Wales and even 465 staff in case of the Taiwanese Control Yuan, compare in detail Fig. 2.5) reflect both the size of the jurisdiction, which differs considerably in the APOR region (the Cook Islands being the least inhabited jurisdiction and Taiwan being the largest one), and the varying extent of the mandate.

In almost all Institutions about half of the staff are female (compare Fig. 2.5 for details). However, for more senior positions, the percentage of female staff tends to be lower. Only three out of the 16 Institutions have a woman as Ombudsman

[69] The budget of the Hong Kong Ombudsman was at an all-time high in 2009 and decreased considerably both in 2010 and 2011. The Tasmanian Ombudsman reported that staffing levels were expected to drop due to budgetary restrictions in the years 2011–2012 and the Ombudsman in the Northern Territory had to close its sub-office in Alice Springs in recent years due to budgetary constraints. The former Commonwealth Ombudsman, Alan Asher, had raised concerns over budget constraints with the Australian Government in 2011, cf report on the Commonwealth Ombudsman, Chap. 7, p. 101.

[70] Tight budgets appear to be a problem since many years. Cf Pearce (2000), p. 94 who described this phenomenon for the Commonwealth Ombudsman already in 2000. Cf also Caiden and Valdes (1999), p. 108.

[71] Full-time equivalents (FTE).

(the Cook Islands, New Zealand and the Northern Territory)[72]; in six Institutions at least one Deputy or Assistant Ombudsman is female.[73] In none of the jurisdictions there is an explicit provision ensuring that the Ombudsman, respectively the staff, reflects the composition of society. Options to achieve this include introducing a quota, limiting the term of office and requiring an alternating appointment of persons as office holders. While there is no simple way of implementing diversity policies in respect of a single office holder, pluralism and diversity in the workforce is easier to be achieved.[74]

2.3 Organisation

The Ombudsman Institutions examined structure their offices in various ways, reflecting the different responsibilities in each jurisdiction. Many Institutions, if large enough, have Assistant Ombudsmen, who are in charge of the different divisions of the office. The structure is usually according to thematic or functional areas (e.g. complaints and investigations, Freedom of Information matters, etc.).[75] In Taiwan, as a peculiarity of the five-powers-system, the audit office (Ministry of Audit) has been set up by the Control Yuan and is subordinated to it. The structure of the Control Yuan mirrors the division of competencies in the executive branch of government. For each Ministry or Government Department a corresponding unit of the Control Yuan is in charge.

References

Besselink LFM (ed) (2000) Human rights commissions and Ombudsman offices. National experiences throughout the world. Kluwer Law International, Dordrecht

Buck T, Kirkham R, Thompson B (2011) The Ombudsman enterprise and administrative justice. Ashgate, Farnham

Caiden GE, Valdes DA (1999) Maturation issues for the Ombudsman. In: Reif LC (ed) The international Ombudsman anthology. Selected writings from the International Ombudsman Institute. Kluwer Law International, Dordrecht

[72] In addition, in Taiwan seven out of the 29 members of the Control Yuan are women.

[73] This is the case in the Australia Commonwealth, New South Wales, South Australia, Western Australia, Cook Islands and Papua New Guinea. In the course of the last nine years, there has been one female Deputy in Hong Kong.

[74] In New South Wales, the Institution reported that under a Government policy to meet the requirements under the Anti-Discrimination Act (New South Wales), also the Ombudsman is encouraged to have policies in place in relation to the employment of women, people with disabilities and Aboriginal people. The Northern Territory Ombudsman has an Equal Opportunity Management Plan.

[75] Cf the respective reports on different jurisdictions in Chaps. 7 to 22 for more details.

Creyke R (2007) Administrative justice—towards integrity in government. Melb Univ Law Rev 31(3):705–732

Gregory R, Giddings P (eds) (2000) Righting wrongs. The Ombudsman in six continents. IOS Press, Berlin

Kucsko-Stadlmayer G (ed) (2008) European Ombudsman-Institutions. Springer, Vienna

McLeod R (2001) Freedom of information—an Ombudsman's perspective, commentary. Fed Law Rev 29(3):359–364

Paterson M (2004) Transparency in the modern state. Happy birthday foi! or commiserations? Altern Law J 29:10–14

Pearce D (2000) Ombudsman in Australia. In: Gregory R, Giddings P (eds) Righting wrongs. The Ombudsman in six continents. IOS Press, Berlin

Reif LC (2004) The Ombudsman, good governance, and the international human rights system. Martinus Nijhoff, Leiden

Sawer G (1968) The Ombudsman and related institutions in Australia and New Zealand. Ann Am Acad Pol Soc Sci 377:62–72

Chapter 3
Mandate

Michael Frahm

3.1 Object of Control

3.1.1 International Standards

The Paris Principles stipulate that an Institution should be given "as broad a mandate as possible [...] specifying [...] its sphere of competence."[1] While the Principles do not explicitly focus on the object of control, this may be derived from the specific responsibilities which shall include *inter alia* "legislative or administrative provisions", "any situation of violation of human rights", and "situations in any part of the country where human rights are violated".[2] Further, Institutions may "be authorized to hear and consider complaints and petitions concerning individual situations" and thus may make "recommendations to the competent authorities [...]".[3] UN General Assembly Resolution 63/169 and UN General Assembly Resolution 65/207 both see the role of the Ombudsman in "promoting good governance in public administrations, as well as improving their relations with citizens, and in strengthening the delivery of public services."[4]

[1] Paris Principles, "Competences and responsibilities", paragraph 2.

[2] Paris Principles, "Competences and responsibilities", paragraph 3.

[3] Paris Principles, "Additional principles concerning the status of commissions with quasi-judicial competence", introductory paragraph and d).

[4] UN General Assembly Resolution 63/169, 2008, on the role of the Ombudsman, mediator and other national human rights institutions and protection of human rights, preamble; UN General Assembly Resolution 65/207, 2010, on the role of the Ombudsman, mediator and other national human rights institutions in the promotion and protection of human rights, preamble.

M. Frahm (✉)
Ludwig Boltzmann Institute of Human Rights, Vienna, Austria
e-mail: michael.frahm@univie.ac.at

International Ombudsman Institute (ed.), *Australasia and Pacific Ombudsman Institutions*,
DOI 10.1007/978-3-642-33896-0_3,

3.1.2 *Public Administration*

3.1.2.1 General Overview

It is a commonplace to state that the main object of control of the Ombudsmen examined is the public administration of the respective jurisdiction. This is the consequence of the focus chosen in this study.[5] Other Ombudsman-like bodies may have their focus on or be exclusively competent to control private entities. These include private sector Ombudsmen in the fields of privatised former government businesses,[6] but also private industry Ombudsmen in areas that have never been considered state business.[7] With this being said, it is worth looking at the details of public administration in the twenty-first century.

In general, it is necessary to distinguish between two aspects of the term "public administration". On the one hand, public administration signifies the entity or entities within jurisdiction (and *de facto* the acts of persons acting on behalf of any such entity). On the other hand, the object of control is limited to *administrative* actions of these entities. I.e., if Ministers, courts or other bodies are partly within jurisdiction, the scope of the Ombudsman's control is limited to the *administrative* actions of these persons or bodies.

The definition of what constitutes "administration" differs in the jurisdictions examined.[8] In most jurisdictions the establishing act determines the object of control as "all Government Departments" or "any state and local government" and includes the term "any public authority." A closer definition of the terminology is usually given in the act's definition chapter.[9] Clarification of what constitutes a Government Department is not needed. The general clauses used to include other entities into the Ombudsman's jurisdiction differ in details but aim at including all variations of entities that are constituted, established, controlled (by way of appointment of holding of shares) or (partly) funded by the executive for a public purpose including any subsidiaries that may exist. In addition, an exclusion clause lists those entities that are explicitly excluded.[10] As one example, see the relevant definitions in the Tasmanian law:

Section 4 (1) of the Ombudsman Act:
"[. . .] public authorities [are. . .]

(d) a body or authority, whether incorporated or not, that is constituted or established by or under an Act for a public purpose;

---

[5] Cf Sect. 1.2, p. 10 above.

[6] Cf the discussion in Buck et al. (2011), p. 7; cf also Reif (2004), p. 26 et seqq.

[7] Cf Reif (2004), p. 27.

[8] For a discussion of the definition, cf Keith (2005), Development of the role of the Ombudsman with reference to the Pacific. Speech held at the 22nd APOR Conference, p. 2 et seq.

[9] All Australian jurisdictions as well as Papua New Guinea, Taiwan and Vanuatu follow this model.

[10] Cf Sect. 3.1.2.4, p. 45 below for more details.

(e) a body or authority, whether incorporated or not, whose members or a majority of whose members are appointed by the Governor or a Minister;" [. . .] and
(j) any other prescribed body or authority, whether incorporated or not (i) to which any money is paid by way of appropriation from the Public Account; or (ii) over which the Government or a Minister exercises control."

The other jurisdictions provide a list which is attached to the establishing act and enumerates the entities under the Ombudsman's jurisdiction.[11] The disadvantage of the latter model is that, with each reform of the public administration and with each establishment of a new public entity, the respective act is in need of updating. In either case, there is always a clarification that staff of the entities are included. All but one Ombudsmen examined have jurisdiction on both the central and the local level.[12] Naturally, the central level legislator establishing the Ombudsman foresees that this body supervises the central level administration. To respect local self-government, in addition, there could be local level Ombudsmen. In the absence of such a model, however, the Ombudsman should have competence for local councils as well. Otherwise, the level of administration which is often most relevant to the people, i.e. the local level, would be excluded from the Ombudsman's control. This would be detrimental to its usefulness and significance for the population.

The Ombudsman Institutions in many jurisdictions derive certain powers also from other pieces of legislation. Insofar, the object of control may differ in detail. For example, under Freedom of Information legislation, Ministers also often fall under the Ombudsman's jurisdiction (e.g. in the Cook Islands, New Zealand,[13] New South Wales, South Australia, Western Australia). In Hong Kong, jurisdiction over the Police, the Independent Commission against Corruption and the Secretariat of the Public Service Commission is limited to Freedom of Information complaints.[14] In Papua New Guinea, Taiwan and Vanuatu, the object of control includes leaders or senior public officials under the jurisdictions' anti-corruption legislation (Leadership Code and Sunshine Laws).[15] In many jurisdictions which have laws regulating telecommunication interceptions and the use of surveillance devices, the Ombudsman Institution has a role with regard to the monitoring of compliance.[16] For an overview of bodies under the Ombudsmen's jurisdictions see Fig. 3.1.

---

[11] Cook Islands, Hong Kong, New Zealand, Samoa and Tonga.

[12] Jurisdiction of the Commonwealth Ombudsman is limited to the central level. There are state/territory level Ombudsmen in all six Australian states as well as in the ACT and the Northern Territory.

[13] In New Zealand this competence extends to the national Intelligence Service.

[14] Cf Chap.15, p. 199 for details.

[15] Cf the respective reports on different jurisdictions, Chaps. 7–22 for details.

[16] This is *inter alia* the case for the Ombudsman of the Australian Commonwealth, New South Wales, the Northern Territory, Tasmania and Western Australia. In New Zealand, for example, the Privacy Commissioner is competent, cf. http://privacy.org.nz/.

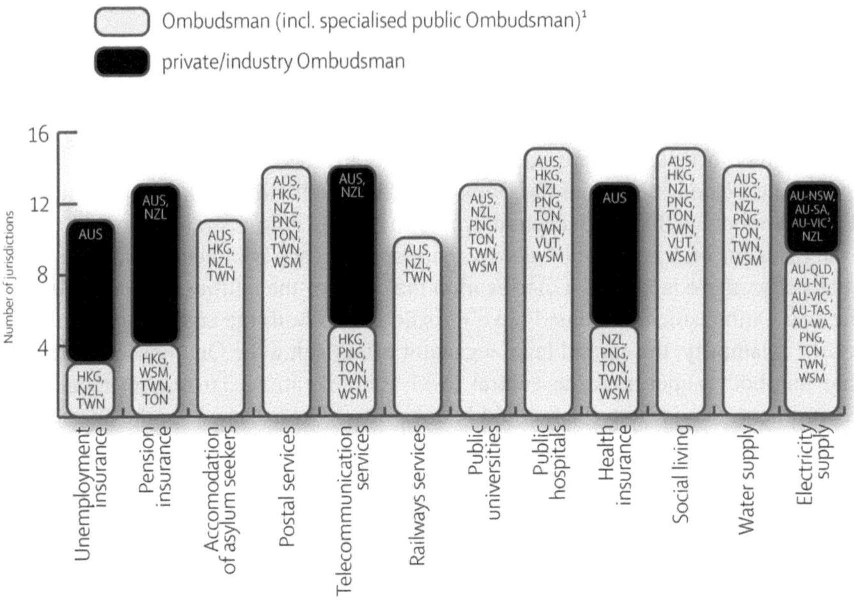

Fig. 3.1 General jurisdiction and competencies

3.1.2.2 Public Service Providers

Public services are services which are of general interest to the public, i.e. which supply the public with essential commodities (potable water, gas or electricity) or essential services (housing, education or transportation). Historically, such public services have almost exclusively been provided by the states. In the last decades, however, many jurisdictions have privatised or outsourced certain services or have used the model of public-private-partnerships to ensure the supply of certain commodities or essential services.[17]

From the individual's point of view and as far as his or her needs to receive these services are concerned at first glance, it is irrelevant whether these services are provided by a private entity, a private entity (partly) owned by the state, a statutory entity or the government.[18] It should thus not make a difference whether an individual can turn to the Ombudsman in case of a complaint. For this reason, a couple of important public services have been selected to be examined in more detail for the purposes of this study.[19] These are unemployment insurance, pension

[17] Cf Stuhmcke (2008), p. 321 et seq.; Villar (2002), p. 5; and McLeod (2001), p. 361.

[18] This being said, from a human rights and democracy perspective, many questions are connected with the outsourcing of government functions and public private partnerships. Cf *inter alia* Stuhmcke (2008), p. 322 and McLeod (2001), p. 362 et seq.

[19] All Institutions examined were asked for information on who supplies these services and whether or not the provider is under the Institution's jurisdiction.

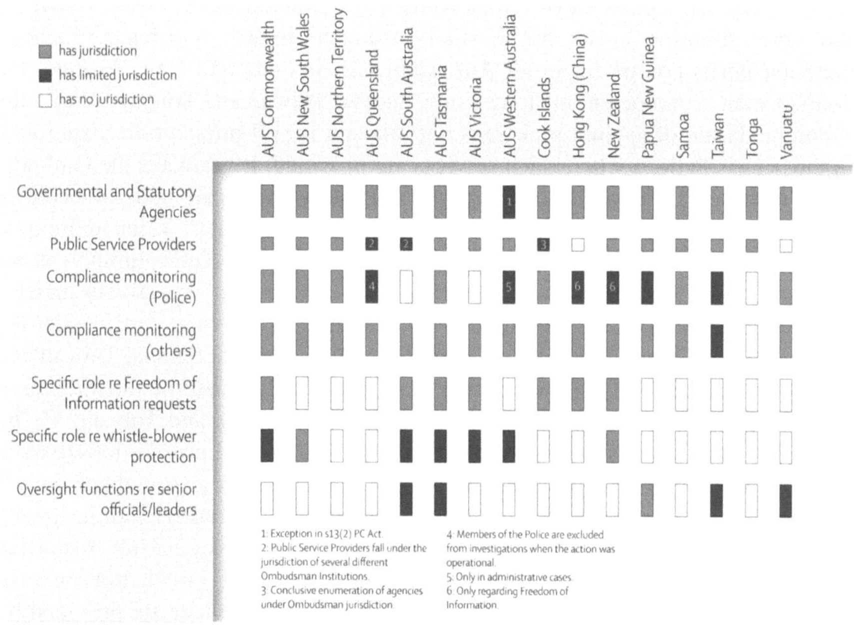

Fig. 3.2 Jurisdiction over different public service providers.
(1) The column "Ombudsman" refers to the Ombudsmen examined in this study, with the following exceptions: "Public hospitals"—the column also includes the public health complaints commissions in the AU-ACT, AU-NSW and AU-QLD; "Water supply"—the column also includes the ACT Civil and Administrative Tribunal and the Energy and Water Ombudsman in AU-NSW and AU-QLD; "Electricity supply"—the column also includes the ACT Civil and Administrative Tribunal and the public Energy Ombudsmen in AU-QLD, AU-TAS and AU-WA.
(2) In AU-VIC the Ombudsman has jurisdiction regarding public sector agencies, whereas a private industry Ombudsman is responsible for the private sector.
(3) The Cook Islands are not included in this overview

insurance, accommodation of asylum seekers, postal services, telecommunication, railways, universities, public hospitals, health insurance, social living, electricity and water supply (see Fig. 3.2).

It can be established that in most jurisdictions, the providers of most of these services are either under the jurisdiction of the Ombudsman, under the jurisdiction of a specialised Ombudsman or under the jurisdiction of another independent complaint body, which provides its services to the population for free.[20] The latter are partly statutory bodies, partly private industry Ombudsmen. In general terms, there is no "one size fits all"-solution, as different conditions require different solutions.

Unemployment insurance, where it exists, is partly under the jurisdiction of a private Financial Ombudsman (all Australian states and territories) and partly under

[20] All the following data does not include the Cook Islands, as the Institution there has not responded to this question.

the Ombudsman's jurisdiction (Hong Kong, New Zealand and Taiwan).[21] Largely the same situation exists for pension insurance issues: a private Financial Ombudsman is competent in all Australian jurisdictions and New Zealand, the Ombudsman is competent in Hong Kong, Samoa, Taiwan and Tonga.[22] While the accommodation of asylum seekers is not relevant for all jurisdictions examined, in those jurisdictions where such services are provided, it is always the Ombudsman that has jurisdiction for investigation.[23] Postal services are under the control of the Ombudsman in all jurisdictions (except for Vanuatu).[24] Telecommunication services are partly under the jurisdiction of a private Telecommunications Industry Ombudsman (all Australian states and territories) respectively under a private Telecom Dispute Resolution Service (New Zealand) and partly under the Ombudsman's jurisdiction (Hong Kong, Papua New Guinea, Samoa, Taiwan and Tonga).[25] Railway services, where they exist, are largely under the jurisdiction of the Ombudsman (all Australian jurisdictions, New Zealand and Taiwan).[26] The Ombudsman may investigate public universities in almost all jurisdictions (except for Hong Kong and Vanuatu). Likewise, the Ombudsman or a specialised body[27] is competent to investigate public hospitals in all jurisdictions. Health insurance issues are under the jurisdiction of a private Health Commissioner (all Australian jurisdictions) respectively the Ombudsman (in the other jurisdictions except for Hong Kong and Vanuatu). Social living and related services are provided by public entities in all jurisdictions and therefore always fall under the Ombudsman's competency. Regarding electricity and water supply, complaints can be directed to different entities. In the case of water supply this mostly is the Ombudsman (except for in the ACT, New South Wales, Queensland and Vanuatu).[28] In case of electricity supply, the picture is more diverse. While in some jurisdictions the Ombudsman is competent,[29] in some others

[21] In Papua New Guinea and Vanuatu, the Ombudsman has no jurisdiction. No clear answers can be provided for Samoa and Tonga.

[22] In Papua New Guinea and Vanuatu, the Ombudsman has no jurisdiction.

[23] No such services are provided in Papua New Guinea, Samoa, Tonga and Vanuatu.

[24] In Australia, the Postal Industry Ombudsman is competent, acting in personal union with the Commonwealth Ombudsman.

[25] In Vanuatu, the Ombudsman has no jurisdiction.

[26] Railway services do not exist or are not under the Ombudsman's jurisdiction in Hong Kong, Papua New Guinea, Samoa, Tonga and Vanuatu.

[27] The ACT, New South Wales and Queensland have established Public Health Complaints Commissions that are competent to investigate complaints with regards to these services.

[28] In the ACT, an individual can turn to the ACT Civil and Administrative Tribunal. In New South Wales and Queensland it is the Energy and Water Ombudsman that has jurisdiction. In Vanuatu the Ombudsman has no jurisdiction in this field.

[29] The Ombudsman is competent in the Northern Territory, Victoria (for public sector agencies), Papua New Guinea, Samoa, Taiwan and Tonga. In the ACT, it is again the ACT Civil and Administrative Tribunal that is competent. The Ombudsman has no jurisdiction in Hong Kong and Vanuatu; there is no information whether another body is competent to investigate complaints.

there are specialised public Ombudsmen[30] or private Industry Ombudsmen respectively.[31]

3.1.2.3 Detention Facilities

All jurisdictions foresee that the Ombudsman may visit facilities which restrict a person's freedom of movement, including hospitals and detention facilities. Responses to the study's questionnaire show that in almost all jurisdictions[32] the Ombudsman or his or her staff may speak to detainees in private.[33] An explicit legal provision only exists in Papua New Guinea (under the Corrections Institutions Service Act), in Taiwan and in South Australia (based on the state's Corrections Services Act 1982), while in the other 13 jurisdictions this right is not explicitly determined by law. In Victoria, Western Australia and Hong Kong two provisions are interpreted as the basis for the entitlement to speak with detainees in private: The rule that Ombudsmen shall conduct all investigations in private, read in conjunction with the rule that Ombudsmen have the power to regulate their procedure in such a way as they think fit. Since these provisions exist in most jurisdictions, they may be a basis for what otherwise can just be regarded as custom and practice.

3.1.2.4 Private Natural Persons and Legal Persons

Generally, private individuals cannot be subject to the control of the Ombudsman. While this statement may sound redundant, in some jurisdictions such situations are not entirely impossible. In Papua New Guinea the Ombudsman Commission is authorised (under the Discriminatory Practices Act) to investigate any case of suspected discriminatory practice in the provision of services. Object of control is any person that is the holder of a licence (e.g. under the Restaurants (Licensing) Act, the Trading Act, or of a public motor vehicle).[34] Insofar, in exceptions, a private person may also be subject to the Ombudsman's jurisdiction. Private legal entities are also excluded from the Ombudsman's jurisdiction except for the cases presented above in Sect. 3.1.2.1.

---

[30] Specialised Public Ombudsmen exist in Queensland, Tasmania and Western Australia.

[31] Private Industry Ombudsmen exist in New South Wales, South Australia and Victoria (for private sector agencies), while in New Zealand a private Electricity and Gas Complaints Commissioner Scheme provides for a complaints mechanism.

[32] As Cook Islands' law is silent in this regard, it remains unclear whether such a right exists. There has been no response to this question from Tonga.

[33] The Australian Commonwealth Ombudsman may also undertake unannounced visits to detention facilities, cf Chap. 7, p. 111.

[34] Cf Chap. 18, p. 240 for more details.

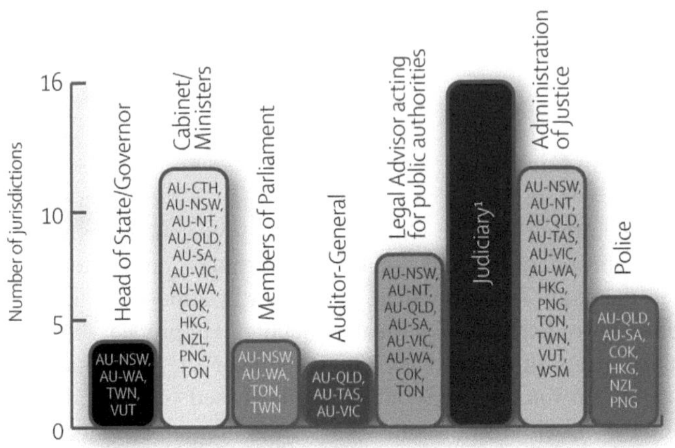

Fig. 3.3 Exclusion from the Ombudsman's jurisdiction. (1) While the judiciary is generally excluded from the Ombudsman's jurisdiction, there is limited control over the judiciary in AU-CTH, AU-NT, PNG, TWN and VUT. (2) This overview is non-exclusive and represents a selection of the most prevalent exclusions

3.1.2.5 Exemptions

All jurisdictions exclude certain persons, bodies and certain categories of actions from the Ombudsmen's jurisdiction, see Fig. 3.3 for more details. The former is achieved by way of a list of excepted bodies in the establishing law. It typically includes the Head of State, Ministers and the judiciary. As far as categories of actions are concerned, these include *inter alia* actions by courts, tribunals or court-like structures headed by a judge (explicitly excluded in all Australian jurisdictions).

3.1.3 Judiciary

3.1.3.1 General Overview

The Ombudsman Institutions' core function is to oversee the administration. Correspondingly, the Institutions do generally not have jurisdiction over the judiciary. As described, the Institutions in the region insofar follow the Danish rather than the Swedish/Finnish model[35]; not one of the Institutions examined has been given control over the judiciary to the extent that exists in the Swedish/Finnish legislation.[36] The only exception is the Control Yuan in Taiwan and, to a limited degree, also the Institutions in Papua New Guinea and Vanuatu.

[35] Cf Chap. 112, p. 4 above for details.

[36] Cf Reif (2004), p. 13 for details.

In Taiwan, the Control Yuan oversees all government levels, including the judiciary.[37] While the Institution cannot intervene in individual proceedings, all personnel of the Judicial Yuan, i.e. all judges and other court staff, fall under the Institution's jurisdiction. Serious suspicion of malfeasance in the course of ongoing proceedings can lead to an immediate investigation by the Control Yuan. The violation of laws by judicial personnel may lead to a censure by the Control Yuan or, in case of more serious violations, to impeachment proceedings.[38]

3.1.3.2 Limited Control Over the Judiciary

In difference to other Australian jurisdictions, the establishing law in the Northern Territory explicitly authorises the Ombudsman Institution to investigate actions by a tribunal or a member of a tribunal if the Ombudsman "is satisfied there has been unreasonable delay by the authority in relation to the action".[39] The exempt provision is explicitly limited to tribunals[40] and does not include the ordinary judiciary. This legal provision takes account of the fact that tribunals may be seen as falling within the area of competence of the executive rather than the judicial branch.

In Papua New Guinea and Vanuatu, the Ombudsman Institution may investigate the behaviour of leaders if they are suspected to have violated provisions of the Leadership Code.[41] Leaders include *inter alia* judges, public prosecutors and chief magistrates.[42]

3.1.3.3 Administration of Justice

The core function of the judiciary, i.e. the substantive aspects of the proceedings in court, is always exempted, except for the deviations mentioned above. Different models can be found when it comes to the question of the administrative aspects of delivering justice. Many jurisdictions have explicitly excluded the judiciary as well as tribunals from the control of the Ombudsman Institutions. However, other jurisdictions make it clear that actions of a purely administrative nature, i.e. actions of preparatory and follow-up character without which no proceeding in front of a judge or magistrate can take place, can be the object of control of the Ombudsman

[37] Cf report on Taiwan, Chap. 20, p. 257 below for details.

[38] Cf ibid.

[39] Cf s16(3) OA (Northern Territory).

[40] Tribunals include the Lands, Planning and Mining Tribunal and the Mental Health Review Tribunal, cf www.nt.gov.au/justice/ntmc/about.shtml for details.

[41] Cf reports on Papua New Guinea, Chap. 18, p. 235 and Vanuatu, Chap. 22; p. 283 for details.

[42] The term "leaders" is defined accordingly in the Constitution of Papua New Guinea, cf. Art.221 Constitution.

Institution.[43] This is the case *inter alia* in the Cook Islands, in New Zealand, the Australian Commonwealth and South Australia. More explicitly it can be said that this jurisdiction comprises the actions of court and tribunal registries,[44] of the Department or Ministry of Justice,[45] of Corrections[46] and acts of the judiciary if these are purely administrative and not "done in the discharge of a judicial authority."[47] In Victoria, the Ombudsman may intervene in review proceedings dealing with Freedom of Information requests at the Victorian Civil and Administrative Tribunal (VCAT).[48]

3.1.4 Legislator

The legislator is not object of control of the Ombudsman. Rather, in many jurisdictions Ombudsmen are Officers of Parliament (in the Cook Islands, New Zealand, the Northern Territory, Queensland, Samoa, Victoria and Western Australia)[49] and report on their activities to Parliament. The Ombudsmen's core function is the control of the administration respectively the executive branch of government. As a rule of law principle, administrative action does not take place without a legal foundation. Typically, an administrative action is the execution or implementation of laws and legal requirements in individual cases. For this reason, overseeing the administration means identifying not only shortcomings in the way legislation is implemented, but also includes the identification of legal ambiguities and legal shortcomings.[50] The legislator is therefore often the addressee of outcomes of the Ombudsmen's work. Often, this is not explicitly regulated in the establishing laws of the Institutions. Mostly, it is stipulated that Ombudsmen shall report to the body which has been the subject of the investigation on any flaws identified. In practice, such information also reaches Parliament either by way of the Annual Report or in special reports.[51] The Institution in New South Wales, for example, may recommend legislative amendments and does so quite frequently by way of special reports to Parliament.[52] Interestingly, in Taiwan the Control Yuan

---

[43] Cf Owen (1999), p. 63.

[44] Australian Commonwealth.

[45] Cook Islands and New Zealand.

[46] New Zealand.

[47] South Australia. According to information provided by the Institution; cf s3(1)(c) OA (South Australia).

[48] Cf report on Victoria, Chap. 13, p. 177 and s57 FOIA (Victoria) for more details.

[49] Cf Sect. 2.2.2, p. 24 above.

[50] Cf Kucsko-Stadlmayer (2008), p. 30.

[51] Cf Sect. 4.1.3.1, p. 74 for more details on legislative initiatives.

[52] According to information provided by the Institution.

has jurisdiction over the public officials working for the Legislative Yuan, but not over Parliamentarians.[53]

3.2 Standard of Control

3.2.1 International Standards

The Paris Principles stipulate that an Institution should be given "as broad a mandate as possible [...] specifying [...] its sphere of competence."[54] Further, responsibilities should include "any matters concerning the promotion and protection of human rights."[55] This explicitly identifies human rights as a basic standard. UN General Assembly Resolution 63/169 and UN General Assembly Resolution 65/207 both see the role of the Ombudsmen in "promoting good governance in public administrations, as well as improving their relations with citizens, and in strengthening the delivery of public services."[56] Further, UN General Assembly Resolution 63/169 refers to the work of the Ombudsmen as "consistent with the principles of justice, equality and rule of law."[57] UN General Assembly Resolution 63/172 acknowledges the role of NHRIs in "the strengthening of the rule of law and the promotion and protection of human rights in all sectors",[58] while UN General Assembly Resolution 65/207 underlines the role of existing Ombudsmen "in contributing to the effective realization of the rule of law and respect for the principles of justice and equality"[59] and encourages them "to operate, as appropriate, in accordance with" the Paris Principles.[60]

---

[53] Cf report on Taiwan, Chap. 20, p. 257 for details.

[54] Paris Principles, "Competences and responsibilities", paragraph 2.

[55] Paris Principles, "Competences and responsibilities", paragraph 3(a).

[56] UN General Assembly Resolution 63/169, 2008, on the role of the Ombudsman, mediator and other national human rights institutions and protection of human rights, preamble, and UN General Assembly Resolution 65/207, 2010, on the role of the Ombudsman, mediator and other national human rights institutions in the promotion and protection of human rights, preamble.

[57] UN General Assembly Resolution 63/169, 2008, on the role of the Ombudsman, mediator and other national human rights institutions and protection of human rights, paragraph 2(b).

[58] UN General Assembly Resolution 63/172, 2008, on national institutions for the promotion and protection of human rights, paragraph 12.

[59] UN General Assembly Resolution 65/207, 2010, on the role of the Ombudsman, mediator and other national human rights institutions in the promotion and protection of human rights, preamble.

[60] UN General Assembly Resolution 65/207, 2010, on the role of the Ombudsman, mediator and other national human rights institutions in the promotion and protection of human rights, paragraph 6(a).

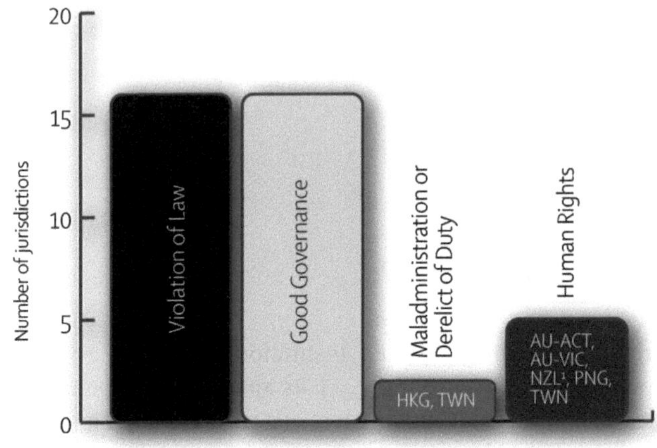

Fig. 3.4 Standard of Control. (1) In the case of NZL this refers to the Ombudsmen's functions as National Preventive Mechanism under the OPCAT and National Mechanism under the CRPD

3.2.2 General Overview

The standard of control is the benchmark against which the Ombudsman measures administrative actions. The jurisdictions examined widely follow the same model in defining this benchmark (see Fig. 3.4).[61] Most legal norms refer to a set of terms, defining in the negative what constitutes an inadequate administrative action (e.g. if an action or conduct was "contrary to law" or "unjust, oppressive or improperly discriminatory").[62] Sometimes an umbrella term (e.g. "maladministration" or "derelict of duty") is used and then defined further[63]; sometimes additional reference is made to human rights obligations.[64] The set of terms used the most represents the endeavour to include all situations that may constitute an inadequate administrative action so as to give the Ombudsman a mandate that is as comprehensive as possible.[65]

Additionally, the subject matter is not always simply called "administrative actions". While in practice there are no significant differences in what represents an administrative action, the laws sometimes attempt to define it further. The standard terms used are "matter of administration," "administrative act" or "administrative functions." Some laws clearly state that an administrative action is understood as

---

[61] Cf Pearce (1999), p. 86 et seq.

[62] This includes all jurisdictions except for Hong Kong and Taiwan, see footnote below.

[63] In Hong Kong the law uses the term "maladministration" which is further specified in the Definition Chapter. In Taiwan, the Constitution requires the Control Yuan to investigate whether there has been any "violation of law or "dereliction of duty".

[64] This is the case in Papua New Guinea and Victoria, cf Chap. 18, p. 235 and Chap. 13, p. 177 for more details.

[65] Cf Gregory (1999), p. 139 who discusses the term "maladministration".

comprising a manner of conduct, decisions, recommendations, acts or omissions relating to a matter of administration (e.g. in New Zealand). Irrespective of the exact wording, administrative actions must be delineated from governmental policies[66] which do not fall under the Ombudsmen's jurisdiction. If the Ombudsman may investigate administrative actions in the area of the judiciary, these must also be delineated from the substantive aspects of the proceedings in court.[67]

3.2.3 *Violation of Law*

Clearly, in all jurisdictions examined the standard of control includes the question of legality of administrative actions. Here, the control standard in almost all jurisdictions (except for Hong Kong) explicitly refers to actions and/or conduct that appears to have been "contrary to law."[68] Also in Hong Kong, where reference is made to "maladministration", any violation of law is covered.[69] The Ombudsman is authorised to investigate any form of maladministration, including an action that "was based wholly or partly on a mistake of law or fact."[70] Thus, he or she must also have the authorisation to point out a blatant violation of law. The question whether such violation would more appropriately be dealt with by a court, is an issue the Ombudsman considers when deciding whether or not to initiate an investigation.[71]

3.2.4 *Good Governance*

The set of terms used to define the standard of control in almost all jurisdictions, while showing variations in the details specified, includes most or all of the following elements (language differs in detail)[72]:

The Ombudsman determines whether the administrative action was:

- unreasonable, unjust, oppressive, or improperly discriminatory
- in accordance with a rule of law or a provision of any act, regulation, or bylaw or a practice that is or may be unreasonable, unjust, oppressive, or improperly discriminatory

---

66 Cf Keith (2005), Development of the role of the Ombudsman with reference to the Pacific, speech held at the 22nd APOR Conference, p. 2.

67 In case of a dispute, the question can be put before the highest court for decision in most jurisdictions, cf Sect. 4.1.3.1, p. 74 for details.

68 Cf e.g. s15(1) OA (Commonwealth).

69 Cf Cooray (2000), p. 77.

70 Cf s2(1) OO (Hong Kong).

71 Cf Sect. 4.1.2.1, p. 66.

72 Quotes from the legislation in New Zealand, New South Wales and the Northern Territory, used as examples for all the legislations that use the same or similar wording. Cf also Pearce (2000), p. 97 et seq. and Gregory (1999), p. 142.

- based on a mistake of law or fact
- based wholly or partly on improper motives, irrelevant grounds or irrelevant consideration
- a conduct for which reasons should be given but are not given
- done in the exercise of a power or discretion and the reasons for the decisions were not but should have been given
- [otherwise] wrong

These provisions clearly share a common objective which is to achieve good governance.[73] The concept of "good governance"[74] includes the rule of law, implying an impartial enforcement of a democratic legal framework, and the assumption that all administrative actions must take place in a transparent way, that those affected must be informed well and comprehensively, that the administration must act in an effective, efficient and timely manner while making best use of the available resources, and that those affected must be informed about their rights and possible legal remedies.[75]

All these elements specifying the standard of control define inadequate administrative actions which can be investigated by the Ombudsman.[76] These negative descriptions provide for deducing a positive standard for good governance: reasonable, just, fair and well-founded decisions which are based on nothing but all the relevant facts, rules/regulations, proper motives,[77] and relevant grounds. The common feature of all these standards is that they are rather vague and thus necessitate interpretation.[78] Hence it is up to the Ombudsman to develop an ever-improving interpretative framework according to which these standards of control can be applied.

The framing of the standards of control in the differing jurisdictions shows widespread similarities caused by the adaptation of the New Zealand model to the jurisdictions in the region. Over the years, the wording used to define the standards of control changed only slightly. Partly, the criterion whether the administrative action was a "conduct for which reasons should be given but [were] not given" was included into the standards of control.[79] In Vanuatu, reference to the Common Law concept of natural justice[80] (or procedural fairness) is made which is

[73] For a discussion of the term good governance cf p. 8 et seq. Cf also Chen (2010), p. 726 et seq.

[74] The Commonwealth Heads of Government advocate good governance and endorsed the "Framework for Principles for Promoting Good Governance and Combating Corruption" in the Durban Communiqué 1999. The Framework refers in paragraph 21 to the importance of Ombudsmen vested with an anti-corruption mandate in combating poor governance.

[75] Cf Reif (2004), p. 63 and p. 78 et seq. for more details on the concept of good governance.

[76] Cf Gregory (1999), p. 144.

[77] Motives are often implied by a law or regulation and must be accurately deduced by those who apply the law.

[78] Except for the legality of an action, cf Sect. 3.2.3, p. 51.

[79] This criterion is not explicit part of the standard of control in s22 of the Ombudsman Act (New Zealand).

[80] Cf www.britannica.com/EBchecked/topic/406273/natural-justice.

an indispensable part of good governance.[81] This set of terms is applicable to each case investigated and the Ombudsmen may refer to any of these criteria to justify their intervention. Interestingly, many laws by now include the catch-all clause about an action simply being "wrong". This very vague term gives the Ombudsman the necessary flexibility — to be used responsibly — to address any situation perceived to be incorrect for whatever reason.

3.2.5 *Maladministration or Derelict of Duty*

In some jurisdictions the terminology used to specify the standard of control differs slightly more from the one listed above (i.e. in Hong Kong and Taiwan). The criterion for the standard of control used in Hong Kong is "injustice in consequence of maladministration" in connection with an administrative action.[82] The term "maladministration" is defined in the law as "inefficient, bad or improper administration." A non-exhaustive enumeration[83] includes a more detailed definition, mirroring many elements contained in the definitions of other jurisdictions examined (analysed above).[84] For the purposes of this study,[85] maladministration can be seen as the antonym of good governance.[86] The standard of control used in Taiwan (in addition to a violation of law) is that of a "dereliction of duty."[87] There is no further definition as to what this includes.

3.2.6 *Human Rights*

3.2.6.1 Human Rights as Standard of Control

Human rights can either be an explicit or an implied standard of control. In a wide interpretation of the concept of good governance, human rights are an inherent part

[81] Cf s34(1) LCA (Vanuatu) which stipulates "contrary to natural justice".

[82] Cf s7(1)(b)(i) OO (Hong Kong).

[83] The legal definition of maladministration includes "unreasonable conduct, including delay, discourtesy and lack of consideration for a person affected by any action, abuse of any power (including any discretionary power) or authority [...] or unreasonable, unjust, oppressive or improperly discriminatory procedures," cf. s2(1) OO (Hong Kong).

[84] Cf Sect. 3.2.4, p. 51.

[85] The concept of good governance was originally developed by the World Bank in a very different context — that of development aid and economic reforms. Back then, good governance was the opposite of what was considered poor or bad governance in many partner countries in the global South. Cf Reif (2004), p. 62 et seq.

[86] Cf Kucsko-Stadlmayer (2008), p. 33 for details; she refers to "good administration" in this context. Cf also Kofler (2008), who states that the Ombudsman in the UK "investigates instances of maladministration," a term not further defined by law, p. 435.

[87] The standard of control is stipulated in the Constitution.

of good governance[88] and can thus be seen as belonging to the set of terms[89] used by most jurisdictions to define the standard of control.[90] Most jurisdictions examined are signatories to various international human rights treaties; the International Covenant on Civil and Political Rights (ICCPR), for example, has been ratified by all jurisdictions except for Taiwan and Tonga.[91] The mentioned set of terms however refers usually to the legal order of the respective jurisdiction only. Reif argues that in this case, it has to be established "whether international law is considered to be part of the domestic legal system. If it can be concluded that these norms are part of the national legal system, either automatically or through the passage of domestic implementing legislation, then the [Ombudsman] can use the 'domestic' model of the international human rights obligations as part of the legal arsenal it employs in the process of undertaking an investigation".[92] Reif concludes that "in this manner, international human rights law can be used [...] by all [Ombudsmen]." This is the case, for example, when it comes to the right to non-discrimination stipulated *inter alia* in Articles 2 and 26 ICCPR. The above-quoted set of norms explicitly refers to discriminative administrative actions twice.

In a somewhat stricter manner, human rights are explicitly part of the standard of control in a few jurisdictions where the Ombudsmen have been given specific tasks in regard to the protection and promotion of human rights.[93]

In Papua New Guinea for example, the Constitution stipulates a set of terms largely congruent with the terms listed above as control criteria. However, the Constitution also explicitly stipulates that in its considerations the Ombudsman Commission shall take the Constitution's "National Goals and Directive Principles, the Basic Rights and the Basic Social Obligations" into account as appropriate.[94] Similarly, in the ACT the Human Rights Act stipulates that "[s]o far as it is possible to do so consistently with its purpose, a Territory law must be interpreted in a way that is compatible with human rights."[95] The Act further stipulates that it is unlawful for a public authority to act in a way that is incompatible with a human right. The Ombudsman has not been vested with specific powers in this regard but shall take the Act's provision fully into account. In Victoria the law also prescribes such a list of control criteria. A sub-section inserted into the Ombudsman Act after the adoption of the Charter of Human Rights and Responsibilities Act 2006

[88] Cf Annual Report of the Secretary General of the UN 1997, UN Doc A/52/1, paragraph 27, (www.un.org/Docs/SG/Report97/97rep2.htm#A). Cf also Reif (2004), p. 64 et seqq.

[89] Cf Sect. 3.2.4, p. 51 above.

[90] Cf also Reif (1999), p. 282; Reif (2004), p. 86 and Oosting cited in Reif (1999), p. 282.

[91] Taiwan has ratified the Covenants, but the deposit was rejected by the UN. Cf Liao (2001), p. 90 for more details on Taiwan and international human rights treaties. The Cook Islands are not a signatory but bound by virtue of their association with New Zealand.

[92] Reif (1999), p. 281.

[93] Cf Reif (2004), p. 87 et seq.

[94] Cf art. 219(1)(a) Constitution (Papua New Guinea).

[95] Cf s40 Human Rights Act (ACT) 2004.

(Victoria) gives the Ombudsman the power to "enquire into or investigate whether any administrative action is incompatible with a human right set out in the [Charter]".[96] Should the Victorian Ombudsman find any such incompatibility in a specific case, his or her role is limited to the standard procedural powers — reporting and recommending remedial action of any sort. Neither the Ombudsman Act (Victoria) nor the Charter itself gives the Ombudsman any subsequent powers. The Ombudsman's function is neither stronger nor weaker than in the standard procedure.

In Taiwan, the members of the Control Yuan have been granted the power to investigate whether the conduct or a policy of the executive[97] is in conformity with the standards contained in the International Covenant on Economic, Social and Cultural Rights (ICESCR) and the ICCPR.[98] This is based on the Act to Implement the ICESCR and the ICCPR that entered into force in 2009.[99] The two Covenants stipulate a comprehensive list of civil and political rights as well as of economic, social and cultural rights that thus have become part of the domestic legal order. Already in 2000, the Control Yuan has established a Human Rights Protection Committee, as one of its eight special committees. Also at this time human rights became a standard of control for the Control Yuan. As in the case of Victoria, there are no special mechanisms foreseen in case of human rights violations; rather, the standard procedures apply.

3.2.6.2 Monitoring the Implementation of Human Rights

Beyond the use of human rights as a control criterion is the monitoring of how human rights are implemented. The purpose of such activities goes hand in hand with the reason for the tendency to put less emphasis on the investigation of individual cases than on the more general approach of investigating systemic deficiencies.[100] The purpose of the latter is to significantly reduce the number of individual complaints related to one issue by addressing one systemic deficiency. Similarly, proactive monitoring of the implementation of specific human rights — and addressing the shortcomings identified — holds the chance of significantly reducing the number of complaints related to these human rights violations. In the region examined this task is only beginning to spread as an explicit statutory function of the Ombudsman. The Papua New Guinea Ombudsman Commission has established a Human Rights Unit, which monitors the implementation of Papua New Guinea's international obligations concerning human rights. The power for

[96] Cf Reif (2011), p. 278 and s13(1A) OA (Victoria).

[97] This competence includes all levels of government both central level and local level.

[98] Cf report on Taiwan, Chap. 20, p. 263.

[99] By way of this Act, the provisions of both covenants become binding law in Taiwan although Taiwan is not a UN member.

[100] Cf p. 61 and 82 for more details.

this monitoring role can be read into the general powers of the Commission which are embedded in the Constitution.[101] In Victoria, such monitoring rests with the Victorian Equal Opportunity and Human Rights Commission.[102] In Samoa there are plans for the Ombudsman to also become the country's Human Rights Commission, which would include an active monitoring role.[103]

The New Zealand Ombudsmen Office has certain explicit human rights monitoring tasks. New Zealand is the only of the sixteen jurisdictions examined that has to date signed and ratified[104] the Optional Protocol to the Convention against Torture and other Cruel, Inhuman or Degrading Treatment or Punishment (OPCAT).[105] In 2007, the New Zealand Ombudsmen Office was designated one of four National Preventive Mechanisms (NPMs) with the task of preventing torture and ill-treatment (by undertaking regular visits to places of detention) and of making recommendations to the authorities. In 2010, the Ombudsmen further assumed the role of one of the independent National Mechanisms to "promote, protect and monitor"[106] the implementation of the Convention of the Rights of Persons with Disabilities (CRPD).[107]

In Taiwan, the Legislative Yuan has passed an Act which implements the Convention on the Elimination of All Forms of Discrimination against Women (CEDAW) in 2011.[108] In the future, Parliament will probably pass legislation to implement the OPCAT as well.[109] Based on this legislation, Control Yuan members investigate whether the executive acts are in compliance with human rights. In addition, its Human Rights Protection Committee has been given the task to proactively advocate and monitor the implementation of human rights.[110] The Committee's functions include the providing of proposals for drafts of human

---

[101] The Institution is involved in the Government's establishing of a Human Rights Commission, in conformity with the Paris Principles. It can be expected that in the future this Commission will adequately exercise monitoring functions.

[102] Cf s41 Charter of Human Rights and Responsibilities Act 2006 (Victoria).

[103] Cf report on Samoa, Chap. 19, p. 249 for more details.

[104] Australia has signed but not yet ratified, cf report on the Commonwealth Ombudsman, Chap. 7, p. 101 for more details; Taiwan may pass legislation to implement OPCAT in the future according to information provided by the Control Yuan. Such legislation would make the provisions of the OPCAT become binding law in Taiwan although Taiwan is not a UN member.

[105] The OPCAT requires signatories to establish fully independent National Preventive Mechanisms (NPMs) to prevent torture and ill-treatment, cf 4.1.3.9, p. 79.

[106] Cf art. 33 UN Convention of the Rights of Persons with Disabilities (CRPD).

[107] The CRPD entered into force on 3 May 2008.

[108] By way of this Act, the provisions of the Convention become binding law in Taiwan although Taiwan is not a UN member. In addition to the 2009 Act implementing the ICESCR and the ICCPR, cf p. 55 above.

[109] Similarly, also by way of such Act, the provisions of the CEDAW would become binding law in Taiwan although Taiwan is not a UN member. Information on these plans of the Parliament was provided by the Institution.

[110] This is stipulated in the Rules Governing the Establishment of the Human Rights Protection Committee, which are based on the Organic Law of the Control Yuan.

rights laws, the researching of how to promote human rights, the promoting of human rights education, the interaction with international human rights institutions and the collecting of relevant information.

3.3 Access

3.3.1 International Standards[111]

The Paris Principles stipulate that an Institution should be given "as broad a mandate as possible [. . .] specifying [. . .] its sphere of competence."[112] Further, to "hear any person and obtain any information and any documents necessary for assessing situations falling within its competence,"[113] to inform "the party who filed the petition of his [or her] rights, in particular the remedies available to him [or her], and promoting his [or her] access to them,"[114] and to hear "any complaints or petitions or transmitting them to any other competent authority."[115] UN General Assembly Resolution 63/169 refers to the work of the Ombudsmen as having to be "consistent with the principles of justice, equality and rule of law."[116] Finally, UN General Assembly Resolution 65/207 gives great importance to the role of existing Ombudsmen "in contributing to the effective realization of the rule of law and respect for the principles of justice and equality"[117] and encourages them "to operate, as appropriate, in accordance with" the Paris Principles.[118] The standards listed here include the different aspects that are part of the access to justice as defined in Sect. 1.1.3.[119] These aspects are the existence of an effective remedy, a *de facto* access to court, the principles of fair trial, judicial protection, due process, legal certainty, absence of undue delay and non-discrimination.

---

[111] UNDP (2005), p. 109 et seq.

[112] Paris Principles, "Competences and responsibilities", paragraph 2.

[113] Paris Principles, "Methods of operation", paragraph (b).

[114] Paris Principles, "Additional principles concerning the status of commissions with quasi-jurisdictional competences, paragraph (b).

[115] Paris Principles, "Additional principles concerning the status of commissions with quasi-jurisdictional competences, paragraph (c).

[116] UN General Assembly Resolution 63/169, 2008, on the role of the Ombudsman, mediator and other national human rights institutions and protection of human rights, paragraph 2(b).

[117] UN General Assembly Resolution 65/207, 2010, on the role of the Ombudsman, mediator and other national human rights institutions in the promotion and protection of human rights, preamble.

[118] UN General Assembly Resolution 65/207, 2010, on the role of the Ombudsman, mediator and other national human rights institutions in the promotion and protection of human rights, paragraph 6(a).

[119] Cf p. 6 for more details.

3.3.2 Accessibility of the Institution

The Ombudsman Institution is only as good as the access to it. The more visible and invisible hurdles there are in the potential complainant's way, the more unlikely the registration of a complaint becomes. Potential obstacles include practical aspects, such as physical barriers (e.g. long distances, travel costs, no barrier-free access to offices), lack of awareness of the Ombudsman Institution and/or its mandate, difficult procedures and offering services only in a restricted number of languages. More formal aspects encompass any requirements for a complaint, the existence of fees and of deadlines as well as eligibility criteria for submitting a complaint.[120]

All Institutions have offices that are accessible to the public and, if no sub-offices exist in the regions,[121] the Ombudsman or his or her staff regularly undertake outreach visits to different parts of the jurisdiction. Potential complainants in places such as detention facilities are visited regularly,[122] and there are statutory procedures in place ensuring that mail from a detainee is immediately forwarded to the Ombudsman by the prison authorities. Information about barrier-free access to the offices is limited.[123] All Ombudsman Institutions have regular opening hours[124] and can also be reached by telephone (in Australia and New Zealand, the Institutions offer toll-free numbers) and via the internet (except for Tonga and Vanuatu). Complainants can always file complaints in writing and mostly also orally, either in person or by telephone (except for New South Wales,[125] Victoria, Western Australia and Samoa[126]). Sometimes complainants are subsequently required to put the complaint in writing (in the Northern Territory, Tasmania, Tonga and Vanuatu). The internet or e-mail can be used in all jurisdictions for submitting a complaint except for in Tonga and Vanuatu. Often the Institutions offer support if a complainant requires an interpreter (e.g. in Queensland, the law even stipulates that anyone who cannot communicate in English has the right to an interpreter).[127] Information is usually available in different languages (including relevant languages for national minorities and immigrants) and in the form of

---

[120] Cf Gregory (1999), p. 136 et seq. and Groves (2002), p. 195.

[121] Only the Commonwealth Ombudsman and the Institutions in New Zealand and Papua New Guinea have regional sub-offices.

[122] Cf Grooves (2002), p. 196 for more details on the activities of the Ombudsmen in Australia.

[123] No information can be given for Tonga and Vanuatu. In other jurisdictions, access is ensured.

[124] Opening hours are usually from between 9 and 10 am to 5 pm (Monday to Friday).

[125] However, the New South Wales Ombudsman has discretion to also accept complaints filed orally.

[126] The Samoan Ombudsman offers support if a person has difficulties in putting the complaint in writing.

[127] In all other Australian jurisdictions, the Ombudsmen offer translation services, partly by using a telephone translation service for non-English speakers. The same goes for the New Zealand, Hong Kong and Taiwan Institutions.

hardcopy flyers, information brochures and online. None of the sixteen Institutions levies fees upon a complainant.[128]

3.3.3 Discretion to Accept and Investigate a Complaint

Following the submission of a complaint, the Ombudsman determines whether the complaint is eligible, whether the matter complained of falls within his or her jurisdiction and, if answered in the positive, whether he or she will investigate the matter. Eligibility to complain is not bound to nationality. In all jurisdictions, any natural and legal person may complain.[129] In some jurisdictions, a third party may submit a complaint on behalf of the aggrieved person (in the Australian Commonwealth, the Northern Territory, in South Australia and Victoria; in New South Wales a Parliamentarian may act on someone else's behalf).

The cut-off period for submissions is usually 12 months (but 24 months in Tasmania and Hong Kong) after the situation complained about had occurred or come to the knowledge of the complainant. In some jurisdictions the law rather vaguely stipulates that the complaint should not be delayed too long (Papua New Guinea, Taiwan and Vanuatu). However, any cut-off period is not an absolute deadline; the Ombudsman has discretion to investigate the matter under exceptional circumstances at any time.

Further eligibility criteria or exclusion clauses leave it to the discretion of the Ombudsman to determine whether or not to investigate the subject matter. The way these criteria and provisions are modelled shows that complaints to the Ombudsman are seen as subsidiary to other formal ways of seeking redress. If there is a formal right to review or appeal against the administrative action complained about, the Ombudsman may decide not to investigate the matter, unless there are special circumstances that make it appear unreasonable to exercise these rights (this applies to all jurisdictions but Samoa). Some laws formulate this in a rather strong way ("must not investigate [...] unless"),[130] others clearly leave the decision to investigate to the Ombudsman's discretion ("may decide..."). Since the question of reasonableness is always included in these provisions, it is, however, not a requirement to first exhaust all legal remedies before turning to the Ombudsman. As an exception, Samoan law stipulates that the Ombudsman has no jurisdiction in cases, in which legal remedies have not been exhausted.[131]

---

[128] Although the law sometimes allows this, all Institutions reported that *de facto* no such fee is levied. E.g. the Hong Kong law allows the levying of a fee and the Ombudsman Act in Samoa explicitly foresees a fee. However, no fee has ever been levied upon a complainant.

[129] The Ombudsman Act (New South Wales) even stipulates that a public authority may also file a complaint, cf. s12(1) OA (New South Wales).

[130] This is the case in Hong Kong, the Northern Territory, Victoria and Western Australia.

[131] Cf s11(6)(a) Ombudsman Act (Samoa).

Another standard criterion in all jurisdictions is the fact that the complainant must have a certain personal interest in the matter. This provision is akin to the right of action in a judicial process. If there are other complaints entities with a function similar to that of the Ombudsman and both have jurisdiction, the law can stipulate that the Ombudsman may not investigate a matter if there is an ongoing investigation in front of the other complaints entity (Queensland and South Australia). Many jurisdictions require the complainant to first address the authority responsible for the action complained of and grant the Ombudsman discretion not to investigate if the complainant has not addressed said authority or, if the complainant has done so, not to investigate until he or she learns that no redress (or no adequate redress) has been granted (Australian Commonwealth, New South Wales, the Northern Territory, South Australia, Tasmania and Vanuatu).

In many jurisdictions, the law contains a clause which leaves it to the discretion of the Ombudsman to decide whether or not to investigate an action. The Ombudsman may decide not to investigate if, under the circumstances, "any further investigation is unnecessary" (Cook Islands, Hong Kong, New Zealand, the Northern Territory,[132] Tonga, Vanuatu and Western Australia) or if "an investigation does not appear to be warranted in the circumstances" (Tasmania). In Papua New Guinea, an issue may not be investigated if there are other, more important cases.[133]

Finally, all jurisdictions contain an anti-abuse clause stipulating that the Ombudsman may not investigate if the matter of the complaint is "trivial, frivolous or vexatious or is not made in good faith" (formulations vary).

3.3.4 *Proprio Motu-Proceedings*

The Ombudsman can initiate investigations on his or her own motion in all jurisdictions researched. This power strengthens the credibility of the Institution. Irrespective of how the Ombudsman learns about a subject matter,[134] it always may become the object of an own motion investigation. The restricting effect of not including the possibility of third party-complaints in most jurisdictions (see above) is thus ameliorated. Also, this provision minimises the risk that issues brought to the attention of the Ombudsman anonymously[135] or complaints which the complainant wishes to withdraw cannot be investigated.[136] In case of *propio motu*-investigations,

---

[132] This also goes for a complaint made by a third party if there is "no substantive issue" or if there is "no first-hand evidence about the subject matter", cf (s33(c)-(e) OA (Northern Territory).

[133] Cf s16(3) OLOC (Papua New Guinea).

[134] Sources typically include press and television as well as individual complaints.

[135] Cf Kucsko-Stadlmayer (2008), p. 21.

[136] In Hong Kong, the latter case is specifically addressed in the law, which stipulates that, if a complainant withdraws a complaint, the Ombudsman shall determine whether it is in the public interest to continue the investigation, s11 OO (Hong Kong).

there are no additional statutory preconditions and the Ombudsman's mandate is the same as in case of investigations following complaints. This gives the Ombudsman wide discretion whenever he or she learns about potential matters of concern.

Propio motu- proceedings allow the Institutions to better address systemic flaws with the aim of improving the public administration in general.[137] They thus contribute to administrative justice.[138] This aspect is also asserted to be an "integrity arm of government"[139] which encompasses all administrative law review institutions of a state, including the Ombudsman.[140] The focus of this integrity arm is, besides addressing individual grievances, the "systemic investigation and audit"[141] of the public administration.

The Control Yuan in Taiwan clearly represents such an integrity arm.[142] In addition to own motion investigations,[143] it has the power to conduct "circuit supervisions" by taking a holistic view at all aspects of the administration. It also has the power of audit.[144] In Australia, as Stuhmcke argues on the basis of statistical data, the Commonwealth Ombudsman has strategically shifted away from the investigation of individual complaints[145] (under his or her discretion) towards the use of his or her resources for own motion investigations for the identification of systemic problems.[146] The empirical data shows that the Commonwealth Ombudsman used his or her discretion not to investigate individual complaints in 19 % of the cases in the 1977/1978 reporting period, but in 73 % of all cases submitted in the 2004/2005 reporting period.[147] A similar trend can be assumed for other jurisdictions.[148] Complainants of cases not investigated are "referred away [...either] back to [the] agency in question or [...] to other complaints bodies."[149] At the same time, the Ombudsman supports the public administration in improving its "complaint-handling skills".[150]

---

[137] Cf p. 82 for more details on the investigation of systemic flaws.

[138] Cf *inter alia* Creyke (2007), p. 705 et seqq. and Stuhmcke (2010), p.143 et seqq. for details.

[139] Cf Creyke, ibid.

[140] Cf Creyke, ibid.

[141] Cf Stuhmcke (2010), p. 144 and Buck et al. (2011), p. 138.

[142] The Control Yuan was established for this purpose, cf report on Taiwan, Chap. 20, p. 257 for more details on the background of Taiwan's five-power system.

[143] Own motion investigations may be carried out by another organisation on behalf of the Control Yuan, by one of its Committees, or by a Control Yuan member.

[144] Cf report on Taiwan, Chap. 20, p. 257 for details.

[145] According to Stuhmcke, in the 1960s and 1970s parliamentary debates in the Australian Commonwealth, there has been the clear picture that the Ombudsman's role is to focus on addressing individual complaints, cf Stuhmcke (2010), p. 147 et seq.

[146] Cf Stuhmcke (2010), p. 159.

[147] Cf Stuhmcke (2010), tables on p. 151 and 153.

[148] Cf Buck et al. (2011), p. 134 et seq. who reports the same for the United Kingdom.

[149] Cf Stuhmcke (2010), p. 152.

[150] Cf Stuhmcke (2010), p. 152.

3.3.5 Proceedings Following Referrals

In most jurisdictions, the Ombudsman may be allocated the task to initiate proceedings by Parliament, one of its Committees, the Governor, or the Prime Minister (except for the Australian Commonwealth, Hong Kong, New South Wales, Papua New Guinea and Taiwan).[151] In this case, the Ombudsman has no discretion but is obligated to investigate the issue and to report back to Parliament (and the referral authority) about the outcome. Other than that, the standard provisions in regard to the Institution's mandate apply. Referral by Parliament does not require the Ombudsman's approval. However, the referral by the Prime Minister requires the prior consent of the respective Ombudsman in New Zealand, Samoa and Tonga.[152]

References

Buck T, Kirkham R, Thompson B (2011) The Ombudsman enterprise and administrative justice. Ashgate, Farnham

Chen M (2010) New Zealand's Ombudsmen legislation: the need for amendments after almost 50 years. Law Rev 41:723–760

Cooray A (2000) Ombudsman in Asia. In: Gregory R, Giddings P (eds) Righting wrongs. The Ombudsman in six continents. IOS Press, Berlin

Creyke R (2007) Administrative justice—towards integrity in government. Melb Univ Law Rev 31(3):705–732

Gregory R (1999) Building an Ombudsman scheme: provisions and operating practices. In: Reif LC (ed) The International Ombudsman Anthology. Selected writings from the International Ombudsman Institute. Kluwer Law International, Dordrechtetal

Groves M (2002) Ombudsmen's jurisdiction in prisons. Monash Univ Law Rev 28(2):181–205

Keith KJ (2005) Development of the role of the Ombudsman with reference to the Pacific. In: Speech held at the 22nd APOR conference, p. 2

Kofler B (2008) United Kingdom of Great Britain and Northern Ireland. In: Kucsko-Stadlmayer G (ed) European Ombudsman-Institutions. Springer, Vienna

Kucsko-Stadlmayer G (ed) (2008) European Ombudsman-Institutions. Springer, Vienna

Liao FF-T (2001) Establishing a national human rights commission in Taiwan: the role of NGOs and challenges ahead. Asia Pac J Hum Rights Law 2(2):90–109

McLeod R (2001) Freedom of information—an Ombudsman's perspective, commentary. Fed Law Rev 29(3):359–364

Owen S (1999) The Ombudsman: essential elements and common challenges. In: Reif LC (ed) The International Ombudsman Anthology. Selected writings from the International Ombudsman Institute. Kluwer Law International, Dordrecht

Pearce D (1999) The Ombudsman: review and preview the importance of being different. In: Reif LC (ed) The International Ombudsman Anthology. Selected writings from the International Ombudsman Institute. Kluwer Law International, Dordrecht

[151] In Vanuatu, a Minister, a Member of Parliament, the National Council of Chiefs or a Local Government Council may refer a subject matter to the Ombudsman for investigation.

[152] In New Zealand it needs the approval of the Chief Ombudsman.

Pearce D, Gregory R, Giddings P (eds) (2000) Righting wrongs. The Ombudsman in six continents. IOS Press, Berlinetal
Reif LC (ed) (1999) The International Ombudsman Anthology. Selected writings from the International Ombudsman Institute. Kluwer Law International, Dordrecht
Reif LC (2004) The Ombudsman, good governance, and the International Human Rights System. Martinus Nijhoff, Leiden
Reif LC (2011) Transplantation and adaptation: the evolution of the human rights Ombudsman. Boston Coll Third World Law J 31(2):269–310
Stuhmcke A (2008) Changing relations between government and citizen: administrative law and the work of the Australian commonwealth Ombudsman. Aust J Public Adm 67(3):321–339
Stuhmcke A (2010) ‘Each for themselves’ or ‘one for all’? The changing emphasis of the commonwealth Ombudsman. Fed Law Rev 38(1):143–167
del Villar K (2002) Who guards the guardians? Recent developments concerning the jurisdiction and accountability of Ombudsmen in Australia. In: Reif LC (ed) (The international Ombudsman yearbook 2002, vol 6. Martinus Nijhoff, Leiden
UNDP (2005) Programming for justice: access for all. A practitioner’s guide to a human rights-based approach to access to justice. United Nations, Bangkok

Chapter 4
Powers

Michael Frahm

4.1 Administration

4.1.1 International Standards

The Paris Principles stipulate that an Institution should have the responsibility to "submit to the Government [and] Parliament [...] on an advisory basis [...] through the exercise of its power to hear a matter without higher referral, opinions, recommendation, proposals and reports on any matters concerning the promotion and protection of human rights; the national institution may decide to publicize them".[1] The Principles further state that an Institution shall "freely consider any questions falling within its competences [and ...] address public opinion directly or through any press organ, particularly in order to publicize its opinions and recommendations".[2] Moreover, the Principles highlight that Institutions should "[s]eek[...] an amicable settlement through conciliation or [...] binding decisions or [...] on the basis of confidentiality" and should "[m]ak[e] recommendations to the competent authorities, especially by proposing amendments or reforms of the laws [...]".[3] UN General Assembly Resolution 64/161 underlines the importance of "giving [Institutions] an investigative role",[4] and UN General Assembly Resolution 65/207 stresses that Institutions "can play an important role in advising the

[1] Paris Principles, "Competences and responsibilities", paragraph 3(a).

[2] Paris Principles, "Methods of operation", sub-paragraphs (a) and (c).

[3] Paris Principles, "Additional principles concerning the status of commissions with quasi-jurisdictional competence", sub-paragraphs (a) and (d).

[4] UN General Assembly Resolution 64/161, 2009, on national institutions for the promotion and protection of human rights, paragraph 10.

M. Frahm (✉)
Ludwig Boltzmann Institute of Human Rights, Vienna, Austria
e-mail: michael.frahm@univie.ac.at

International Ombudsman Institute (ed.), *Australasia and Pacific Ombudsman Institutions*,
DOI 10.1007/978-3-642-33896-0_4, © Springer-Verlag Berlin Heidelberg 2013

Government with respect to bringing national legislation and national practices in line with their international human rights obligations."[5]

4.1.2 *Standard Functions*

In the following, the standard functions that form the basis for the Ombudsman's work are presented. The functions, universally recognised as forming the foundation for an office to be associated with an Ombudsman irrespective of its name, include the power to investigate, to recommend remedial action and to report on his or her activities.[6]

4.1.2.1 Investigation

The investigative function usually endows the Ombudsman with far-reaching powers to ascertain all relevant facts related to the subject-matter under investigation.[7] In many jurisdictions, the Ombudsman may preliminarily inquire into the subject matter to determine whether it falls under jurisdiction and whether, using his or her discretion, to investigate the matter (Hong Kong, Taiwan and all Australian Institutions). Before initiating a formal investigation it is always necessary to inform the head of the body concerned.[8] Investigations are always to be conducted in private; other than that, the Ombudsmen may freely determine the procedures.

Collecting of Information

The Ombudsman may hear any person and obtain any material or document from this person. In this context, he or she may administer an oath in all jurisdictions. The body concerned as well as any person summoned by the Ombudsman is legally bound to support the Ombudsman by giving the requested information and by rendering any material requested. The obligation to support the Ombudsman can (except for South Australia, Taiwan, Vanuatu, Victoria and Western Australia) be

---

[5] UN General Assembly Resolution 65/207, 2010, on the role of the Ombudsman, mediator and other national human rights institutions in the promotion and protection of human rights, paragraph 11.

[6] Cf Reif (2004), p. 3.

[7] Cf Besselink (2000), p. 161.

[8] The Commonwealth Ombudsman is explicitly authorised by law to have a standing arrangement with agencies, which sets out the manner of informing the agency; cf. report on the Commonwealth Ombudsman, Sect. 7.2.3.1, p. 110. The body concerned may be an agency, a Department or any other entity under jurisdiction, cf Sect. 3.1, p. 39 above.

limited in most jurisdictions *inter alia* for reasons of "security, defence or international relations."[9] In these cases, the Ombudsman cannot require a person to provide any such information.[10] However, a professional privilege claiming material to be subject to secrecy obligations by other laws can often not be held against an Ombudsman's request. In Samoa and Tonga, however, before passing on information of a personal nature to the Ombudsman, any consent required by any law must be obtained by the person concerned.

Access to Premises

In all jurisdictions,[11] the Ombudsman is authorised to enter any premises of agencies within jurisdiction, including correction facilities.[12] In the course of investigations he or she may inspect documents and take away or photocopy relevant documents.[13] Access is usually allowed at "any reasonable time", while the laws in Papua New Guinea,[14] South Australia, Victoria and Western Australia explicitly allow access at "any time".

In many jurisdictions, access further requires advance notice (except for Taiwan, New South Wales and Victoria),[15] while in South Australia, no such notice is required at least for preliminary investigations. In many jurisdictions, the right of access can be limited for the same reasons as in case of the obligation to support the Ombudsman[16] (e.g. in the case of the Commonwealth Ombudsman, in the Cook Islands, Hong Kong, New Zealand, Papua New Guinea, Samoa and Tonga).

All Ombudsmen have jurisdiction over correction facilities because prisons are part of the bodies within jurisdiction. The power to access prisons is thus mostly part of the general clause to enter any premises of agencies within jurisdiction. In some jurisdictions, however, there are special provisions which regulate the access to prisons (e.g. in the ACT, Papua New Guinea, New South Wales and South Australia). For example, in the ACT the ACT Corrections Management Act 2007

---

[9] Cf Pearce (2000), p. 96. This is done by way of a decision of the Prime Minster (Papua New Guinea), the Attorney-General (Australia, New Zealand, Samoa and Tonga) or the Minister of Justice (Cook Islands).

[10] In Vanuatu, the law stipulates that, while such information may be given to the Ombudsman, he or she shall not disclose any such matters.

[11] In Vanuatu, the law stresses a cooperational approach and thus allows access to premises only if there is no cooperation, based on a court warrant.

[12] Cf Groves (2002), p. 196.

[13] Cf Reif (2004), p. 4.

[14] Access to places of detention at any time is authorised under the Correctional Institutions Service Act (Papua New Guinea).

[15] In the function of Immigration Ombudsman the Commonwealth Ombudsman has the power to make unannounced visits to immigration detention centres. In Papua New Guinea, for visits of places of detention prior notice should be given, if possible.

[16] Cf p. 66 above for more details.

grants entry and inspection powers to the Ombudsman for correctional centres at any reasonable time. Additionally, in the capacity of the Immigration Ombudsman,[17] the Commonwealth Ombudsman may also visit immigration detention centres, including for unannounced visits. In New South Wales, the Crimes (Administration of Sentences) Regulation 2008 allows the Ombudsman and his or her staff to enter correction facilities without prior authorisation.[18] In New Zealand, the Ombudsmen are vested with special powers in regard to prisons and monitor the process of investigations of deaths in custody.[19]

In all jurisdictions the Ombudsman can meet and communicate with prison inmates in private. This is usually not explicitly regulated by law, but standard practice. It is explicitly regulated in Papua New Guinea, South Australia and Taiwan. This power can, however, be deduced from reading different provisions of the laws together, as done by the Victorian Ombudsman[20] — the right to freely determine his or her own procedure and the rule that all investigations shall be conducted in private.[21]

Sanctions

It is a big challenge for Ombudsmen that they must depend on the willingness of administrations to cooperate in order to effectively carry out investigations. A high standing and reputation of the Ombudsman him- or herself may often be supportive. However, without the threat of sanctions, compliance with requests of Ombudsmen is likely to be lower than it is today.[22] All Ombudsmen can summon a person to appear before the Ombudsman, administer an oath and examine said person under oath. In most jurisdictions failure to comply with such a request constitutes a punishable offence sanctioned by a fine (see Fig. 4.1). If the threat of punishment does not lead to compliance, options are usually limited. Only few Ombudsmen may turn to courts for a court order to enforce their request (the Commonwealth Ombudsman, South Australia, Tasmania, Queensland and Vanuatu).[23] If even a court order has no effect, these Ombudsmen (except for the Commonwealth Ombudsman and Vanuatu) may apply to court for a warrant for an arrest of said person. In Freedom of Information cases, the New Zealand Ombudsmen may set a 20-day deadline for complying with a request. If there is no compliance, however, they can only report on this to the Prime Minster and to Parliament.

---

[17] Cf report on the Commonwealth Ombudsman, Chap. 7, p. 101 for details.

[18] The Correctional Services Act 1982 (South Australia) contains a similar provision.

[19] Cf report on New Zealand, Chap. 21, p. 221 for more details.

[20] Information provided by the Institution.

[21] Cf report on Victoria, Chap. 13, p. 177 for more details.

[22] Cf Sect. 4.1.2.2, p. 69 below for details.

[23] In addition, in Taiwan the Control Yuan can directly turn to the Police for support.

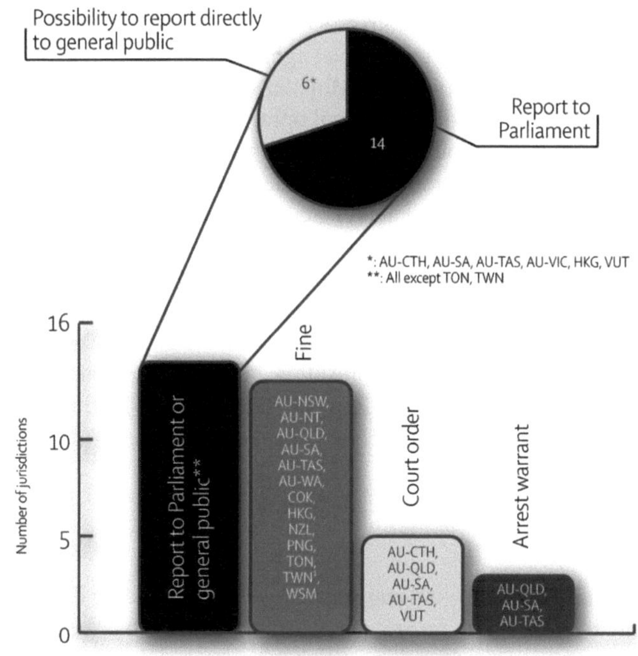

Fig. 4.1 Coercive powers during the investigation. (1) In TWN, the Ombudsman Institution may also initiate an impeachment procedure

4.1.2.2 Recommendation

During investigation, the Ombudsman may come to different conclusions.[24] Depending on the established facts, he or she may decide to discontinue the investigation, to attempt to solve the issue by way of conciliation or mediation if this is foreseen by law,[25] to find any other informal solution (i.e. without written recommendations) or to put his or her opinion in the form of recommendations.[26]

Process

Before drafting the recommendations, the Ombudsman shall always consult with the body (or individual) concerned if he or she intends to expressly or implicitly criticise this body or person in the report. To hear anybody adversely affected by an

---

[24] Sometimes, the announcement to investigate may already lead to a resolution of the matter. For example, if the body concerned decides to reinvestigate the matter and comes to a different decision that is favourable to the complainant.

[25] Cf Sect. 4.1.3, p. 74 below.

[26] Cf Reif (2004), p. 4.

action is part of the principle of fair proceedings.[27] Usually, the Ombudsman is authorised to discuss the matter under investigation with the responsible Minister at any time during the investigation. If a Minister requests so, the Ombudsman shall consult said Minister before forming a final opinion with adverse recommendations (except for in Hong Kong, South Australia, Taiwan, Tasmania and Vanuatu). The establishing laws give the Ombudsman wide discretion and stipulate that the Ombudsman may recommend whatever he or she believes necessary to remedy the situation.[28] The report with the recommendations is usually addressed to both the body concerned and the supervisory authority, usually the responsible Minister (except for in the Northern Territory).[29] Other addressees include e.g. the Chairperson of an organisation if that organisation was investigated (Cook Islands, New Zealand and Tonga), the Mayor (or presiding member of a council)[30] in case of local issues under investigation (New Zealand, the Northern Territory and Victoria) or a provincial or local government body (Papua New Guinea).

Consequences

A recommendation is, as the word suggests, not a legally binding decision that must be implemented. However, there are mechanisms ensuring that the body concerned will seriously consider any recommendation made by the Ombudsman. In all jurisdictions, the Ombudsman may request the authority concerned to report back to the Ombudsman on the steps taken (or planned to be taken) to give effect to the recommendations within a reasonable time. This ensures that the body concerned cannot simply ignore a recommendation. Non-compliance must be duly justified vis-à-vis the Ombudsman. All examined Institutions reported that recommendations are usually highly persuasive, and those that provided figures stated that compliance with recommendations made is close to 100 %.[31] In case of non-compliance with the requirement to report back, the laws foresee that the Ombudsman may inform the Prime Minister[32] and Parliament (in all jurisdictions

[27] Cf Buck et al. (2011), p. 129.

[28] For example, monetary compensation may be recommended. This is explicitly regulated e.g. for the Commonwealth Ombudsman and in New South Wales, cf s26A OA (New South Wales). However, such recommendation is limited to the individual case. Often, on the occasion of an individual case, the underlying root causes are addressed and recommendations become much more complex. Such recommendations, however, have the potential to improve systematic flaws existing in the administrative process. Cf Buck et al. (2011), p. 129 et seq.

[29] In Vanuatu, instead of the responsible Minster the Prime Minster shall be informed.

[30] In the Northern Territory, the presiding member of the council shall be the addressee if the authority investigated is a council.

[31] Cf reports on different jurisdictions, Chaps. 7 to 22 for more details.

[32] The Chief Executive (Hong Kong), the Chief Minister (ACT), the Governor (Victoria) or the Premier, respectively. In Victoria, in case of municipal issues the Mayor shall be informed. In New South Wales and the Northern Territory, instead of the Premier the responsible Minster shall be informed. In Tasmania, the responsible Minister shall be informed in addition to the Premier.

except for in Taiwan and Tonga) by way of a report. In a few jurisdictions, the law additionally foresees that the Ombudsman may directly inform the public in such a case (Australian Commonwealth, Hong Kong, South Australia, Tasmania, Victoria and Vanuatu).[33] In New Zealand and the Cook Islands, the Ombudsman may require an organisation under scrutiny (at the local level) to make a summary of the report (including the recommendations) available to the public.

In Taiwan, if the Control Yuan has proposed corrective measures, the body concerned must implement these measures or take other actions to remedy the shortcomings identified and shall inform the Control Yuan of this in writing. If there is no response within two months, the Control Yuan may question or summon the respective official in charge. If there is no cooperation whatsoever, the Control Yuan may initiate an impeachment procedure against the official that refuses to take appropriate action.[34]

4.1.2.3 Reporting

Annual Reports

In the jurisdictions where the Ombudsmen are Officers of Parliament, these Officers report to Parliament on their work annually and may do so on other occasions as well.[35] Also, in all jurisdictions examined except for Taiwan, the Ombudsmen report to Parliament at least once a year (see Fig. 4.2). This reporting obligation is irrespective of the fact, whether an Ombudsman is an Officer of Parliament or whether Parliament is involved in the appointment process.[36] They mostly report directly to Parliament. Sometimes, the procedure foresees that the Ombudsman reports through the Prime Minister (the Australian Commonwealth, Hong Kong, the Northern Territory, Papua New Guinea, Tonga and Vanuatu),[37] who is then obliged to table the report before Parliament. In Taiwan, the Control Yuan does not report to Parliament, but annually publishes three reports, which are aimed directly at the general public. This reflects that the Control Yuan, as one of the five powers, is not responsible to the legislator to the extent as in the other jurisdictions.[38]

---

[33] Cf Pearce (2000), p. 101.

[34] Cf report on Taiwan, Chap. 20, p. 257 for more details.

[35] Cf Pearce (2000), p. 103 who states that "the primary accountability of Ombudsmen [...] is achieved" through this reporting obligation.

[36] Cf Sect. 2.2.3, p. 25 for details.

[37] In Hong Kong it is the Chief Executive, in Papua New Guinea the Head of State and in the Northern Territory the Minister responsible for the Ombudsman.

[38] The Control Yuan may also address the general public on other occasions as appropriate. Cf report on Taiwan, Chap. 20, p. 257.

Fig. 4.2 Annual reports and special reports

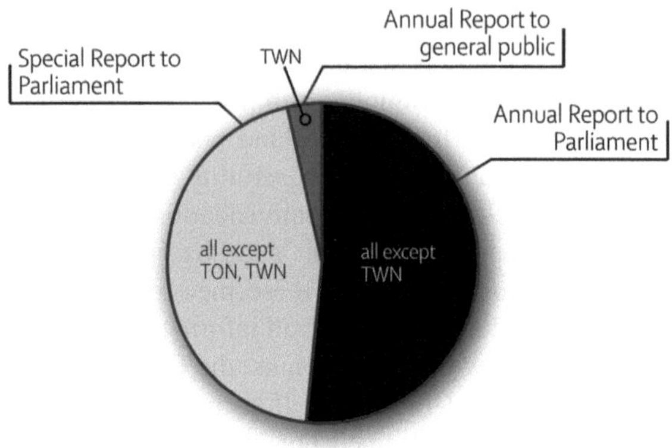

Other Reports

In addition to the Annual Report, all Ombudsmen have the power to submit other reports to Parliament when they consider this necessary. Some laws also specify the power to submit special reports. In Tasmania, for example, the law stipulates that the Ombudsman may publish a report addressed to the general public about any particular case or generally in relation to the execution of his or her functions if this is in the public interest.[39] In Queensland, the Ombudsman must obtain permission by the Speaker of Parliament to do so.[40] In Tonga, the law does currently not foresee reports relating to cases investigated to be made public.[41] A special report is considered a last resort for severe issues of particular concern that cannot wait until the next Annual Report is due. Submitting such a report is a means of calling particular attention to a specific issue of concern to the Ombudsman.

Purpose

The annual reporting obligation serves different yet complementary purposes.[42] First of all, the Annual Report is an *accountability mechanism*, as the Ombudsman, an appointee, reports on the general performance of the office and on the spending of the allocated budget. Both the appointment authority and Parliament[43] must have a means to assess the performance of the incumbent. To this end, the Report includes statistical information as well as a narrative part on the exercise of the statutory functions of the Ombudsman. Further, the Ombudsman informs about staffing level, budget and other activities of the office.

[39] Cf s31 OA (Tasmania).

[40] Cf s54 OA (Queensland).

[41] Cf Sect. 21, p. 276 for more details concerning reform plans to include this power.

[42] Cf Kucsko-Stadlmayer (2008), p. 48.

[43] Respectively all those involved in the appointment and dismissal of the Ombudsman.

In addition, the Annual Report regularly highlights specific cases investigated by the Ombudsman during the reporting period. This way the Ombudsman informs the legislator of administrative shortcomings and at the same time *addresses issues in need of reform*. The latter is partially done by proposing legislative amendments.[44] At the same time, the general public is also informed.[45] The fact that unresolved issues may be published lastly also exerts some pressure on the administration to implement recommendations or to remedy a situation and "may have a considerable preventive effect."[46]

Lastly, there is also a conditioned sanctioning mechanism element contained in some form of reports. As described, in some jurisdictions there is the possibility to directly inform the public in individual cases if non-compliance of the body concerned with the requirement to take a position on the Ombudsman's recommendation.[47] Here, the threat of publication is supposed to have a preventive function.

In jurisdictions where the Ombudsmen have been vested with additional functions,[48] the Annual Reports also cover these functions and any respective reporting obligations that may exist under additional legislation. In New South Wales, for example, the Ombudsman's Annual Report also covers his or her reporting requirements under the Police Act (NSW), the Public Interest Disclosure Act (NSW), the Law Enforcement (Powers and Responsibilities Act (NSW) 2002 and the Disability Service Act (NSW) 1993. Sometimes Ombudsmen have specific reporting obligations to other entities as well. In the Northern Territory, for example, the Ombudsman shall report on his or her inspection of the Police's Telecommunication Interception Records to the Police Minister regularly.[49] The Ombudsman shall further report on the inspection of records of the Police service to the responsible Minister bi-annually.[50]

In jurisdictions where Ombudsmen have explicit functions in the field of human rights protection,[51] these aspects may be outlined in a special section of the Annual Report (e.g. in the ACT, Papua New Guinea, Taiwan and Victoria). The New Zealand Ombudsmen, however, report to Parliament on their human rights function under the Crimes of Torture Act in a separate Annual Report.[52] The Annual Reports and other reports (with the exceptions described above) are usually made available

[44] Cf Sect. 4.1.3.5, p. 75 below for more information.

[45] Cf Buck et al. (2011), p. 131.

[46] Cf Kucsko-Stadlmayer (2008), p. 48.

[47] This is foreseen by law for the Australian Commonwealth, South Australia, Victoria and Vanuatu as well as for New Zealand and the Cook Islands at a local level.

[48] Cf Chaps. 4.1.3 and 4.1.4, p. 74 and p. 79 below for details.

[49] However, by law these reports are not to be made public.

[50] These reports must subsequently be tabled before Parliament. Cf report on the Northern Territory, Chap. 9, p. 131 for details.

[51] Cf Sect. 4.1.3.8, p. 78 below for details.

[52] The law enables the country to meet its obligations under the UN Convention Against Torture and designates the Ombudsmen as a National Preventive Mechanism, cf Sect. 4.1.3.9, p. 79 for more details.

to the general public both in hardcopy and online via the Institutions' websites. Most Institutions proactively address the general public throughout the year as well as at the occasion of the publication of the Annual Report.[53]

4.1.3 Additional Functions

The standard functions described above form the basis and core of the Ombudsmen's work. As already described in the introduction, most Ombudsmen have developed far beyond these standard powers. The legislator has vested them with additional functions, which are described below.

4.1.3.1 Power to Refer to Court a Question of Law

Most Ombudsmen in the APOR region have the power to turn to the courts if a question arises in regard to the legality of the exercise of one of his or her powers (except in Taiwan and Vanuatu).[54] The competent court is usually the Supreme Court, respectively the High Court in the Cook Islands, the Constitutional Court in Papua New Guinea and the Federal Court of Australia in case of the Commonwealth Ombudsman. The Ombudsmen in Papua New Guinea and Tasmania additionally have the power to refer a question of law relevant to their proceedings to the Supreme Court (Tasmania) respectively the Constitutional Court (Papua New Guinea) for an interpretative decision. In Papua New Guinea this includes submitting questions of legality, validity and interpretation of constitutional law, including any question as to the validity of a law or a proposed bill.[55]

4.1.3.2 Power to Apply to Court for an Injunction

In the course of an Ombudsman investigation situations can arise which carry the imminent risk of new and irreversible facts being created by the agency which is subject of the investigation. This can seriously undermine the very purpose of an Ombudsman investigation. To strengthen his or her position in such a situation, some jurisdictions (New South Wales, the Northern Territory and South Australia) grant the Ombudsman the possibility to have such actions stopped by a court or on his or her own initiative. In New South Wales, the Ombudsman can apply to the

[53] Cf Chap. 5, p. 87 for details.

[54] Also, the party subject to the investigation may submit an application to court for a determination of this question.

[55] Cf art. 19 Const. (Papua New Guinea) and report on Papua New Guinea, Sect. 18, p. 235 for more details.

Supreme Court for "an injunction restraining any conduct in which a public authority is engaging or [...] appears likely to engage, where that conduct is the subject of, or affects the subject of, an investigation or proposed investigation by the Ombudsman."[56] In South Australia and the Northern Territory, the Ombudsman him- or herself has the power to "direct an agency [...] to refrain from performing an administrative act specified in the notice for any period specified in the notice"[57] for up to 45 days.

4.1.3.3 Power to Intervene in Court Proceedings

The Ombudsman is usually not competent to intervene in any court proceeding. However, in the Northern Territory the Ombudsman has the power to investigate actions of courts, tribunals or the prosecution in cases in which there is, to the Ombudsman's conviction, an unreasonable delay by the authority.[58] Further, the Ombudsman Victoria has the power to intervene before the Victorian Civil and Administrative Tribunal (VCAT) in matters concerning Freedom of Information if he or she is of the opinion that such an intervention is warranted (s57(1) FOIA (Victoria)) . Such an intervention supports an applicant's case; when deciding whether or not to intervene, the Ombudsman shall thus consider *inter alia* the financial means of the applicant and the applicant's prospects of success.

4.1.3.4 Conciliation and Mediation

In a couple of jurisdictions, the Ombudsman has the power to deal with a complaint by conciliation or mediation (Hong Kong, New South Wales, the Northern Territory, South Australia, Tasmania and Vanuatu).[59] The rationale is to resolve a matter permanently by a binding agreement reached between the parties involved, as such solution has a significant peace-making effect.[60] Precondition is that the matter is suitable, i.e. that it does not represent a systemic flaw which cannot be overcome by a case-by-case approach.[61] Further, the subject matter should involve only minor maladministration on the side of the body concerned,[62] and finally, the procedure is

---

[56] Cf s 21C OA (New South Wales).

[57] Cf s19A OA (South Australia). The Ombudsman Act in the Northern Territory contains a similar provision, cf s55 OA (Northern Territory).

[58] Cf s16(3) OA (Northern Territory).

[59] Cf Groves (2002), p. 197.

[60] Cf Hill (2001), p. 149. He underlines that mediation is "particularly well suited to disputes" where those involved "will continue to encounter each other".

[61] In Vanuatu, the Ombudsman may also mediate between a leader and the complainant if the complaint relates to the conduct of a leader.

[62] Expressly foreseen in s11B OO (Hong Kong).

fully voluntary, i.e. both parties must consent to the procedure (and may abandon it at any time). Cooray describes mediation as "the remedy of first resort"[63] when the main issue at stake is "a personal grievance not revealing any systemic fault in the administration".[64] The laws allow for a quite flexible procedure, as they do not contain strict rules regarding the conciliation or mediation process as such or regarding what a settlement agreement between the parties must contain as a minimum requirement. The conciliator or mediator may be the Ombudsman, one of his or her officers or, with the agreement of the complainant, an external mediator.

4.1.3.5 Legislative Initiative

The right to propose legislative amendments derives from the general recommendation power to address deficits identified in an investigation,[65] be it following a complaint or as part of an own motion investigation.[66] Increasingly, Ombudsmen undertake own motion investigations to address what they consider systemic flaws and weaknesses in public administration.[67] Consequently, not only administrative standard operating procedures but the very law behind an administrative question becomes a focus of investigation. As a result, Ombudsmen may propose the repairing of flaws by amending the legislation. While, according to the standard process, recommendations are first and foremost addressed to the body under investigation, in practice, all Ombudsmen also address Parliament when proposing amendments to laws.[68] In some jurisdictions, this competence has been recognised by involving the Institution in more formal ways in reviewing new draft legislation or in auditing newly promulgated legislation (e.g. in New Zealand).[69] Mostly, however, this function is limited to including such recommendations into the Annual Report or to reporting to Parliament on the issue in a Special Report.[70] Following submission of such a proposal, it is up to Parliament, respectively the executive, to consider the recommendations.

---

[63] Cf Cooray (2009), p. 59.

[64] Cf Cooray (2009), p. 59.

[65] Cf Sect. 4.1.2.2, p. 69 for details.

[66] Most legislation contains a clause allowing the Ombudsman to act if he or she is "of the opinion that an administrative action has produced unfair or objectionable results and that the action was caused wholly or partly by legislation".

[67] Cf Sect. 3.3.4, p. 60 for details.

[68] In Samoa, this is excised with caution and only if absolutely necessary. Information provided by the Samoan Institution.

[69] Beyond mere legislative initiatives, Ombudsmen often also make informal submissions to public bodies which can be useful to influence certain administrative practices, cf Buck et al. (2011), p. 144.

[70] In New South Wales, the Ombudsman makes submissions for legislative changes to Parliament quite often. This is done either by way of a special report or in a letter to Parliament.

In New Zealand, the Cabinet Manual and the Guidelines of the Legislation Advisory Committee entail a wider-ranging provision according to which the Ombudsmen shall be involved "in their areas of interest"[71] and, in case of a new public body being established, in regard to the application of the Ombudsman Act (New Zealand) and the application of Freedom of Information legislation.[72] In Taiwan, the Ombudsman has a special position, and the proposing of legislative amendments derives directly from the Control Yuan's specific role.

4.1.3.6 Power to Recommend Disciplinary Proceedings and Power to Initiate Impeachment Procedures

Maladministration or poor administrative performance can have multiple reasons. If the Ombudsman identifies individually attributable behaviour in regard to the subject matter of the investigation that warrants disciplinary proceedings, or if he or she encounters resistance in the course of the investigation, or if there is no reaction to recommendations made to a body under investigation, in many jurisdictions the Ombudsman has the power to recommend disciplinary proceedings (in the Cook Islands, New South Wales, the Northern Territory, Papua New Guinea, Samoa, South Australia, Tonga and Vanuatu), or to initiate an impeachment procedure against a public official (Taiwan), respectively (see Fig. 4.3). In some jurisdictions, while there is no explicit statutory power to do so, recommending disciplinary proceedings is a standard practice (Hong Kong, New Zealand and Victoria).

While the Ombudsman does not possess strong coercive powers, non-compliance with an Ombudsman's request regularly constitutes a punishable offence.[73] Concurrently, such non-compliance may call for disciplinary sanctions on behalf of the person's employment authority.

In these cases, the Ombudsman shall regularly inform the supervisor of the person in question and, in more serious cases, the responsible Minister shall be informed. For example, the Ombudsman New South Wales has the statutory obligation to report cases of serious misconduct warranting dismissal or punishment to the responsible Minster and to the head of the agency in question. In South Australia, on the other hand, the Ombudsman is only obliged to inform the head of the agency in question. The Control Yuan in Taiwan in turn proposes corrective measures which range from submitting a censure to the most serious consequence of initiating an impeachment procedure against an official.[74] If corrective measures are proposed and no action is taken, the Control Yuan may also initiate an impeachment procedure against the superior who obstructs the proposal.[75]

---

[71] Cf the Cabinet Manual of New Zealand for details. Information provided by the Institution.

[72] Cf the Guidelines of the Legislation Advisory Committee (New Zealand) for details.

[73] Cf Sect. 4.1.2, p. 68 above.

[74] Cf Yueh-chin (1995), p. 26 for details.

[75] Cf report on Taiwan, Chap. 20, p. 257 for details.

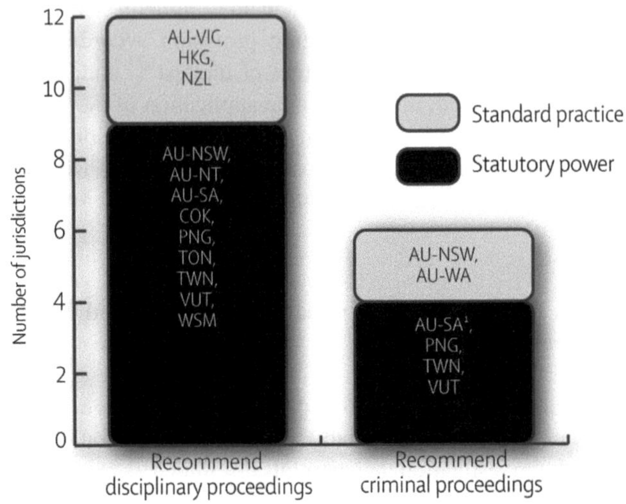

Fig. 4.3 Power to recommend disciplinary and criminal proceedings. (1) In AU-SA, the statutory power to recommend criminal proceedings is limited to cases of fraud and corruption

4.1.3.7 Power to Recommend Criminal Proceedings

If an Ombudsman suspects criminal behaviour, he or she will usually refer the matter to the competent authorities. Many jurisdictions report this to be common practice, but, it is a legal obligation in a few jurisdictions only. The Ombudsman in South Australia, for example, is obliged to report any allegation of fraud or corruption to the Anti-Corruption Branch of the Police.[76] Also, in Papua New Guinea the law stipulates that the Ombudsman Commission shall refer a matter to the Prosecutor if it suspects a criminal offence.[77] The Control Yuan in Taiwan also has the statutory obligation to refer criminal acts to the judiciary for further action.[78]

4.1.3.8 Power to Report on Human Rights Issues

In a few jurisdictions, human rights are an explicit standard of control.[79] In these jurisdictions (the ACT, New Zealand, Papua New Guinea, Taiwan and Victoria), the Ombudsman has the standard powers available, i.e. he or she may recommend remedial action and report on the matter if he or she identifies an infringement of human rights by an entity under jurisdiction. None of the Institutions examined has

[76] Information provided by the Institution.

[77] Cf s22 OLOC (Papua New Guinea). Similarly in the law in Vanuatu, cf s31 OA (Vanuatu).

[78] Cf report on Taiwan, Chap. 20, p. 257 for details.

[79] Cf Sect. 3.2.6, p. 53.

the power to declare the violation of human rights in a legally binding way. Those Ombudsmen vested with this power regularly report on human rights issues in their Annual Reports. This creates increasing awareness of the importance of human rights obligations on the part of the administration and the public, which shall lead to a more human rights compliant administration in the long term.

4.1.3.9 National Preventive Mechanism (OPCAT)

The New Zealand Ombudsmen office is a National Preventive Mechanism (NPM) in compliance with OPCAT.[80] Under this scheme, the Ombudsmen are tasked to prevent torture and ill-treatment by undertaking regular visits to places of detention and by making "recommendations to the relevant authorities with the aim of improving the treatment and the conditions [...] and to prevent torture" by taking into consideration the relevant international norms (Article 19 OPCAT). The NPM's rights include "access to all information concerning the number of persons" held in places of detention and regular "access to all places of detention" as well as the right to speak with detainees in private (Article 20 OPCAT).[81] OPCAT further codifies basic principles, privileges and working methods essential to an effective independent inspection of places of detention. The Ombudsmen have the power to make recommendations to the relevant authorities in New Zealand.

4.1.4 Additional Roles and Functions under other Legislation

4.1.4.1 Freedom of Information

Freedom of Information legislation grants citizens the general right to access information held by the public administration.[82] This right, however, is not unlimited, and the administration may claim that information requested falls under an exemption clause.[83] In several jurisdictions, the Ombudsman has been vested with the power to review the initial decision taken by the agency concerned (in the

---

[80] Cf Sect. 3.2.6.2, p. 55 and report on New Zealand, Chap. 17, p. 221.

[81] Australia has signed OPCAT in May 2009, but has yet to ratify it. There is political commitment to do so and to set up the necessary system of NPMs, cf report on the Australian Commonwealth, Chap. 7, p. 101.

[82] One important aspect is the right to have personal information disclosed which is held by an agency. With the general trend to outsource Government services to private contractors, the question whether the legislation in place adequately addresses this situation arises. Cf *inter alia* McLeod (2001), p. 359 et seqq.

[83] Such as sensitive Government information relating to national security, defence, international relations, information compromising the privacy of natural persons or information that would disclose a trade secret.

Australian Commonwealth, the Cook Islands, Hong Kong, New Zealand, South Australia, Tasmania and Victoria). In New Zealand, for example, if an Ombudsman recommends to grant the requester access to information the agency withheld, the agency concerned may seek a veto to the Ombudsman's recommendation by the Governor-General respectively by the competent local authority in case of local government issues.[84] If said veto is not granted or if the agency remains inactive, the recommendation to release the information becomes binding and can be enforced by a court.[85] Usually, Freedom of Information laws also stipulate that the Ombudsman shall have the standard powers (as under the Ombudsmen's establishing legislation) to review and investigate requests.

4.1.4.2 Whistle-Blower Protection

In some jurisdictions, Ombudsmen have certain tasks in the area of whistle-blower protection (the ACT, New South Wales, New Zealand, South Australia, Tasmania, Victoria and Western Australia). The laws aim at protecting those who identify wrongdoing within an agency or organisation and who reveal (or consider to reveal) this wrongdoing to the public. Such public interest disclosures have the potential to strengthen accountability and good governance. To this end, the Ombudsmen in New Zealand, for example, provide advice and guidance to any employee who is considering to make a disclosure about serious wrong-doing at his or her workplace. All these Ombudsmen are also competent to receive public interest disclosures and may investigate matters disclosed to them using their standard powers. Further, the Ombudsman often shall monitor and audit the exercise of functions by public officials under the respective laws and their compliance with them. Often, also advice is given to public officials who deal with disclosures (e.g. in New South Wales), or the Institution issues guidelines on the process to assist public authorities in complying with this legislation (Tasmania and Victoria).[86]

4.1.4.3 Anti-Discrimination

In Papua New Guinea, the Ombudsman Commission has a specific power embedded in the Constitution to investigate any case of an alleged or suspected

[84] If, on the other hand, an Ombudsman concurs with the initial decision to withhold information, the requester may seek judicial review of both the initial decision and the Ombudsman's determination. Cf also Owen (1999), p. 61.

[85] In case of inactivity, the recommendation of an Ombudsman becomes legally binding from the 21st working day after the recommendation has been made. A similar provision is contained in the respective law of the Cook Islands. In the Cook Islands, the Queen's Representative has the authority to veto the Ombudsman's recommendation.

[86] Cf Buck et al. (2011), p. 141 et seqq. Buck et al. argue that Ombudsmen are in particularly competent to "produce general good practice guides".

discriminatory practice concerning the provision of services, going beyond the standard function of Ombudsmen to examine matters of administration *inter alia* against the benchmark of discrimination.[87] Under these provisions, also private individuals may be subject to an investigation if they are licensed to undertake certain business activities (e.g. the sale of meat, the sale of alcohol, the keeping of a restaurant or of a place of entertainment). The Ombudsman Commission may initiate such proceedings either on its own initiative or following a complaint by a person affected. This function shall assist government bodies to eliminate unfair legislation or discriminatory practices against individuals.[88]

4.1.4.4 Leadership Code and Anti-Corruption Activities

In some jurisdictions, Ombudsmen are vested with special powers to oversee the conduct of senior public officials and to curb corruption (Papua New Guinea, Taiwan and Vanuatu). These powers shall ensure transparency, prevent actions by officials in case of conflicts of interest and increase public confidence in those in power. The objective of preventing corrupt behaviour of leaders and senior public officials is mainly pursued in two ways.

Firstly, as a pre-emptive measure these persons are exposed to rigorous and repeated controls of their assets, irrespective of any suspicion. For example, in Papua New Guinea the constitutional Leadership Code places explicit obligations for good conduct and ethical behaviour on senior officials. The Leadership Code is a distinct feature of the Pacific region and was first introduced in Papua New Guinea with the purpose of finding a way to prevent those in power from abusing the system for their personal benefit.[89] Any person to whom the Leadership Code[90] applies shall submit a comprehensive statement to the Ombudsman Commission on assets and income, including information about business connections, business transactions undertaken, gifts received and positions held.[91] Such statement must also include relevant information about the Ombudsman's spouse and any underage children and must be submitted within three months after accepting the position and thereafter at least once a year. To make this provision effective, the Commission has the power to examine each statement.

---

[87] Cf Sect. 3.2.2, p. 50.

[88] Cf report on Papua New Guinea, Chap. 18, p. 245 for details.

[89] Cf Jonge (1998), p. 12 et seqq. and Maino in Reif (1995), p. 53 et seqq. for more details on the background and the development of the Leadership Code. In addition to Papua New Guinea and Vanuatu, a Leadership Code is also part of the legislative frameworks of Fiji and the Solomon Islands.

[90] The constitutional Leadership Code is implemented by the Organic Law on the Duties and Responsibilities of Leadership (OLDRL). Art. 26 Constitution defines the group of persons to which the Leadership Code applies including *inter alia* the Prime Minister and all other Ministers, the Members of Parliament, the members of Provincial Assemblies, the heads of Departments of the National Public Service and senior diplomatic and consular officials.

[91] Cf s4 OLDRL (Papua New Guinea).

Secondly, if there is suspicion that legal obligations have been violated by a leader, the Ombudsman shall investigate the matter. Investigative powers as well as reporting rights are largely similar to the standard investigation powers. In Papua New Guinea, however, information, consultation and participation rights are limited, i.e. no advance notification of the intention to investigate or consultation with a Minister is foreseen. Additionally, the Commission can give binding instructions to leaders to undertake or to abstain from certain actions. A violation of such an instruction in itself constitutes a breach of the Leadership Code, and the Commission may initiate an impeachment procedure by referring a case of an alleged breach to the Prosecutor, who subsequently shall prosecute violations. In Vanuatu, a similar Leadership Code is embedded in the Constitution, while in Taiwan the Control Yuan has similar control and supervisory powers to fight corruption and to make procedures transparent to the public, which are based on Taiwan's Anti-Corruption Laws (or Sunshine Laws).[92]

4.1.4.5 Oversight and Audit Functions

In several jurisdictions, the Ombudsmen have been granted specific powers to oversee government bodies and/or to conduct audits and review administrative practices and procedures of government bodies.[93] The purpose of these functions is to further the public administration's compliance with the applicable legislation by considering practices and procedures and by lending support, allowing the administration to improve these practices and procedures. At the same time, the Ombudsmen's audit functions shall increase public confidence in the proper execution of powers that have a particularly high risk of infringing upon an individual's human right (e.g. the right to privacy). As stated above,[94] Ombudsmen are increasingly described by scholars as the "integrity arm of government".[95] This is all the more true if Ombudsmen have been vested with explicit audit powers. Such audit and compliance functions may include the supervision of actions of the Police and of other law enforcement agencies which use covert powers (telecommunications interceptions and stored communications), surveillance devices and implement Police-controlled operations (e.g. the Commonwealth Ombudsman and the Ombudsmen in New South Wales, Tasmania and Western Australia).[96] To this end, Ombudsmen regularly inspect the records of the body in question (e.g. the

---

[92] These laws include the Act on Property-Declaration by Public Servants, the Act on Recusal of Public Servants due to Conflicts of Interest, the Political Donations Act and the Lobbying Act.

[93] Cf Buck et al. (2011), p. 146.

[94] Cf Sect. 3.3.4, p. 60.

[95] Cf Creyke (2007), p. 722 for more details on this notion and its origins. Cf also Stuhmcke (2010), p. 233 et seq.

[96] In addition, the Samoan Ombudsman has the obligation to regularly review and report on the investigations of the Professional Standards Unit (PSU) of the Police, cf report on Samoa, Chap. 19, p. 249 for details.

Telecommunication Interception Records of the Police) to verify compliance with the legislation.

Other Ombudsmen have been vested with more general audit and oversight functions (e.g. in the Northern Territory, Queensland, South Australia and Taiwan).[97] These functions include the power to review administrative practices and procedures, irrespective of individual cases. In the exercise of these functions, Ombudsmen usually have the same powers like in the investigation of a concrete administrative action. In Queensland, the law makes it an explicit task of the Ombudsman "to consider the administrative practices and procedures of agencies generally and to make recommendations or provide information or other help to the agencies for the improvement of the practices and procedures",[98] and in South Australia, the law stipulates that "if the Ombudsman considers it to be in the public interest to do so, the Ombudsman may conduct a review of the administrative practices and procedures of an agency to which this Act applies."[99] This task is for example implemented by way of "sample auditing"[100] of files of a specific agency under jurisdiction, by reporting to Parliament on significant outcomes of such an audit, by "encourag[ing] and assist[ing] agencies to develop effective internal complaints management systems",[101] and by providing training to agencies on how to foster "good decision-making and complaints management."[102]

4.2 Judiciary

The judicial branch of government is generally not an object of the Ombudsman's control.[103] Thus, powers vis-à-vis the judiciary are very limited. However, Taiwan's Control Yuan, the Northern Territory Ombudsman (with the power to investigate actions by a tribunal or one of its members in case of unreasonable delays),[104] and the Papua New Guinea and Vanuatu Ombudsmen (with their power to investigate the behaviour of leaders, including judges and prosecutors) deviate from this model.[105] In all these cases, the Ombudsmen may make use of all the

[97] For details on the procedure in Taiwan, cf Sect. 3.3.4, p. 60 above. Furthermore, in Vanuatu the law stipulates that the Ombudsman may participate in any general study or enquiry that could improve the functioning of a public authority, s37 OA (Vanuatu), cf report on Vanuatu, Chap. 22, p. 283.

[98] Cf s12(c) OA (Queensland).

[99] Cf s14A(1) OA (South Australia).

[100] Cf APOR Manual (2009), p. 29.

[101] Cf APOR Manual (2009), p. 29.

[102] Cf APOR Manual (2009), p. 29.

[103] Cf Reif (2004), p. 13.

[104] Cf Sect. 3.1.3, p. 46, report on the Northern Territory, Chap. 9, p. 131 and Reif (2004), p. 13.

[105] Cf Sect. 3.1.3, p. 46 and reports on Papua New Guinea and Vanuatu, Chaps. 18 and 22, p. 235 and p. 283.

standard investigative powers vested in them.[106] In Taiwan, the powers include the censure of an official and the initiation of an impeachment procedure, whereas in Papua New Guinea and Vanuatu the powers include referring a matter where there is evidence for misconduct to the Prosecutor. In addition, the powers of the Ombudsman in Vanuatu include full access to relevant government documents and other material that is relevant to the investigation at all times and not being limited by any secrecy provision, thus going beyond the provisions in the Ombudsman Act.[107]

Further, the administration of justice is partly the object of control of the Ombudsman (the Australian Commonwealth, the Cook Islands, New Zealand and South Australia).[108] In these jurisdictions, the Ombudsmen have all the standard powers at their disposal to effectively undertake investigations.

4.3 Legislator

The legislative branch of government is not object of control of the Ombudsman as described above.[109] While the legislator may be the addressee of the Ombudsman's work — e.g. in cases of identified shortcomings in existing legislation — the Ombudsman's power ends as soon as he or she has reported to Parliament and has pinpointed an issue of concern. It is not within his or her power to put any kind of pressure on Parliament to react to any recommendation made, as, ultimately, the legislator is responsible only to its electorate.

This is reflected in the fact that in none of the jurisdictions examined the Ombudsman is entitled by law to participate in debates in Parliament. While in practice in many jurisdictions he or she may appear before Parliament or one of its committees to a varying extent, this always has to be initiated by an invitation by Parliament. In New Zealand, for example, the Ombudsmen' involvement in regard to the amending or drafting of new legislation is quite extensive. However, also in this case, this is due to the Parliament's express wish to involve the Institution to be able to make use of its knowledge.[110] In Taiwan, the Control Yuan is entitled to supervise all functionaries working in the Legislative Yuan (but not the Members of Parliament). This means that the administration within the legislative branch of government may be controlled, similar to those jurisdictions where the administration of justice (but not the core functions of the judiciary) is under the

[106] Cf Sect. 4.1.2, p. 66 for details.

[107] Cf s34(4)(a) Leadership Code Act (Vanuatu).

[108] Cf Sect. 3.1.3, p. 46 for details.

[109] Cf Sect. 3.1.4, p. 48 for details.

[110] Parliament has formalised the Ombudsmen's involvement in its Cabinet Manual and in the Guidelines of the Legislation Advisory Committee. However, both can be amended by Parliament and do not qualify for granting a subjective right. Cf Sect. 4.1.3.5, p. 76 for details.

Ombudsman's jurisdiction.[111] The investigative powers of the Control Yuan in this case are the same as the standard powers.[112]

References

Commonwealth Ombudsman (2009a) Australasia and Pacific Ombudsman Region Information Manual 2009. Commonwealth Ombudsman, Canberra, Australia http://www.ombudsman.gov.au/docs/APOR-Manual_20091009.pdf

Besselink LFM (2000) Types of national institutions for the protection of human rights and Ombudsman institutions: an overview of legal and institutional issues. In: Hossain K, Besselink LFM, Selassie HSG, Völker E (eds) Human rights commissions and Ombudsman offices. National experiences throughout the world. Kluwer Law International, Dordrecht

Buck T, Kirkham R, Thompson B (2011) The Ombudsman enterprise and administrative justice. Ashgate, Farnham

Cooray A (2000) Ombudsman in Asia. In: Gregory R, Giddings P (eds) Righting wrongs. The Ombudsman in six continents. IOS Press, Berlin

Cooray A (2009) Some reflections on the legislative context of the Hong Kong Ombudsman. Asia Pac Law Rev 17(1):53–72

Creyke R (2007) Administrative justice—towards integrity in government. Melb Univ Law Rev 31(3):705–732

Groves M (2002) Ombudsmen's jurisdiction in prisons. Monash Univ Law Rev 28(2):181–205

Hill ER (2001) The Ombudsman as mediator—challenges, limitations and opportunities in Vanuatu. In: Reif LC (ed) The international Ombudsman yearbook 2001, vol 5. Martinus Nijhoff, Leiden

de Jonge A (1998) Ombudsmen and leadership codes in Papua New Guinea: keeping government accountable in a rapidly changing world. Melanesian Law J 6:1–33

Kucsko-Stadlmayer G (ed) (2008) European Ombudsman-Institutions. Springer, Vienna

Maino C (1995) Ethical considerations: the leadership code of Papua New Guinea. In: Reif LC (ed) The Ombudsman concept. International Ombudsman Institute, Edmonton

McLeod R (2001) Freedom of information—an Ombudsman's perspective, commentary. Fed Law Rev 29(3):359–364

Owen S (1999) The Ombudsman: essential elements and common challenges. In: Reif LC (ed) The international Ombudsman anthology. Selected writings from the International Ombudsman Institute. Kluwer Law International, Dordrecht

Pearce D (2000) Ombudsman in Australia. In: Gregory R, Giddings P (eds) Righting wrongs. The Ombudsman in six continents. IOS Press, Berlin

Reif LC (2004) The Ombudsman, good governance, and the international human rights system. Martinus Nijhoff, Leiden

Stuhmcke A (2010) 'Each for themselves' or 'one for all'? The changing emphasis of the commonwealth Ombudsman. Fed Law Rev 38(1):143–167

Yueh-chin H (1995) Role and responsibility of the control yuan. In: Reif LC (ed) The Ombudsman concept. International Ombudsman Institute, Edmonton

[111] Cf Sect. 3.1.3, p. 46 for details.

[112] Cf Sect. 4.1.2, p. 66 for details.

Chapter 5
Awareness and Outreach

Michael Frahm

5.1 International Standards

The Paris Principles stipulate that an Institution should "cooperate with the United Nations [. . .], regional institutions and the national organisations of other countries", "to assist in the formulation of programmes for the teaching of, and research into, human rights and to take part in their execution in schools, universities and professional circles", and to "publicize human rights and efforts to combat all forms of discrimination [. . .] by increasing public awareness, especially through information and education and by making use of all press organs".[1] Further, an Institution shall "address public opinion directly or through any press organ, particularly in order to publicize its opinions and recommendations", "maintain consultation with the other bodies [. . .] responsible for the promotion and protection of human rights (in particular [O]mbudsmen, mediators and similar institutions)", and "develop relations with [NGOs]".[2] UN General Assembly Resolution 63/169 encourages UN member states to "consider conducting communication campaigns [. . .] to enhance public awareness on the importance of the role of the Ombudsman"[3] and UN General Assembly Resolution 65/207 underlines the "role played by regional and international associations of the Ombudsm[e]n [. . .] in promoting cooperation and sharing best practices" and encourages UN member

[1] Paris Principles, "Competences and responsibilities" (3)(e), (f) and (g).

[2] Paris Principles, "Methods of operation" (c), (f) and (g).

[3] UN General Assembly Resolution 63/169, 2008, on the role of the Ombudsman, mediator and other national human rights institutions and protection of human rights, paragraph 2(a).

M. Frahm (✉)
Ludwig Boltzmann Institute of Human Rights, Vienna, Austria
e-mail: michael.frahm@univie.ac.at

International Ombudsman Institute (ed.), *Australasia and Pacific Ombudsman Institutions*, 87
DOI 10.1007/978-3-642-33896-0_5, © Springer-Verlag Berlin Heidelberg 2013

states to "develop and conduct, as appropriate, outreach activities at the national level, in collaboration with all relevant stakeholders, in order to raise awareness" of the Ombudsmen's role.[4]

5.2 Publications

All Ombudsman Institutions publish their Annual Reports and those who are present on the internet make them available to the general public via their websites. Most Institutions also publish other reports on specific topics or on special investigations.[5] For raising public awareness and informing the public as well as public officials, many Ombudsmen also use at least one or more of the following means: electronic newsletters, information leaflets, brochures, fact sheets, media statements/press releases and awareness campaigns in the media.

5.3 Training and Outreach Activities

Most Ombudsmen (except for the Cook Islands, Samoa, Tonga and Vanuatu) have designated officers or — in case of larger Institutions — a separate unit for communication and outreach activities. These units have two main target groups: public administration staff and the civil society. The first group is addressed by way of regular training activities on e.g. different aspects of good public administration and good complaint handling.[6] All Institutions reach out to the civil society in varying degrees by way of awareness raising, information campaigns and promotion activities.[7] They give regular presentations on the Ombudsman's role and functions, participate in community events and regularly offer workshops aimed at increasing public awareness of the roles and functions of the Ombudsman.

In Hong Kong, for example, the Institution sponsored TV clips and advertisements in buses and local newspapers.[8] Ombudsman Institutions further consult and cooperate with the civil society and NGOs in various forms and to varying degrees. In New South Wales, for example, the Institution has an Aboriginal Unit, a Youth Liaison Officer, a Community Education and Training Unit, all of

[4] UN General Assembly Resolution 65/207, 2010, on the role of the Ombudsman, mediator and other national human rights institutions in the promotion and protection of human rights, paragraph 12 and 2(b).

[5] Cf Sect. 4.1.2.3, p. 71 for details.

[6] Cf Buck et al 2011, p. 97.

[7] Cf Buck et al 2011, p. 96 et seq. and the respective reports on different jurisdictions, Chaps. 7–22, for more details.

[8] Cf report on Hong Kong, Chap. 15, p. 199 for details.

which reach out to the civil society by attending community and cultural events, giving workshops, etc.[9] In the 2010–2011 reporting period, these units delivered 140 presentations and participated *inter alia* in Aboriginal Community Information and Assistance Road Shows in different towns and visited 59 regional and remote communities in New South Wales.[10]

Many Ombudsmen also regularly visit correctional centres, usually as part of their outreach activity respectively under their own motion investigative power (e.g. in Queensland, South Australia and Western Australia). The New Zealand Ombudsmen, whose duties include those of a designated National Preventive Mechanism (NPM),[11] visited 17 places of detention in the 2010–2011 reporting period and produced ten inspection records. Under their mandate as NPM they also visit immigration detention facilities, institutions where persons are held on grounds of disability or impaired health, child care and protection residences and youth justice facilities.

The staff of all public sector agencies, Departments and Ministries is addressed by way of regular workshops and seminars. E.g. in Papua New Guinea, the Ombudsman Commission has been cooperating with the Police service for several years to establish a new accountability and review mechanism. Over the course of several years, mutual confidence has increased, both actors have improved their information sharing and undertake joint investigations into serious allegations against the Police. Following formalisation of the cooperation by way of a Memorandum of Understanding, the need for legislative reform to perpetuate the cooperation has been discussed and may ultimately follow. This step should further increase public confidence in the Police's accountability.[12]

5.4 Cooperation with other Institutions and Organisations

The relationship with other Institutions and organisations is of differing intensity, according to the data provided by the Institutions examined in their questionnaires. Interaction with the community of Ombudsmen facilitates the "sharing of experience in handling complaints" and in fostering good governance.[13] All Ombudsmen cooperate with each other in the forum of the IOI as well as in regional activities in the APOR region. Many are also active in regional and topical networks such as the Pacific Ombudsman Alliance (POA)[14] and the Australia and New Zealand

[9] Cf report on Hong Kong, Chap. 15, p. 199 for details.

[10] Cf Annual Report (New South Wales) 2010/2011, p. 92 for details.

[11] Cf Sect. 3.2.6.2, p. 55 for details on NPM.

[12] Cf report on Papua New Guinea, Chap. 18, p. 235 for details.

[13] As reported by the Commonwealth Ombudsman in the study's questionnaire.

[14] Members are: the Commonwealth Ombudsman and the Institutions of the Cook Islands, New South Wales, New Zealand, Papua New Guinea, Samoa, Solomon Islands, Tonga and Vanuatu.

Ombudsman Association (ANZOA).[15] In addition, all Australian Ombudsmen meet regularly and confer with the heads of other public integrity bodies[16] in their respective states or territories. The Queensland Ombudsman, for example, cooperates with the Commission for Children and Young People and Child Guardian, the Health Quality and Complaints Commission, the Anti-Discrimination Commission and the Crime and Misconduct Commission.[17] Those Australian Ombudsmen with Freedom of Information powers, such as the South Australian Ombudsman, meet regularly with the other Australian Information Commissioners in the forum of the Australian Association of Information Access Commissioners. The Commonwealth Ombudsman, for example, also runs an international programme that includes a twinning scheme with the Papua New Guinea Ombudsman Commission, secretariat support to the POA, and support of the Indonesian Ombudsmen.[18] The New Zealand Ombudsmen in turn provide training and assistance to Pacific countries. The Cook Islands, for example, were supported in the investigation of complaints and in formulating standard operating procedures, while the pacific island of Niue was assisted in regard to a complaints handling system.[19]

The activities described are only a small selection of what the Ombudsmen examined do in regard to awareness raising and outreach activities. All these activities have one imperative aim: an ever-improving public administration and a higher public awareness of the Ombudsman. Sharing best practices among Ombudsmen means mutual learning, based on which daily routines are improved and sometimes even legislation is amended, strengthening an Ombudsman's independence. Increased public awareness of the functions of the Ombudsman by the means of information and education reduces the likelihood of exclusion, discrimination, and human rights violations. It ultimately leads to higher public confidence in and acceptance of the existing system of government.

References

Buck, Kirkham, Thompson (2011) The Ombudsman enterprise and administrative justice. Ashgate, Farnham

Stuhmcke A, Tran A (2007) The commonwealth Ombudsman. An integrity branch of government? Alternative Law J 32(4):233–236

[15] Members are: the Parliamentary and Industry-based Ombudsmen of the two countries.

[16] Cf Stuhmcke and Tran 2007, p. 233 et seq. for more details.

[17] According to information provided by the Institution.

[18] Cf Annual Report (Commonwealth) 2010/2011, p. 158 et seq. for details.

[19] Cf Annual Report (New Zealand) 2010/2011, p. 56 for details.

Chapter 6
Good Practice Examples

Michael Frahm

6.1 General Overview

In all jurisdictions examined there are some specific features that are worth highlighting. Each of them strengthens the respective Ombudsman's independence, makes his or her mandate more comprehensive, or endows the Ombudsman with additional powers which enlarge his or her possibilities to protect a complainant or any person cooperating with the Ombudsman. This chapter presents a selection of these features in reference to the respective reports on the different jurisdictions in Chaps. 7–22.[1] These features may serve as a catalogue of good practice examples and encourage peer-learning. The examples shed light on — or offer particularly good answers to — different aspects of elements that constitute an Ombudsman Institution in compliance with international standards.

6.2 Legal Status and Independence

6.2.1 Appointment and Removal Procedure

The appointment and removal procedures stipulated in the Queensland legislation go beyond the standard processes foreseen in most jurisdictions[2] (disregarding differences in detail) and ensure great transparency, fairness and inclusiveness. The law requires obligatory national press advertisements calling for applications

[1] Cf reports on different jurisdictions, Chaps. 7–22 for detailed information on all jurisdictions.

[2] Cf Sect. 2.2.3, p. 25 and 2.2.7, p. 29 for details.

M. Frahm (✉)
Ludwig Boltzmann Institute of Human Rights, Vienna, Austria
e-mail: michael.frahm@univie.ac.at

International Ombudsman Institute (ed.), *Australasia and Pacific Ombudsman Institutions*, DOI 10.1007/978-3-642-33896-0_6, © Springer-Verlag Berlin Heidelberg 2013

by qualified persons.[3] It further establishes an obligatory consultation process between the Minister and the Parliamentary Committee responsible.

The law likewise foresees a meticulous procedure in case of removal. As a first step in such a situation, the Premier must inform the Ombudsman in writing about the reasons for the intended motion. Subsequently, the Premier must request an address by Parliament and include his or her statement sent to the Ombudsman and the Ombudsman's response. Further, the Premier shall consult the responsible Parliamentary Committee about the motion and obtain agreement from all its members or from "a majority of its members other than a majority consisting wholly of members of the political party or parties in government in the Assembly".[4] These elements of procedural fairness guarantee that the Ombudsman is heard and not merely subjected to the process. Further, it ensures that new parliamentary majorities cannot easily remove an Ombudsman from office, in effect stabilizing the Ombudsman's tenure and strengthening his or her independence. This is in line with international standards, which call for a strengthening of the Ombudsman's independence.[5]

6.2.2 *Conflict of Interest*

The Queensland legislation contains further an exemplary provision which aims at preventing any potential conflict of interest. The Ombudsman must issue a written statement about his or her interests and the interests of persons related to him or her within one month after taking office.[6] If the Ombudsman has an interest that may conflict with the exercise of the Ombudsman's responsibilities, he or she must disclose the nature of the interest and conflict to the Speaker of Parliament and to the responsible Parliamentary Committee. This provision underlines the personal independence of the incumbent and increases public confidence in the Ombudsman.

6.3 Mandate

6.3.1 *Review of the Administration*

Over time, the Ombudsmen have increasingly moved away from merely investigating individual cases. As described above,[7] there has been a development towards more

---

[3] Cf report on Queensland, Chap. 10, p. 145 for details.

[4] Cf s67 OA (Queensland).

[5] Cf Sect. 2.2.1, p. 23.

[6] Cf report on Queensland, Chap. 10, p. 145 for details.

[7] Cf Sect. 3.3.4, p. 60 for details.

systematic investigations and the addressing of systemic shortcomings in the public administration. A growing number of scholars and also office holders refer to Ombudsman Institutions and other independent offices as the "integrity arm of government."[8] The aim of a more systemic approach is to improve the overall quality and to further the integrity of the administration by supporting the improvement of practices and procedures. Many Ombudsmen use their power of own motion investigations to do exactly this — audit the administration.[9] In the Northern Territory, Queensland and South Australia as well as in Taiwan, the Institutions have been given a more explicit mandate in this field, as was described in Sect. 4.1.4.5 above.[10] The law in South Australia, for example, stipulates:

> If the Ombudsman considers it to be in the public interest to do so, the Ombudsman may conduct a review of the administrative practices and procedures of an agency to which this Act applies.[11]

Such clarification strengthens the role of Ombudsmen in this field and should not be seen as a shift in the focus of attention. The Ombudsman must remain the contact person for people who wish their grievances to be addressed.[12] However, addressing systemic flaws to improve the administration in general can make many individual complaints obsolete. The potential of the general review provision lies in this aspect. Further, such provision appears to reflect the reality of the work of many Ombudsmen. This clarification signifies the recognition of this function by the legislator and endows the Ombudsman with a broader mandate.

6.3.2 Investigation of Human Rights Violations

In a small but growing number of jurisdictions[13] human rights are an *explicit* standard of control (Papua New Guinea, Taiwan and Victoria).[14] Further, it is argued here that, in a broad interpretation, the set of terms used by all jurisdictions to define the

---

[8] Cf Creyke 2007, p. 722 and Stuhmcke 2010, p. 233 et seq.

[9] Cf Sect. 3.3.4, p. 60 for details.

[10] Cf reports on different jurisdictions, Chaps. 9, 10, 11 and 20 for details.

[11] Cf s14A(1) Ombudsman Act (South Australia). In the Northern Territory (s10 OA (Northern Territory)) and in Queensland (s12(c) OA (Queensland)) similar provisions exist while in Taiwan, the power of audit is exercised by the Control Yuan, which is empowered by the Constitution.

[12] Cf Buck et al. 2011, p. 92 who assessed that "proposals to downgrade the complaint-handling role has found little favour in the [O]mbudsman community [. . .]".

[13] In Samoa, the Government has started an initiative to set up the Samoa Human Rights Commission within the Ombudsman office, which will vest the Ombudsman with investigative powers also in regard to human rights.

[14] Cf Sect. 3.2.6, p. 53 for details. New Zealand has also included human rights in regard to the role of the Ombudsmen as National Preventive Mechanism under OPCAT and as National Mechanism under the CRPD, cf ibid.

standard of control *imply* human rights.[15] Yet, an explicit reference in the law better reflects the importance of human rights for the Ombudsman's work and strengthens his or her position. It makes human rights an explicit benchmark for complaints, recognises their importance, and ultimately also empowers people in the sense of a rights-based approach. In the three jurisdictions mentioned above, the Ombudsman has been authorised to investigate questionable administrative actions which may infringe human rights. In none of these jurisdictions this is connected with granting the Ombudsman new powers. Thus, the finding that an administrative action has violated a human right as well as any recommendations for corrective actions have the same standing as any other recommendation made according to the standard procedure. The importance of such findings should nevertheless not be underestimated. As already described,[16] the findings of the Ombudsmen are usually highly persuasive, and will continue to be so if it is concluded that there has been a violation of a human right. This is in line with international standards, which call for the inclusion of the protection of human rights in the responsibilities of Institutions.[17]

6.3.3 Protection of the Term "Ombudsman"

The term "Ombudsman" is a promise. The term stands *inter alia* for independence, accessibility and for fast, fair and free procedures. Using this term, Ombudsmen in the APOR region have gained a good reputation over the last 50 years of their existence. The more popular the Ombudsman model became, the more the risk of similar bodies which however lack certain essential aspects also using the name and prestige connected with it grew. In 2010, the Australian and New Zealand Ombudsman Association (ANZOA) began a campaign which aimed at a better protection of the name in Australia.[18]

In New Zealand, South Australia and Tonga, the name Ombudsman is protected by law.[19] In New Zealand and Tonga, no person other than the person appointed under the law may use the term. Violation of this provision constitutes a punishable offence. In South Australia, protection is limited to all agencies under the jurisdiction of the Ombudsman. No such agency is allowed to use the term "Ombudsman" for any internal procedure aiming at the investigation and remedy of complaints. Protecting the name indirectly increases public confidence in the Ombudsman. The public cannot get confused and misled by Ombudsman-like schemes that do not live

---

[15] Cf Sect. 3.2.6, p. 53 for details.

[16] Cf Sect. 4.1.2.2, p. 69 for details.

[17] Cf Sect. 3.2.1, p. 49 for details.

[18] ANZOA points out the growing use of the term by e.g. "bodies with regulatory functions and/or advocacy roles", cf www.anzoa.com.au/Use_of_term_Ombudsman.html. Cf also Reif 2004b, p. 53.

[19] In Tonga, the protected term currently is "Commissioner for Public Relations", a name that has been considered misleading for a long time, cf report on Tonga, Chap. 21, p. 273.

up to what the name promises. Once disappointed by any such process, public confidence in the public-sector Ombudsman could decrease. Therefore, the legal protection of the term is included here as an example of good practice that may ensure the continued good reputation of the Ombudsman.

6.3.4 Conciliation and Mediation

In several jurisdictions, the Ombudsman may, with the consent of both parties, decide to deal with a complaint by conciliation and mediation. This power, described in more detail above,[20] gives the Ombudsman the flexibility to attempt to resolve matters[21] by way of a conciliation or mediation process which ends with an agreement between the complainant and the administrative body complained about. The advantage of this option is the involvement of both parties in the entire process. Conciliation and mediation include the consideration of the position of "the other side" and the reaching of an agreement. This process empowers people who may otherwise feel rather uninvolved in the Ombudsman's investigation. The fact that the outcome has been commonly agreed on has a significant peace-making effect.

6.4 Powers

6.4.1 Protection against Victimisation

Some jurisdictions sanction any victimisation of persons complaining to or supporting the work of the Ombudsman. In Western Australia for example, it is a punishable offence to prejudice the safety or career of any person providing information to or assisting the Ombudsman, or to intimidate, harass or threaten to do so or undertake any other act that is to the detriment of any person for his or her complaining to, providing information to or assisting the Ombudsman.[22] A similar provision in New South Wales outlaws the performance of "any violence, punishment, damage, loss or disadvantage" vis-à-vis any person for his or her complaining to, giving evidence to or assisting the Ombudsman or, for employers, to dismiss any employee for assisting the Ombudsman.[23] Anyone found guilty of this offence faces punishment with a fine or imprisonment of up to two (Western Australia)

---

[20] Cf Sect. 4.1.3.4, p. 75 for details.

[21] Matters involving minor maladministration only and not representing a systemic flaw.

[22] Cf s30B PC Act (Western Australia).

[23] Cf s37 OA (New South Wales).

respectively five (New South Wales) years. Such provisions facilitate making a complaint respectively supporting an investigation, as they reduce the fear of victimisation individuals may have.

6.4.2 *Injunction*

A few jurisdictions endow the Ombudsman with the power to temporarily stop administrative actions from being performed while he or she investigates or considers an investigation. This power, described in more detail above,[24] allows the Ombudsman to investigate a matter without the risk of irreversible facts being created which may in consequence adversely and irreversibly affect the complainant. In such cases, either an injunction can be issued by a court, or the Ombudsman him- or herself can issue a binding instruction to the agency concerned. This complementation of the mandate fills a gap with potentially severe consequences. It strengthens the Ombudsman's mandate, ensures that in any such situation the Ombudsman has the tools to effectively carry out the investigation, and ensures a better protection of the rights, including human rights, of complainants.

6.4.3 *Compensation*

The Ombudsman can freely decide what he or she recommends at the end of an investigation in order to remedy the situation.[25] This includes the recommendation of a monetary compensation for the complainant, if this Ombudsman considers this appropriate.[26] Such a recommendation is usually based on the general power to make any recommendation considered appropriate. In New South Wales, the legislator decided to emphasise this option and thus inserted a sub-section to the Ombudsman Act which explicitly stipulates that the Ombudsman may recommend "that compensation be paid to any person".[27] The subsequent section regulates the procedure by which the authority concerned may authorise such a payment.[28] Such a provision which recognises the payment of a monetary compensation as one of the potential outcomes strengthens the Ombudsman's case when recommending the payment of compensation. It also facilitates the implementation of such a recommendation, as the necessary authorisation procedures for payments are stipulated in

---

[24] Cf Sect. 4.1.3.2, p. 74.

[25] Cf Sect. 4.1.2.2, p. 69 for details.

[26] Cf Buck et al. 2011, p. 116.

[27] Cf s26(2)(d1) OA (New South Wales).

[28] Cf s26A OA (New South Wales).

the law. Ultimately, in certain situations compensation is the only remedy available if a violation of rights has been occurred. Its inclusion in the legal framework therefore ensures that in such cases the determination of an infringement of rights does not remain without consequences.

References

Buck, Kirkham, Thompson (2011) The Ombudsman enterprise and administrative justice. Ashgate, Farnham

Creyke R (2007) Administrative justice – towards integrity in government. Melbourne Univ Law Rev 31(3):705–732

Reif LC (2004) The Ombudsman, good governance, and the international human rights system. Martinus Nijhoff, Leiden

Stuhmcke A (2010) 'Each for themselves' or 'one for all'? The changing emphasis of the commonwealth Ombudsman. Federal Law Rev 38(1):143–167

Part II
Reports on Different Jurisdictions

Chapter 7
Australia: Commonwealth Ombudsman

Michael Frahm

7.1 General Information

Aboriginal settlers from Southeast Asia arrived on the continent approximately 40,000 years before the first Europeans started exploration in the seventeenth century. In 1770, Captain James Cook occupied Australia in the name of the United Kingdom. Six colonies were created in the late eighteenth and nineteenth centuries, which became the Commonwealth of Australia in 1901. Today Australia is a federal parliamentary democracy and constitutional monarchy, with Queen Elizabeth II, in personal union also the Queen of Australia, as its Head of State, represented by the Governor-General at federal level and the Governors at state level (Fig. 7.1).[1]

The population of the Commonwealth of Australia is estimated at 22.6 million, with a population density of only 2.7/km^2.[2] Australia's population is diverse with the following dominating ethnic groups: White, mostly of British or Irish ancestry 92 %, Asian 7 % and Aboriginals 1 %. While English is the *de facto* national language, other languages spoken include Chinese 2.5 %, Italian 1.6 %, Greek 1.3 %, Arabic 1.2 %, Vietnamese 1 %, other 8.2 % and unspecified 5.7 %.[3]

In addition to the Federal Australian Government of the Commonwealth with the Prime Minister as Head of Government, there are six states[4] (representing the six British colonies that created the Commonwealth) which each have their own Parliaments and administration. In addition, there are territories within the Australian border consisting of land not claimed by one of the states. According to the

[1] Cf BBC country profile Australia (http://news.bbc.co.uk/2/hi/country_profiles/default.stm) and CIA World Factbook (Australia).

[2] Australian Bureau of Statistics June 2011.

[3] According to the 2006 Census.

[4] New South Wales, Queensland, South Australia, Tasmania, Victoria and Western Australia.

M. Frahm (✉)
Ludwig Boltzmann Institute of Human Rights, Vienna, Austria
e-mail: michael.frahm@univie.ac.at

International Ombudsman Institute (ed.), *Australasia and Pacific Ombudsman Institutions*, 101
DOI 10.1007/978-3-642-33896-0_7, © Springer-Verlag Berlin Heidelberg 2013

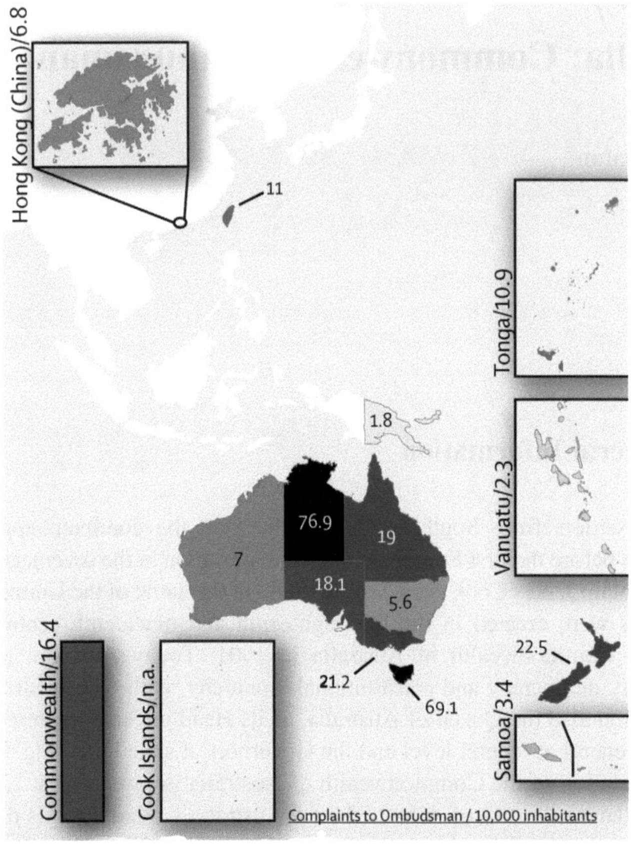

Fig. 7.1 Overview of the region including number of complaints per inhabitants

Constitution, these territories do not have the right to convene their own government and administer themselves. There are, however, two territories[5] which have been granted the right of self-government.[6]

In addition, there is a third level of government—namely that of local governments, which are called "local councils." The six states each have domestic administrators, the Governors, and Premiers as Head of Government. While the Governors are recommended by the state Premiers and appointed by the Queen, each state's Premier is in turn appointed by the state's Governor. In contrast, territories have administrators appointed by the Governor-General.[7] Except for the two self-governing territories mentioned above, whose Head of Government is a Chief Minister, territories are directly subject to the Commonwealth Government, and the Commonwealth Parliament has powers to legislate in territories.

[5] The Australian Capital Territory (ACT) and the Northern Territory.

[6] Other than in the case of the states, the power of these territories is defined by ordinary law and not guaranteed by the Constitution.

[7] ACT has neither a Governor nor an Administrator; it is the Governor-General who represents the Queen.

The capital of the Commonwealth of Australia is Canberra, which administratively belongs to the Australian Capital Territory (ACT). Like the Commonwealth, each state (except for Queensland[8]) has a bicameral system with an Upper and a Lower House.[9] Powers are distributed between the Federal Government and the states. There are exclusive[10] and concurrent powers. The states (as well as the self-governing territories) have full legislative power in all those subject matters which the Constitution does not specifically assign to the Federal Government. If any inconsistencies with concurrent powers emerge, federal law prevails (art. 109 Const.).

The Constitution of Australia, written in 1901, does not contain a Bill of Rights but rather several express as well as implied protections of human rights (especially legal protection). Australia has nine legal systems, i.e. one federal system and eight state and territory systems. All are based on English Common Law. At federal level, the High Court of Australia has jurisdiction over Commonwealth law. It is the highest court with appellate jurisdiction over all other courts and some original jurisdiction. Additionally, it also has the power of constitutional review. Other federal level courts include the Federal Court of Australia, the Family Court of Australia and the Federal Magistrates Court of Australia.

There are also states and territory court systems, each of which operates independently. For more information compare the respective report below.

7.2 The Ombudsman Institution

Commonwealth Ombudsman
Street: Level 5, Childers Square, 14 Childers Street[11]
Postal address: GPO Box 442, Canberra ACT 2601
Zipcode: ACT 2601 City: Canberra
Phone: +61.1300 362 072
Fax: +61.2 62760123
E-mail: ombudsman@ombudsman.gov.au
Website: www.ombudsman.gov.au/

Toll free line: 1300 362 072[12]

---

[8] Queensland has a single-chamber Parliament, the "Legislative Assembly". The upper chamber was abolished in 1922. The self-governed territories ACT and Northern Territory also only have a unicameral Parliament.

[9] In the Commonwealth Parliament the two Houses are called the "Senate" and the "House of Representatives." The states call them the "Legislative Council" and "Legislative Assembly", respectively.

[10] For example defence, external affairs, immigration and citizenship.

[11] This is the Canberra and National office. In addition there are seven offices, cf footnote 29, p. 107 for details.

[12] Calls from mobile phones are charged at mobile phone rates.

7.2.1 Overview

7.2.1.1 Legal Basis

The Commonwealth Ombudsman was established by the Commonwealth Ombudsman Act 1976 (OA) and began its activity in 1977. Together with the seven other state and territorial Ombudsman Institutions in Australia examined in this study, the office joined the IOI in 1985. The office has federal level jurisdiction only. At state level respectively territory level there are eight[13] additional Ombudsmen with state level (respectively territory level) jurisdiction.

The Institution was originally modelled after the Ombudsman office in New Zealand. However, over the years numerous modifications of its mandate have taken place, a few of which are listed here as examples:

Since 1982, the office has had jurisdiction over the field of Freedom of Information, i.e. since then any individual has been allowed to complain to the Ombudsman about the handling of Freedom of Information requests by government agencies. Since November 2010, the Ombudsman has been transferring most complaints to a new statutory agency, the office of the Australian Information Commissioner[14] while retaining jurisdiction. In 1989, the Ombudsman assumed the position of ACT Ombudsman based on the authorisation in s5(1) (c) OA. In April 2011, the latest substantial amendment has added jurisdiction over private registered education providers with regard to overseas students to the powers of the Ombudsman.[15]

In addition to the Commonwealth Ombudsman there are other Ombudsmen with special mandates at federal level. What is interesting to note is that these Institutions are structurally amalgamated with the Commonwealth Ombudsman, who therefore today "wears different hats" and the office's activities are thus governed by a number of different Commonwealth and ACT laws. The Commonwealth Ombudsman acts also as the Defence Force, Immigration, Law Enforcement, Taxation, Postal Industry, ACT, and Overseas Students Ombudsman. Besides the OA, the most important laws are the ACT Ombudsman Act 1989 (ACT-OA), the Australian Federal Police Act 1979, the Telecommunications (Interception and Access) Act 1979 (TIAA) and the ACT Freedom of Information Act 1989 (ACT-FOIA). In the past years, the office has been led by one Ombudsman[16] and two Deputies.[17]

---

[13] In the ACT, New South Wales, Northern Territory, Queensland, South Australia, Tasmania, Victoria and Western Australia. The ACT Ombudsman is administered by the Commonwealth Ombudsman.

[14] This office was formed as part of a larger reform of the federal Freedom of Information Act. The reform has merged powers relating to Freedom of Information and privacy into one office and has added new functions relating to information policy. The office of the Privacy Commissioner was integrated into the new office of the Australian Information Commissioner.

[15] Other amendments have added competences which are described below.

[16] The last Ombudsman resigned on 28 October 2011, the appointment of Colin Neave as the new Ombudsman was announced on 16 August 2012.

[17] One Deputy position was left vacant from March 2010.

In Australia there is an ICC-accredited[18] National Human Rights Institution (NHRI),[19] the Commonwealth of Australia's Human Rights Commission.[20] It was established as an independent statutory body in 1986 and operates in compliance with the Paris Principles.

7.2.1.2 Legal Status and Independence

The Ombudsman and all Deputy Ombudsmen[21] are appointed by the Governor-General (s21 OA). The law does not foresee a consultation process for any such appointment. The legal provisions governing the functions of the Defence Force Ombudsman and the office of Postal Industry Ombudsman are found in the OA itself, which merely stipulates that these two positions shall be held "by the person who holds the office of Commonwealth Ombudsman" (s19B and s19L OA). The Minister[22] may designate one Deputy Ombudsman as the "Deputy Ombudsman (Defence Force)" (s23 OA). As far as the other Ombudsmen are concerned, the OA stipulates that the Ombudsman may, if he or she so chooses, be called the Taxation Ombudsman, the Immigration Ombudsman or the Law Enforcement Ombudsman in performing his or her functions in relation to the Australian Tax office, Immigration and the Australian Federal Police respectively (s4(3–5) OA). According to an arrangement between the ACT Government and the Federal Government, the Commonwealth Ombudsman is also the ACT Ombudsman. In April 2011, the office assumed its latest function, namely the competence of Overseas Students Ombudsman based on a reform of the Education Services for Overseas Students (ESOS) legislation (s19ZI OA).

The Ombudsman is appointed for a term of up to seven years (s22 OA) and may be reappointed (s22 OA).[23] There are no provisions in the legal basis limiting the number of reappointments or ensuring that members or the staff of the Institution reflect the composition of society. The law is also silent as far as incompatibilities are concerned.

The Governor-General may, with the consent of the (Deputy) Ombudsman, retire the respective Ombudsman on the grounds of physical or mental incapacity (s27 OA). Furthermore, the Governor-General may remove a(n) (Deputy)

[18] The International Coordinating Committee of National Institutions for the Promotion and Protection of Human Rights (ICC) was established under the auspices of the UN Office of the High Commissioner for Human Rights (OHCHR) in 1993. It is incorporated as a legal entity under Swiss law, with a Bureau of 16 voting members representing the four regions of the ICC ("status A" NHRIs), cf www.ohchr.org/en/countries/nhri/pages/nhrimain.aspx.

[19] The Human Rights Commission is accredited as a "status A" NHRI, cf Sect. 1.1.3, p. 6 for details on the Paris Principles and NHRI.

[20] Cf www.hreoc.gov.au/.

[21] There shall be at least one, and not more than three Deputies (s4(1b) OA).

[22] The Ombudsman is currently part of the portfolio administered by the Prime Minister.

[23] The practice is to appoint the Ombudsman for a 5-year term, cf APOR Manual (2009), p. 1.

Ombudsman from office. However, he or she can do so only following an address by both Houses of Parliament and only on the grounds of misbehaviour or physical or mental incapacity (s28(1) OA). For the same reasons and acting on his or her own, the Governor-General may (temporarily) suspend a(n) (Deputy) Ombudsman (s28(2) OA), but must seek approval by both Houses thereafter. Parliament must confirm the suspension within seven sitting days after the suspension, turning it into a permanent removal from office (s28(3) and (4) OA). If this step is not confirmed by Parliament, the suspension terminates (s28(5) OA). The Governor-General on his or her own shall also remove the (Deputy) Ombudsman from office if he or she becomes bankrupt (s28(7) OA) and may do so if the (Deputy) Ombudsman is absent from duty for longer periods of time without authorisation (s28(7A) OA).[24]

The (Deputy) Ombudsman and any staff or delegate are immune from legal process with regard to the exercise of their functions when acting with good faith under the OA or under the Australian Federal Police Act 1979[25] (AFP) (s33 OA). Similarly, they are immune for actions under the ACT-OA (s31 ACT-OA). The Ombudsman cannot be compelled to provide any information or documents obtained by the office in exercising his or her functions to any court or tribunal (s35 OA, s33 ACT-OA).

The Ombudsman may hire staff to fulfil his or her functions. Any person shall be engaged under the Public Service Act 1999[26] (s31 OA). An Ombudsman shall be paid such remuneration as is determined by the Remuneration Tribunal (s24 OA).

7.2.1.3 Organisation

The office is led by the Ombudsman who shall have at least one and a maximum of three Deputies; in 2011 there was one Deputy.[27] They are assisted by five Senior Assistant Ombudsmen, each of whom is responsible for one of the five teams:

- The Justice, Finance and Territories Branch,
- The Community Services Branch,
- The Operations Branch,
- The Immigration and Overseas Students Branch, and
- The Corporate Services.[28]

[24] Absent from duty for more than 14 consecutive days or for 28 days in any twelve months of service.

[25] Division 7 of Part V of the Federal Police Act regulates the Ombudsman's power to review the professional standards and AFP conduct and practices issues annually and on an ad hoc basis as necessary.

[26] For the purpose of the Public Service Act, the office and its staff are considered to constitute a statutory agency.

[27] Until 2010 two Deputies were appointed.

[28] This reflects the office structure as of October 2012.

Besides its headquarters in Canberra, the office has sub-offices in each state and the two self-governed territories.[29] The office, including its sub-offices, comprises 182 employees including the Ombudsman and Deputy Ombudsman (this equals 173.63 full-time equivalents (FTE) in 2010–2011).[30] The office is largely[31] financed from public funds appropriated by Parliament. In addition, funding is received from the ACT Government and the Australian Federal Police for the provision of services under the ACT-OA and when providing services in relation to the Police (s5(7) OA).[32] The resources available to the office are determined by the Federal Government. Pearce[33] reports that there has been a "constant battle to obtain funding that is adequate" to the performance of the duties of the office.[34] The former Ombudsman stepped down in October 2011. He had previously also expressed concerns related to budgetary limitations. The budget for the financial year 2010–2011 was AUS$ 22,510,531 (US$ 23,075,545 as of 4 May 2012).[35]

Since "the title Commonwealth Ombudsman reflects the naming practice of the time"[36] and nowadays nationwide agencies are rather referred to as "Australian" agency, it may be that the office will be re-named the "Australian Ombudsman" should there be a more general overhaul of the relevant legislation.[37]

7.2.2 *Mandate*

7.2.2.1 Object of Control

By virtue of the OA the Ombudsman office has jurisdiction over all agencies of the Federal Government, including the Australian Federal Police (s5(1) as read with s3 OA).

Under its other hats, the office's jurisdiction includes, subject to some exceptions, all ACT agencies (s5(1)(a)(i) ACT-OA) defined as administrative units or bodies established for a public purpose or a territory-owned corporation or a subsidiary. The Ombudsman may exercise his or her powers under the OA also

[29] That is in Adelaide (South Australia), Alice Springs (Central Australia), Brisbane (Queensland), Darwin (Northern Territory), Hobart (Tasmania), Melbourne (Victoria), Perth (Western Australia) and Sydney (New South Wales).

[30] As of 30 June 2011, cf Annual Report 2010/2011, p. 37.

[31] The office receives some funding from the Australian Agency for International Development (AusAID) to support the work of Ombudsmen in Indonesia, Papua New Guinea and other Pacific Islands states.

[32] Cf Annual Report 2010/2011, p. 40.

[33] Dennis Pearce was the Commonwealth Ombudsman from 1988 to 1991.

[34] Cf Pearce (2000), p. 94.

[35] Cf Annual Report 2010/2011, p. 186.

[36] Cf APOR Manual (2009), p. 1.

[37] Cf APOR Manual (2009), p. 1.

in relation to Freedom of Information complaints in accordance with the OA (confirmed by s89F FOIA) vis-à-vis all Departments. The same applies to investigations in relation to the ACT-FOIA. In the latter case agencies exempted are listed in s6 ACT-FOIA. For compliance monitoring tasks in the field of law enforcement, the Ombudsman has jurisdiction over the Australian Federal Police, the Australian Crime Commission and the Australian Commission for Law Enforcement Integrity (s15HS Crimes Act 1914).[38] Under the Surveillance Devices Act 2004 (SDA) specific jurisdiction of the Ombudsman is even broader and besides aforementioned agencies also includes other law enforcement agencies (s6 SDA).[39]

In addition, non-government contractors providing public services under a contract with an Australian government agency generally fall under the Ombudsman's jurisdiction. In 2005, jurisdiction was extended in s3BA OA to regulate this.[40] In the field of employment assistance and the management of immigration detention centres, there are service providers whose actions are deemed to be the actions of the agency, thus falling under the jurisdiction of the Ombudsman (s3(4B) OA).[41] In case of registered private providers of education to overseas students, the Ombudsman has had jurisdiction since 2011 (s19ZI OA). In case of unemployment insurance and pension insurance, the (private) Financial Ombudsman[42] is competent in case of complaints. In case of electricity and water supply in the ACT, the ACT Civil and Administrative Tribunal (ACAT) has jurisdiction for investigations. Complaints in the field of telecommunications services are investigated by the (private) Telecommunications Industry Ombudsman. As far as health insurance is concerned, the Private Health Insurance Ombudsman is competent except for public hospitals, which fall under the jurisdiction of Health Complaints Commissioners in the states and territories.

Private persons cannot be subject to investigations by the Ombudsman unless they are service providers as defined in s3BA OA. Excluded from jurisdiction are also actions taken by a Minister (s5(2)(a) OA and s5(2) ACT-OA),[43] public service employment actions (s5(2)(d) OA),[44] actions of courts and tribunals headed by a judge (s5(2)(b)–(c) OA),[45] and the actions of the intelligence agencies.[46]

---

[38] The Ombudsman shall inspect the records of each agency.

[39] The Ombudsman has the obligation to inspect the records of the agencies. Additional law enforcement agencies include the Police of each state or territory, the NSW Crime Commission, the Independent Commission against Corruption, the Police Integrity Commission, the Crime and Misconduct Commission and the Corruption and Crime Commission.

[40] Cf Stuhmcke (2008), p. 321 et seq. for details on privatised public services.

[41] Cf APOR Manual (2009), p. 2.

[42] Cf www.fos.org.au/centric/home_page.jsp.

[43] However, an advice given to a Minister and an action taken to implement a Minister's decision may be investigated (s5(3) and 5(3A) OA).

[44] However, pre-employment issues (e.g. unsuccessful application), post-employment issues (e.g. super-annuation) and the exercise of civic rights by an employee (e.g. Freedom of Information request, whistleblower disclosure) may be investigated, cf APOR Manual (2009), p. 2.

[45] However, the actions of court and tribunal registries may be investigated.

[46] The Inspector-General of Intelligence and Security is responsible for the agencies (Inspector-General of Intelligence and Security Act 1986).

7.2.2.2 Standard of Control

The Ombudsman shall assess whether any administrative conduct "appears to have been contrary to law", was "unreasonable, unjust, oppressive or improperly discriminatory", based "on a mistake of law or of fact", or "otherwise wrong" (s15(1) OA). Further, he or she shall act if it appears that "a discretionary power had been exercised for an improper purpose or on irrelevant grounds" or in exercising a discretionary power "that irrelevant considerations were taken into account, or that there was a failure to take relevant considerations into account" (s15(1) OA).

Procedures can be initiated by individual complainants, be it from private individuals or companies. Even a third party may make a complaint on somebody else's behalf — with the approval of the person concerned. Complaints may be submitted both in writing, including using the online complaint form, or orally (s5(1)(a) and s7 OA). They should include copies of all relevant correspondence with the agency complained about. Also, the Ombudsman may act by own motion (s5(1)(b) OA).

The law foresees that, before initiating formal investigations, the Ombudsman may also commence so-called "preliminary inquiries" (s7A OA). Prior to investigation, he or she must inform the head of the body in question that the office is planning to commence an investigation (s8(1) OA). There are similar procedures under the ACT-OA (s7-s9 ACT-OA). There is no fee for submitting a complaint. The Postal Industry Ombudsman may charge Australia Post or a registered private postal operator a fee in relation to an investigation (s19ZE (1) OA).

Generally, a complaint should be made within twelve months after the action complained about has happended, otherwise the Ombudsman may decide not to investigate the matter (s6(1)(a) OA). The Ombudsman further has discretion not to investigate complaints which are "frivolous, vexatious or not made in good faith," in relation to matters in which the complainant has no sufficient interest or if the complainant has not raised the matter with the agency concerned. Even if the complainant has addressed the agency concerned, the Ombudsman may not investigate unless and until he or she learns that no (adequate) redress has been granted (s6 (1A) and (1B) OA).

If the complainant may pursue other means of reviewing the decision (e.g. court, tribunal) and it would be reasonable to exercise that means of review taking into account all circumstances of the case,[47] the Ombudsman may (in his or her discretion) decide not to investigate. Otherwise, the Ombudsman shall forward the complaint to the respective office if there is another office having jurisdiction[48] and the Ombudsman considers it better that the matter be dealt with by this office (s6 (4D-21) OA).

---

[47] E.g. the nature of the complaint, the costs related to that procedure and the time necessary for pursuing the review.

[48] E.g. the Telecommunications Ombudsman, Privacy Commissioner, Industry Ombudsman, Australian Communications and Media Authority, Public Service Commissioner, Integrity Commissioner or AFP Commissioner.

7.2.3 *Powers*

7.2.3.1 Relation to the Administration

Before initiating a formal investigation, as a first step the Ombudsman may initiate a preliminary inquiry into the subject matter (s7A(1) OA). This shall allow the Ombudsman to decide whether the matter falls within the office's jurisdiction or whether the Ombudsman decides in his or her discretion to investigate the matter. If the Ombudsman subsequently believes formal investigation to be warranted, he or she shall inform the head of the agency concerned of these intentions before starting a formal investigation (s8(1) OA, s9 ACT-OA). The office may have a standing arrangement with the agency, which would contain the manner of informing the agency (s8(1A) OA.[49]

The Ombudsman shall conduct all investigations in private. Other than that, he or she is fairly free in the procedures (s8(2) OA, s9(3) ACT-OA). Any person may be summoned to give evidence or produce documents (s8(3) and s9(1) OA), and failure to comply is an offence punishable with a penalty of AUS$ 1,000 or imprisonment for 3 months (s36 OA). If appropriate, the Ombudsman may administer an oath (s13 OA). The law foresees that a person cannot refuse to answer a question or to produce a document on either basis of self-incrimination or because of secrecy obligations in another statute (s8(2A-2E) OA).[50] However, exceptions are possible for security reasons (s9 OA). The Ombudsman has the power to enter premises of agencies to carry out an investigation, and he or she may inspect documents there; limitations are possible for security reasons (s14 OA and s17 ACT-OA).

In the course of the investigations, the Ombudsman may discuss any relevant matter with the responsible Minister (s8(8) OA and s9(10) ACT-OA). If a Minister requests this, the Ombudsman shall consult this Minister before he or she forms a final opinion according to which a matter needs to be rectified (s8(9) OA and s9(11) ACT-OA). At the end, the Ombudsman may draft a report including an adverse finding and recommending remedial action (s15(3) OA and s18(3) ACT-OA). However, any agency or person who will be expressly or implicitly criticised in such a report must be given an opportunity to comment on the issue before the Ombudsman prepares such a report (s8(5) OA and s9(6) ACT-OA). The final report is to be submitted to the agency concerned. The Ombudsman may request that agency to provide him or her with particulars of any action that it proposes to take with respect to the matters and recommendations included in the report, within a specified time (s15(4) OA) and s18(4) ACT-OA). He or she shall also provide a copy of the report to the Minister concerned (s15(6) OA) and s18(6) ACT-OA).

---

[49] Cf Pearce (2000), p. 96 and s8(1A) OA.

[50] This includes any legal advice or documents to which a claim of legal professional privilege might be made and also Cabinet and other governmental high-level policy documents.

In the final report, the Ombudsman may recommend the payment of a compensation on an act-of-grace basis.[51] However, due to financial concerns, it appears that it is often difficult to get such a recommendation implemented.[52] The Ombudsman may also recommend that agencies reconsider decisions not to award compensation under the "Compensation for Detriment Caused by Defective Administration Scheme" (CDDA Scheme), which is another avenue through which government agencies can compensate individuals or groups (on a discretionary basis) who have suffered loss as a result of defective government administration.[53]

The outcome is legally non-binding, but if no appropriate action is taken within reasonable time or if the agency does not accept the recommendation, the Ombudsman may inform the Prime Minister (s16 OA) respectively the ACT Chief Minister (s19 ACT-OA) in writing. The Ombudsman may also thereafter inform Parliament (s17 OA) respectively the ACT Legislative Assembly (s20 ACT-OA). Following such presentation, the Ombudsman may have further discussions with the principal officer concerned (s18 OA). The Ombudsman can also release any information in the public interest (s35A(1) OA and s34(1) ACT-OA), i.e. can publish an investigation report without necessarily having to present the report to Parliament respectively the ACT Legislative Assembly.

Of note, the Commonwealth Ombudsman and a state Ombudsman may jointly conduct an investigation into an issue that arises within the jurisdiction of both (s8A OA). As an interesting feature the law foresees that, if an agency fails to act and there is no statutory time limit for it to act, the Ombudsman can issue a certificate in the absence of any decision constituting a negative decision for the purpose of enabling the complainant to have a tribunal review of the decision (s10 OA).

The powers described under the OA apply also to any Ombudsman investigation under the Australian Federal Police Act 1979, see s40TS(3) Australian Federal Police Act 1979. Any specific powers of the Ombudsman with respect to inspections are also stipulated in other relevant legislation. For example, in relation to telecommunications interceptions the Ombudsman has the power to enter premises occupied by an agency, to have full and free access to all records, the General Register and the Special Register of the agency (s86 TIAA). In relation to the regular inspection of records of law enforcement agencies (compliance monitoring) to be conducted by the Ombudsman under the Crimes Act 1914 and under the Surveillance Devices Act 2004, the Ombudsman has similar powers to obtain relevant information from officers concerned (s15HT Crimes Act 1914 and s56 SDA).

The ACT Corrections Management Act 2007 provides for entry and inspection powers for the Ombudsman at any reasonable time for a correctional centre. There are no specific provisions in the law in regard to speaking to detainees in private.

---

[51] In cases in which the Government has no legal obligation to compensate, but the Ombudsman sees compensation as an adequate remedy.

[52] Cf Pearce (2000), p. 98.

[53] Cf www.finance.gov.au/financial-framework/discretionary-compensation/finance-submission.html for details.

In his or her capacity as the Immigration Ombudsman (s4(4) OA), the Ombudsman may visit immigration detention centres.[54] This power includes making unannounced visits.

7.2.3.2 Relation to the Judiciary

The Ombudsman has no competence to investigate decisions of courts or of tribunals that have the power to take evidence on oath and are required or permitted to have as a member a judge, or actions of magistrates or coroners (s5(2)(b), (ba), (c) OA), although "the office can investigate the actions of court and tribunal registries".[55] The Ombudsman may request information in pending court cases if necessary for an investigation. The Ombudsman has no general right to appeal; rather, appeals are only possible in cases in which the Ombudsman has been a party to a proceeding.

If a question arises between the Ombudsman and the head of a Department or authority regarding the exercise of a power or performance of a function of the Ombudsman, the Ombudsman (and also the respective head) may file an application with the Federal Court of Australia (s11A(1) OA). In case of the ACT-OA the application is made to the ACT Supreme Court (s14(1) ACT-OA).

If a person fails to comply with a requirement to appear made by the Ombudsman, or provide information and/or documents (s9 OA and s11 ACT-OA), the Ombudsman may file an application with the Federal Court of Australia (s11A(2) OA) or with the ACT Supreme Court (s14(2) ACT-OA), respectively, for an order directing that person to comply with these requirements.

Under the Public Interest Disclosure Act 1994 (ACT) the ACT Ombudsman can commence proceedings to seek a remedy for a person who has suffered an unlawful reprisal in the ACT Supreme Court (s30 Public Interest Disclosure Act 1994 (ACT)).

The Ombudsman's decisions can be reviewed by the Federal Magistrates Court or the Federal Court under the Administrative Decisions (Judicial Review) Act 1977. Decisions made by the Ombudsman under the Freedom of Information Act 1982 (FOIA) are reviewable by the Australian Information Commissioner.

7.2.3.3 Relation to the Legislator

The Ombudsman shall submit an Annual Report to Parliament and can make special reports if desired.[56] These reports are directed to the Prime Minister, who tables them before Parliament. In case the Ombudsman fails to submit a report in time as stipulated by the law, the Ombudsman shall make a written statement to the

[54] Cf Taylor (2000), p. 64 for more details.

[55] Cf Ombudsman Report, Commonwealth Courts and Tribunals, Report No 12/2007, p. 5.

[56] The Ombudsman increasingly uses this power to submit comments to Parliament concerning administrative proceedings, cf Stuhmcke and Tran (2007), p. 235.

Prime Minister in which he or she explains the reasons (s19(7B) OA). The Ombudsman has no strong legislative initiative powers, however, under s15 of the OA, the Ombudsman must report to the relevant agency when he or she is of the opinion that a specific provision of a law should be altered.

There is not one single Parliamentary Committee exclusively competent in relation to the Ombudsman. Parliamentary review of the budget and annual reports of the Ombudsman is assigned primarily to the Senate Standing Committee on Finance and Public Administration. The Ombudsman is required to report to and appear annually before two other Parliamentary Committees in relation to the oversight of controlled operations: to the Parliamentary Joint Committee on Law Enforcement[57] and the Parliamentary Joint Committee on the Australian Commission for Law Enforcement Integrity.[58] The Ombudsman is also required to provide other reports to Parliament on matters such as immigration detention, telephone interception and Police complaint handling.

7.2.4 *Other Characteristics*

In May 2009, Australia signed the Optional Protocol to the Convention against Torture and other Cruel, Inhuman or Degrading Treatment or Punishment (OPCAT),[59] but has not ratified it yet. In the context of the Universal Periodic Review of Australia,[60] the Australian delegation stated that Australia was "committed to ratifying the OPCAT as a matter of priority". A report to the Australian Human Rights Commission describes options for the implementation of OPCAT.[61] As far as National Preventive Mechanisms (NPMs)[62] are concerned, options include designating the Australian Human Rights Commission or the Commonwealth Ombudsman with the function of national coordinating NPM. On the political level, the ratification and implementation process is still under discussion.

With his or her different functions, the Commonwealth Ombudsman has broad jurisdiction and manifold functions in various fields. Particularly of note are his or her functions in overseeing law enforcement agencies which use covert powers (telecommunications interceptions and stored communications), use surveillance

[57] Formerly, the Parliamentary Joint Committee on the Australian Crime Commission.

[58] Cf s10 Parliamentary Joint Committee on Law Enforcement Act 2010 and s218 Law Enforcement Integrity Commissioner Act 2006.

[59] Cf Sect. 3.2.6.2, p. 56 for more details.

[60] Cf www.ohchr.org/EN/HRBodies/UPR%5CPAGES%5CAUSession10.aspx.

[61] Cf www.hreoc.gov.au/human_rights/publications/opcat/opcat.pdf.

[62] The OPCAT requires signatories to establish fully independent NPMs to prevent torture and ill-treatment, cf Sect. 4.1.3.9, p. 79 for more details.

devices and implement Police-controlled operations. Furthermore, the Ombudsman oversees immigration detention facilities and has the power to review the circumstances of detained immigrants.

The very practice-oriented provision in the OA which allows for a standing arrangement with an agency regulating the manner of informing the agency of any new complaint appears quite unique (s8(1A) OA). Another special feature is the Ombudsman's power to directly release information to the public if it is in the public interest — without first addressing Parliament (s35A OA).

Any agency that provides information to the Ombudsman in good faith, believing that the information is relevant to an investigation, is not in breach of privacy or secrecy laws (s8(2A-2E) OA) — this amendment to the Act in 2005 was made in response to the growing tendency of agencies not to volunteer information to the Ombudsman due to concerns about breaches of the Privacy Act 1988.

Very relevant for a federal state system and a system with various Ombudsman-like Institutions is the provision that the Ombudsman may, jointly with a state Ombudsman, conduct an investigation in case of an issue touching upon jurisdiction of both Institutions (s8A OA).

7.2.5 Workload

In the reporting period 2010–2011, the office registered a total of 38,919 approaches and complaints,[63] which related mainly to the following executive branches of the Australian Government: Human Services[64] (7,270 approaches), Treasury[65] (3,092 approaches) and Immigration (2,178 approaches).

7.2.6 Publications

The Ombudsman is obliged to report annually to Parliament on the office's exercise of its statutory functions by submitting his or her report to the Prime Minister (s19(1) OA). In addition, the Ombudsman may report to Parliament on his or her operations at any time during the year via the Prime Minister (s19(2) OA). There are some specifics regarding the Postal Industry Ombudsman reporting obligations in s19X OA. Further reporting obligations in the form of an Annual Report arise in regard to the Ombudsman's functions under the Federal Police Act (s40XD Australian Federal Police Act 1979) and in form of a bi-annual report regarding surveillance device

---

[63] Of the 38,919 approaches, a total of 19,098 were out of jurisdiction, cf Annual Report 2010/11, p. 173.

[64] Of these, the majority was referred to CentreLink and the Child Support Agency.

[65] Of these, the majority was referred to the Australian Taxation office.

inspections under the SDA (s61 SDA). Lastly, also an Annual Report on controlled operations is required and must be tabled before Parliament (s15HO Crimes Act 1914). Under the ACT-OA, the Ombudsman is to report to the ACT Legislative Assembly on his or her activities (s19 ACT-OA). The reports regularly contain statistics, workload and financial and performance information. The report under the ACT-OA contains a short section on human rights deriving from the ACT Human Rights Act 2004.[66]

7.2.7 *Annotations*

There are currently no annotations.

References

Commonwealth Ombudsman (2009a) Australasia and Pacific Ombudsman Region Information Manual 2009. Commonwealth Ombudsman, Canberra. www.ombudsman.gov.au/docs/APOR-Manual_20091009.pdf. Accessed 10 Nov 2011

Pearce D (1999) The Ombudsman: review and preview the importance of being different. In: Reif LC (ed) The international Ombudsman anthology. Selected writings from the international Ombudsman institute. Kluwer Law International, Dordrecht

Pearce D (2000) Ombudsman in Australia. In: Gregory R, Giddings P (eds) Righting wrongs. The Ombudsman in six continents. IOS, Berlin

Stuhmcke A (2008) Changing relations between government and citizen: administrative law and the work of the Australian commonwealth Ombudsman. Aust J Publ Admin 67(3):321–339

Stuhmcke A, Tran A (2007) The commonwealth Ombudsman. An integrity branch of government? Alternative Law J 32(4):233–236

Taylor S (2000) Protecting the human rights of immigration detainees in Australia: an evaluation of current accountability mechanisms. Sydney Law Rev 22(1):50–92

Further Reading

Overview of Legislation: http://www.ombudsman.gov.au/pages/our-legislation/
OA: http://www.comlaw.gov.au/Details/C2005C00403
ACT-OA: http://www.legislation.act.gov.au/a/alt_a1989-45co/current/pdf/alt_a1989-45co.pdf
Australian Federal Police Act 1979: http://www.comlaw.gov.au/Details/C2011C00530
FOIA: http://www.comlaw.gov.au/Details/C2011C00488
TIAA: http://www.comlaw.gov.au/Details/C2011C00146
ACT-FOIA: http://www.legislation.act.gov.au/a/alt_a1989-46co/current/pdf/alt_a1989-46co.pdf

[66] The ACT was the first jurisdiction in Australia to enact a Human Rights Act. It provides an explicit statutory basis for protecting and promoting civil and political rights.

Annual Reports

Commonwealth Ombudsman (2003–2011): http://www.ombudsman.gov.au/pages/publications-and-media/reports/annual/index.php

ACT Ombudsman (2002–2011): http://ombudsman.act.gov.au/pages/publications-and-media/reports/annual/index.php

Postal Industry Ombudsman (2006–2010): http://www.pio.gov.au/publications-and-media/annual-reports.php

Chapter 8
Australia: Ombudsman New South Wales

Michael Frahm

8.1 General Information

New South Wales is one of six states of the Commonwealth of Australia.[1] Australia has a federal system of government with legislative powers distributed between the Federal Government (Commonwealth) and the states (with exclusive and concurrent powers).[2] The legal system is based on English Common Law.

New South Wales has a bipartite administrative system with both a state and a local government level. The state has approximately 7.3 million inhabitants,[3] which corresponds to a comparably high population density of $9.04/km^2$ — the Australian average being $2.7/km^2$. New South Wales has a domestic administrator called the Governor, who is the representative of and appointed by the Queen. The Premier is the Head of Government and is appointed by the Governor. There is a bicameral Parliament vested with legislative power and comprised of the Upper House, or Legislative Council, and the Lower House, or Legislative Assembly. The state capital and largest Australian city is Sydney.

New South Wales has its own Constitution which is based on the Constitution Act of 1902[4]; it codifies a system of local government (art. 51 Const.). The Supreme Court of New South Wales is the superior court of the state, exercising original and appellate jurisdiction. It also rules on state constitutional issues.[5] The New South Wales District Court is the principal trial court and has appellate jurisdiction.

---

[1] Cf Sect. 7, p. 101 for more information on the Commonwealth.

[2] Cf Sect. 7, p. 101 for more information on the Commonwealth legal system.

[3] Australian Bureau of Statistics (June 2011).

[4] Cf www.legislation.nsw.gov.au/viewtop/inforce/act+32+1902+FIRST+0+N/.

[5] Cf www.Parliament.nsw.gov.au/prod/web/common.nsf/key/ResourcesSystemCourtsTheJudiciary for more information on the judicial system.

M. Frahm (✉)
Ludwig Boltzmann Institute of Human Rights, Vienna, Austria
e-mail: michael.frahm@univie.ac.at

International Ombudsman Institute (ed.), *Australasia and Pacific Ombudsman Institutions*, 117
DOI 10.1007/978-3-642-33896-0_8, © Springer-Verlag Berlin Heidelberg 2013

At local level there are Local Courts with criminal (regarding summary offences) and civil jurisdiction.

The New South Wales Ombudsman has no constitutional basis and is a statutory office established by the Ombudsman Act 1974 (OA).

8.2 The Ombudsman Institution

Ombudsman New South Wales
Street: Level 24, 580 George Street
Zipcode: NSW 2000, City: Sydney
Phone: +61.2 9286 1000
Fax: +61.2 92832911
E-mail: nswombo@ombo.nsw.gov.au
Website: www.ombo.nsw.gov.au/

Toll free line: 1800 451 524

8.2.1 Overview

8.2.1.1 Legal Basis

The office of the New South Wales Ombudsman was established in 1974. The office opened to the public the following year, in 1975. Like other Australian Ombudsman offices, it became member of the IOI in 1985. Its enabling legislation modelled the office after the New Zealand Ombudsman office and granted it jurisdiction at the New South Wales state and local government level. In addition to this office, there are also other institutions to which people may refer, depending on the subject matter. These include the Commonwealth Ombudsman if its office has jurisdiction, as well as several Industry Ombudsmen such as the Energy and Water Ombudsman NSW, the (Commonwealth) Fair Work Ombudsman and the (Commonwealth) Telecommunications Industry Ombudsman.[6] For more details on this, see Sect. 8.2.2 below.

The Ombudsman draws his or her powers not only from the OA, but, after several extensions of the mandate over the last 30 or so years, from the following laws:

- Community Services (Complaints, Reviews and Monitoring) Act 1993 (hereinafter CS-CRAMA),
- Police Act 1990 (hereinafter PA),
- Commission for Children and Young People Act 1998,
- Public Interest Disclosures Act 1994 (hereinafter PIDA),

[6] Cf www.fairwork.gov.au/ for details.

- Witness Protection Act 1995 (hereinafter WPA),
- Children and Young Persons (Care and Protection) Act 1998,
- NSW universities' enabling Acts as amended by the Universities Legislation Amendment (Financial and Other Powers) Act 2001,
- Government Information (Public Access) Act 2009,
- Government Information (Information Commissioner) Act 2009,
- Freedom of Information Act 1989 (applied by the Government Information (Public Access) Act 2009),
- Law Enforcement (Controlled Operations) Act 1997 (hereinafter LECOA),
- Telecommunications (Interception) (NSW) Act 1987 (hereinafter TIA),
- Law Enforcement (Powers and Responsibilities) Act 2002,
- Surveillance Devices Act 2007,
- Terrorism (Police Powers) Act 2002 and
- Criminal Procedure Act 1986.

8.2.1.2 Legal Status and Independence

The Ombudsman is appointed by the Governor on the recommendation of the Premier (s6(1) OA).[7] While Parliament initially was not formally involved in the appointment process, the Parliamentary Committee on the Office of the Ombudsman and the Police Integrity Commission (the "Joint Committee", s31A OA) have had the power to veto the appointment since 1992 (s6A and s31BA OA). The appointment is for a term that does not exceed seven years and an office holder is eligible for reappointment (s6(2) OA). Persons are ineligible if they are either older than 65 years or a Member of any House of Parliament (s6 OA). To highlight his or her independence, the law stipulates that the Ombudsman is exempted from public service provisions (s6(6) OA).[8] There are no qualificational requirements for this position laid down in the law.

The OA does not contain an explicit provision which ensures that members or staff of the Institution reflect the composition of the New South Wales society. However, the New South Wales Government has issued a policy with benchmarks to meet the requirements under the Anti-Discrimination Act 1977 and compels government agencies, including the Ombudsman, to work towards achieving these benchmarks.[9]

The Ombudsman must vacate the office on the day on which he or she reaches the age of 65, if he or she is nominated for election as a Member of any Australian

[7] The office is "part of the legislative portfolio of the Premier". However, the Premier does not take any "direct role in relation to [the office's] work". Cf APOR Manual (2009), p. 9.

[8] S6(6) OA stipulates that the Public Sector Management Act 1988 does not apply to the Ombudsman.

[9] Agencies are encouraged to install policies in connection to the employment of women, of people with disabilities and of Aboriginal people.

Parliament, if he or she engages in any paid employment outside the duties of the office (without approval of the Premier[10]), or if he or she resigns from office and the Governor accepts the resignation (s6(4) OA). The Ombudsman may only be removed from office by the Governor upon addresses from both Houses of Parliament (s6(5) OA). The law does not stipulate more details as to the procedure in such a case.

The Ombudsman cannot, without the leave of the NSW Supreme Court, be sued in relation to any matter done or omitted to be done for the purpose of executing the OA or any other Act (s35A OA). The same applies to any member of the Ombudsman's staff. Neither the Ombudsman nor the staff members are competent or compellable to give evidence or produce any document in any legal proceedings in respect to their work (s35 OA).

Remuneration of the Ombudsman is determined by the Statutory and Other offices Remuneration Tribunal[11] (s6(7) OA). Remuneration is not aligned to that of any senior official; for purposes of comparison, it is comparable with other statutory officers and heads of public organisations in New South Wales.[12]

8.2.1.3 Organisation

There are three Deputy Ombudsmen appointed by the Ombudsman in accordance with s8(1) OA, allowing for the appointment of one or more Deputies and Assistant Ombudsmen. One of the Deputies is the Community and Disability Services Commissioner for the purposes of the CS-CRAMA (s8(1A) OA). The senior staff additionally consists of two Directors. There are no sub-offices in New South Wales; however, office staff regularly visit regional centres as well as remote areas to assist the community in critical issues.[13] The office is divided into four branches: Police and Compliance, Human Services, Public Administration and Strategic Projects, and Corporate services.

Staff are appointed by the Ombudsman as necessary for the fulfilment of his or her functions (s32 OA). Other than the Ombudsman him- or herself, the staff is employed under the Public Sector Employment and Management Act 2002. The Ombudsman cannot determine the salary and conditions for his or her staff. At the end of the financial year 2010–2011, the Ombudsman New South Wales employed 185.19 full-time equivalent staff, 133.37 of who were female.

The Ombudsman office is subject to the same budget process as all public sector agencies. Based on the standard New South Wales Government budget cycle of

[10] Cf s6(9) OA.

[11] Established pursuant to the Statutory and Other Offices Remuneration Act 1975.

[12] According to information provided by the office, the remuneration is higher than that of the Chief Justice of the Supreme Court of New South Wales.

[13] In the 2010–2011 reporting period, Ombudsman staff visited 59 regional centres and remote communities in New South Wales.

four years, the budget is allocated for the current year and the three following years.[14] While the standard is to allocate the same budget for every year, the office may request additional funding. Ultimately, it is the Cabinet's Budget Committee that determines any changes in the budget. It is the Ombudsman's authority to determine how the budget is spent.[15] The budget for the financial year 2010–2011 was AUS$ 23,567,000 (US$ 24,170,315 as of 4 May 2012).[16]

The statutory tasks of the office have been modified — and extended — repeatedly over the last years. In 2011, the office became responsible for supporting the work of the Child Death Review Team (CDRT), following an amendment of the respective laws.[17] Following the amendment of the Public Interest Disclosures Act 1994 (PIDA), the Ombudsman acquired a new function in relation to public interest disclosures.[18] There are currently no further plans to reform the office.

8.2.2 *Mandate*

8.2.2.1 Object of Control

The Ombudsman's jurisdiction spans state and local government as well as private sector bodies involved in the provision of public services to children and in the provision of community welfare services more generally. At present it includes all Government Departments and statutory authorities, local councils, both public and private community service providers, the NSW Police Force, correctional centres, child care centres, NSW universities and public as well as private schools (s12 read in conjunction with s5 OA).

In connection with public service providers, the jurisdiction of the Ombudsman includes overseeing the Rail Corporation NSW, a statutory authority. In the area of community welfare, the Ombudsman oversees the Department of Family and Community Services. Other important, partially privately organised providers of public services relevant to the inhabitants of New South Wales fall under the jurisdiction of other Ombudsmen: postal services (Postal Industry Ombudsman[19] in personal union with the Commonwealth Ombudsman), telecommunications (the [private Commonwealth] Telecommunications Industry Ombudsman[20]), accommodation of asylum seekers (Commonwealth Ombudsman), health insurance (private

[14] Cf Appropriation Act (NSW) for details.

[15] The Public Finance and Audit Act 1983 and relevant procurement policies apply to all financial decisions.

[16] Cf Annual Report 2010/2011, p. 119.

[17] Children Legislation Amendment (Wood Inquiry Recommendations) Act 2009.

[18] Cf Annual Report 2010/2011, p. 2.

[19] Cf s19ZE(1) Ombudsman Act (Commonwealth).

[20] Cf www.tio.com.au/ for details.

Commonwealth Health Insurance Ombudsman[21]), electricity and water supply (Energy and Water Ombudsman NSW[22]), pension insurance (Commonwealth Financial Ombudsman[23]) and public hospitals (NSW Health Care Complaints Commission[24]).

The Ombudsman's jurisdiction is limited to administrative actions except in relation to the oversight of NSW Police Force investigations of Police misconduct under Part 8A of the Police Act 1990 (PA). The Ombudsman is excluded by the OA from investigating the administrative conduct of the Governor, Parliament, Ministers and Members of Parliament, courts or court like bodies or judges, legal advisors acting for public authorities, individual employment issues,[25] the Independent Commission Against Corruption (ICAC), legal services commissioners etc. under the OA.[26] However, Freedom of Information legislation[27] also includes Ministers, and courts,[28] which is only relevant for complaints and review requests made to the Ombudsman before 1 July 2010. Since then, the Information Commissioner has been in charge of investigating Freedom of Information complaints. Private agencies outside the Ombudsman's jurisdiction and private individuals cannot be subject to an investigation.

8.2.2.2 Standard of Control

The New South Wales Ombudsman has the power to investigate whether an "administrative conduct" is "contrary to law", was "unreasonable, unjust, oppressive or improperly discriminatory", was "in accordance with any law or established practice but the law or practice is or may be, unreasonable, unjust, oppressive, or improperly discriminatory" or was "based wholly or partly on improper motives, irrelevant grounds or irrelevant consideration" or "based wholly or partly on a mistake of law or fact", or was a "conduct for which reasons should be given, but are not given" or was "otherwise wrong" (s26(1) OA). Such conduct is generally described as "maladministration". The protection of fundamental rights is not

---

[21] Cf www.phio.org.au/ for details.

[22] Cf www.ewon.com.au for details.

[23] Cf www.fos.org.au/centric/home_page.jsp for details.

[24] Cf www.hccc.nsw.gov.au/ for details.

[25] However, the exercise of civic rights such as a whistle-blower disclosure by an employee may be investigated.

[26] Schedule 1 of the OA contains the full list of excluded bodies. For ease of reference, cf also www.ombo.nsw.gov.au/complaints/whatcantcomplainabt.html.

[27] Cf s4(1) Government Information (Public Access) Act. For details on the new office see also Government Information (Information Commissioner) Act 2009.

[28] Between 1989 and 2010, the office's responsibilities fell under the Freedom of Information Act 1989. With the introduction of the Government Information (Public Access) Act 2009 this responsibility has been placed with the newly formed Information Commissioner.

specifically stipulated as a function of the Ombudsman. However, the Ombudsman may need to consider human rights obligations in so far as they are relevant.

Any person (including a public authority) with sufficient interest in the matter (s13(4)(b)(vi) OA) may make a complaint. Members of Parliament are explicitly mentioned as authorised to submit a complaint on behalf of a person (s12(2) OA). In addition to initiating procedures following a complaint, procedures may also be started on the Ombudsman's own initiative (s12 and s25G(2) OA).[29] There are no fees for submitting a complaint. Complaints should be made in writing (s12(4) OA). However, other submissions may be accepted if it is considered appropriate to do so. A complaint should be lodged within twelve months of the incident which is the subject of the complaint (s12(1) OA).

The Ombudsman has discretion whether to commence or discontinue an investigation. If the incident occurred more than twelve months prior to the submitted complaint, the matter may only be investigated under special circumstances. The Ombudsman may refuse to investigate the matter if there is an adequate and reasonable remedy or right of review or appeal available to the complainant or if an investigation does not appear to be warranted, for example if the agency is still investigating the complaint, or a complaint has not yet been made to the agency, or if another body may be more appropriate to handle the complaint. Another reason to decide against an investigation of a complaint may be lack of sufficient personal interest on the part of the complainant in the matter. A misuse clause lastly allows to reject a complaint if it appears to be frivolous, trivial, vexatious, or not made in good faith (s12 and s13(4) OA).

8.2.3 *Powers*

8.2.3.1 Relation to the Administration

The Ombudsman may first decide to take up a preliminary investigation of the matter (s13AA OA). Before a full investigation is initiated, the Ombudsman shall then inform the head of the relevant agency of the decision (s16 OA). In the course of the investigation, which always is to be conducted in private (s17 OA), he or she shall give the agency the chance to be heard (s24 OA). The Ombudsman may, however, also decide not to investigate a complaint. In such a case, he or she shall inform the complainant about the reasons (s15(1b) OA). As a rather rare feature, the Ombudsman may at any time also decide to attempt to deal with a complaint by conciliation (s13A OA). The Ombudsman has the power to access and obtain information and documents held by an agency (s18 OA), and to enter premises and inspect any item on the premises of an agency (s20, s21A OA). In addition,

[29] In the 2010–2011 reporting period, the New South Wales Ombudsman finalised 35 direct investigations.

the Ombudsman has certain of the powers of a Royal Commissioner under Division 1 of Part 2 of the Royal Commission Act 1923 (RCA) and when exercising this power, the Ombudsman can summon any person to appear before the Ombudsman, to provide any document, and to give evidence under oath or affirmation (s19(2) OA and s9–s12 RCA).

Upon request by the responsible Minister, the Ombudsman shall consult said Minister on the matter investigated (s25 OA). When the Ombudsman finalises the investigation, he or she shall report his or her opinion and the reasons for it to the responsible Minister and to the head of the agency and make recommendations as he or she thinks fit (s26(3) OA). In addition, he or she may give a copy of the report to the complainant and to the public authority to whose conduct the report relates (s26(4) OA). The report may, as explicitly stipulated in the founding legislation, also recommend that compensation be paid (s26(2)(d1) OA). While the outcome is legally non-binding, the integrity and standing of the Ombudsman's office is such that the recommendations are highly persuasive. The responsible person may, and on request of the Ombudsman shall, notify him or her of the steps taken to implement the recommendation. If no appropriate action has been taken in due time after the recommendation, the Ombudsman may inform both Houses of Parliament and the responsible Minister in writing.[30] Within twelve sitting days, the Minister must report to Parliament on the issue (s27 OA). In case of serious misconduct warranting dismissal or punishment (s28 OA), the Ombudsman shall report this to the responsible Minister, the head of the public authority and to the Premier's Department.[31] In case of alleged criminal behaviour, the Ombudsman may refer the matter to the Police or Prosecutor as appropriate. This is, however, not a statutory requirement. In the course of investigations, the Ombudsman may give a progress report to the complainant from time to time (s29 OA).

The public is generally not the addressee of reports and outcomes are only released publicly if there is significant public interest. To this end, the Ombudsman may make a recommendation to Parliament that the report be made public in any special report (s31 OA), or in any report to Parliament in case of an inadequate response to an Ombudsman report (s31(2) OA). Anonymised versions of reports may be published in the Annual Report.

In addition to the standard investigation procedure summarised above, the Ombudsman has further powers related to several more specific subject matters. Under Part 3A of the OA on employment related child protection, the Ombudsman has the task to audit and keep under scrutiny the systems installed "for preventing reportable conduct by employees" of government and certain non-government agencies and "for handling and responding to" child abuse allegations by employees of those agencies (s25B OA). To this end, heads of agencies have strict

[30] Implementation figures show that in the 2010–2011 reporting period, approximately 80 % of the recommendations made in investigations reports were implemented.

[31] The latter is only possible if the public authority is employed under the Public Sector Management Act 1988.

deadlines for their reporting obligations to the Ombudsman. In the course of any investigation conducted, the Ombudsman may be present as an observer. If so, he or she must receive a copy of the final report and must be informed of actions taken with respect to the reportable allegation (s25F OA). The Ombudsman may also decide to investigate a case him- or herself or conduct an investigation concerning any inappropriate handling of a reportable allegation (s25G OA).

Somewhat similar procedures have been established under the CS-CRAMA in relation to the delivery of community services and related complaints[32] as well as under the PA in regard to Police conduct.[33] In both cases, one of the Ombudsman's core functions is to scrutinise the systems in place and support the agencies in improving the performance of their duties. In performing the functions under both the CS-CRAMA and the PA, the Ombudsman may use the powers provided by the OA (s20 CS-CRAMA and s156(1) and s160 PA). In the exercise of jurisdiction in relation to the provision of community welfare services, the Ombudsman may also apply for and be issued a search warrant to inspect premises, if there are reasons for doing so (s18 CS-CRAMA).

Under s36 CS-CRAMA, the Ombudsman shall "monitor and review reviewable deaths", "formulate recommendations" as to policies and practices, "maintain a register" and "undertake research" in this field with a view to "reduce or remove risk factors associated with reviewable deaths that are preventable". Since 2011, the Ombudsman has also been responsible for convening and supporting the work of the NSW Child Death Review Team, which reviews the deaths of all children in New South Wales.[34]

The Ombudsman office also reviews the implementation of (new) legislation. This is usually done over a period of one to two years. Subsequently, a report is provided to the responsible Minister. Parliament determines which new laws the Ombudsman shall review and how long such a review shall take. The office focuses on acts that give increased powers to Police and correctional officers for example.[35]

Under the PIDA, the Ombudsman oversees the exercise of functions under the PIDA and compliance with the PIDA by public authorities (s6B PIDA). The Ombudsman also provides information, advice, assistance and training to public authorities, investigating authorities and public officials on any matters relevant to their functions under PIDA. The Ombudsman is one of the authorities to whom disclosures concerning maladministration may be made (s11 PIDA). The Ombudsman may also investigate certain matters disclosed to him or her under the PIDA, using the powers conferred to the Ombudsman under the OA.

---

[32] The Ombudsman, in his or her function as the Community and Disability Services Commissioner, has the task of monitoring, reviewing and investigating complaints in regard to the delivery of community services.

[33] Under the PA, the Ombudsman has, among others, the task of auditing complaint mechanisms to make sure the Police handle a complaint effectively and fairly.

[34] Established under Part 7A of the Commission for Children and Young People Act 1998.

[35] Cf www.ombo.nsw.gov.au/aboutus/reviewimplemlegislatn.html for details.

Under the WPA, the Ombudsman hears appeals against decisions made by the Commissioner of Police in relation to inclusions in or removals from the witness protection program (s6(4) and s12(5) WPA).

Under the audit function of the office, the Ombudsman audits the records of agencies authorised to intercept telephone communications under the Telecommunications (Interception) (NSW) Act 1987, the records of agencies authorised to use surveillance devices under the Surveillance Devices Act 2007 and the records of agencies authorised to conduct controlled operations under the Law Enforcement (Controlled Operations) Act 1997 to ensure compliance with the procedural and information security requirements of the Acts.[36]

The Ombudsman may enter and inspect any premises occupied by an agency to which the OA applies (s20 and s21A OA) which includes detention facilities. The Ombudsman may enter without prior announcement under s20 OA.[37] Ombudsman staff can also be admitted to a correctional centre without the prior authorisation of the Commissioner under s74 of the Crimes (Administration of Sentences) Regulation 2008. While the law does not explicitly stipulate such power, in practice Ombudsman staff regularly speak with detainees in private.

It is an offence punishable with a fine of up to ten penalty units "to wilfully obstruct, hinder or resist the Ombudsman [. . .] in the exercise of [his or her] functions", to "fail to comply with any lawful requirement" or to "make any false statement" or to mislead the Ombudsman (s37(1) OA). It is also an offence for a person to misrepresent themselves as being the Ombudsman, a Deputy Ombudsman and Assistant Ombudsman or an officer of the Ombudsman or to be engaged in the exercise of powers under the OA (s37(2) OA).

It is further an offence punishable with a fine or imprisonment of up to five years to use any violence against, punish or disadvantage any person for his or her complaining to, giving evidence to or assisting the Ombudsman. The same punishment is possible for an employer who dismisses any employee for assisting the Ombudsman (s37 OA).

8.2.3.2 Relation to the Judiciary

If a question arises in regard to the Ombudsman's jurisdiction, the Ombudsman or any interested party may make an application to the Supreme Court for determining this question (s35B OA). The Supreme Court has jurisdiction to review the actions of the Ombudsman in the execution of functions under the OA and other Acts, subject to leave being obtained under s35A of the OA.

In New South Wales, another specific feature of the Ombudsman is the possibility, to make an application to the Supreme Court for an injunction restraining the conduct in which a public authority is engaging (or is likely to engage) if said conduct is the

[36] Cf www.ombo.nsw.gov.au/aboutus/legislation.html for details.

[37] In practice, however, this is rarely done.

subject of an investigation or proposed investigation of the Ombudsman under s21C OA.

If necessary for the purposes of an Ombudsman investigation or for an initial assessment of a complaint by the Ombudsman (but not to investigate judicial actions), the Ombudsman is entitled to request information in pending court cases.

Local courts are competent to deal with proceedings for an offence under the OA in case of obstruction of or resistance to the Ombudsman (s37 and s38 OA).

8.2.3.3 Relation to the Legislator

Via the Presiding Officer of each House, the Ombudsman reports directly to Parliament on an annual basis (s30 OA) and on other occasions if necessary (s31 OA). The Parliamentary Joint Committee oversees the operation of the office, reports annually to Parliament, examines each annual and other reports made by the Ombudsman and reports to Parliament on any matter appearing in or arising out of any such report (s31B OA). There is no statutory provision entitling the Ombudsman to participate in debates in Parliament.

The Ombudsman is entitled to initiatives in the legislative field by way of recommendations in a special report to Parliament or by letter to Parliament, based on the mandate in the enabling legislation.[38] Following any proposal to amend legislation by the Ombudsman it is the Department of the Premier and the Cabinet that may subsequently draft and table a law. However, there is no legal obligation to do so.

8.2.4 Other Characteristics

The legislation of New South Wales contains a few special features which are worth stressing. Firstly, there is the option to deal with a complaint by conciliation (s13A OA). The conciliator may be the Ombudsman, one of his or her officers or, with the agreement of the complainant, the Ombudsman may arrange for an external mediator.

Another noteworthy feature is the possibility to apply to the Supreme Court for an injunction restraining the conduct in which an authority is engaging, with the aim of avoiding that such conduct prejudices or negates the effect or the implementation of a recommendation the Ombudsman may make (s21C OA).

The OA explicitly stipulates the option that the Ombudsman may recommend that compensation be paid to a person (s26(2)(d1) OA). The subsequent section regulates the procedure by which the authority concerned may authorise such payment (s26A OA).

---

[38] Information provided by the Institution.

Further, there is the possibility of issuing a progress report in the course of investigations. The Ombudsman may — in addition to informing a complainant of the outcome of the investigation — inform the complainant of the progress of the investigation from time to time (s29 OA).

It is worth to be noted that the law contains special clauses for the protection against victimisation. Individuals supporting the Ombudsman are protected by way of the provisions on punishable offences (s37(4) OA).

8.2.5 Workload

In the 2010–2011 reporting period, the office was approached a total of 33,064 times, 8,917 of which were formal complaints. Of all formal complaints, most cases referred to the Police (2,596), to Departments and authorities (1,381) and to correctional centres and justice health[39] (864). 430 complaints were outside of jurisdiction (and 6,934 of all approaches).[40] The issues complained about mostly referred to customer service (198), object to decision (195), charges/fees (117) and complaint-handling (205).[41] While there currently is no systematic process for collecting data on all complaints, in its complaints database the office has mechanisms to identify a complainant who fits into a vulnerable or disadvantaged group. Precondition is that the complainants voluntarily identify that they belong to a vulnerable or disadvantaged group. The information is only used in the context of the investigation of the complaint or in some circumstances may be used to identify broader issues.[42]

8.2.6 Publications

The Ombudsman annually reports on the exercise of his or her statutory functions under the OA to Parliament (s30 OA). The report also covers financial statements, statistics, information on work carried out during the year, staff statistics and general information on the activities of the office. In addition, s31 OA allows the Ombudsman to table special reports at any time.

Additional reporting requirements are met by way of inclusion of these reports into the Annual Report pursuant to s30 OA under the following laws: the PA, the Annual Reports (Departments) Act 1985, Annual Reports (Departments)

[39] Justice health provides health care services for those in contact with the criminal justice system, cf www.justicehealth.nsw.gov.au/ for details.

[40] Cf Annual Report 2010/2011, p. 9.

[41] Cf Annual Report 2010/2011, p. 30.

[42] Information provided by the Institution.

Regulation 2005, Government Information (Public Access) Act 2009, PIDA, Law Enforcement (Powers and Responsibilities) Act 2002 and Disability Services Act 1993.

The Ombudsman also publishes a Law Enforcement (Controlled Operations) Act Annual Report under s23(1) of that Act. Under the Surveillance Devices Act 2007, the Ombudsman bi-annually reports on the compliance with the Act by law enforcement agencies to the responsible Minister (s49(1) of that Act). The Minister shall submit the report to Parliament.

The Ombudsman also publishes reports on legislative reviews, on consultations with stakeholders as well as on discussions and issues papers, submissions, guidelines, fact sheets and newsletters.[43]

8.2.7 Annotations

For many years the New South Wales Ombudsman was the only Ombudsman in Australia who was not allowed to require the submission of information over which an agency claimed legal professional privilege. For several years, the Ombudsman has attempted to have the respective clause in the founding Act abolished. Finally, in October 2010 the respective amendment to the OA was passed, and the decisive nine words disappeared from s21 OA and s21A OA, putting the Ombudsman more on par with his or her colleagues in other parts of Australia.[44]

Reference

Commonwealth Ombudsman (2009a) Australasia and Pacific Ombudsman Region Information Manual 2009. Commonwealth Ombudsman, Canberra. www.ombudsman.gov.au/docs/APOR-Manual_20091009.pdf. Accessed 10 Nov 2011

Further Reading

Overview of Legislation: www.ombo.nsw.gov.au/aboutus/legislation.html
Constitution: www.legislation.nsw.gov.au/viewtop/inforce/act+32+1902+FIRST+0+N/
Annual Reports: www.ombo.nsw.gov.au/publication/annualreports.asp

[43] Cf www.ombo.nsw.gov.au/publication/index.html for a comprehensive list.

[44] Cf Annual Report 2009/2010, p. 3, and the Ombudsman Amendment (Removal of Legal Professional Privilege) Act 2010.

Chapter 9
Australia: Northern Territory Ombudsman

Michael Frahm

9.1 General Information

The Northern Territory with its capital Darwin is a self-governing territory[1] and one of eight states and territories which make up the Commonwealth of Australia.[2] It has a two-tiered political system with both a territory and a local government level. The Administrator of the Northern Territory, appointed by the Governor-General of Australia, fulfils functions widely similar to that of a Governor. The Head of Government of the territory is the Chief Minister, who is appointed by the Administrator. The Northern Territory's Parliament consists only of the Lower House, the Legislative Assembly. The Australian Parliament has powers to legislate in territories but has granted the Northern Territory and the ACT the right to self-government.

The Northern Territory has approximately 230,000 inhabitants,[3] which corresponds to a population density of 0.17/km^2. The legislative system is based on English Common Law with a federal system of government. The powers are distributed between the Federal Government and the states, with specifics in regard to the power of the Northern Territory Government. As a territory, the Northern Territory does not have its own Constitution, however, the Basic Law governing the territory is the Northern Territory (Self-Government) Act 1978. It does not foresee an Ombudsman.

The court system of the Northern Territory consists of different levels of courts. The superior court is the Supreme Court. It exercises original and appellate jurisdiction in both criminal and civil matters. The District Court is the principal trial

[1] The other self-governing territory is the ACT. Cf the report on the Commonwealth Ombudsman for more information as to the difference between territories and states, Chap. 7, p. 101.

[2] Cf. Chap. 7, p. 101 for more information on the Commonwealth.

[3] Australian Bureau of Statistics (June 2011).

M. Frahm (✉)
Ludwig Boltzmann Institute of Human Rights, Vienna, Austria
e-mail: michael.frahm@univie.ac.at

International Ombudsman Institute (ed.), *Australasia and Pacific Ombudsman Institutions*, 131
DOI 10.1007/978-3-642-33896-0_9, © Springer-Verlag Berlin Heidelberg 2013

court of the Northern Territory. The local Magistrates Courts hear civil and criminal cases (dealing with summary offences).

9.2 The Ombudsman Institution

Northern Territory Ombudsman
Street: 12th Floor, NT House, 22 Mitchell Street
Postal address: PO Box 1344, Darwin NT 0801
Zipcode: NT 0800, City: Darwin
Phone: +61.8.8999 1818
Fax : +61.8.8999 1828
E-mail: nt.ombudsman@nt.gov.au
Website: www.ombudsman.nt.gov.au/
Toll free line: 1800 806 380

9.2.1 Overview

9.2.1.1 Legal Basis

The Northern Territory Ombudsman was installed in 1978. The Institution is based on the New Zealand model. The office became a member of the IOI in 1985. The Ombudsman has jurisdiction at the regional and local level and oversees Government Departments, agencies and boards. There are other bodies with special mandates in the Northern Territory to which people may submit their complaints. The Health and Community Services Complaints Commission (HCSCC),[4] for example, investigates complaints by individuals about health and community services.

The principal legislation from which the Ombudsman draws its powers is the Ombudsman Act 2009 (OA) together with the respective Ombudsman Regulations. Regarding other functions, the Telecommunications (Interception) Northern Territory Act and the Telecommunications (Interception and Access) Act (Commonwealth) as well as the Surveillance Devices Act 2007 endow the Ombudsman with the relevant powers.

[4] This Commission was established as an independent statutory body by the Health and Community Services Complaints Act 1998. It also used to be situated within the Ombudsman office, cf www.hcscc.nt.gov.au/about/. In August 2011, the Ombudsman's contract as the HCSC Commissioner expired and the office of the Ombudsman separated from the HCSCC. Since January 2011, the HCSCC — the functions and duties of which have been expanded with the entering into force of the National Registration Scheme on 1 July 2010 — has become a division of the Department of Justice; cf Annual Report 2009/2010, p. 7 and HCSCC Annual Report 2009/2010, p. 5 for more details.

9.2.1.2 Legal Status and Independence

The Ombudsman is appointed by the Administrator on the recommendation of the Legislative Assembly for a term of seven years (s132 and s134 OA) and is not eligible for reappointment. One cannot become Ombudsman if one has been a member of any Parliament or any council in Australia or the holder of an equivalent office in the Commonwealth or a state or territory within the preceding three years (s133 OA). The OA contains no further qualificational requirements and no "pluralism" provisions. However, the office has an Equal Opportunity Management Plan.[5] Also, the Ombudsman shall not hold any office of profit or engage in any occupation for reward outside official duties, except in so far as he or she is authorised to do so by Parliament (s136 OA).

In regard to removal from office, the establishing act stipulates that the Ombudsman must be removed permanently from office by the Administrator (s140 OA) or may be removed from office following a suspension by the Administrator if the Legislative Assembly consents (s141 OA). The first case applies if the Ombudsman is found guilty of an indictable offence, becomes bankrupt or engages in remunerative employment outside the duties of office without the Chief Minister's approval (s140 OA). The second case allows the Administrator to temporarily suspend the Ombudsman from his or her office in case of misbehaviour or misconduct or physical or mental incapacity. In this case, the temporary suspension can only be turned into a permanent dismissal if the Legislative Assembly passes a corresponding resolution by a two-thirds majority (s141(4) OA). Otherwise, the Ombudsman must resume his or her duties (s141(5) OA).

The office becomes vacant if the Ombudsman becomes a candidate for any Australian Parliament, for any council or for an equivalent office (s142 OA).

The Ombudsman, and any of his or her staff, cannot be sued unless the action in question was taken in bad faith (s160 OA).

Salary and allowances of the Ombudsman are determined by the Administrator. The conditions of employment shall not be altered to the Ombudsman's detriment during his or her term of office (s135 OA).

9.2.1.3 Organisation

The office is headed by the Ombudsman and also includes the two senior functions of Deputy Ombudsman and Assistant Ombudsman, who manage the following topical areas: (1) Conciliation and Complaint Resolution, Ombudsman Enquiries and Complaints, Corporate Support and (2) Police Complaints and Ombudsman

[5] The plan aims at fostering "an understanding and commitment to equity and diversity principles, activities and outcomes by all employees in the agency". The objective is to include "equity and diversity in all Human Resource Management policies and practices" and to "eliminate workplace discrimination and harassment". Cf Annual Report 2010/2011, p. 97 for details.

Investigations, Own Motion Investigations, Telecommunications Interceptions and Surveillance Devices, Training and Development.[6] In addition, there are four Senior Investigation Officers, two Investigation Officers, two Resolution Officers, one Police Administration Officer, one Business Manager, one Records/Finance Officer and one trainee.[7] Officers of the Ombudsman are public sector employees (s145 OA). The total number of staff is 17 full-time equivalents as of June 2011.[8] All staff are public sector employees but shall be subject to direction only by the Ombudsman (s145 and s146 OA).

The Ombudsman used to have a sub-office in Alice Springs, which has however been closed due to budgetary restraints. As part of the office's activities undertaken to provide accessibility to its services, the Ombudsman visits rural and remote communities. The office is funded by parliamentary appropriations. The office also "provides administrative support to a representative of the Commonwealth Ombudsman's office" ,[9] which is also situated within the office of the Ombudsman in Darwin. The budget for the financial year 2010–2011 was AUS$ 2,025,000 (US$ 2,077,245 as of 4 May 2012).[10]

The Ombudsman will be tasked with the oversight of Controlled Operations and Assumed Identities by the Police on enactment of two bills before Parliament.

9.2.2 Mandate

9.2.2.1 Object of Control

The Ombudsman is competent to investigate complaints about matters of administration in relation to public authorities[11] (s10 OA). This means that Government agencies and statutory authorities, boards, local councils, public universities, government-run services such as prisons and schools, water providers, and the Police are under the Ombudsman's jurisdiction. In relation to bodies under his or her jurisdiction, the Ombudsman shall also more generally consider and help to improve their practices and procedures. In addition, the Ombudsman is also in charge of investigating and dealing with complaints about the conduct of Police officers (s10(d) and s65-s116 OA). Private persons are only under the Ombudsman's jurisdiction if they are providing public services.[12]

---

[6] Cf APOR Manual (2009), p. 22.

[7] Cf www.ombudsman.nt.gov.au/about-us/our-structure/ for details.

[8] Cf Annual Report 2010/2011, p. 21.

[9] Cf APOR Manual (2009), p. 21.

[10] Cf Annual Report 2010/2011, p. 143.

[11] Public authorities are defined in s5 OA and include an agency, the Police service, the Power and Water Corporation, a council or another entity that is constituted or established for a public purpose by or under a law of the Territory or declared to be a public authority by other legislation.

[12] Cf APOR Manual (2009), p. 20.

Other important, partially privately organised providers of public services are dealt with at the Commonwealth level and fall under the jurisdiction of the following Ombudspersons: postal services (Postal Industry Ombudsman[13] in personal union with the Commonwealth Ombudsman), accommodation of asylum seekers (Commonwealth Ombudsman), health insurance (Health Insurance Ombudsman[14]), pension insurance and unemployment insurance (Financial Services Ombudsman[15]).[16]

The OA explicitly excludes certain bodies from jurisdiction (s15 and s16 OA): These include the judiciary, the coroner and the Anti-Discrimination Commission. In addition, some specific subject matters do not fall under the Ombudsman's jurisdiction, such as any decision made by Cabinet or by a Minister, any action taken by a person acting as legal adviser or any matters of public service employment.

9.2.2.2 Standard of Control

The Ombudsman investigates whether administrative conduct (s6 OA) was "contrary to law", "unreasonable, unjust, oppressive, or improperly discriminatory", "in accordance with any law or established practice but the law or practice is, or may be, unreasonable, unjust, oppressive, or improperly discriminatory", was based "wholly or partly on improper motives, irrelevant grounds or irrelevant consideration", was done "in the exercise of a power or discretion, and the reasons for the decision were not, but should have been, given" or was "based wholly or partly on a mistake of law or fact" or was "conduct[ed] for which reasons should be given but are not given" or was "otherwise wrong" (s59 OA).

These standards also by and large apply in relation to Police conduct investigations. In these cases, the Ombudsman shall also consider whether the conduct of a Police officer constitutes an offence or breach of discipline (s101 OA). There is no additional provision relating to the protection of fundamental and human rights.

A complaint can be made by any natural or legal person who has been personally aggrieved by an administrative action or a third person[17] representing the aggrieved (s21 OA). A Police officer may only make a complaint about the conduct of another Police officer if the conduct constitutes an offence punishable by imprisonment, is likely to bring the Police into disrepute or diminish public confidence in it (s21(2) OA). Procedures may be initiated also by *proprio motu* (s14 OA) and must be initiated in case Parliament or any of its committees refer the matter to the Ombudsman for investigation (s17 OA). Complaints may be

---

[13] Cf s19ZE(1) Ombudsman Act (Commonwealth).

[14] Cf www.phio.org.au/ for details.

[15] Cf www.fos.org.au/centric/home_page.jsp for details.

[16] The office's jurisdiction has been extended over the years; last extensions include the Telecommunications Interception Inspection and Surveillance Devices Inspections in 2007, respectively 2008.

[17] A third party may only make a complaint if the complaint raises a substantive issue or if the party has first-hand evidence about the matter complained about. Also, a deceased person may be represented by a third party (s22 OA).

made orally or in writing (s23(2) OA). However, the Ombudsman may require that the complaint is to be made in writing (s23(3) OA). A complaint about Police conduct can be made to either the Ombudsman or to a Police officer (s24 OA). There is no requirement to identify the Police officer whose conduct is the subject of the complaint.

After receiving a complaint, the Ombudsman decides at his or her discretion whether to commence an investigation or to refer it to another complaints authority (s32 OA). The law establishes a cut-off period, stipulating that the Ombudsman shall not, except in special circumstances, investigate a complaint that has not been lodged within twelve months of the incident (s25(1) and (3) OA). The Ombudsman has discretion to refuse investigation if the complaint is "trivial, or frivolous or vexatious, or not made in good faith" or if the complainant does not have sufficient personal interest in the matter (s33(a) and (b) OA). Further, he or she may decide not to investigate if the complainant has not directly complained to the agency concerned in an attempt to resolve the issue, if any further investigation is unnecessary or unjustifiable or if, in case of a complaint made by a third party, the complaint does not raise a substantive issue or there is no first-hand evidence about the subject matter of the complaint (s33(c–e) OA).

Also, if there is an ongoing investigation or one that will be submitted to a complaints entity of equal level to the Ombudsman, he or she may decide not to investigate the matter (s34 OA). If the complainant has directly complained to the respective authority, the Ombudsman may decide not to investigate until he or she learns that either no redress or no adequate redress has been granted (s35 OA).

9.2.3 Powers

9.2.3.1 Relation to the Administration

The Ombudsman has the function to investigate complaints received regarding administrative practices and to improve the public administration by way of own motion investigations (s10(a) and (b) OA). The law differentiates between preliminary (s28 OA) and formal investigations (s47 OA). In the first case, the principal officer of the authority concerned must give the Ombudsman reasonable support during the preliminary inquiries procedure (s29 OA). Following these inquiries, the Ombudsman may decide to investigate, to refer the case to another complaints entity (s32 OA),[18] to deal with the complaint by conciliation or mediation or not to investigate the matter.[19]

Before starting a formal investigation, the Ombudsman shall inform the body concerned and also the Minister responsible for the authority in question of the decision to investigate in writing (s47 OA). The Ombudsman shall conduct

[18] The Ombudsman shall inform all parties involved of the referral (s32(2) OA).

[19] In the case of a referred complaint, the Ombudsman must deal with such a complaint (s18 OA).

investigations in private and may regulate the procedure of an investigation in such a manner as he or she thinks fit (s49 OA). He or she shall consult the respective Department, a Minister who asks to be consulted respectively a presiding member of a council who so asks in the case of an administrative action taken by a council (s50(1) OA). The Ombudsman shall in any case consult with the aforementioned if the Ombudsman is considering issuing an adverse report about an administrative action (s50(2) OA).

The Ombudsman shall inform the complainant about the reasons if he or she decides not to investigate a complaint (s36 OA).

The Ombudsman may, at any time on his or her own initiative or upon request, decide to deal with a complaint by conciliation or mediation, given the consent of the parties to the complaint (s37 OA). The investigation is suspended during this time (s40 OA). If the attempt fails, the investigation must be resumed and the conciliator or mediator must be excluded from the process (s46 OA). If an agreement has been reached, it must be recorded in writing and will become binding after a cooling-off period of 14 days, in the course of which the agreement may be cancelled by either side (s44 OA).

In the course of the investigation process, the Ombudsman has extensive powers to investigate complaints (s11 OA). He or she may enter and inspect any item on the premises of any Government Department or authority within jurisdiction (s54 OA). In addition, the Ombudsman can require any person to attend before him or her, to render any document or other thing and to give evidence under oath by written notice (s52 and s53 OA).

The Ombudsman has the power to direct a public authority to stop performing an administrative action for a stated period[20] in order to prevent the establishment of irreversible facts (s55 OA).

Upon concluding an investigation, the Ombudsman shall make a report to the principal officer of the authority concerned, and may therein make such recommendations as he or she thinks fit (s60 OA). If there is evidence of a breach of duty or misconduct, the Ombudsman must also report this to the principal officer (s60 OA). The principal officer must, at the Ombudsman's request, report back within a certain time period on what steps have been taken to give effect to the recommendations (s63(2) OA). If, within a reasonable period of time, no adequate or appropriate action has been taken, the Ombudsman may send a copy of the report to the responsible Minister and, if the authority concerned is a council, to the presiding member of the council (s63(3) OA). In this case, the Ombudsman may also table a report on the matter before Parliament (s63(4) OA). After completing the investigation, the Ombudsman must also inform the complainant of the outcome (s57 OA).

In Part VII (s65-s116 OA) the law contains special provisions for the investigations of Police complaints. These are largely similar to the procedures described above. What is of note is that, according to s66 OA, the Ombudsman must

[20] The period is limited to a maximum of 45 days by law.

assess a Police complaint and decide how to deal with it, i.e. whether to decline dealing with it (s67 OA) or to deal with it by conciliation (s69 OA), by utilising the Police complaints resolution process (s78 OA), by investigation by a Police Standards Command member (s80 OA) or by an Ombudsman investigation.

The Ombudsman may supervise the Police complaints resolution process and investigation (s85 OA). The Ombudsman may decide to investigate the complaint him- or herself if a senior officer or a Police Standards Command member is involved in the matter or if the complaint concerns the practices, procedures or policies of the Police (s86(1) OA). There are several reporting obligations within the Police and vis-à-vis the Ombudsman (s91-s97 OA) if Police structures are used to investigate the matter. Otherwise, the Ombudsman is to report to the Police Commissioner if the Ombudsman investigates the matter (s98-s101 OA).

Besides the functions under the OA, the Ombudsman undertakes a variety of audit/integrity and oversight functions vis-à-vis the administration. These functions are based on various laws. Under s63(1) Surveillance Devices Act 2007, the Ombudsman has the responsibility to inspect records of the Northern Territory Police and to report on compliance of the Police with the legal provisions on the use of surveillance devices to the Legislative Assembly via the Minister (s64 Surveillance Devices Act). Under the Telecommunications (Interception) Northern Territory Act (s9) and the Commonwealth Telecommunications (Interception and Access) Act, the Ombudsman shall monitor and report on the compliance of law enforcement agencies with these laws to the responsible Minister.

In the course of an investigation the Ombudsman may enter correction facilities at any time, as they fall under his or her jurisdiction (s54 OA). The law does not specifically stipulate that the Ombudsman may speak to detainees in private.[21]

The Ombudsman and any staff members are privileged and must not be called to give evidence in any civil, criminal or disciplinary proceeding about any matter that he or she has gained knowledge about in the course of his or her official capacity (s119 OA).

The law makes it an offence to violate provisions of the OA, such as the obligation to maintain secrecy over confidential information (s120-s122 OA). It is also a punishable offence to give misleading information (s123 OA), to prevent or obstruct someone from making a complaint (s124 OA), to commit any act of reprisal against another person who has made or intends to make a complaint or who has cooperated or intends to do so with any member of the Ombudsman's staff (s125 OA), to fail to comply with any lawful requirement (s126-s128 OA), and to obstruct the Ombudsman or any of his or her staff in the exercise of official functions (s129 OA).

A special provision foresees the liability of executive officers of a corporate body in case that corporate body commits an offence against the OA. The officers may exculpate themselves if they did not have knowledge of the violation or have exercised due diligence (s131 OA).

[21] It could be assumed that this is possible in practice as, pursuant to s49 OA, every investigation is to be conducted in private.

9.2.3.2 Relation to the Judiciary

The Ombudsman has no competence to investigate actions of the judiciary (s16(1) OA). However, there are some exceptions which allow the Ombudsman to investigate an action of the judiciary, including the prosecution, if to the Ombudsman's conviction there has been an unreasonable delay by the authority (s16(3) OA).

If a question arises with regard to the Ombudsman's competence to conduct an investigation, the Ombudsman, the principal officer of the authority concerned respectively the Police officer concerned, or the complainant may file an application with the Supreme Court for determining this question (s20 OA).

9.2.3.3 Relation to the Legislator

The Ombudsman is an independent Officer of Parliament. He or she has no jurisdiction over the House or any Member of Parliament. The Ombudsman reports to Parliament annually (s152 OA) and may generally report on the performance of his or her functions or relating to a particular case investigated by him or her at any time (s153 OA). If Parliament refers an issue to the Ombudsman for investigation,[22] the Ombudsman must carry out an investigation into such matter and report to Parliament on the outcome (s155 OA).

The Ombudsman contacts Parliament via the responsible Minister, according to the Administrative Arrangements Orders, which is the Chief Minister. This is purely an administrative responsibility and thus "does not impact on the Ombudsman's independence".[23] Under specific circumstances, his or her counterpart may also be the Speaker of the Assembly.[24] During the budget appropriation process, the Ombudsman may be invited to appear before the Estimates Committee.[25] There is, however, no entitlement in the law that allows the Ombudsman him- or herself to participate directly in debates in Parliament or its committees. There are no statutory obligations on Parliament to react to any material submitted by the Ombudsman.

9.2.4 Other Characteristics

What is of note is that the Ombudsman has the explicit function to further the public administration's integrity by considering its administrative practices and procedures and lending support with the aim to improve its practices and procedures. The Ombudsman also serves as the body which receives and investigates complaints about the conduct of Police officers.

---

[22] Cf Sect. 9.2.2.2, p. 135 for details.

[23] Cf APOR Manual (2009), p. 19.

[24] Cf s155 OA.

[25] Cf APOR Manual (2009), p. 19.

As a new feature,[26] the Ombudsman has been given the power to direct a public authority to stop performing an administrative action for a stated time period to prevent irreversible facts to be realised. Further, the power of the Ombudsman to investigate actions of courts, tribunals or the prosecution in cases where there has been, to the Ombudsman's conviction, an unreasonable delay by the authority is noteworthy.

The OA also contains the option to deal with a matter by conciliation or mediation with the aim to come to a binding agreement between the parties involved. In general, these and other procedural issues seem to be better and more concretely determined than in other, similar legal provisions in other Australian states or territories.

Further, the law contains special clauses for the protection against victimisation. Individuals supporting the Ombudsman are protected by way of the provisions on punishable offences (s124-s125 OA).

Last but not least, the OA addresses the question of liability of the executive of corporate bodies by including a special offence provision, stipulating that executive officers generally are liable if the corporate body commits an offence against the OA. However, they may exculpate themselves for lack of knowledge or on the grounds of having exercised due diligence (s131 OA).

9.2.5 Workload

In the 2010–2011 reporting period, the office was approached 1,768 times.[27] These first contacts resulted in the investigation of 264 cases.[28] Of all approaches, 162 were about Correctional Services, 49 complaints concerned the Department of Justice (except prisoners' complaints), 108 complaints were made in regard to the Department of Housing, Local Government and Regional Services and 60 complaints were about power and water companies. As far as Police cases are concerned, there were a total of 427 complaints.

9.2.6 Publications

The Ombudsman shall report on the exercise of his or her statutory functions to Parliament annually (s152 OA) and on other occasions, as considered appropriate

[26] Included in the OA following the reform of the establishing legislation in 2009, cf APOR Manual (2009), p. 24.

[27] Of the 1,768 initial approaches, 977 were made by men (55.3 %) and 791 were made by women (44.7 %).

[28] Cf Annual Report 2010/2011, p. 31.

(s153 OA). In the case of an investigation after referral by Parliament, the Ombudsman shall submit a report to Parliament (s155 OA).

The Ombudsman shall furthermore report on the results of his or her inspection of the Telecommunications Interception Records of the Police to the Police Minister regularly.[29] By law, the result of these inspections must not be made public.[30] Under the Surveillance Devices Act 2007, the Ombudsman shall report bi-annually on the inspection of records of the Northern Territory Police service to the responsible Minister (s64(1) Surveillance Devices Act).[31] These reports must subsequently be tabled before Parliament by the Police Minister within seven sitting days after receiving the report.

The office has also made available different publications with the aim to assist complainants in submitting a complaint. There is a Procedures Manual, an Accounting and Property Manual and an Employment and Training Policy and Procedures Manual. These publications are available on the Ombudsman's website, where the office also makes available other public reports and brochures.

9.2.7 Annotations

There are currently no annotations.

Reference

Commonwealth Ombudsman (2009a) Australasia and Pacific Ombudsman Region Information Manual 2009. Commonwealth Ombudsman, Canberra. www.ombudsman.gov.au/docs/APOR-Manual_20091009.pdf. Accessed 10 Nov 2011

Further Reading

Overview of Legislation: http://www.comlaw.gov.au/Details/C2011C00309; http://www.ombudsman.nt.gov.au/about-us/legislation/

Annual Reports (2002–2011): http://www.ombudsman.nt.gov.au/publications-reports/annual-reports/

[29] The law requires the Ombudsman to report on the results of inspections that were carried out (s10 Telecommunications (Interception) Northern Territory Act).

[30] Cf Annual Report 2010/2011, p. 90.

[31] The law requires the Ombudsman to inspect the records to determine the extent of compliance with the Act by the agency and its law enforcement officers (s63 Surveillance Devices Act 2007).

Chapter 10
Australia: Queensland Ombudsman

Michael Frahm

10.1 General Information

Queensland is one of six states within the Commonwealth of Australia[1] and has a two-tiered political system with both a state and a local government level. Its capital is Brisbane. The state has a population of approximately 4.6 million people corresponding to a population density of 2.6/km^2 (close to the Australian average of 2.7/km^2); almost half of the population lives in the capital.[2] Queensland has a domestic administrator called Governor, who is appointed by the Queen on advice of the state Premier. The Head of Government or Premier in turn is appointed by the Governor. The Queensland Parliament is the only single chamber Parliament in Australia.[3] The Constitution foresees a system of local government (art. 70 Const.); currently there are 73 local governments in Queensland.[4]

Queensland has its own Constitution, dating from 2001. Like all Australian jurisdictions, the legislative system is based on English Common Law with a federal system of government and powers distributed between the Federal Government and the states.[5] The Supreme Court of Queensland is the superior court exercising original and appellate jurisdiction (art. 57 Const.). There are Magistrates Courts with criminal and civil jurisdiction, which deal with summary offences. The Queensland District Court is the principal trial court. The Ombudsman has no constitutional basis, but is based on ordinary law, the Ombudsman Act.

---

[1] Cf Chap. 7, p. 101 for more information on the Commonwealth.

[2] Australian Bureau of Statistics (June 2011).

[3] It consists of the Queen and the Legislative Assembly. The Upper Chamber was abolished in 1922.

[4] Cf www.dlgp.qld.gov.au/local-government-directory.html.

[5] Cf Chap. 7, p. 101 for more information on the Commonwealth legal system.

M. Frahm (✉)
Ludwig Boltzmann Institute of Human Rights, Vienna, Austria
e-mail: michael.frahm@univie.ac.at

International Ombudsman Institute (ed.), *Australasia and Pacific Ombudsman Institutions*,
DOI 10.1007/978-3-642-33896-0_10, © Springer-Verlag Berlin Heidelberg 2013

10.2 The Ombudsman Institution

Queensland Ombudsman
Street: Level 17, 53 Albert Street
Postal address: GPO Box 3314, Brisbane QLD 4001
Zipcode: QLD 4000, City: Brisbane
Phone: +61.7 3005 7000
Fax: +61.7 3005 7067
E-mail: ombudsman@ombudsman.qld.gov.au
Website: www.ombudsman.qld.gov.au/

Toll free line: 1800 068 908

10.2.1 Overview

10.2.1.1 Legal Basis

The Institution of the Queensland Ombudsman was established in 1974, and the office was opened in the same year as the fourth Institution of its kind in Australia.[6] Together with other Australian offices, it became a member of the IOI in 1985. The office has jurisdiction at the regional (i.e. Queensland) and local level. Its legal basis is the Ombudsman Act (OA), which came into effect in 2001 and replaced the Parliamentary Commissioner Act 1974. In addition to the Queensland Ombudsman, legislation provides for other statutory offices with special mandates in the field of children's rights, anti-corruption, anti-discrimination, health quality as well as energy and water. The Commission for Children and Young People and Child Guardian (CCYPCG) was established in 2000 to promote and protect the rights, interests and the wellbeing of minors.[7] The Crime and Misconduct Commission (CMC) has far-reaching powers to investigate complaints of misconduct and/or corruption in the public sector.[8] The Anti-Discrimination Commission Queensland (ADCQ) has the statutory duty to protect people from unlawful discrimination, sexual harassment and certain other related behaviour under the Anti-Discrimination Act 1991. The Health Quality and Complaints Commission (HQCC) was established in 2006 and provides for an independent investigation

[6] The first jurisdiction to install the position of an Ombudsman in Australia was Western Australia (1971), followed by South Australia (1972) and Victoria (1973).

[7] As established by the Commission for Children and Young People and Child Guardian Act 2000.

[8] Its jurisdiction under the Crime and Misconduct Act, the Witness Protection Act 2000 and the Criminal Proceeds Confiscation Act 2002 includes the state's Police service, state Government Departments, public sector agencies, local councils, universities and Members of the Legislative Assembly.

of healthcare complaints for consumers as well as oversight and review of the quality of health services.[9] The Energy and Water Ombudsman Queensland (EWOQ), established in 2006, is an independent dispute resolution service for private energy customers[10] across Queensland and water customers in the South-East of Queensland.[11]

10.2.1.2 Legal Status and Independence

Statutory provisions for the appointment and removal of the Queensland Ombudsman are more detailed than in many other jurisdictions of the region. For example, the appointment process foresees obligatory national press advertisements calling for applications from qualified persons (s58 OA). Furthermore, the responsible Minister shall consult with the respective Parliamentary Committee[12] about the selection process and the appointment of the person as Ombudsman (s59 OA). However, such advertisement is not necessary in case of reappointment (s59(2) OA). Following these obligatory consultations, the Ombudsman is appointed by the Governor. One term of office shall be no more than five years. Reappointment is possible up to a total tenure not exceeding ten years (s61 OA). There are no qualificational requirements for the Ombudsman, nor any legislated provisions ensuring that the Institution's staff reflects the composition of society.

The law prohibits the appointment of a person as Ombudsman if, within three years prior to the envisaged appointment, the person has been a parliamentarian in the Commonwealth, in Queensland, or in any other federal state of Australia or the holder of "the office of the chairperson, the Mayor, the president, a councillor or a member of a local [g]overnment" or the holder of an office in another federal state equivalent to the mentioned offices (s60 OA).[13] The position of Ombudsman is generally incompatible with any other paid undertaking. To hold "any other office of profit" or "engage in any remunerative employment or undertaking outside official duties" the Ombudsman requires the prior consent of the Minister (s64 OA).

As another means of ensuring independence and avoiding any conflict of interest, the Ombudsman must, within one month after taking office, make a statement that informs about his or her interests and the interests of persons related to him or her.[14]

[9] Established by the Health Quality and Complaints Commission Act 2006.

[10] Also small business energy customers are covered.

[11] Under the Energy and Water Ombudsman Act 2006.

[12] The Legal Affairs, Police, Corrective Services and Emergency Services Committee of the Legislative Assembly is the committee in charge of overseeing the Ombudsman office.

[13] Likewise, the Ombudsman has to resign on becoming a candidate for any of these positions (s72 OA), respectively in case of running for the Parliament of Queensland, he or she must resign under s67(1) Parliament of Queensland Act 2001.

[14] A related person is the Ombudsman's spouse or a person who is totally or substantially dependent on the Ombudsman. This person can either be the Ombudsman's child, or the person's affairs are so closely connected with the Ombudsman's affairs that a benefit derived by the person, or a substantial part of it, could pass to the Ombudsman (s63A(11b) OA).

If the Ombudsman has an interest that conflicts or may conflict with the discharge of the Ombudsman's responsibilities, the Ombudsman must disclose the nature of the interest and conflict to the Speaker of Parliament and to the responsible Parliamentary Committee.

The Ombudsman can be removed from office by the Governor for proved incapacity, incompetence, misconduct or conviction of an indictable offence (s66 OA) following a meticulous procedure. Precondition to such removal is an address by Parliament, which can be requested only by the Premier. Prior to requesting such a motion, the Premier shall inform the Ombudsman in a statement about the reasons for the motion and then table this statement and any written response by the Ombudsman before the Assembly. The Premier needs to consult with the responsible Parliamentary Committee about the motion and to obtain agreement from all its members or from "a majority of its members other than a majority consisting wholly of members of the political party or parties in government in the Assembly" (s67 OA).[15] For the same reasons, the Governor may alternatively suspend the Ombudsman from office (s68 OA). The procedure is similar to the removal procedure.

If the Legislative Assembly is not sitting, the Governor may temporarily suspend the Ombudsman according to s69 OA. The only condition in such case is that the Premier must hitherto have given the Ombudsman a statement which explains the reasons for the suspension and that he or she has considered any response to the statement by the Ombudsman. Once Parliament has commenced sitting, the Premier must table the statement and any written response by the Ombudsman before the Assembly within three sitting days. Unless the Ombudsman is suspended or removed from office on an address by Parliament, the suspension ceases at the end of the sixth sitting day (s69 OA). In the opposite case, the Ombudsman may, at any time, resign from office by addressing the Governor in writing (s71 OA).

The law stipulates that the Ombudsman is not subject to direction by any person about the way he or she performs the functions of Ombudsman or the priority the Ombudsman gives to investigations (s13 OA). The Ombudsman and the office's staff, including secondees from the public service and temporary staff, are not considered public servants, and the Public Service Act 2008 does not apply to them, which ensures their independence from the executive (s58(2), s76(2), s77 and s78 OA). The Ombudsman and any member of the Ombudsman's staff are protected under the OA from liability for any act done, or omission made honestly and without negligence (s93 OA).

The Ombudsman receives a salary and allowances determined by the Governor (s62 OA). The Governor has approved the current Ombudsman's remuneration to be equivalent to a chief executive in public service.

---

[15] Cf APOR Manual 2009, p. 26.

10.2.1.3 Organisation

In addition to the Ombudsman and the Deputy Ombudsman, the office consists of four Assistant Ombudsmen and two managers. Each of the latter six leads a separate team in the office, the Administrative Improvement Unit, the Communication and Research Unit, the Corporate Services Unit, the Assessment and Resolution Team, the Local Government and Infrastructure Team, and the Community Services and Corrections Team.[16] The office, located in the capital of Queensland, Brisbane, has no sub-offices. 53.7 staff (full-time equivalents) work in the office,[17] 63 % of who are female.

Funding for the Queensland Ombudsman is provided by parliamentary appropriations as part of the annual Queensland Government budget process. Each year, the Ombudsman must prepare estimates of proposed revenues and expenditures and pass these on to the Minister responsible for the administration of the Financial Accountability Act 2009 (s88 OA). Subsequently, the Minister must consult with the Legal Affairs, Police, Corrective Services and Emergency Services Committee of the Assembly, which is responsible for developing the proposed budget of the Ombudsman. The budget for the financial year 2010–2011 was AUS$ 7,069,000 (US$ 7,249,259 as of 4 May 2012).[18]

There are currently no plans to reform the Ombudsman Institution in Queensland.

10.2.2 Mandate

10.2.2.1 Object of Control

The Queensland Ombudsman has jurisdiction over Queensland public agencies and their staff, i.e. state Government Departments and public authorities, including universities and local councils (s12 OA). The terms "agency" and "public authority" are further defined in the OA.[19] Private individuals and actions of Commonwealth or interstate Departments or agencies are not under the Ombudsman's jurisdiction.

---

[16] Cf APOR Manual 2009, p. 30 et seq.

[17] As of 30 June 2011.

[18] Cf Annual Report 2010/2011, p. 119.

[19] An agency is a Department, a local government or a public authority. The term "agency" includes any entity, that is not an incorporated entity or an individual and that was established under an Act as a board, council, committee, subcommittee or any other similar entity for supporting or for performing functions connected with the agency (s8 OA). Public authority is exactly defined in s9 OA.

As far as public service providers are concerned, the Queensland Ombudsman investigates complaints about universities and railways.[20] While there are other important providers of public services relevant to the people living in Queensland, these mostly fall under the jurisdiction of other statutory officers: postal services and accommodation of asylum seekers (Commonwealth Ombudsman), health insurance (Private Health Insurance Ombudsman), electricity and water supply (Energy and Water Ombudsman Queensland), pension insurance (Financial Services Ombudsman) and public hospitals (Health Quality and Complaints Commission).

Excluded from jurisdiction are actions taken by courts and judges, a tribunal,[21] legal advisers to the state or counsel to the state in legal proceedings, decisions of Ministers and the Cabinet, the Auditor-General, a member of the Police service, if the action is operational, a mediator at a mediation session under the Dispute Resolution Centres Act 1990, a conciliator operating under the Health Rights Commission Act 1991, or the Health Quality and Complaints Commission Act 2006 and the Information Commissioner in the performance of the Commissioner's functions under the Right to Information Act 2009 (s16 OA).

10.2.2.2 Standard of Control

The Ombudsman assesses "administrative actions" (s12 OA) against the requirements stipulated in s49(2) OA. Accordingly, the Ombudsman shall assess whether any administrative action was "contrary to law", was "unreasonable, unjust, oppressive or improperly discriminatory", was "in accordance with a rule of law or a provision of an Act or a practice that is unreasonable, unjust, oppressive, or improperly discriminatory in the circumstances" or was "taken for an improper purpose or on irrelevant grounds or having regard to irrelevant considerations", was "an action for which reasons should have been given, but were not given", was based "on a mistake of law or of fact", or was "wrong" (s49(2) OA). The law does not specifically stipulate the protection of human rights as a function of the Queensland Ombudsman.

According to the OA, any person or any body of persons, whether incorporated or not, may make a complaint if apparently directly affected by the action (s20(1)(b) OA). Before commencing formal investigations, the Ombudsman may also initiate preliminary inquiries (s22 OA). In such a case, the principal officer of the agency concerned is obliged to support the Ombudsman in the conduct of the preliminary inquiry (s22(2) OA). Before beginning a full investigation, the Ombudsman shall inform that principal officer of his or her intention (s27(2) OA). Complaints may be submitted verbally or in writing, i.e. by telephone, letter, fax, in person or by using the online complaint form. Complaints should be clear and concise and be lodged within

[20] Those provided by the Queensland state Government only.

[21] This includes the action of a tribunal member relating to the tribunal's deliberations.

twelve months of the incident which is the subject of the complaint (s20 (1)(c) as read with s20(3)(c) OA). There is no fee related to submitting a complaint.

Besides acting upon receipt of a complaint, the Ombudsman may start investigations on his or her own initiative at any time (s12(a)(iii) OA) or upon referral by Parliament or one of its statutory committees (s12(a)(i) OA). The Ombudsman has discretion whether to commence (or, once commenced, whether to continue) an investigation and may decide in the negative if it appears that the complaint is trivial, frivolous, vexatious, or not made in good faith, if the "complainant does not have a sufficient direct interest in the action complained of" or if the complainant has a right of review or appeal and it appears reasonable in the circumstances to expect him or her to resort to that remedy (s23 OA).

10.2.3 Powers

10.2.3.1 Relation to the Administration

The Ombudsman may initiate a preliminary inquiry "to decide whether a complaint should be investigated" (s22 OA). Before initiating a formal investigation, the Ombudsman shall inform the head of the relevant agency of this intention (s27(2) OA). The Ombudsman may also decide not to investigate a complaint. In this case, the complainant shall be informed of this decision and of the reasons thereof (s23(4) OA). Investigations are conducted in private and, subject to the OA, the Ombudsman may determine the procedures to be used in an investigation (s25 OA).

The Ombudsman may require[22] a person to hand over certain documents or information (s28 OA) under oath and administer the oath (s33 OA). Further, he or she may request an officer of the agency in question to provide the Ombudsman with reasonable support in exercising his or her powers. The Ombudsman may consult any Minister[23] concerned at any time, but he or she must consult with a Minister if either the Minister so requests or if an investigation relates to a recommendation made to the Minister; and if the Ombudsman is considering to make recommendations for remedial action in connection with reporting about the investigation (s26 OA). If, during an investigation, the Ombudsman thinks there may be grounds for making a report that will affect an agency, the Ombudsman must give the head of the agency an opportunity to comment on the matter under investigation before making the report (s26(3) OA). In case of adverse comments

[22] If a person does not appear before the Ombudsman as requested, the Magistrate Court may issue a *subpoena* requiring the person's attendance before the Ombudsman (s30 OA). Ultimately, an arrest warrant may be issued (s36 OA) on the Ombudsman's request.

[23] This provision refers also to any local government chairperson, Mayor or president (s26(4) OA).

about a person in a report, the Ombudsman shall give the respective person the chance to be heard (s55 OA).

After the completion of an investigation, the Ombudsman may submit a report with recommendations to the appropriate agency and may send a copy of the report to the responsible Minister (s50 OA). The Ombudsman may ask the principal officer to notify him or her within a stated period of time of the steps taken to implement the recommendation. In case of a breach of duty or misconduct, however, the Ombudsman must submit a corresponding report to the agency (s50(2) OA).[24] The recommendations are not legally binding, but if no appropriate action is taken to rectify the situation within a reasonable period of time, the Ombudsman may pass on a copy of the report to the Premier, including any comments made by the agency (s51(3) OA). In this case, the Ombudsman may also provide the Speaker with an additional report for tabling before Parliament. This report shall deal with the original report and the comments (s51(4) OA). The Ombudsman may also him- or herself table an investigative report (including recommendations) before Parliament.

To effectively carry out the function of Ombudsman, the Ombudsman may, after prior notice, enter and inspect a place occupied by an agency and take extracts or copies of documents located there (s34 OA). Based on this rule, the Ombudsman may also visit prisons in connection with an investigation. In practice, the Ombudsman regularly monitors prisons in Queensland; at least one visit to each adult prison is carried out each year. In the 2010–2011 reporting period, Ombudsman officers undertook further visits to several centres to investigate particular complaints.[25] While there is no specific statutory provision regarding speaking to detainees in private, this is *de facto* usually allowed.

It is an offence to state anything to the Ombudsman that the person knows to be false or misleading or to hand over a document containing false or misleading information (s41–s42 OA). The OA penalises obstructing the Ombudsman or any officer of the Ombudsman in the performance of their duties with up to six months of imprisonment (s43 OA).

10.2.3.2 Relation to the Judiciary

The Ombudsman may not investigate actions of judicial authorities and courts (s9(2) OA). In case there is ambiguity about the Ombudsman's jurisdiction in the course of an investigation, the Ombudsman may apply to the Supreme Court to decide the question in closed court (s17 OA). The Ombudsman has the power to request information from agencies in relation to pending court cases.

[24] If the agency concerned is a local government, the Ombudsman may send a copy to the local government's chairperson, Mayor or president (s50(2) OA).

[25] Cf Annual Report 2010/2011, p. 39.

In the course of an investigation, the Ombudsman can turn to a Magistrate Court on two occasions: The Ombudsman may request the issue of a *subpoena* requiring a person to appear before the Ombudsman (s31(2) OA). Further, the Ombudsman may apply to a Magistrate Court for an arrest warrant for a person who has neither complied with an investigation requirement (s29 OA) nor with a *subpoena* issued due to the failure to comply with the investigation requirement (s36(1) OA).

10.2.3.3 Relation to the Legislator

The Ombudsman is an independent (s13 OA) Officer of Parliament (s11(2) OA) and therefore directly reports to Parliament on an annual basis (s87 OA) as well as on other occasions as deemed necessary (s52 OA). The Legislative Assembly's Legal Affairs, Police, Corrective Services and Emergency Services Committee oversees the office of the Ombudsman and examines each Annual Report tabled before the Assembly and, if appropriate, comments on any aspect of the report (s89(c) OA). The Ombudsman is not entitled to participate in debates in the Queensland Parliament. However, in practice, the Ombudsman responds to questions posed by the overseeing Committee either in writing or in person at a hearing of the Committee and during the annual budget review process. As an Officer of Parliament, the Ombudsman may also make submissions to any other committee at his or her discretion.

The Ombudsman has no explicit statutory power to render proposals for legislative change. However, in the course of his or her work, the Ombudsman may make recommendations for administrative improvements which may also include proposals for legislative amendments. Generally, such recommendations are made to the agency concerned. That agency then is responsible for developing and implementing legislative amendments. While the Ombudsman cannot force agencies to accept recommendations, in practice, most of the recommendations are accepted and implemented (in the 2010–2011 reporting period about 99 %).[26]

10.2.4 Other Characteristics

In addition to the function of investigating administrative actions of agencies (as described above), the law stipulates the overall consideration of administrative practices and procedures of agencies and the issue of recommendations or provision of information or other help for the agencies to improve their practices and procedures as an additional and explicit mandate of the Ombudsman (s12(c) OA). This provision shows that the legislator has originally wished for a broader mandate for the Ombudsman in order to contribute to improving the overall quality of administrative practices in the public sector. This is for example implemented by

[26] Information provided by the institution.

the Ombudsman's systemic examination of specific issues and "often by [sample auditing] of the agency's files for compliance with legislation, [... internal] procedures, and recognised standards".[27] To this end, the office also offers training "on good decision-making and complaints management".[28]

In case of lack of cooperation, the Queensland Ombudsman has stronger options available to make that person appear before the Ombudsman than most other Ombudsmen in the region. The Ombudsman may turn to court and request the issue of a *subpoena* that requires a person's attendance before the Ombudsman. Also, the Ombudsman may apply to court for an arrest warrant if a person has not complied with an investigation requirement and with a previously issued *subpoena* (s36 OA, see above Sect. 10.2.3.2).

Further, the detailed statutory provisions for the appointment and removal of the Ombudsman (see above Sect. 10.2.1.2) allow for a very transparent and inclusive process.

While the law does not contain a formal requirement to this effect, in practice a complainant's written request that a decision be reviewed internally will be answered and a more senior officer will review the case.

10.2.5 Workload

In the 2010–2011 reporting period, the Ombudsman was contacted 20,382 times and received 8,354 complaints. Out of the 8,354 complaints, 4,587 (55 %) related to the Queensland Government, 2,126 (25 %) to local councils, and 270 (3 %) to universities.[29] Demographic data such as percentage of complaints submitted by women and by vulnerable and disadvantaged groups is not regularly collected.

10.2.6 Publications

The Ombudsman must report directly to the Legislative Assembly on the exercise of his or her functions on an annual basis (s87 OA) and may do so on other occasions if necessary (s52 OA). The report also covers the requirements under the Financial Accountability Act 2009.[30] In case of an investigation following a

[27] Cf APOR Manual 2009, p. 28 et seq.

[28] Cf APOR Manual 2009, p. 28 et seq.

[29] The remaining 1,371 complaints related to "others", which includes Police service, private sector, Commonwealth, or were out of jurisdiction.

[30] It also meets the requirements of the Financial and Performance Management Standard 2009 and the detailed requirements set out in the Annual Report Requirements for Queensland Government Agencies.

parliamentary referral, the Ombudsman must give a report on the investigation to the Speaker for tabling before Parliament (s53 OA). The content of and recommendations given in reports to agencies are not generally published. The Ombudsman may, however, publish an investigative report in the public interest, if, after a written request by the Ombudsman, the Speaker of Parliament has authorised the Ombudsman to do so (s54 OA). Statistical information about the number of recommendations and the rate of acceptance is published in the Annual Report. In addition to these Annual Reports, the office publishes certain investigation reports, brochures, newsletters, a Local Government Casebook, guides for agencies, such as the "Good-Decision-Making Guide", an "Unreasonable Complaint Conduct Manual" and others.

10.2.7 Annotations

There are currently no annotations.

Reference

Commonwealth Ombudsman (2009) Australasia and Pacific Ombudsman Region Information Manual 2009. Commonwealth Ombudsman, Canberra. www.ombudsman.gov.au/docs/APOR-Manual_20091009.pdf. Accessed 10 Nov 2011

Further Reading

Overview of Legislation:
Constitution: www.legislation.qld.gov.au/LEGISLTN/CURRENT/C/ConstofQA01.pdf
Ombudsman Act: www.ombudsman.qld.gov.au/AboutUs/OurLegislation/tabid/65/Default.aspx
Annual reports 2001–2011: www.ombudsman.qld.gov.au/PublicationsandReports/AnnualReport/AnnualReport20102011/tabid/426/Default.aspx

Chapter 11
Australia: South Australian Ombudsman

Michael Frahm

11.1 General Information

South Australia, one of the six Australian states, is situated in the country's southern central part; its capital is Adelaide. Its political system consists of two levels — the South Australian Government and local governments. The state's population is about 1,660,000 people, with a population density of 1.67/km^2.[1] The domestic administrator is called Governor and is appointed by the Queen on advice of the state Premier. The Premier in turn is appointed by the Governor. Parliament consists of two chambers, the Legislative Council (Upper House) and the Legislative Assembly (Lower House).

The state's fundamental principles are enshrined in the South Australian Constitution Act of 1934. As part of the Commonwealth of Australia, the state's legal system is based on English Common Law. South Australia has independent legislative powers in all matters which are not specifically assigned to the Australian Federal Government, as powers are distributed between the Federal Government and the states.[2] The court system consists of the Supreme Court, exercising original and appellate jurisdiction, the District Court as the principal trial court of South Australia, Magistrate Courts with criminal and civil jurisdiction, and Country Courts. The Ombudsman is not enshrined in the Constitution but was established by the Ombudsman Act 1972.

---

[1] Australian Bureau of Statistics (June 2011).

[2] Cf Chap. 7, p. XX for more information on the Commonwealth legal system.

M. Frahm (✉)
Ludwig Boltzmann Institute of Human Rights, Vienna, Austria
e-mail: michael.frahm@univie.ac.at

International Ombudsman Institute (ed.), *Australasia and Pacific Ombudsman Institutions*, 155
DOI 10.1007/978-3-642-33896-0_11, © Springer-Verlag Berlin Heidelberg 2013

11.2 The Ombudsman Institution

South Australian Ombudsman
Street: Level 5 East Wing 50 Grenfell Street
Postal address: PO Box 3651 Rundle Mall SA 5000 Adelaide
Zipcode: SA 5000, City: Adelaide
Phone: +61.8 8226 8699
Fax: +61.8 8226 8602
E-mail: ombudsman@ombudsman.sa.gov.au
Website: www.ombudsman.sa.gov.au/

Toll free line: 1800 182 150

11.2.1 Overview

11.2.1.1 Legal Basis

The South Australian Ombudsman office was established as early as 1972 and opened to the public the same year. After Western Australia,[3] it was the second office in the Commonwealth[4] to be established. Its establishing act models the office on the New Zealand Ombudsman office and grants jurisdiction at the state and local level. In 1985, together with the other Australian offices, it acceded the IOI. Today, the Ombudsman draws power not only from the Ombudsman Act (OA), but also from other legislative acts such as the Freedom of Information Act (FOIA), the Royal Commissions Act (RCA), the Local Government Act (LGA) and the Whistleblowers Protection Act (WPA).

Despite the expansion of the mandate into the fields of Freedom of Information, whistle-blowers and public access to both council meetings and to minutes of those meetings, in South Australia there are also other Ombudsmen with special mandates. The Workcover Ombudsman,[5] an independent statutory officer, is appointed by the South Australian Government to "provide free advice and assistance to injured workers and employers" if they want to complain about the state's workers compensation scheme. The Employee Ombudsman[6] provides individuals with advice about and support for workplace issues. The Energy Industry

[3] The Western Australian Ombudsman — Parliamentary Commissioner for Administrative Investigations was established as the first Australian Ombudsman in 1971.

[4] Cf Chap. 7, p. 101 for more information on the Commonwealth.

[5] Established pursuant to Part 6D of the Workers Rehabilitation and Compensation Act 1986 (South Australia), cf www.wcombudsmansa.com.au/ for more details.

[6] Cf www.employeeombudsman.sa.gov.au/ for details.

Ombudsman South Australia[7] has the task to investigate and resolve disputes between electricity and gas companies and their customers.

11.2.1.2 Legal Status and Independence

The Ombudsman is appointed by the Governor upon recommendation of both Houses of Parliament (s6(1) OA). Inside Parliament, it is the Statutory Officers Committee that shall identify a suitable person for appointment (s6(1a) OA). The requirements for a "suitable person" in s6 OA are not further defined in the law nor are there provisions to ensure that members and staff reflect the composition of society. There is no fixed term of office prescribed in the law, but the Ombudsman is appointed to hold office until he or she reaches 65 years of age (s10(1) OA). Consequently, there is no provision for any reappointment.

It is incompatible with the position of the Ombudsman to engage in any remunerative employment outside his or her official duties (s7 OA). Any exceptions require prior consent of the Attorney-General.[8] Furthermore, the position of the Ombudsman becomes automatically vacant when the Ombudsman resigns by written notice to the Governor, becomes bankrupt, is convicted of an indictable offence, becomes a member of any Australian Parliament, or becomes — in the opinion of the Governor — mentally or physically incapable of carrying out the duties of office (s10(4) OA). To ensure his or her independence, the Ombudsman is exempted from public service regulations (s11 OA).

The Ombudsman may only be removed from office by the Governor on addresses from both Houses of Parliament (s10(2) OA). The Governor may temporarily suspend the Ombudsman from office on the ground of "incompetence or misbehaviour" (s10(3) OA). In this case, Parliament must be given "a full statement of the reason" within seven days of the suspension. It is Parliament who subsequently decides about the removal of the Ombudsman. If Parliament does not seek the Ombudsman's removal within one month, the Ombudsman must be restored to office (s10(3b) OA). The Ombudsman cannot be sued for any act or omission done in good faith, nor can he or she be called to give evidence in any judicial proceeding (s30 OA). The same applies to all office staff.

Salary and allowances of the Ombudsman are determined by the Governor (s6(2) and (3) OA). In practice, remuneration is determined by the independent Remuneration Tribunal, and is currently linked to that of a magistrate. For comparison, it is approximately 185 % of the basic salary of a Member of the South Australian Parliament.[9]

---

[7] Cf www.eiosa.com.au/ for details.

[8] The Attorney General is responsible for the administration of the OA; the Ombudsman is an independent statutory officer within his or her Department, cf Annual Report 2009/2010, p. 55.

[9] Cf s4 Parliamentary Remuneration Act 1990 (South Australia). Cf www.remtribunal.sa.gov.au/ for information on Parliamentary allowances.

11.2.1.3 Organisation

The office, which has no sub-offices, is headed by the Ombudsman, who is in turn assisted by a Deputy Ombudsman. There are two main teams, General Investigations and Administration, plus a specialist legal unit working principally on Freedom of Information matters.[10] While the office's investigating officers deal with complex complaints, there are assessment officers addressing the more straightforward issues. In total, the office permanently employs 14 full time equivalents, ten of who are female. Six of the 14 are lawyers. While the Ombudsman is excluded from public service regulations, all staff are employed under the Public Sector Management Act 1995. For administrative purposes the office forms a unit of the Attorney-General's Department, and corporate services are provided by the Department.

The Ombudsman office is funded by parliamentary appropriations (s6(3) OA). Spending within the allocated budget is determined autonomously by the Ombudsman. The Attorney-General submits the Ombudsman's budget, after consultation with the Ombudsman. The budget for the financial year 2010–2011 was AUS$ 1,829,041 (US$ 1,876,047 as of 4 May 2012).[11]

In March 2010, the Attorney-General announced an intention to reform "the public integrity arm of government". However, as of April 2012, no draft legislation to this effect had been published. The initial plans foresaw a stronger role of the office with respect to local councils.

11.2.2 Mandate

11.2.2.1 Object of Control

The Ombudsman's jurisdiction under the OA includes state Government Departments and authorities, local councils and statutory office holders. Also, administrative units established under the Public Sector Act 2009 and such incorporated or unincorporated bodies established for public purposes that are subject to control by the executive fall under the Ombudsman's jurisdiction. Other bodies may be declared to be subject to the OA by regulations. Under the FOIA, any South Australian agency, including Ministers of the Crown, and under the LGA any local council is subject to the Ombudsman's jurisdiction.

Public service providers under the Ombudsman's jurisdiction include bodies providing railway services, water supply, universities, public hospitals[12] and social living. Other relevant service providers fall under different schemes. The Commonwealth Ombudsman has jurisdiction regarding complaints of asylum seekers and

[10] Cf APOR Manual 2009, p. 40.

[11] Cf Annual Report 2010/2011, p. 52.

[12] In relation to administrative issues only.

concerning postal services. In regard to private health insurance, the Private Health Insurance Ombudsman[13] is competent. Regarding pensions, the Commonwealth Financial Ombudsman[14] may be addressed, telecommunication issues are taken care of by the (private Commonwealth) Telecommunications Industry Ombudsman,[15] and complaints regarding electricity or gas may be submitted to the Energy Industry Ombudsman of South Australia.[16]

An area generally excluded from investigation by the Ombudsman is the judiciary, i.e. decisions of a court (s13(3) OA read in conjunction with s5 OA). However, the Courts Administration Authority is a body within the Ombudsman's jurisdiction, which means that administrative aspects may be investigated. Complaints about most employee–employer matters, actions of the Police,[17] of a Minister,[18] and of legal advisors to the Crown are also excluded. Actions of private persons can not be subject to an investigation, except for the cases explained above (providers of public services).

11.2.2.2 Standard of Control

The Ombudsman assesses "administrative acts" (s13 OA) against the requirements of s25(1) OA. Accordingly, the Ombudsman investigates whether any act was "contrary to law", "unreasonable, unjust, oppressive, or improperly discriminatory", "in accordance with a rule of law or a provision of an enactment or a practice which is or may be unreasonable, unjust, oppressive, or improperly discriminatory", was done "in the exercise of a power or discretion, and was so done for an improper purpose or on irrelevant grounds or on the basis of irrelevant considerations", was done "in the exercise of a power or discretion, and the reasons for the decision were not, but should have been, given" or was "based wholly or partly on a mistake of law or fact or was wrong". There is no additional provision relating to the protection of fundamental and human rights.

Any person, group, body or organisation who or which is directly affected by a decision or failure to act by an agency within the Ombudsman's jurisdiction may make a complaint (s13(2) and s15(1) OA). Also, a third person may file a complaint on someone else's behalf under certain conditions (s15(2) OA). The Ombudsman may also act on his or her own initiative (s13(2) OA) or an issue may be referred to the Ombudsman by Parliament (s14 OA). A complaint is received in any

[13] It is an Australian Government agency, cf s230–s256 of the Private Health Insurance Act 2007. Cf www.phio.org.au/ for more information.

[14] Cf www.fos.org.au/centric/home_page.jsp for details.

[15] Cf www.tio.com.au/ for details.

[16] Cf footnote 6 above.

[17] The Police Complaints Authority is competent to investigate such complaints.

[18] However, a Minster may be subject to investigation in respect of external reviews under the FOIA.

understandable form. It may be submitted not only in writing but also via phone or fax, in person, or using an online form. It should be lodged within twelve months of the incident since otherwise it is generally not admissible (s16 OA). In exceptional circumstances, the Ombudsman may nevertheless accept the complaint even after this deadline. A Freedom of Information complaint should be made within 30 days of the agency's decision (s14(2) FOIA), a deadline that may be extended in certain circumstances (s14A FOIA). All services of the Ombudsman are free.

The Ombudsman decides at his or her discretion whether to commence (or continue) an investigation (s17(2) OA). Apart from the above mentioned deadline of twelve months, the Ombudsman also considers whether the complainant has access to any legal remedy or right of review and whether it can be reasonably expected that he or she will resort to that remedy under the given circumstances, whether the complainant has sufficient personal interest in the matter and whether there are other, more appropriate bodies to investigate the issue. The Ombudsman may reject investigation also in cases in which the complaint is still investigated by the agency in question, or if no complaint has yet been filed with the respective agency and if the complaint appears to be "trivial", "frivolous, or vexatious or [...] not made in good faith".[19]

11.2.3 Powers

11.2.3.1 Relation to the Administration

In each case in which the Ombudsman is approached, staff assesses whether the issue is within jurisdiction and whether an investigation is warranted. If this is answered in the positive, a preliminary investigation is undertaken (s18(1) OA). Prior to proceeding with a full investigation, the Ombudsman must inform the relevant agency of the decision to investigate the matter (s18(2) OA). The Ombudsman may also decide not to investigate a complaint, in which case he or she shall inform the complainant about the reasons (s17 OA). All investigations are to be conducted in private. The Ombudsman may determine the procedure to be used in an investigation (s18(6) OA). Before finalising and reporting on a matter, the agency must be given the chance to be heard (s18(4) OA).

Alternatively, the Ombudsman may decide to attempt to deal with a complaint by conciliation (s17A OA). In such cases, the Ombudsman or a third person may act as conciliator. In certain situations, the Ombudsman can also direct an agency to refrain from performing an action for up to 45 days to allow the Ombudsman to undertake an investigation (s19A OA).

In the course of investigations, the Ombudsman may access information held by an agency (s20 and s22 OA) and may enter and inspect any item on the premises of an agency (s23 OA). He or she may enter and inspect any relevant premises at any time

[19] S17(2) OA. Cf also Annual Report 2009/2010, p. 55 et seq for more details.

(s23 OA read together with the RCA). In addition, having all of the powers of a Royal Commission, the Ombudsman can summon any person to attend before him or her, to provide any document and to give evidence under oath (s19 OA as read with the RCA). If a person fails to comply with such a request, the Ombudsman may issue a warrant (s11(2) RCA) or apply to a magistrate court to have a warrant issued.

After the completion of an investigation, the Ombudsman must report his or her opinion to the agency concerned and may make recommendations (s25(2) OA). The Ombudsman shall also furnish a copy of the report to the Minister concerned (s25(3) OA). The agency must, at the Ombudsman's request, report within a certain time period on what steps have been taken to rectify the situation (s25(4) OA). While the outcome is legally non-binding, the Ombudsman may, if no appropriate action is taken within reasonable time, inform the Premier in writing, attaching a copy of the report (s25(5) OA). Finally, the Ombudsman may also thereafter forward copies of the report for presentation to both Houses of Parliament (s25(6) OA). The Ombudsman can publish an investigation report, which may include a release of a report to the media or publication to the complainant or any other party, if the Ombudsman considers this to be in the public interest (s26 OA).

The investigation procedures and powers of the Ombudsman under both the LGA and the FOIA are very similar.[20]

Under the LGA, the Ombudsman has the power to review and investigate decisions made by councils under s90 and s91 LGA in regard to public access to council meetings and access to minutes of council meetings; and, under s187B LGA, to investigate whether a council's declaration of a rate or service charge has an unfair or unreasonable impact on a particular ratepayer. The Ombudsman may determine that a council has unreasonably excluded members of the public from its meetings or unreasonably prevented access to minutes of meetings. The Ombudsman may also deal with complaints about alleged conflicts of interest of elected council members with regards to matters decided by the council (s73 LGA). During an investigation, the Ombudsman has similar powers as under the OA (s93A LGA). At the conclusion of a review, he or she may prepare a report and may make recommendations to a council. At the end of an investigation he or she must prepare a written report, must supply a copy of any report to the Minister and the council, and may publish any report (or parts or a summary thereof) in such manner as he or she thinks fit (s94, 187A(5) and 187B(5) LGA).

Under the FOIA, the Ombudsman has the power to investigate the subject matter of an application to review a Freedom of Information decision of any agency.[21] He or she may confirm, vary or reverse an agency's decision under the FOIA. The review includes three types of decisions — a determination to charge for the provision of information, a determination to reveal information relating to a person's personal or business affairs to a third person or a determination not to amend personal information

[20] The powers of the Ombudsman are mostly the same as those under the OA, cf s74(5B), s93A, s94, s187A(2) and s187B(2) LGA, and cf s39(5)(a) FOIA.

[21] Except for the Police, for which the Police Complaints Authority is responsible.

in respect of the person. When undertaking investigations under the FOIA, the law foresees that the Ombudsman has the same powers as under the OA (s39(5a) FOIA). In addition, the Ombudsman may exercise other rights as described in s39 FOIA.

Under the WPA, the Ombudsman is one of the "appropriate authorities" to whom public interest information can be made (s5(4)(g) WPA). His or her main function is to receive and investigate "public interest information" as described under the WPA, when the information relates to public officers (other than Police officers or members of the judiciary).

In case of misconduct, the Ombudsman is required to bring any breach of duty or misconduct by an agency member to the attention of the head of the agency (s18 (5) OA). However, any allegation of fraud or corruption must be referred to the Anti-Corruption Branch of the Police.[22] Under s5(5) WPA, a disclosure of possible fraud or misconduct must be reported to the Anti-Corruption Branch of the Police.[23] Preventing another person from making a complaint or hindering or obstructing another person in making a complaint under the OA is a punishable offence (s15A OA). Further, failure to comply with any lawful requirement of the Ombudsman is an offence, punishable with a penalty of AUS$ 2,000 (s24 OA).

S23 OA allows the Ombudsman to enter correction facilities. There are also powers of entry available under s10 RCA read together with s19 OA. The necessity to inform the principal officer of the relevant agency of this intention prior to an investigation also applies to prisons (s18(1a) OA), however, a preliminary investigation may be commenced without notice. The Ombudsman is entitled to communicate in private with persons in custody (s33(7) and (8) Correctional Services Act 1982). Even without an explicit statutory obligation, the Ombudsman regularly audits correction facilities and exercises own motion investigations.

In addition to handling individual complaints and undertaking own motion investigations, the legislator has also authorised the Ombudsman to conduct reviews of administrative practices and procedures of any agency within the Ombudsman's jurisdiction (s14A OA). If the Ombudsman considers this to be in the public interest, he or she may initiate such administrative audits any time. To this end, the Ombudsman has the same powers as described above (s14A(2) OA).

11.2.3.2 Relation to the Judiciary

The Ombudsman cannot investigate judicial actions (s3(1) OA), but may investigate certain administrative actions by judicial authorities. In case there is ambiguity about the exercise of a power of the Ombudsman, the Ombudsman or the principal officer of the agency concerned may make an application to the Supreme Court for a determination of the question (s28 OA).

---

[22] This averagely occurs five times a year.

[23] This occurs approximately 25 times a year.

Further, the Ombudsman may, under the powers vested in him or her under the RCA, apply to a magistrate court to have a warrant issued for a person to be apprehended and brought before the Ombudsman (s11A(1) RCA).

Decisions of the Ombudsman under the OA may not be appealed. However, the parties to an Ombudsman Freedom of Information determination may appeal to the District Court (s40 FOIA).

11.2.3.3 Relation to the Legislator

The Ombudsman is an independent statutory officer within the Attorney-General's Department and reports directly to Parliament on an annual basis (s29 OA) as well as on other occasions as necessary (s29 OA). If Parliament refers an issue to the Ombudsman for investigation,[24] the Ombudsman must carry out an investigation into said matter (s14 OA). The Ombudsman usually appears before the Statutory Officers Committee, which is responsible for overseeing the office's operation, on an annual basis. On occasion he or she is also invited to appear before other committees. There is no obligation on the Parliament to respond to material submitted by the Ombudsman. When an administrative error has been found in the course of an investigation, the Ombudsman may make recommendations to Parliament for legislative amendment either by way of a report on complaints or by way of the Annual Report.[25]

11.2.4 Other Characteristics

A special feature of the Ombudsman in South Australia is the power to conduct administrative audits and review administrative practices and procedures of any agency (s14A OA).

The term "Ombudsman" is protected in South Australia. No agency under jurisdiction of the Ombudsman is allowed to use the word "Ombudsman" in describing an internal procedure or a person in charge of such process by which the agency attempts to investigate and remedy complaints (s32 OA).

Other features worth mentioning are the option to attempt to deal with a complaint by conciliation (s17A OA) and the power to direct an agency to refrain from performing an action for up to 45 days to allow the Ombudsman to investigate with the purpose of preventing that such action may prejudice or negate the outcome of an investigation (s19A OA).

---

[24] Cf Sect. 11.2.2.2 p. 159.

[25] Such recommendation is averagely made twice a year.

Further, the explicit provision in the Freedom of Information legislation needs to be mentioned which foresees the providing of occasional training to public officials on the application of the law (s54A FOIA).

11.2.5 Workload

In the 2010–2011 reporting period, the Ombudsman received 9,238 approaches, 3,167 of which were complaints under the OA and 233 of which were requests for reviews under the FOIA. Out of these, 23 % related to local government, 18 % to corrections and 12 % to housing.

11.2.6 Publications

The Ombudsman annually reports to Parliament on the exercise of his or her statutory functions (s29 OA). In addition, the Ombudsman has the power to have a report published in such a manner as the Ombudsman thinks fit (s26 OA). Occasionally, he or she may thus table individual investigation reports under the OA, the FOIA and the LGA. There are no other statutory reporting obligations. On its website, the office also publishes presentations, special reports and FOIA determinations.

11.2.7 Annotations

Amendments to the Ombudsman Act are anticipated as part of a package of legislation covering public integrity issues. This legislation is expected to be introduced to Parliament by the Attorney-General in May 2012.[26]

Reference

Commonwealth Ombudsman (2009) Australasia and Pacific Ombudsman Region Information Manual 2009. Commonwealth Ombudsman, Canberra. www.ombudsman.gov.au/docs/APOR-Manual_20091009.pdf. Accessed 10 Nov 2011

Further Reading

Overview of Legislation: www.ombudsman.sa.gov.au/about-the-office/legislation
Annual reports (2004–2010): www.ombudsman.sa.gov.au/publications/annual-reports

[26] Information as of April 2012, provided by the Institution.

Chapter 12
Australia: Tasmanian Ombudsman

Michael Frahm

12.1 General Information

Tasmania is an island[1] and is the smallest state in Australia, with a population of approximately 500,000,[2] corresponding to a population density of 7.36 persons/km^2. The state has a two-tiered political system, with both a state and a local government level. The Government of Tasmania exists within the federal parliamentary democracy and constitutional monarchy of Australia.[3] The domestic administrator, called Governor, is appointed by the Queen on advice of the state Premier. The Head of Government or Premier is appointed by the Governor.

The capital of Tasmania is Hobart. The state is administratively divided into 29 Local Government Areas.[4] There is a bicameral Parliament consisting of the Legislative Council (or Upper House) and the Legislative Assembly (or Lower House). The legal system is based on English Common Law and the Australian federal system of government, with powers distributed between the Federal Government and the states. Tasmania has its own Constitution, which was put down in writing in the Constitution Act of 1934. The court system consists of the Supreme Court as the superior court of the state, exercising original and appellate jurisdiction, and the Magistrates Court with criminal and civil jurisdiction.[5]

---

[1] The state of Tasmania consists of the main island and of the surrounding islands and islets.

[2] According to the Australian Bureau of Statistics population was at 510,600 in June 2011.

[3] Cf Chap. 7, p. 101 for more information on the Commonwealth.

[4] Cf www.service.tas.gov.au/ for more details.

[5] Cf www.courts.tas.gov.au/ for details.

M. Frahm (✉)
Ludwig Boltzmann Institute of Human Rights, Vienna, Austria
e-mail: michael.frahm@univie.ac.at

International Ombudsman Institute (ed.), *Australasia and Pacific Ombudsman Institutions*,
DOI 10.1007/978-3-642-33896-0_12,

12.2 The Ombudsman Institution

Tasmanian Ombudsman
Street: Ground Floor 99 Bathurst St, Hobart 7000 and
111 Cameron St, Launceston 7250
Postal address: GPO Box 960, Hobart 7001
Zipcode: 7250, City: Launceston
Phone: +61.1300 766 725
Fax: +61.3. 6233 8966
E-mail: ombudsman@ombudsman.tas.gov.au
Website: www.ombudsman.tas.gov.au/

Toll free line: 1800 001 170

12.2.1 Overview

12.2.1.1 Legal Basis

The Ombudsman office was established in 1978 and opened to the public in 1979. The establishing legislation modelled the office after the New Zealand Ombudsman office. The office has jurisdiction at the regional and local level. Over the years, the competences of the office have been expanded numerous times. Today, the Ombudsman serves also as the Health Complaints Commissioner and the Energy Ombudsman. The Ombudsman subsequently draws power from a range of laws. Besides the Ombudsman Act 1978 (OA), these include the Commissions of Inquiry Act 1995, the Right to Information Act 2009 (RTI Act),[6] the Adoption Act 1988, the Corrections Act 1997, the Integrity Commission Act 2009, the Personal Information Protection Act 2004, the Public Information Disclosures Act 2002, the Water and Sewerage Industry Act 2008, and the Witness Protection Act 2000. In regard to the additional function of auditing Police compliance, the Police Powers (Controlled Operations) Act 2006, the Police Powers (Surveillance Devices) Act 2006 and the Telecommunications (Interception) Tasmania Act 1999 endow the Ombudsman with additional powers.

For the function of Health Complaints Commissioner, the relevant legislation is the Health Complaints Act 1995 and related acts. For the Energy Ombudsman, the legal basis is the Energy Ombudsman Act 1998 (EOA).

[6] The former Freedom of Information Act 1991 has been repealed.

Other complaint bodies[7] to which people in Tasmania may refer are the Integrity Commission,[8] the Commonwealth Ombudsman, the (Commonwealth) Telecommunications Industry Ombudsman,[9] the Financial Ombudsman Service,[10] the Office of the Anti-Discrimination Commissioner,[11] and the Office of Consumer Affairs and Fair Trading.[12]

12.2.1.2 Legal Status and Independence

The Ombudsman is appointed by the Governor (s5(1A) OA). The appointment is for a term not exceeding five years, reappointment for a further term not exceeding five years is possible (s5(2) OA). The Governor may additionally appoint a Deputy Ombudsman (s8A OA).[13] The law does not stipulate specific qualification requirements for a candidate. There are also no requirements that the Ombudsman him- or herself or his or her staff are to reflect the composition of society. The Ombudsman shall not engage in any remunerative employment outside official duties (s5(7) OA). A person is disqualified from holding or being appointed to the office of Ombudsman if he or she is a member of any Australian Commonwealth, state or territory Parliament or a candidate for election as such a member (s5(4) OA).

The Ombudsman may only be permanently removed from office by the Governor on addresses from both Houses of Parliament (s6(1) OA). In addition, the Governor may temporarily suspend the Ombudsman from office if the Governor is convinced that the Ombudsman is "incapable of properly performing the duties of his office, has shown himself incompetent properly to perform, or has neglected, those duties, has become bankrupt, has been convicted of a crime or an offense that is punishable by imprisonment for a term of twelve months or more, or has been guilty of misconduct" (s6(2) OA). In such a case "a statement of the grounds of his suspension" must be tabled before each House of Parliament within seven sitting days of the suspension. Unless both Houses of Parliament pass an "address praying for his removal" within one month, the Ombudsman is restored to office (s6(3) OA). Ultimately, the office becomes vacant if the Ombudsman resigns by written notice to the Governor (s5(6) OA) or if he or she becomes a candidate for election as a Member of Parliament (s5(4) OA).

---

[7] Cf Annual Report 2010/2011, p. 13.

[8] The Commission was established under the Integrity Commission Act 2009 to improve the standard of conduct and ethics in public authorities, cf www.integrity.tas.gov.au/ for more details.

[9] Cf www.tio.com.au/ for details.

[10] Cf www.fos.org.au/centric/home_page.jsp for details.

[11] The office was established under the Anti-Discrimination Act 1998 to promote the development of transparent and fair processes and services, cf www.antidiscrimination. tas.gov.au/ for details.

[12] Cf www.consumer.tas.gov.au/ for details.

[13] Something which has not yet been done in practice.

The Ombudsman is immune from legal proceedings (s33 OA). The same applies to any member of the Ombudsman's staff. The salary and allowances of the Ombudsman are determined by the Governor (s5(8) OA).

Administratively, the office of the Ombudsman for a long time was an operational unit within the Department of Justice. In July 2007, it became a separate agency within the Government to reinforce its independence.[14]

12.2.1.3 Organisation

As the Ombudsman also serves as the Health Complaints Commissioner and the Energy Ombudsman, his or her office is divided into six teams: Ombudsman investigations; Freedom of Information, public interest disclosure and personal information protection; health complaints; energy complaints; corporate functions; and conciliation.[15] Due to the fact that no Deputy Ombudsman has been appointed,[16] the former principal officer has been reclassified to "Director – Office of the Ombudsman"; after the Ombudsman this position is the most senior post in the office.[17] Ombudsman staff may be appointed or employed under the State Service Act 2000. Also, state service officers or employees may "be made available to enable the Ombudsman to perform the functions of office" (s9 OA). As of July 2011, the office comprises 25 members of staff, which equals 19.6 full-time equivalents (FTE).[18] The office has no sub-offices in the territory of Tasmania.

The office of the Ombudsman is predominantly funded by parliamentary appropriations.[19] In addition, the office receives funding from the energy entities which are under the Energy Ombudsman's jurisdiction and are thus obligated to fund the Ombudsman's work through payment of Energy Entities Membership and Complaint Levy Fees.[20] The budget for the financial year 2010–2011 was AUS$ 2,528,000 (US$ 2,591,705 as of 4 May 2012).[21]

Since 1 July 2009, the Ombudsman has also been the Coordinating Official Visitor of the Mental Health Official Visitors Scheme under the Mental Health Act 1996.[22]

---

[14] Cf APOR Manual 2009, p. 43.

[15] Cf APOR Manual 2009, p. 47.

[16] Cf footnote 12 above.

[17] Cf Annual Report 2010/2011, p. 9.

[18] As of 30 June 2011, cf Annual Report 2010/2011, p. 9. For the current 2011–2012 financial year, a decrease of staff by 1.4 FTE was expected due to budgetary restrictions, ibid.

[19] Cf Annual Report 2010/2011, p. 17 of the attached Financial Statements 2010/2011.

[20] Cf Annual Report 2010/2011, p. 17 of the attached Financial Statements 2010/2011.

[21] Cf Annual Report 2010/2011, p. 5 of the attached Financial Statements 2010/2011.

[22] Cf Annual Report 2010/2011, p. 50.

12.2.2 *Mandate*

12.2.2.1 Object of Control

The Tasmanian Ombudsman has jurisdiction over public authorities and their staff, i.e., *inter alia*, over state service agencies, the Police service, local authorities, the prison service, state-owned companies, and any body the members of which (or most of its members) are appointed by the Governor or a Minister (s12 read in conjunction with s4 OA). Private individuals or private businesses and actions of Commonwealth or interstate Departments or agencies are not under the Ombudsman's jurisdiction.

Under the Energy Ombudsman Act, electricity and natural gas consumers may address the Ombudsman with regard to their energy retailer or distributor. Under the Health Complaints Act, the Ombudsman has jurisdiction over health services in both the public and the private sector.

Excluded from jurisdiction are, amongst others, actions taken by courts and tribunals, the prosecution, the audit office and councils (s4(2) OA).

12.2.2.2 Standard of Control

The Ombudsman assesses "administrative actions" (s12(1) OA) against the requirements stipulated in s28(1) OA. Accordingly, the Ombudsman shall assess whether any administrative action was "contrary to law", was "unreasonable, unjust, oppressive or improperly discriminatory", was "in accordance with a rule of law or a provision of an enactment or a practice which is or may be unreasonable, unjust, oppressive, or improperly discriminatory" or was "taken in the exercise of a power or discretion, and was so taken for an improper purpose or on irrelevant grounds or on the basis of irrelevant considerations", was "a decision that was made in the exercise of a power or discretion, and the reasons for the decision were not, but should have been, given", was based "on a mistake of law or of fact", or was "wrong" (s28(1) OA). The law does not specifically stipulate the protection of human rights as a function of the Ombudsman.

Any person who or body which is directly affected by an administrative action by an agency within the Ombudsman's jurisdiction may make a complaint (s14 OA). Complaints may be made in writing or orally (s14(1) OA). However, the Ombudsman may require an oral complaint to be confirmed in writing. Complaints should be lodged within 24 months of the incident which is the subject of the complaint (s19(1) OA). There is no fee levied in the context of submitting a complaint to the Ombudsman. In addition to investigations following a complaint, the Ombudsman may also conduct an investigation on his or her own initiative (s13 OA) or following a referral by the Governor or by Parliament (s15–s16 OA).

The Ombudsman has discretion whether to commence or continue an investigation. Unless special circumstances exist for matters that are older than 24 months, he or she may not investigate such subject matters (s19 OA). The Ombudsman is not obliged to investigate matters if the complainant has a legal remedy or right of review or appeal and it is reasonable to expect the complainant to resort to that remedy (s20 OA); if a complaint appears to be "trivial", "frivolous, [. . .] vexatious, or [. . .] not made in good faith"; if the complainant "does not have a sufficient [personal] interest in the matter"; or if an investigation does not appear to be warranted under the given circumstances (s21 OA).

The standard of control under the Health Complaints Act 1995 which entitles the Ombudsman to undertake investigations is by and large similar (s25 Health Complaints Act 1995).

Under the Freedom of Information legislation, an application for external review to the Ombudsman shall be made within 20 days (s44 RTI Act).[23]

Under the Energy Ombudsman Act, the Ombudsman may investigate a wide range of complaints against an energy entity (s3 EOA), including disputed accounts and high bills, debts and arrears and disconnection or restriction of supply (s5 EOA).[24]

12.2.3 *Powers*

12.2.3.1 Relation to the Administration

Before launching a formal investigation, as a first step the Ombudsman may initiate a preliminary investigation of the subject matter (s20A OA). This allows the Ombudsman to decide whether to investigate the matter further. The principal officer of the authority concerned shall provide all necessary assistance (s20A (2) OA). If the Ombudsman subsequently believes a formal investigation to be warranted, he or she shall inform the head of the authority concerned of this intention before starting the investigation (s23 OA). He or she may also, however, resolve the complaint without investigating (s20A(3) OA). If the Ombudsman decides not to investigate a complaint, he or she shall inform the complainant about the reasons (s19–s21 OA). Finally, the Ombudsman may decide to attempt to deal with a complaint by conciliation (s22A–22E OA).

If the Ombudsman decides to deal with a complaint by conciliation, he or she requires the consent of all parties to the complaint (s22B OA). Any person with the appropriate qualifications may be authorised by the Ombudsman, who can also act him- or herself, to act as conciliator. If the attempt fails, investigations must be resumed and the conciliator must be excluded from the process (s22C OA).

[23] Similarly, an application for review to the principal officer shall also be made within 20 days of the agency's determination (s43(1) RTI Act).

[24] Cf www.energyombudsman.tas.gov.au/about_us/our_role for details.

The costs of the process are to be born by the parties in such proportions as the parties may agree, or in equal shares, or as otherwise directed by the Ombudsman (s22E OA).

In case of a formal investigation, the Ombudsman may determine the procedure to be used in an investigation (s23A(1) OA) and shall give the public body the chance to be heard (s23A(6) OA). All investigations shall be conducted in private (s23A(3) OA). In case of an own motion investigation or a referral under s15 or s16 OA, the Ombudsman must also inform the principal officer and the Minister. The Ombudsman may also consult any Minister concerned at any time (s23(8) OA). In the cause of the investigation, the Ombudsman may enter and inspect any item on the premises of an agency (s25 OA). In carrying out an investigation, the Ombudsman may exercise the powers given to a Commission of Inquiry under Part 3 of the Commissions of Inquiry Act 1995 (s24(1) OA). These powers include the power to hold public hearings, to control public reporting, to summon witnesses, to give evidence and produce documents, to apply for a warrant from a magistrate to enter and search premises, vehicles and vessels, to take possession of evidence, and to examine witnesses under oath. In case of the application of the Commissions of Inquiry Act 1995, the Ombudsman must inform the principal officer and the Minister.[25]

At the end of the investigation, the Ombudsman may either resolve the matter informally with the principal officer responsible (s28(1A) OA) or, in more serious cases (sub-paragraph 2), he or she shall report his or her opinion and the reasons for it to the principal officer and issue recommendations (s28(2) OA). If the responsible Minister was informed of the launch of the formal investigation, the Ombudsman shall send a copy of the report to him or her (s28(3) OA). The principal officer must, at the Ombudsman's request, report within a certain time period on the steps taken to rectify the situation (s28(4) OA). If the answer is not satisfactory, the Ombudsman may report to the Premier and the responsible Minister on the matter (s28 (5) OA). In this case, the Ombudsman may bring a report on the matter before each House of Parliament (s28(6) OA). The Ombudsman may also publish a report, if he or she considers this to be in the public interest (s31 OA).

In the course of an investigation, the Ombudsman has the power to enter premises, including correction facilities, at any reasonable time. However, he or she has to inform the principal officer of the authority beforehand (s25(2) OA). The law does not specifically stipulate that the Ombudsman may speak to detainees in private.[26]

Any person who obstructs, hinders or resists the Ombudsman or any of his or her staff without lawful justification or excuse, who fails to comply with any lawful requirement made, or who gives false or misleading information, is guilty of an offence liable to a fine not exceeding 20 penalty units (s27 OA).

[25] Cf APOR Manual 2009, p. 45 et seq.

[26] It could be assumed that in practice this is possible as, pursuant to s23A(3) OA, every investigation is to be conducted in private.

Under Part 3 of the Commissions of Inquiry Act 1995,[27] the Ombudsman has additional powers, namely those of a Commission of Inquiry. Failure to comply with the Ombudsman's notice under this act is contempt, s27 Commissions of Inquiry Act 1995.

The Ombudsman also undertakes investigations under other laws, following largely similar procedures:

Under the Energy Ombudsman Act 1998, the Ombudsman receives complaints relating to the sale and supply of gas or electricity (or about services provided). He or she may assist energy entities to develop procedures to resolve such complaints. Eventually, the Ombudsman has the power to make an decision which is binding on the energy entity concerned.

Under the Right to Information Act 2009, a person whose request to be provided with information in the possession of a public authority or a Minister has been refused may apply to the Ombudsman for a review of that decision. While most reviews occur at the request of the applicant for assessed disclosure, also third parties who do not want information to be released may request a review. The Ombudsman has the power to issue guidelines on the process and to provide advice on the operation of the RTI Act to a public authority or Minister.

Under the Public Interest Disclosures Act 2002, the Ombudsman may determine whether a disclosure submitted to the Ombudsman by a whistle-blower warrants investigation. He or she may further investigate disclosures and monitor investigations undertaken by other public bodies. Additionally, it is the Ombudsman's function to publish guidelines to assist public authorities in interpreting and complying with this legislation.

Under the Personal Information Protection Act 2004, the Ombudsman may investigate complaints received on alleged breaches of stipulated principles regarding the protection of personal information.

Under legislation relating to Police functions,[28] the Ombudsman is required to audit the Police's compliance with recordkeeping requirements under the respective legislation.

Under the Health Complaints Act 1995, the Commissioner (i.e. the Ombudsman acting as Commissioner) has the power to investigate complaints about health service providers in both the public and the private sector. Investigations may be initiated not only following complaints, but the Commissioner may also act on his or her own initiative.

Under the Official Visitors to State Prisons Scheme, the Ombudsman provides administrative support for the Official Visitors to the State's Prisons and to Mental Health Official Visitors, who are appointed under the Mental Health Act 1996.[29]

---

[27] Cf s24 OA.

[28] Telecommunications (Interception) Tasmania Act 1999, Police Powers (Surveillance Devices) Act 2006 and Police Powers (Controlled Operations) Act 2006.

[29] Cf APOR Manual 2009, p. 44 et seqq. Cf also http://officialvisitors.tas.gov.au/ for details.

12.2.3.2 Relation to the Judiciary

The Ombudsman is only authorised to investigate administrative acts. He or she has no authority to investigate actions of judicial authorities and courts (s12(1) and (5) OA).

The Ombudsman may refer to the Supreme Court during an investigation in two cases. Firstly, if a question arises regarding the legality of the exercise of a power of the Ombudsman, the Ombudsman or any interested party may submit an application to the Supreme Court for a determination of the question (s32 OA). Secondly, he or she may also refer a question of law to the Supreme Court for decision under s24(1) OA, read in conjunction with s16 of the Commissions of Inquiry Act 1995.

There are other occasions in which the Ombudsman may, under the powers vested in him or her under the Commissions of Inquiry Act 1995, refer to a magistrate. According to s24 of the Commissions of Inquiry Act 1995 the Ombudsman may apply to a magistrate to have a warrant issued. Under s27(3) of the Commissions of Inquiry Act 1995, the Ombudsman may apply to a magistrate to have a person apprehended and brought before the Ombudsman.

12.2.3.3 Relation to the Legislator

The Ombudsman is appointed by the Governor, and answerable to Parliament. He or she reports to Parliament on an annual basis (s30 OA) and on other occasions, including in relation to specific investigations (s31 OA). While there is currently no specific Parliamentary Committee in charge of overseeing the Ombudsman's work, the Ombudsman reports on his or her work to the Estimates Committees each year.[30] If Parliament or any of its committees has referred a matter to the Ombudsman, the Ombudsman must investigate and report back (s16(2) OA).

12.2.4 Other Characteristics

What must be noted, is the option given to the Ombudsman by the OA which enables him or her to deal with a matter by conciliation with the aim of resolving a matter in that way by an agreement between the parties involved.

Furthermore, the powers vested in the Ombudsman under the Commissions of Inquiry Act 1995 allow him or her to refer to a magistrate if a person does not comply with a lawful request of the Ombudsman.

Another specific feature is the Ombudsman's competence to refer a question of law arising in the course of its inquiry to the Supreme Court for decision.

[30] Cf APOR Manual 2009, p. 43.

12.2.5 Workload

In the 2010–2011 reporting period the office was approached 2,953 times.[31] These contacts resulted in 702 complaints received under the Ombudsman Act, 295 complaints received by the Health Complaints Commissioner, and 465 complaints received by the Energy Ombudsman.[32] Of all complaints under the Ombudsman Act, 65 % concerned Departments, 14 % concerned local governments, and 19 % concerned other public authorities. Of all Government Departments 46 % of all complaints concerned justice, 26 % concerned health and human services and 17 % concerned Police and emergency management.

12.2.6 Publications

The Ombudsman is obliged to report to Parliament on the exercise of his or her statutory functions annually (s30 OA). In addition to reporting obligations under the OA, the Ombudsman shall also report on his or her investigations of complaints concerning health service providers under the Health Complaints Act 1995 (s12 Health Complaints Act 1995). Further, the Ombudsman publishes an Annual Report as the Energy Ombudsman under the Energy Ombudsman Act 1998.

The Annual Report to Parliament under s30 OA covers the exercise of the Ombudsman's statutory functions as well as those of the Health Complaints Commissioner and of the Energy Ombudsman in the many jurisdictions covered by them. In addition, there are the two specific reports of the Health Complaints Commissioner and the Energy Ombudsman which cover the specific jurisdictions in much more detail.

According to s31 OA, the Ombudsman may also publish other special reports and have them published in the public interest in such manner as the Ombudsman thinks fit. In practice, they can be found at the Ombudsman's website.

12.2.7 Annotations

There are currently no annotations.

---

[31] Cf Annual Report 2010/2011, p. 54.

[32] Cf Annual Report 2010/2011, p. 62.

Reference

Commonwealth Ombudsman (2009) Australasia and Pacific Ombudsman Region Information Manual 2009. Commonwealth Ombudsman, Canberra. www.ombudsman.gov.au/docs/APOR-Manual_20091009.pdf. Accessed 10 Nov 2011

Further Reading

Overview of Legislation: www.thelaw.tas.gov.au/tocview/index.w3p;cond=ALL;doc_id=94%2-B%2B1934%2BAT%40EN%2B20110919180000;histon=;prompt=;rec=;term=constitution and www.ombudsman.tas.gov.au/legislation

Annual reports (2001–2011): www.ombudsman.tas.gov.au/publications_and_media/annual_reports

Annual reports under Health Complaints Act 1995 (2002–2011): www.healthcomplaints.tas.gov.au/

Chapter 13
Australia: Victorian Ombudsman

Michael Frahm

13.1 General Information

Victoria is one of the six states of the Australian Commonwealth[1] and is situated in the South-East of the country. While it is the smallest state by size, its population is comparably high, with 5.6 million people and a population density of 22/km^2.[2] Below the Government of Victoria, based in the capital Melbourne, there are local governments. There is a domestic administrator, called Governor, who is appointed by the Queen on advice of the state Premier. The Premier in turn is appointed by the Governor, a decision based on the vote in the Lower House. Besides the Lower House or Legislative Assembly, there is also an Upper House, the Legislative Council.

The legislative system of Victoria is based on English Common Law with a federal system of government and powers distributed between the Federal Government and the states. Victoria has its own Constitution Act of 1975. The Constitution implies the existence of the Ombudsman by stipulating rules ensuring the Ombudsman's independence in art. 94E Constitution. The highest court is the Supreme Court, which exercises both original and appellate jurisdiction: it has two divisions, the Trial Division and the Court of Appeal. Appeals from the Supreme Court are heard by the High Court of Australia, the national appeals court. Below it are the County Court which hears middle-tier criminal matters and civil disputes, and the Magistrates' Court as the local court with criminal and civil jurisdiction in minor matters and disputes.

---

[1] Cf Chap. 7, p. 101 for more information on the Commonwealth.

[2] Australian Bureau of Statistics (June 2011).

M. Frahm (✉)
Ludwig Boltzmann Institute of Human Rights, Vienna, Austria
e-mail: michael.frahm@univie.ac.at

International Ombudsman Institute (ed.), *Australasia and Pacific Ombudsman Institutions*,
DOI 10.1007/978-3-642-33896-0_13,

13.2 The Ombudsman Institution

Victorian Ombudsman
Street: 9/459 Collins Street (North Tower)
Zipcode: 3000, City: Melbourne
Phone: +61.3.9613 6222
Fax: +61.3.9614 0246
E-mail: ombudvic@ombudsman.vic.gov.au
Website: www.ombudsman.vic.gov.au

Toll free line: 1800 806 314

13.2.1 Overview

13.2.1.1 Legal Basis

The Institution of the Ombudsman was established in 1973 and opened office the same year. It became a member of the IOI in 1985. Its establishing legislation was modelled after the New Zealand office and Scandinavian models. The Ombudsman thus has jurisdiction over the Victorian state and local level. In addition to the Ombudsman, the Office of Police Integrity[3] has a somewhat similar mandate with regards to Police matters.

The legal basis for the Ombudsman's tasks is established by the Constitution Act 1975, the Ombudsman Act 1973 (OA), the Whistleblowers Protection Act 2001 (WPA), and the Freedom of Information Act 1982 (FOIA).

13.2.1.2 Legal Status and Independence

The Ombudsman is appointed by the Governor. The law does not foresee involvement of the Parliament. The term of office is ten years, and the person is not eligible to be reappointed (s3(4) OA). There are no qualifications required by law for the appointment as Ombudsman.

It is incompatible with the function of Ombudsman to be a Member of Parliament in any Australian state or territory or in the Commonwealth (s3(3) OA). Further, the Ombudsman shall not engage in any remunerative employment outside the duties of his or her office without the Governor's prior consent.[4] To ensure his or her independence, the Ombudsman is exempted from public service regulations (s8(1) OA).

[3] The Office of Police Integrity is an independent statutory body that investigates complaints regarding serious Police misconduct and corruption.

[4] This also applies to any officer of the Ombudsman.

The Ombudsman ceases to hold office if he or she resigns in writing, is nominated for election for any House of Parliament, be it in Victoria, the Commonwealth or any other state (s3(5) OA), or if he or she is removed from office or suspended and not restored. He or she may only be removed from office upon request of both Houses of Parliament (3(5) OA). If Parliament is not in session, the Governor may temporarily suspend the Ombudsman on the grounds of disability, bankruptcy, neglect of duty or misconduct or on any other grounds which makes him or her unfit to be the Ombudsman in the opinion of the Governor.

In case of a suspension, the Governor shall inform Parliament of the grounds for the suspension in writing within the first seven sitting days following the suspension. The Ombudsman shall be restored to office unless both Houses pass an address asking for the Ombudsman's removal within the subsequent 20 sitting days (s4 (2) OA). This is guaranteed by the Constitution, which prescribes that removal or suspension may only be made in accordance with these rules (art. 94E(7) Const.). The Ombudsman, and any of his or her officers, cannot be sued unless the action in question was undertaken in bad faith (s29 OA).

Remuneration of the Ombudsman is determined by the Governor. The rate of the salary shall not be reduced during his or her term in office (s5 OA). It is comparable to that of Members of Parliament and judges.

13.2.1.3 Organisation

The office consists of the Ombudsman, one Deputy Ombudsman and three Directors; their respective responsibilities structure the office as follows: Corporate Services, Investigations (Assessment and Investigations) and Investigations (Major Investigations). In addition to the Ombudsman the office employs 69 staff (full-time equivalents) as of 30 June 2011.[5] All employees are employed by the Ombudsman under the Public Administration Act 2004.

The office is located in the state capital Melbourne, and there are no sub-offices. However, the Ombudsman undertakes regular regional visits.[6] The Ombudsman is funded by appropriations from Parliament; this is the office's only link to the executive arm of government. The Ombudsman autonomously decides how the budget is spent. The budget for the financial year 2010–2011 was AUS$ 9,246,556 (US$ 9,483,267 as of 4 May 2012).[7]

The Government has plans to review the Ombudsman Act to make it fit for the decades to come, as it has not been fundamentally reviewed since its passing in 1973.[8]

[5] Cf Annual Report 2010/2011, p. 27.

[6] Cf Annual Report 2010/2011, p. 60. In addition, officers are regularly undertaking outreach activities.

[7] Cf Annual Report 2010/2011, Part 2, p. 40.

[8] Information provided by the Institution.

13.2.2 *Mandate*

13.2.2.1 Object of Control

The Ombudsman investigates complaints concerning all Government Departments and most statutory bodies and municipal councils (s13 OA). Among the statutory bodies included are *inter alia* WorkSafe Victoria, school councils, universities, selected professional boards such as the Legal Services Board, VicRoads[9] and the Transport Accident Commission. Under the WPA, the conduct of Members of Parliament or elected councillors is also included. Under the FOIA, Departments, councils and other authorities as prescribed under s5(1) FOIA are included.

Public service providers under the Ombudsman's jurisdiction include those public sector agencies responsible for electricity and water supply, railways, public hospitals and social living. The Commonwealth Ombudsman is competent in regard to complaints of asylum seekers. As the Postal Industry Ombudsman, he or she also has jurisdiction concerning postal services.[10] Issues of private health insurance and pensions can be addressed to one of two national Ombudsmen, namely either the Private Health Insurance Ombudsman[11] or the Commonwealth Financial Ombudsman.[12]

The Ombudsman has no jurisdiction over the judiciary (s13(3) OA),[13] legal advisors or counsels of the Crown, Ministers or officers of the Governor, the Auditor-General or a person acting as a trustee.[14] Private natural or legal persons cannot be subject to an investigation. If the Ombudsman investigates a matter referred to him or her by Parliament, the Ombudsman shall investigate the matter, even if outside his or her normal jurisdiction[15] (s16(2) OA).

13.2.2.2 Standard of Control

The Ombudsman assesses "administrative acts" (s13 OA) against the requirements of s23 OA. Accordingly, the Ombudsman investigates whether any action was "contrary to law", "unreasonable, unjust, oppressive, or improperly

---

[9] VicRoads is the Roads and Licensing Regulatory Body established under the Transport Act 1983.

[10] Cf s19ZE Ombudsman Act (Commonwealth).

[11] Cf s230 to s256 Private Health Insurance Act 2007 and, for more information, cf www.phio.org.au/.

[12] Cf www.fos.org.au/centric/home_page.jsp for details.

[13] This does not only include courts and tribunals, but also other boards or commissions established by a statute and chaired by a lawyer.

[14] I.e. a trustee under the Trustee Act 1958; although, according to s13(2A) OA, the Ombudsman may investigate administrative actions by state trustees.

[15] However, even Parliament may not refer a matter concerning a judicial proceeding under this provision.

discriminatory", "in accordance with the law but that law is or may be unreasonable, unjust, oppressive, or improperly discriminatory" or was "wrong". Under s13 (1A) OA, the Ombudsman has the specific function of investigating whether an administrative action is "incompatible with a human right set out in the Charter of Human Rights and Responsibilities". The Charter[16] establishes 20 basic civil and political rights for all citizens. At the same time it obliges public administration, including private entities which provide public services under a contract of a public body, to act in a manner compatible with the rights established.

An investigation may be initiated on receipt of a complaint or on the Ombudsman's own initiative (s14(1) OA). It may also be initiated by referral by Parliament (s16 OA). Complaints to this effect can be submitted by any member of the public or by a group of persons, be they a natural or legal persons (s14(2) OA). A complaint shall be made in writing (s14(2) OA). Furthermore, the complaint shall be submitted within twelve months of the incident, since it otherwise may not be investigated at the Ombudsman's discretion.

Requests for a referral of a disclosure under the WPA shall be made within 28 days of the notification according to s36 WPA (s35(1)(b) WPA). All Ombudsman services are free.

In addition to delayed complaints, the Ombudsman may decide not to investigate a complaint if it is "trivial, frivolous, vexatious and not made in good faith" (s15 OA). He or she may also refer a complaint either to the Privacy Commissioner or to the Health Services Commissioner if the complaint could be made the subject of an application under the Information Privacy Act 2000 or the Health Records Act 2001 (s15A and s15B OA). Under the WPA, the Ombudsman may also refer an investigation to another more appropriate body such as the Police or the Office of Police Integrity.

The Ombudsman shall not investigate a complaint, unless under special circumstances, if the complainant has any legal right of appeal or review available to him or her (s13(4) OA), if the person has no personal interest in the matter, or if a matter relates to terms and conditions of employment (s13(5) OA). A complaint submitted by a third person who is not affected by the action complained of him- or herself, shall not be investigated (s14(3) OA) unless the third person is a Member of Parliament acting on behalf of the aggrieved person or is a person considered suitable by the Ombudsman to represent the interest of an aggrieved person who has died or is unable to act for him- or herself or if, with regard to all the circumstances, the Ombudsman considers it proper to investigate the complaint (s14(4) OA).

[16] Charter of Human Rights and Responsibilities Act 2006, entry into force 1 January 2008.

13.2.3 Powers

13.2.3.1 Relations to the Administration

Before launching a full investigation, the Ombudsman may first initiate an enquiry to determine whether a formal investigation should be conducted (s13A(1)(a) OA) or whether the matter may be resolved informally (s13A(1)(b) OA). Such enquiry may be conducted following a complaint or on the Ombudsman's own motion. Undertaking such enquiry allows making phone calls, contacting persons via e-mail, fax or letter and may also involve review of files and conducting informal interviews. The principal officer of the body in question must assist the Ombudsman in the conducting of such an enquiry (s13A(3) OA). Depending on the outcome of the enquiry, the Ombudsman may have solved the issue, may decide not to investigate (s15 OA) or may decide to initiate a formal investigation.[17]

In the latter case, the Ombudsman must inform the relevant person in charge of the decision to investigate the matter before commencing the investigation (s17 (1) OA). The Ombudsman may determine the procedure to be used in an investigation (s17(7) OA). The investigations are to be conducted in private. In the course of an investigation, the Ombudsman may enter and inspect any item on the premises of an agency (s21 OA). Before finalising and reporting on a matter, the agency must be given the chance to be heard (s18(4) OA). In addition, the provisions of sections 17, 18, 19, 20 and 20A of the Evidence (Miscellaneous Provisions) Act 1958 apply to any of the Ombudsman's investigations (s18(1) OA). Accordingly, the Ombudsman can summon any person to attend before him or her, to provide any document and to give evidence under oath. The Ombudsman may consult any Minister concerned at any time, but he or she must consult with a Minister if the Minister so requests (s17(5) OA).

After completing an investigation, the Ombudsman must report his or her opinion to the agency concerned and may make recommendations (s23(2) OA). The Ombudsman shall also supply a copy of the report to the Minister, respectively the Mayor of the municipality concerned, and may send a copy to the Premier (s23(3) OA). The agency must, at the Ombudsman's request, report on the steps taken to rectify the situation within a certain time period (s23(4) OA). If the answer is not satisfactory and no appropriate action has been taken within a reasonable period of time, the Ombudsman may inform the Governor, respectively the Mayor of the Municipal Council, in writing (s23(5) OA). If a copy of the report was sent to the Governor, the Ombudsman may also thereafter report to Parliament on the issue (s23(6) OA). The Ombudsman can finally publish an investigation report, which may include a release of a report to the media or publication to the complainant or any other party if the Ombudsman considers this to be in the public interest

[17] Additionally, if it is decided to refer a complaint to either the Privacy Commissioner or the Health Services Commissioner, the Ombudsman shall notify the complainant and the respondent of the referral in writing (s15A and s15B OA).

(s26 OA). The Ombudsman shall also inform the complainant about the outcome of any investigation or any other action taken in relation to the complaint (s24 OA).

Under the FOIA, the Ombudsman *inter alia* investigates complaints about decisions on Freedom of Information requests such as any public authority's refusal to grant access to a document (s25A(8) OA).

Under the WPA, the Ombudsman investigates, respectively oversees investigations of complaints by whistle-blowers. The main powers include determining whether disclosures are of public interest as specified by law, preparing guidelines for procedures to be followed by public bodies in relation to disclosures and investigations, and monitoring investigations by public bodies and the Chief Commissioner of the Police (s39 WPA).

Under the Melbourne City Link Act 1995[18] and the Transport (Compliance and Miscellaneous) Act 1983 and other laws, the Ombudsman has various statutory auditing and oversight functions (s13(2AA) OA).[19] The Ombudsman further has certain monitoring roles relating to the compliance of relevant officials with the Prevention of Brutality to Animals Act 1986 (s13(2AAA) OA) and the Domestic Animals Act (s13(2AC) OA).

The Ombudsman may at any time enter and inspect any premises of an agency under his or her jurisdiction, including detention facilities (private and public prisons). There is no requirement for prior notice. The Ombudsman may speak with detainees alone when conducting an investigation.[20]

A person who fails to comply with the Ombudsman's requests without a reasonable excuse under the Evidence (Miscellaneous Provisions) Act 1958 is guilty of an offence punishable with a fine of up to 15 penalty units or with imprisonment for a term of no more than three months.

A person who commits an offence against the OA is liable to a penalty up to AUS$ 1,000 or imprisonment for up to twelve months (s30 OA).

13.2.3.2 Relations to the Judiciary

The Ombudsman cannot investigate judicial actions (s13(3) OA). In case of ambiguity regarding whether or not the Ombudsman has jurisdiction, the Ombudsman or the party subject to the investigation may make an application to the Supreme Court for determining the question (s27 OA).

[18] The Melbourne City Link is a modern, 22 km-long automated toll way connecting different freeways in the city.

[19] Cf also APOR Manual 2009, p. 52 et seq.

[20] The power derives from s17 OA, in particular s17(2) OA, according to which the Ombudsman shall conduct investigations in private, and s17(7) OA, allowing for the Ombudsman to regulate his or her procedure in such a way as he or she thinks fit.

The Ombudsman may intervene before the Victorian Civil and Administrative Tribunal (VCAT) in matters concerning the Freedom of Information, if he or she is of the opinion that such intervention is warranted (s57(1) FOIA).

13.2.3.3 Relations to the Legislator

The Ombudsman is an independent Officer of Parliament (art. 94E Const.) and reports directly to Parliament on an annual basis and on any other occasions as appropriate, including specific investigations (s23(5) and s25(2) OA).[21] The Ombudsman is not entitled to participate in parliamentary debates. He or she may give evidence to parliamentary committees, if so requested.

While the Ombudsman cannot initiate legislative amendments, he or she can make recommendations for legislative change, following the identification of any such need in the cause of individual investigations. In practice, the Ombudsman makes regularly use of this possibility. There is no formal process laid down in the law for dealing with such recommendations except for the consideration of recommendations by the relevant Minister.

13.2.4 Other Characteristics

After a 2006 amendment to the OA, the functions of the Ombudsman now include the explicit "power to enquire into or investigate whether any administrative action is incompatible with a human right set out in the Charter of Human Rights and Responsibilities" (s13(1A) OA).[22] A finding according to s13(1A) does not have any legal effect as such.

13.2.5 Workload

In the 2010–2011 reporting period, the office was approached 25,557 times and received 13,439 complaints. Out of these complaints, 26.6 % related to justice, 24.8 % to local government and 13.5 % to human services. No specific data is collected as to complaints received from women or from vulnerable and disadvantaged groups.

[21] Cf Clark and De Martinis (2003), p. 33 and p. 37 for more details.

[22] This means that the Victorian Ombudsman is the only Australian Ombudsman so far who deals with "complaints with respect to alleged breaches of the state's Charter of Human Rights and Responsibilities" by public authorities; cf Reif (2011), p. 278.

13.2.6 Publications

The Ombudsman annually reports to Parliament on the exercise of his or her statutory functions (s25 OA). This report includes a specific section on human rights in accordance with the Ombudsman's obligations under s13A OA. In addition, the Ombudsman may make a report on any matter arising in connection with the performance of his or her functions at any time (s25(2) OA). Similarly, under s103 WPA, the Ombudsman may have a report tabled before Parliament on any matter arising in connection with the performance of his or her functions under the WPA at any time. Occasionally, if a report is made to Parliament, Parliament may decide to make such report available to the public (see also s26 OA).

The Ombudsman furthermore shall annually report to the Minister administering the Melbourne City Link Act 1995 on the results of the reviews undertaken (s25A OA). On its website, the office also publishes fact sheets, newsletters, presentations and published parliamentary reports.

13.2.7 Annotations

There are currently no annotations.

References

Clark C, De Martinis M (2003) A framework for reforming the independence and accountability of statutory officers of parliament: a case study of Victoria. Aust J Public Admin 62(1):32–42

Commonwealth Ombudsman (2009) Australasia and Pacific Ombudsman Region Information Manual 2009. Commonwealth Ombudsman, Canberra. www.ombudsman.gov.au/docs/APOR-Manual_20091009.pdf. Accessed 10 Nov 2011

Reif LC (2011) Transplantation and adaptation: the evolution of the human rights ombudsman. Boston Coll Third World Law J 31(2):269–310

Further Reading

Overview of Legislation: www.austlii.edu.au/au/legis/vic/consol_act/ca1975188/ and www.legislation.vic.gov.au

Annual reports (2002–2011): www.ombudsman.vic.gov.au/www/html/255-annual-report-2010.asp

Chapter 14
Australia: Western Australian Ombudsman

Michael Frahm

14.1 General Information

Western Australia, with its capital Perth, is one of eight states and territories that make up the Commonwealth of Australia.[1] It has a two-tiered political system with both a central and a local government level. The domestic administrator is the Governor, appointed by the Queen on the advice of the Premier. The Premier is appointed by the Governor on the advice of the Lower House. Western Australia has a bicameral Parliament with a Lower House, the Legislative Assembly and an Upper House, the Legislative Council.

Western Australia has approximately 2.3 million inhabitants, which corresponds to a population density of 0.91/km^2.[2] The legislative system is based on English Common Law with a federal system of government and powers distributed between the Federal Government and the states. The state's Constitution Act of 1889 does not foresee an Ombudsman. The court system of Western Australia consists of different levels of courts. The highest court is the Supreme Court. It has responsibility for both criminal and civil matters and is Western Australia's main appeal court. It exercises original and appellate jurisdiction. The District Court has responsibility for all serious criminal offences the maximum penalty for which is 20 years imprisonment, and for civil matters. It also hears appeals from the local Magistrates Courts and some tribunals.

---

[1] Cf Chap. 7, p. 101 for more information on the Commonwealth.

[2] Australian Bureau of Statistics (June 2011).

M. Frahm (✉)
Ludwig Boltzmann Institute of Human Rights, Vienna, Austria
e-mail: michael.frahm@univie.ac.at

International Ombudsman Institute (ed.), *Australasia and Pacific Ombudsman Institutions*,
DOI 10.1007/978-3-642-33896-0_14,

14.2 The Ombudsman Institution

Western Australian Ombudsman — Parliamentary Commissioner for Administrative Investigations
Street: 2nd Floor, Albert Facey House, 469 Wellington Street
Postal address: PO Box Z5386, St Georges Terrace
Zipcode: WA 6000, City: Perth
Phone: +61.8 9220 7555
Fax: +61.8 9220–7500
E-mail: mail@ombudsman.wa.gov.au
Website: www.ombudsman.wa.gov.au/

Toll free line: 1800 117 000

14.2.1 Overview

14.2.1.1 Legal Basis

Western Australia was the first state in Australia to establish an Ombudsman in 1971. The office began to operate the following year. The Institution was initially based on the New Zealand model. The office joined the IOI in 1985. The Ombudsman has jurisdiction over Government Departments, agencies and boards, as well as over government services such as hospitals, prisons, schools, public universities and local governments.

Under a service delivery arrangement with the Government of the Commonwealth of Australia, the Ombudsman also handles complaints from residents of the two Indian Ocean Territories that are part of the Commonwealth, the Christmas Islands and Cocos (Keeling) Islands. Under a service agreement with the Board of the Energy Industry Ombudsman (Western Australia) Limited, the Ombudsman also acts as the Energy Ombudsman. The Energy Ombudsman can be addressed by electricity and gas consumers in case of a dispute with the respective providers.

In Western Australia, there are other state bodies with special mandates to which people may submit their complaints. The Health and Disability Services Complaints Office investigates complaints about health and disability services, and the Equal Opportunity Commission can be addressed by individuals who claim they have been discriminated against.

The principal legislation from which the Ombudsman draws power are the Parliamentary Commissioner Act 1971 (PC Act) and the Royal Commissions Act 1968 (RC Act). Regarding the Indian Ocean Territories, the Indian Ocean Territories (Administration of Laws) Act 1992, the Christmas Island Act 1958 and the Cocos (Keeling) Islands Act 1955 are of relevance. As the Energy Ombudsman, the Ombudsman draws power from the Economic Regulation Authority Act

2003, the Electricity Industry Act 2004 and the Energy Coordination Act 1994.[3] In regard to other functions, the Telecommunications (Interception) Western Australia Act 1996 and the Telecommunications (Interception) Act 1979 (Commonwealth), the Public Interest Disclosure Act 2003 (PIDA), the Terrorism (Preventative Detention) Act 2006 and the National Code of Practice for Registration Authorities and Providers of Education and Training to Overseas Students 2007 (authorising the review of appeals by overseas students) endow the Ombudsman with the relevant powers.

14.2.1.2 Legal Status and Independence

The Parliamentary Commissioner (or Ombudsman) is appointed by the Governor for a term of five years (s5(2, 3) PC Act).[4] The law is silent in regard to any reappointment of the incumbent. However, in practice the Ombudsman can be, and in the past has been reappointed. The law is also silent in regard to any involvement of parliamentarians in the appointment process. No one may become Ombudsman who has been a member of any Parliament in Australia within the preceding three years (s5(8) PC Act). No further qualificational requirements and no "pluralism" provisions are contained in the PC Act. As a Western Australian statutory authority, the Equal Opportunity Act 1984 applies to the Ombudsman office. The Equal Employment Opportunity Management Plan required under the legal provisions of Part IX of the Equal Opportunity Act includes staff diversity issues.

When it comes to removal from office, the establishing act stipulates that the Ombudsman may only be removed from office by the Governor on addresses from both Houses of Parliament (s6(1) PC Act). The Governor may also temporarily suspend the Ombudsman from his or her office if the Governor is convinced that the Ombudsman is incapable of properly performing the duties of his or her office, has shown him- or herself incompetent to properly perform his or her duties, or has neglected those duties, is bankrupt or has been guilty of misconduct (s6(2) PC Act). In this case, within seven days of the suspension, Parliament must be given "a statement of the grounds". Based on this statement, Parliament must decide whether or not to remove the Ombudsman. If Parliament does not seek the Ombudsman's removal within one month, the Ombudsman must be restored to office (s6(3) PC Act).

The office becomes vacant when the Ombudsman becomes a candidate for any Australian Parliament (s5(8) PC Act). Also, the Ombudsman shall not hold any office of profit or engage in any occupation for reward outside official duties, except if he or she is authorised to do so by Parliament (s5(9) PC Act).

---

[3] Cf s34 Parliamentary Commissioner Act 1971 which authorises the Ombudsman to enter into an agreement with the governing body of the Energy Ombudsman Scheme.

[4] This rule and the following rules in this chapter are similarly applicable to the Deputy Ombudsman.

Generally, the Ombudsman can not be sued; the only exception are cases in which the Ombudsman has acted in bad faith and if the Supreme Court has granted permission (s30 PC Act). The same applies to any member of the Ombudsman's staff.

Salary and allowances of the Ombudsman and the Deputy Ombudsman are determined by the Governor. The salary shall not be reduced during his or her term of office (s5(5) PC Act). In practice, the Ombudsman's salary is set by the Western Australia Salaries and Allowances Tribunal, which also determines the salaries of the Members of Parliament, including all Ministers and the Premier. The Ombudsman's salary is comparable to that of Members of Parliament.

14.2.1.3 Organisation

The office is lead by the Ombudsman. Senior staff includes one Deputy Ombudsman and four Assistant Ombudsmen, who manage the following divisions: Administrative Improvements, Complaint Resolution (Access and Resolution Team and Investigations and Resolution Team), Child Death Review (Child Death Review Team) and Strategic Services (Strategic Services and Communications Team; Business Services Team and Energy Team). Staff are appointed by the Ombudsman (s9 PC Act); the total number of staff as of 30 June 2011 is 60.3 full-time equivalents (27 % male and 63 % female).[5]

The Ombudsman maintains no sub-offices. As part of the office's activities to provide accessibility to its services, the Ombudsman regularly visits rural areas and remote communities.

The office is funded by parliamentary appropriations and the Ombudsman is accountable to Parliament for all expenditure undertaken under the normal and financial management budget processes for statutory authorities, including compliance with the Financial Management Act 2006 and auditing by the Auditor-General. As the Ombudsman does not report via a Minister, budget submissions are made directly to the Treasurer, and the Ombudsman appears before Parliament during the budget process. The budget approved by Parliament does not include costs incurred for the work of the Energy Ombudsman; these expenses are born by the members of the Energy Ombudsman scheme. The budget for the financial year 2010–2011 was AUS$ 7,731,430 (US$ 7,926,262 as of 4 May 2012).[6]

The office is in the process of being allocated new responsibilities. It has been tasked with monitoring the Criminal Penalty Infringement Notices[7] scheme and with undertaking family and domestic violence fatality reviews. Further, there are two new draft laws before Parliament which provide for two new inspection and/or review functions for the Ombudsman. These are the Criminal Investigation (Covert Powers) Bill 2011 and the Criminal Organisations Control Bill 2011. Additionally,

[5] Cf Annual Report 2010/2011, p. 137.

[6] Cf Annual Report 2010/2011, p. 109.

[7] Under the Criminal Code Amendment (Infringement Notices) Act 2011.

the Water Services Bill 2011 proposes to extend the mandate of the Energy Ombudsman to include complaints about water services.

14.2.2 Mandate

14.2.2.1 Object of Control

The Ombudsman is competent to investigate complaints about matters of administration in relation to all Departments and authorities, unless they are enumeratively exempted in s13(2) PC Act. This means that Government Departments, agencies and boards, government-run services such as hospitals, prisons and schools, public universities, the government railways, water providers, local governments[8] and the Western Australia Police[9] (regarding matters of administration only) are under the Ombudsman's jurisdiction. Private persons are only under the Ombudsman's jurisdiction if they are engaged in a private/public partnership with the state's government agencies. The Energy Ombudsman jurisdiction comprises all members of the Energy Ombudsman scheme.

Other important, partially privately organised providers of public services are dealt with at the Commonwealth level and fall under the jurisdiction of the following Ombudspersons: postal services (Postal Industry Ombudsman[10] in personal union with the Commonwealth Ombudsman), telecommunications (Telecommunications Industry Ombudsman), accommodation of asylum seekers (Commonwealth Ombudsman), health insurance (Health Insurance Ombudsman[11]), pension insurance and unemployment insurance (Financial Ombudsman[12]).

In its s13(2), the PC Act explicitly excludes certain bodies from with jurisdiction. These include the judiciary, the coroner, Parliament and the Governor. This section furthermore refers to Schedule 1 of the Act, which contains a list of other authorities exempted. In addition, some specific subject matters do not fall under the Ombudsman's jurisdiction, such as any decision made by Cabinet or by a Minister or any action undertaken by a person acting as legal adviser (s14 PC Act).

14.2.2.2 Standard of Control

The Ombudsman investigates actions based on the requirements of s25(1) PC Act. Accordingly, the Ombudsman investigates whether any act was "contrary to law",

[8] Cf s4A PC Act.

[9] The Corruption and Crime Commission deals with other complaints regarding the Police.

[10] Cf s19ZE(1) Ombudsman Act (Commonwealth).

[11] Cf www.phio.org.au/ for details.

[12] Cf www.fos.org.au/centric/home_page.jsp for details.

"unreasonable, unjust, oppressive, or improperly discriminatory", "in accordance with a rule of law or a provision of an enactment or a practice that is or may be unreasonable, unjust, oppressive, or improperly discriminatory", was done "in the exercise of a power or discretion, and was so taken for an improper purpose or on irrelevant grounds, or on the taking into account of irrelevant considerations", was done "in the exercise of a power or discretion, and the reasons for the decision were not, but should have been, given" or was "based wholly or partly on a mistake of law or fact or was wrong". There is no additional provision relating to the protection of fundamental and human rights.

A complaint can be made by any natural or legal person or group of people personally affected by the action to which the complaint relates (s17(1) PC Act). Procedures may be initiated not only by individual complaints but also by *proprio motu* (s16(1) PC Act), by referral by Parliament (s15(1) PC Act) or by the review of an investigable child death (s19B(2) PC Act). Complaints shall be made in writing (s17(1) PC Act); this includes the use of an online complaint form. The Ombudsman's services are free.

After the receipt of a complaint, the Ombudsman decides at his or her discretion whether to commence an investigation. The law gives some guidance by establishing a cut-off period which stipulates that the Ombudsman shall not, except under special circumstances, investigate a complaint that has not been lodged within twelve months of the incident (s17(5) PC Act). He or she shall not investigate a complaint again, except under special circumstances, if the complainant has any right of appeal or any legal remedy available to him or her and if it can be reasonably expected that he or she will resort to that remedy (s14(4) and (5) PC Act). Finally, the Ombudsman has discretion to refuse investigation if the complainant does not have sufficient personal interest in the matter, if any further investigation is unnecessary or unjustifiable or if the complaint is "trivial, frivolous or vexatious, or not made in good faith" (s18(1) PC Act).

When a decision has to be made on how to best invest limited resources and whether an investigation into a matter is warranted under the given circumstances, the office also considers the number of complaints received by the Ombudsman, the assumed public interest in the issue of concern and the number of people that may be affected by investigating the issue. Additionally, the overall potential for the Ombudsman's investigation to improve administration in public authorities is considered.[13]

[13] Cf Annual Report 2009/2010, p. 57.

14.2.3 Powers

14.2.3.1 Relation to the Administration

The Ombudsman has the function to investigate complaints received in regard to administrative practices, to investigate certain child deaths and to improve the public administration by way of own motion investigations and by education programmes for public officials. Before investigation, he or she shall inform the body concerned of the decision to investigate. The law thus differentiates between formal and expedited, informal investigations. In the first case, the Ombudsman shall also inform the Minister responsible for the authority in question in writing (s19(1) PC Act). In the latter case, the Ombudsman shall also inform the body concerned, but may do so orally. In this case it is in his or her discretion to also inform the Minister (s19(2) PC Act). The Ombudsman shall conduct investigations in private (s19(2) PC Act) and give the respective agency the chance to be heard (s19(4) PC Act). The Ombudsman may regulate the procedure of an investigation in such a manner as he or she thinks fit (s19(8) PC Act) and may also decide not to investigate a complaint. If so, he or she shall inform the complainant about the reasons (s18(2) PC Act).

The Ombudsman has extensive powers to investigate complaints (s14 PC Act) and to undertake own motion investigations (s16(1) PC Act). He or she may enter and inspect any item on the premises of any Government Department or authority within jurisdiction (s21 PC Act). In addition, having all of the powers of a Royal Commission,[14] the Ombudsman can summon any person to attend before him or her, to provide any document and to give evidence under oath or affirmation (s20(1) PC Act read together with s9, s11 RC Act). The Ombudsman may also have a written notice served to a public authority or public officer, requiring them to produce certain information (s8A RC Act). Likewise, a written notice may be served to a person, requiring the person to attend before the Ombudsman and to render documents and other things (s8B RC Act).

To maintain secrecy, the Ombudsman may direct any person to whom a document is sent by the Ombudsman in writing not to disclose any information contained in the document, except for the purposes of the investigation to which the document relates (s23(1a) PC Act). In the course of an investigation, the Ombudsman may from time to time give a progress report to the complainant (s26 PC Act). The Ombudsman may consult any Minister concerned at any time, but he or she must consult with a Minister if the Minister so requests (s20(5) and (6) PC Act). If the Ombudsman encounters serious misconduct relating to matters under investigation, he or she may refer them to the Corruption and Crime Commission.[15]

---

[14] Cf Royal Commissions Act 1968.

[15] This is not explicitly foreseen in the law, but standard practice. Information provided by the Institution.

Upon concluding an investigation the Ombudsman shall make a report to the principal officer of the authority concerned, and may make therein such recommendations as he or she thinks fit (s25(2) PC Act). A copy of any report containing recommendations must also be provided to the responsible Minister (s25(3) PC Act). In case of a referral by Parliament, the Ombudsman must report to Parliament upon finalisation of the investigation (s15 PC Act). The principal officer must, at the Ombudsman's request, report back within a certain time period on what steps have been taken to give effect to the recommendations (s25(4) PC Act). If, within a reasonable time, no adequate or appropriate action has been taken, the Ombudsman may send a copy of the report to the Premier (s25(5) PC Act). In this case, the Ombudsman may also table a report on the matter before Parliament (s25(6) PC Act).[16]

Under the provisions relating to child death reviews, the Ombudsman reviews investigable deaths of children in Western Australia (s19A and s19B PC Act). In particular, the Ombudsman reviews the circumstances under which and the reasons why the deaths occurred, works towards identifying patterns or trends in relation to the deaths and makes recommendations about ways to prevent or reduce investigable deaths.

Besides the functions under the PC Act, the Ombudsman undertakes a variety of audit/integrity and oversight functions vis-à-vis public administration. These functions are based on various laws and service delivery arrangements.

According to the two Telecommunications (Interception) Acts,[17] the Ombudsman has the duty to inspect the records of the Western Australia Police and the Corruption and Crime Commission at least twice a year to ensure compliance with the respective legislation.

According to the National Code of Practice for Registration Authorities and Providers of Education for Overseas Students 2007, the Ombudsman reviews appeals from overseas students in cases where their internal appeals remained unsuccessful.

According to the PIDA, the Ombudsman is one of the authorities to whom disclosures concerning maladministration may be made (s5(3)(c) PIDA). In this context, the Ombudsman provides advice to potential whistle-blowers and, if a public interest disclosure has been made to the Ombudsman, he or she is to investigate the matters disclosed to him or her (s8 PIDA).

According to a service delivery arrangement between the Ombudsman and the Commonwealth Government, the Ombudsman handles complaints from residents of the Indian Ocean territories (Christmas and Cocos (Keeling) Islands) about public authorities within the Ombudsman's jurisdiction. In this regard the Ombudsman has the powers under the PC Act and RC Act as described above.

---

[16] In practice, most issues are resolved and appropriate remedial action is taken without the need to make formal recommendations or reports. Between 2008 and 2011, all recommendations made by the Ombudsman to improve practices or procedures were accepted.

[17] Cf Sect. 14.2.1.1, p. 188.

According to the Terrorism (Preventative Detention) Act 2006, the Ombudsman receives and investigates complaints about administrative matters connected with the detention from a person detained under that law.

According to a service agreement with the Board of the Energy Industry Ombudsman (Western Australia) Limited, the Ombudsman in the function of Energy Ombudsman considers complaints about electricity and gas providers. The Ombudsman may request a supplier to act or not to act, depending on the outcome of the investigation, and thus can prevent disconnections of consumers from the power supply system in case of an unresolved complaint. The Energy Ombudsman also has the power to make a financial award of up to AUS$ 20,000 or AUS$ 50,000 with the agreement of the parties to the dispute, which is binding for the energy company.

The Ombudsman may in the course of an investigation, enter correction facilities at any time, as they fall under his or her jurisdiction (s21 PC Act). Although the law does not specifically stipulate that the Ombudsman may speak to detainees in private, in practice he or she may do so since, pursuant to s19(2) PC Act, every investigation is to be conducted in private.

It is an offence punishable with a fine of AUS$ 1,000 (s31 PC Act) to wilfully obstruct, hinder or resist the Ombudsman in the exercise of his or her functions, to fail to comply with any lawful requirement or to make any false statement or mislead the Ombudsman (s24 PC Act).

It is further an offence punishable with a fine or imprisonment of up to two years to prejudice the safety or career of, or to intimidate, harass or to threaten to do so another person for his or her complaining to, providing information to or assisting the Ombudsman (s30B PC Act).

14.2.3.2 Relation to the Judiciary

The Ombudsman has no competence to investigate actions of the judiciary (s13(2) PC Act). If a question with regard to the Ombudsman's competence to conduct an investigation arises, in the course of an investigation under the PC Act, the Ombudsman or the party under investigation may file an application with the Supreme Court for a determination of this question (s29 PC Act).

14.2.3.3 Relation to the Legislator

The Ombudsman is an independent Officer of Parliament. He or she has no jurisdiction over either House or over Members of Parliament. The Ombudsman annually[18] reports to Parliament (s61 and s63 Financial Management Act 2006) and

[18] Parliament must be advised of the inability to table an Annual Report within the prescribed period and the reasons for this (s65 Financial Management Act 2006).

may report any time on any matter arising in connection with the exercise of his or her functions (s27(1) PC Act). If Parliament refers an issue to the Ombudsman for investigation,[19] the Ombudsman must carry out an investigation into such matter (s15 PC Act).

The Ombudsman usually contacts Parliament through the Speaker of the Legislative Assembly and the President of the Legislative Council. During the budget appropriation process, the Ombudsman may appear before the Estimates Committee and, if requested, he or she may also appear before the Standing Committee on Public Administration and other parliamentary committees to provide information on specific areas within his or her jurisdiction.[20] The information provided by the Ombudsman may subsequently be used by parliamentarians in their debates. However, the Ombudsman him- or herself is not entitled to participate directly in debates in Parliament or its committees. There are no statutory obligations on Parliament to react to any material submitted by the Ombudsman.

As part of his or her recommendations following an investigation, the Ombudsman may also make a recommendation to change certain legal provisions. However, in practice such recommendations are rare. In such cases it is up to the responsible Minister or body concerned to make use of such proposals, as they are directed to them and not directly to the legislator.

14.2.4 Other Characteristics

One interesting feature is the fact that the law foresees progress reports. The Ombudsman may — in addition to informing a complainant of the outcome of the investigation — from time to time during the course of investigations inform the complainant about the progress of the investigation (s26 PC Act).

Also, the provisions on punishable offences are worth mentioning. The victimisation of individuals who have made, or will or may in the future, make a complaint and/or provide information to the Ombudsman is explicitly prohibited.

14.2.5 Workload

In the 2010–2011 reporting period, the office was contacted approximately 6,000 times. These first contacts resulted in 1,970 formal complaints. Out of these, 1,138 (79.4 %) related to the public sector, 234 (16.3 %) related to the local government sector and 62 (4.3 %) related to the university sector.[21] The public sector complaints

[19] Cf Sect. 14.2.2.2, p. 191.

[20] Cf APOR Manual 2009, p. 57.

[21] Of the 1,970 complaints, 1,434 were within the Ombudsman's jurisdiction.

may be broken down into the following areas: Corrective Services 363 complaints (32 %), Police 147 complaints (13 %) and Public Housing 129 complaints (11 %).

14.2.6 Publications

The Ombudsman shall report to Parliament on the exercise of his or her statutory functions annually (s61 and s63 Financial Management Act 2006) and on other occasions as considered appropriate (s27 PC Act). In case of an investigation upon referral by Parliament, the Ombudsman shall submit a report to Parliament (s15 PC Act).

As the Energy Ombudsman, the Ombudsman also has to submit an Annual Report to the Australian Securities and Investments Commission.

The Ombudsman shall furthermore annually report on the results of his or her inspection of the telecommunications interception records of the Police[22] and of the Corruption and Crime Commission[23] to the respective authorities.

The office has also issued different publications, with the aim to assist both complainants and public authorities. These publications are available on the Ombudsman's website, where the office also makes available other guidelines and information sheets, press releases and newsletters as well as the reports of the Ombudsman.

14.2.7 Annotations

There are currently no annotations.

Reference

Commonwealth Ombudsman (2009) Australasia and Pacific Ombudsman Region Information Manual 2009. Commonwealth Ombudsman, Canberra. www.ombudsman.gov.au/docs/APOR-Manual_20091009.pdf. Accessed 10 Nov 2011

[22] The report is submitted to the Commissioner of Police and the state Minister for Police.

[23] The report is submitted to the state Attorney-General and the Corruption and Crime Commissioner.

Further Reading

Overview of Legislation: www.slp.wa.gov.au/legislation/statutes.nsf/main_yrbyyrsall.html
Constitution: www.slp.wa.gov.au/pco/prod/Filestore.nsf/Documents/MRDocument:19644P/$FILE/ConstitutionAct1889_06-c0-00.pdf?OpenElement
Annual reports Ombudsman (2000–2011): www.ombudsman.wa.gov.au/Publications/Annual_Reports.htm
Annual Reports Energy Ombudsman (2004–2011): www.ombudsman.wa.gov.au/energy/publications/annual_reports.htm

Chapter 15
Hong Kong (Special Administrative Region of China): Ombudsman

Michael Frahm

15.1 General Information

The territory of Hong Kong was occupied by the United Kingdom in 1841 and became a British Crown Colony in 1843. The agreement of 1984 between the United Kingdom and the People's Republic of China paved the way for the reunification of Hong Kong with China in 1997. According to that agreement, Hong Kong will be governed as a Special Administrative Region (SAR) for at least 50 more years.[1] The population is estimated at 7,071,000 people[2] with a population density of 6,544/km^2. The population is predominantly Chinese (93.2 %); in addition there are Filipinos (1.9 %), Indonesians (1.9 %) and others (3.9 %).[3] The official languages are Chinese and English.

Hong Kong has a parliamentary body, the Legislative Council, which has 60 Members. Of these, 30 are directly elected by geographical constituencies and 30 are elected by functional, occupation-based constituencies. The Chief Executive is the Head of the Hong Kong Special Administrative Region. He or she is elected by an Election Committee and is appointed by the Central People's Government of China. Hong Kong is administratively divided into 18 geographic districts which are represented by District Councils. The legal system is based on English Common Law. Hong Kong has a Basic Law, comparable with a state's constitution. The Basic Law contains a list of Fundamental Rights and Freedoms. It was promulgated by the National People's Congress of the People's Republic of China and contains the underlying principle of "one country, two systems". The highest court in Hong

[1] Cf CIA World Factbook (Hong Kong).

[2] According to the 2011 Population Census by the Census and Statistics Department, Hong Kong SAR.

[3] Ibid.

M. Frahm (✉)
Ludwig Boltzmann Institute of Human Rights, Vienna, Austria
e-mail: michael.frahm@univie.ac.at

International Ombudsman Institute (ed.), *Australasia and Pacific Ombudsman Institutions*, DOI 10.1007/978-3-642-33896-0_15, © Springer-Verlag Berlin Heidelberg 2013

Kong is the Court of Final Appeal in the Hong Kong SAR. On a lower level there is the High Court which consists of a Court of Appeal and the Court of First Instance, the District Courts with limited jurisdiction in both civil and criminal matters, and Magistrate Courts with limited jurisdiction in criminal matters. In addition, there is a Lands Tribunal which deals with land disputes, including questions of compensation.[4]

15.2 The Ombudsman Institution

Office of The Ombudsman, Hong Kong[5]
Postal address: 30/F, China Merchants Tower
Shun Tak Centre, 168-200 Connaught Road Central
Zipcode: N/A, City: Hong Kong SAR
Phone: +852.2629 0555
Fax: +852.2882 8149
E-mail: complaints@ombudsman.hk and enquiry@ombudsman.hk
Website: www.ombudsman.hk

15.2.1 Overview

15.2.1.1 Legal Basis

The Institution was established in 1989 and opened to the public the same year. It also became a member of the IOI in 1989. The establishing act, the Ombudsman Ordinance (OO), modelled the office after the British Parliamentary Commissioner for Administration (or Parliamentary Ombudsman) and also drew on the respective New Zealand laws.[6] It has jurisdiction in all of Hong Kong SAR.

In addition to the Ombudsman, there is the Hong Kong Equal Opportunities Commission which has been accredited by the ICC as an NHRI.[7] The Equal Opportunities Commission implements laws in the field of equality and anti-discrimination.[8] Further, there is the Office of the Privacy Commissioner for Personal Data, which oversees the protection of privacy in the use of personal

[4] Cf www.doj.gov.hk/eng/legal/ for more details.

[5] Prior to a legislative amendment in 1996, the office was called "Office of the Commissioner for Administrative Complaints".

[6] The role of the Ombudsman has been strengthened in the post 1997-era, cf Wong and Yuen (2009), p. 115.

[7] Cf Sect. 1.1.3, p. 6 for details.

[8] *Inter alia*, the Sex Discrimination Ordinance, the Disability Discrimination Ordinance, the Family Status Discrimination Ordinance and the Race Discrimination Ordinance.

data.[9] In the area of Freedom of Information, the Ombudsman is empowered by the OO to monitor Government's compliance with the Code on Access to Information (CAI).

15.2.1.2 Legal Status and Independence

The Ombudsman is appointed by the Chief Executive of the Hong Kong SAR (s3(3) OO). The Legislative Council is not involved in the appointment process. There is no fixed procedure for the Chief Executive to be guided by any consultation process.[10] However, once appointed, the Ombudsman can only be removed from office by the Chief Executive with the approval of the Legislative Council on the grounds of the Ombudsman being unable to discharge the functions of his or her office or in case of misbehaviour (s3(4) OO). There are no further details on the exact dismissal procedure prescribed by law.

The Chief Executive may also temporarily fill the position of the Ombudsman if the person appointed dies, resigns, is removed from office, is absent from Hong Kong or is unable to perform his or her functions for any other reason (s5 OO). The Ombudsman shall serve a term of five years and may be reappointed indefinitely (s3(3A) OO). There are no qualificational requirements or any provisions in the OO that ensure that the office staff reflects the composition of society.

The Ombudsman shall not, without the specific approval of the Chief Executive, hold any office of profit other than his or her office as the Ombudsman, or engage in any occupation for reward outside the duties of his or her office (s4 OO). To ensure his or her independence, the law prescribes that the Ombudsman shall not be regarded as public servant or agent of the Government (s6B OO).[11]

The Ombudsman may appoint staff and determine their terms and conditions of appointment, including their salaries (s6 OO). The Ombudsman may do all things that are necessary for the performance of his or her functions, including the entering into contracts, agreements or other obligations, the acquisition and holding of property, the creation of a reserve and the investment of surplus funds (s7(1A) OO and Schedule 1A to the OO).

Under the OO, the Ombudsman and any of the office's staff shall not be personally liable for any civil liability or claim whatsoever in respect to any act or omission undertaken in the performance of any function under the OO if acting in good faith (s18A OO). For the purposes of the Law on Defamation, absolute privilege is attached to the publication of any matter by the office (s18 OO).

[9] Cf the Personal Data (Privacy) Ordinance.

[10] Cf Cooray (2000), p. 56.

[11] However, for the purposes of the Prevention of Bribery Ordinance and the Public Finance Ordinance, the Ombudsman is deemed to be a public servant and a public officer, respectively according to the definitions of those laws.

The salary and remuneration of the Ombudsman as well as the terms and conditions of the appointment are determined by the Chief Executive (s3(5) and (6) OO). The salary is comparable to the highest rank in the civil service of the Hong Kong SAR Government.

15.2.1.3 Organisation

The office is led by the Ombudsman and the Deputy Ombudsman and consists of two Investigation Divisions, the Administration and Development Division and the Assessment Team. Each Investigation Division is headed by an Assistant Ombudsman who is responsible for supervising the investigations. The Assessment Team screens all incoming enquiries and complaints to determine whether they are subject to the office's jurisdiction. This Team arranges for duty officers to receive complainants who come to the office in person.

The Administration and Development Division, headed by a Chief Manager, provides support services in resource management, accounting, general administration and external relations. The Chief Manager also processes complaints against staff. The Translation Section deals with English and Chinese translations.[12]

The office has 111 staff members (full-time equivalents), 44 of whom are male (39.6 %) and 67 of whom are female (60.4 %). 77 of the employees (69.4 %) have academic qualifications at the level of at least a bachelor degree [34 male (44.2 %) and 43 female (55.8 %)].[13]

The Ombudsman annually submits his or her estimates of expenditure to the responsible office, the Financial Services and the Treasury Bureau, for preparation of the annual budget. The estimate is later included in the overall estimates of expenditure and presented to the Legislative Council in an Appropriation Bill for scrutiny and approval. If requested, the Ombudsman attends a meeting of the Council's Finance Committee to answer questions about the budget. The Legislative Council then appropriates the budget for the office as part of the general revenue in form of a one-line-vote (s6(3) OO). This means that internally, the Ombudsman is flexible in the use of the allocation during the year. He or she determines the terms of conditions of all staff hired (s6(2) OO). The Ombudsman must follow the financial and report provisions set out in Schedule 1A to the OO (s3(7) OO) and, within six months after the end of a financial year, submit a report on his or her activities and an audited statement of accounts to the Chief Executive for tabling before the Legislative Council. The budget of the office was Hong Kong $ 95,315,284 in 2011 and Hong Kong $ 103,031,920 (US$ 13,262,662 as of 4 May 2012) in 2012.

[12] Cf www.ombudsman.hk/images/organisation_structure.jpg for details.

[13] As at 31 March 2011.

15.2.2 Mandate

15.2.2.1 Object of Control

Under the OO, the Ombudsman has jurisdiction over all Government Departments and over the 23 public organisations listed in Part I of Schedule 1 to the OO. In addition, according to the Code on Access to Information (CAI), the Ombudsman may also investigate complaints against Government Departments about non-compliance with the CAI. Jurisdiction over the Police Force and Auxiliary Police Force, the Secretariat of the Public Service Commission and the Independent Commission Against Corruption is limited to investigations related to the CAI (according to Part II of Schedule 1 to the OO).[14]

Private enterprises providing public services such as electricity and railway services do not fall under the Ombudsman's jurisdiction. As health insurance is not provided by a public institution, the Ombudsman is not competent to investigate complaints in this area. Tertiary education, i.e. universities, do not generally fall under his or her jurisdiction. The office does, however, investigate complaints against the Student Financial Assistance Agency.[15]

Other relevant public services are provided by Government Departments or public organisations and fall under the Ombudsman's jurisdiction as follows: labour issues (Labour Department); immigration, including asylum seekers-related issues (Immigration Department); postal services (Post Office); public hospitals-related issues (Hospital Authority); water supply-related issues (Water Supplies Department); the administration of provident fund schemes (Mandatory Provident Fund Schemes Authority) and social living issues (Social Welfare Department).

Although the jurisdiction is generally quite broad, there are certain specific actions that are expressly excluded from the jurisdiction according to the establishing act. Schedule 2 to the OO entails all actions excluded (s8 OO). These include actions related to security, defence or international relations, any civil or criminal proceedings, actions related to employment, personal actions of the Chief Executive, actions undertaken by the Police and the Independent Commission Against Corruption in relation to the prevention, detection or investigation of any crime or offence, and actions relating to land grants, takeovers and mergers.[16] Professional judgments, such as medical and legal issues, are not considered administrative matters and therefore fall outside the Ombudsman's jurisdiction. Private persons and entities cannot be subject to an investigation.

[14] Annex A to the CAI lists all Government Departments to which the CAI applies.

[15] This Government Department is responsible for the administration of financial assistance schemes and scholarships.

[16] Wong and Yuen question the rationality of excluding issues such as land grants, takeovers and mergers from the Ombudsman's jurisdiction, given the importance of the financial sector and the land development in Hong Kong, cf Wong and Yuen (2009), p. 125.

15.2.2.2 Standard of Control

The Ombudsman may investigate complaints of maladministration from a person who claims to "have sustained injustice in consequence of (the) maladministration". He or she can also investigate acts of maladministration in the absence of any complaint, if he or she is of the opinion that "any person may have sustained injustice in consequence of (such) maladministration" (s7(1)(b)(ii) OO). The term "maladministration" is defined as "inefficient, bad or improper administration" and covers "unreasonable conduct, including delay, discourtesy and lack of consideration for a person affected by any action; abuse of any power (including any discretionary power) or authority, including any action which is unreasonable, unjust, oppressive or improperly discriminatory or is in accordance with a practice that is or may be unreasonable, unjust, oppressive or improperly discriminatory, or any action based wholly or partly on a mistake of law or fact; or unreasonable, unjust, oppressive or improperly discriminatory procedures" (s2(1) OO).

In case of complaints related to Freedom of Information, the Institution investigates decisions concerning requests for access to information. The standard of control is the question whether "a [D]epartment has failed to properly apply any provision" of the CAI (para. 1.26 CAI).

Procedures can be initiated by complaints from the public, or *proprio motu* by the Ombudsman (s7(1) OO),[17] prompted by significant issues of concern to the community. Both natural persons and legal persons are entitled to register a complaint. The law prescribes that they must have a link to Hong Kong. Anybody who was a resident or had a place of business in Hong Kong, or was physically present in Hong Kong at the time the action under complaint was taken, or who was aggrieved by an action taken in relation to any right or obligation which accrued or arose in Hong Kong is entitled (s10(1)(db) OO).

The Ombudsman has discretion to determine whether a complaint has been duly made under the OO (s9 OO). The law does not contain further specifications as to the format of complaints. While s9A OO authorises the charging of a reasonable fee, in practice the office does not charge the public for making complaints.[18]

The Ombudsman shall not investigate an issue that the complainant has had knowledge of for more than 24 months, unless particular circumstances make it appropriate to investigate nevertheless. He or she shall further not investigate an anonymous complaint, a complaint made by a third party on another natural person's behalf, unless that person is unable to act for him- or herself, or a complaint made on behalf of a corporate body unless the Ombudsman is convinced that the corporate body has authorised the making of the complaint (s10(1) OO). Lastly, a complaint shall not be investigated if the complainant can pursue other

[17] Prior to legislative amendments in 1994, individuals could only complain indirectly by complaining to a Member of the Legislative Council. Cf Wong and Yuen (2009), p. 119.

[18] Charges on photocopying or duplication of voice/video recordings may be levied, depending on the individual conditions.

means of reviewing the decision (e.g. right of appeal or objection, except judicial review) and if it were reasonable to exercise this means of review when taking into account all circumstances of the case (s10(1) OO). The Ombudsman may refuse an investigation if the issue has been previously investigated and he or she has not identified a case of maladministration. He or she may also refuse investigation if the subject matter is trivial, the complaint is frivolous or vexatious or is not made in good faith or if any (further) investigation appears unnecessary (s10(2) OO).

15.2.3 Powers

15.2.3.1 Relation to the Administration

Before initiating an investigation, the Ombudsman shall determine whether the complaint has duly been made under the OO and whether to commence an investigation (s9 OO). For this purpose, he or she may conduct preliminary inquiries (s11A OO). If the Ombudsman decides not to investigate a complaint, he or she shall inform the complainant of this decision (s10(3) OO). Otherwise, the Ombudsman shall inform the head of the organisation concerned of his or her intention to investigate the matter (s12(1) OO). Under exceptional circumstances, the Ombudsman may decide not to inform the head but to inform the Chief Secretary for Administration instead (s12(2) OO). The Ombudsman shall conduct all investigations in private. Other than that, he or she is fairly free in the choice of procedures (s12(3)(b) and (4) OO). If the complainant withdraws the complaint, the Ombudsman shall determine whether it is in the public interest to continue the investigation (s11 OO).

In the course of the investigation the Ombudsman may obtain information from any person as he or she thinks fit and may make inquiries as he or she considers appropriate (s12(3)(a) OO). He or she may also require persons and authorities to render certain documents or provide certain information under oath and may administer the oath (s13(1) and (2) OO). After the Ombudsman has notified the head of the organisation concerned, the Ombudsman has the power to enter the organisation's premises and may inspect and obtain documents there; limitations are possible for security and other reasons as determined by the Chief Executive (s20 OO).

The Ombudsman shall determine whether it may be appropriate to deal with the complaint by mediation (s11B OO). In this case, provided both parties agree to a mediation attempt, he or she may authorise any of his or her staff as a mediator (s11B(2) OO).

The Ombudsman himself or herself shall not act as mediator in any case (s11B (3) OO). If mediation is not successful, the complaint is to be investigated as if no mediation had taken place, and the mediator is excluded from the investigation process (s11B(6) OO).

After the investigation is completed, the Ombudsman may draft a report, including his or her findings and recommendations for remedy (s16(1) OO).[19] However, before the Ombudsman makes any comment or recommendation that is adverse to any person, that person must be given an opportunity to be heard (s12(6) OO). The final report with recommendations is to be submitted to the organisation concerned. The Ombudsman may require said organisation to report on the steps intended to implement the recommendations in the report within a specified period of time (s16(2) OO). When there is no adequate reaction to the report, the Ombudsman may submit the report to the Chief Executive (s16(3) OO). For cases concerning serious irregularity or injustice, the Ombudsman may submit a further report to the Chief Executive (s16(5) OO). A copy of such further report shall be tabled before the Legislative Council (s16(6) OO). The Ombudsman shall also inform the complainant of the outcome of the investigation (s17(1) OO). Further, the Ombudsman may publish a report, if he or she considers this to be in the public interest (s16A OO).

The Ombudsman's powers also include entry to prisons (s20 OO), as the Correctional Services Department is listed in Schedule 1 Part I to the OO. However, before entering, the Ombudsman shall notify the head of the Department (s20(2) OO). While the OO does not contain a specific provision on the question of whether or not the Ombudsman can speak to detainees alone, in practice the Ombudsman is allowed to speak with detainees in private, as s12(4) OO foresees investigations to be conducted in private.

A person who "without lawful excuse, obstructs, hinders or resists the Ombudsman or any other person in the exercise of his [or her] powers under this Ordinance; [. . .] fails to comply with any lawful requirement [. . .] or makes a statement which he [or she] knows to be false or does not believe to be true or otherwise knowingly misleads the Ombudsman or any other person in the exercise of his or her powers under th[e] Ordinance" commits an offence and is liable to a fine of Hong Kong $ 10,000 and to imprisonment for six months (s23 OO).

15.2.3.2 Relation to the Judiciary

The Ombudsman has no competence to investigate actions of courts and tribunals and has no special functions and powers relating to the judiciary. Schedule 2 to the OO, which entails all actions excluded, covers the commencement or conduct of any proceedings, including any decision whether to prosecute any person for an offence. Nevertheless, all registries and administrative offices of courts and tribunals for which the Judicial Administrator has responsibility do come within the Ombudsman's purview (Schedule 1 Part I to the OO).

[19] There is no formal time limit for the investigations. However, the Ombudsman aims to complete a minimum of 60 % of investigations within three months and the rest within six months. In 2010/2011, 74.5 % of investigations were completed within three months, 24.6 % within six months, and only 0.9 % took longer.

Although the Ombudsman's decision is final, this does not prevent those not satisfied with the decision of the Ombudsman from requesting a review or from seeking judicial review by a court.[20]

If there is suspicion that the Ombudsman may be acting *ultra vires*, courts are competent to review the question.[21]

15.2.3.3 Relation to the Legislator

The Ombudsman is required to report to the Legislative Council through the Chief Executive on the exercise of his or her functions annually. The Annual Report contains a list of the Ombudsman's investigations and summaries of some of the investigation reports. The Government may then also submit to the Legislative Council its comments on any issue raised therein. Its response, the "Government Minute", describes if and how the Government has accepted and implemented the Ombudsman's recommendations.[22]

The Ombudsman also meets Members of the Legislative Council every year, updates them on the work of the office and answers any questions raised by members. Further, the Ombudsman attends the annual meeting of the Council's Special Finance Committee that approves the appropriation of funds for, *inter alia*, the Ombudsman's office.

The law does not explicitly foresee legislative initiatives by the Ombudsman. In practice, he or she may propose legislative amendments to the Government, i.e. to the Chief Secretary for Administration's Office, for consideration as a consequence of his or her investigations. The Government may add comments and then table such proposal before the Legislative Council for approval.[23] The Government is not obliged to act upon any such proposal and is free to propose amendments to the Legislative Council.

15.2.4 Other Characteristics

The People's Republic of China has not signed or ratified the OPCAT.[24]

---

[20] There have been some attempts of judicial review against the Ombudsman. For instance, three complainants applied for judicial review against the Ombudsman's decision in 2009. None succeeded in obtaining leave from the High Court.

[21] Cf Cooray (2000), p. 69.

[22] Cf Cooray (2000), p. 56.

[23] The latest amendments to the OO were made in 2010 upon the Ombudsman's initiative.

[24] Cf Sect. 3.2.6.2, p. 55 for details.

A provision in the enabling legislation explicitly stipulates that the Ombudsman may continue an investigation despite the fact that the complainant has withdrawn the complaint if it is in the public interest (s11 OO).

A special feature in the enabling legislation is the possibility for the Ombudsman to deal with a complaint by mediation under the condition that the Ombudsman is of the opinion that the subject matter involves no, or only minor, maladministration (s11B OO) and that both parties consent to this procedure (s11B(4) OO).

15.2.5 Workload

In the 2010–2011 reporting period, the office received 5,339 complaints, including 39 CAI-related complaints. The complaints mainly related to land matters (12 %), environmental hygiene (11 %) and housing (11 %). Thus the areas investigated mainly concerned unauthorised development works, water seepage and public housing management.[25] Other areas included social welfare, public health services, environmental issues and leisure and cultural facilities.

15.2.6 Publications

The Ombudsman shall annually submit a report on his or her activities and an audited statement of accounts to the Chief Executive for tabling before the Legislative Council (Schedule 1A, s3 OO). The Annual Report includes figures on performance and results, reports on rewards, challenges and office administration, as well as information on the office's external relations activities.

There is no requirement for other reports. However, the Ombudsman may, at his or her discretion, publish reports on any investigation if they do not disclose the identity of any person aggrieved, any complainant or any officer of the organisation under investigation and if the Ombudsman considers it to be in the public interest to do so (s16A OO). In practice, such reports are published in the form of selected case summaries in the Annual Report, or in press conferences which are held approximately four times per year. In addition, selected decisions are available on the Ombudsman's website. Furthermore, the office issues various publications such as a fact sheet on the office, performance pledges and a publicity leaflet.[26]

---

[25] Cf Summary of Annual Report 2011, p. 2.

[26] In 2011, the office also launched a publicity campaign to inform the public of the competences of the Ombudsman. Short publicity videos about the office's function and jurisdiction were broadcast on TV and on buses and trains. Print advertisements were published in local newspapers.

15.2.7 Annotations

There are currently no annotations.

References

Cooray A (2000) Ombudsman in Asia. In: Gregory R, Giddings P (eds) Righting wrongs. The Ombudsman in six continents. IOS, Berlin

Wong W, Yuen R (2009) The Ombudsman in Hong Kong: role and challenges under the transformation of governance in the post-1997 era. Asia Pac Law Rev 17(1):115–133

Further Reading

Overview of Legislation: www.legislation.gov.hk/blis_ind.nsf/WebView?OpenAgent&vwpg=CurAllEngDoc*397*0*397.1#397.1 and www.access.gov.hk/doc/code.pdf

Basic Law: www.basiclaw.gov.hk/en/basiclawtext/images/basiclaw_full_text.pdf

Annual reports (2000–2012): www.ombudsman.hk/annual_reports.shtml

Chapter 16
Cook Islands: Ombudsman

Michael Frahm

16.1 General Information

The Cook Islands are a self-governing parliamentary democracy in free association with New Zealand.[1] The Islands became independent in 1965. The Head of State is Queen Elizabeth II, represented by the Governor-General of New Zealand (art. 2 Const.). The Parliament of the Cook Islands consists of 24 Members elected by universal suffrage. The Government is lead by the Prime Minister. The Cook Islands consist of 15 small islands, the capital Avarua is situated on Rarotonga Island. In 2008, the population was estimated at 20,000 respectively at 11,488,[2] with a population density[3] of 83.5 persons/km^2. Ethnic groups include the Cook Island Maori (Polynesians), representing 87.7 % of the population, 5.8 % part Cook Island Maori [*sic*!] and 6.5 % others.[4] Languages spoken are English (official language) and Maori. Due to the Islands' small size there is no further administrative division.

The Cook Islands have their own Constitution, laid down in the Cook Island Constitution Act 1964. The Constitution lists fundamental human rights and freedoms in its art. 64.[5]

The Cook Islands' legal system is based on New Zealand Law and English Common Law. The court system includes Justices of the Peace (art. 61 Const.), the High Court (art. 47 Const.), and the Court of Appeal (art. 56 Const.) as the superior court which hears any appeal from the High Court. While an Ombudsman Institution has not been established in the Constitution *expressis verbis*, art. 67 of

[1] In consultation with the Cook Islands, New Zealand is responsible for foreign affairs and defence.

[2] UN estimate 2008, respectively CIA World Factbook July 2010 estimate.

[3] UN estimate 2008.

[4] According to the 2001 Census.

[5] These were added in 1981, cf New Zealand Law Commission (2006), p. 36.

M. Frahm (✉)
Ludwig Boltzmann Institute of Human Rights, Vienna, Austria
e-mail: michael.frahm@univie.ac.at

International Ombudsman Institute (ed.), *Australasia and Pacific Ombudsman Institutions*, DOI 10.1007/978-3-642-33896-0_16, © Springer-Verlag Berlin Heidelberg 2013

the Constitution[6] mentions the Ombudsman, taking the existence of the office for granted.

16.2 The Ombudsman Institution

Te Mato Akamoeau, Ombudsman of the Cook Islands
Postal address: PO Box 748, Rarotonga, Avarua
Street: 1st floor, Ingram House, Rarotonga, Avarua
Phone: +682.20605
Fax: +682.21605
E-mail: complaint@ombudsman.gov.ck
Website: www.ombudsman.gov.ck/

16.2.1 Overview

16.2.1.1 Legal Basis

The Ombudsman of the Cook Islands was established in 1984, with the first incumbent appointed in 1985, when the office opened its doors to the public. The Institution joined the IOI in 1986. The establishing legislation follows the New Zealand model. The office has federal jurisdiction; due to the small size of the Cook Islands, there are no other regional Ombudsmen. The Ombudsman draws power not only from the Ombudsman Act 1984 (OA), but, after the implementation of two new laws, also from the Official Information Act 2008 (OIA) and the Disability Act 2008 (DA).[7]

16.2.1.2 Legal Status and Independence

The Ombudsman is appointed as Officer of Parliament by the Queen's Representative on the advice of the Prime Minister, who shall convey the recommendations of Parliament (s3(1) and (2) OA). The appointment is for a term of three years, and infinite reappointment is possible. However, the Ombudsman must retire at the age of 72 (s5 OA). The establishing act does not foresee any qualificational requirements. It is incompatible with the position of Ombudsman to be a Member of Parliament or of an island council. Furthermore, the Ombudsman "shall not, without the approval of the Prime Minister, hold any office of trust or profit other than his

[6] On the Cook Islands Public Service Board of Appeal.

[7] The Cook Islands have become the first Pacific Island country to develop a rights-based disability policy and action plan. Cf New Zealand Law Commission (2006), p. 68.

office as the Ombudsman, or engage in any occupation for reward outside the duties of [the] office" (s4 OA). The Ombudsman shall, before entering office, confirm on oath before the Speaker of Parliament that he or she will perform the functions of Ombudsman impartially and will not divulge any information received (s9 OA).

The Ombudsman may be removed from office in case of "inability to discharge the functions of his office (whether arising from infirmity of body or mind or from any other cause) or misbehaviour". Only the Queen's Representative, who shall act on the advice of the Prime Minister, may remove the Ombudsman. The Prime Minister shall also convey the recommendation of Parliament in this procedure (s6(1) OA). If Parliament is not in session, the Representative may suspend the Ombudsman from office for the same reasons, but not "beyond two months after the commencement of the next ensuing session of Parliament" (s6(2) OA).

Under the OA, no proceeding or decision of the Ombudsman may be challenged, reviewed, quashed or called into question in a court, except on the ground of lack of jurisdiction (s22 OA). The Ombudsman is generally immune to legal proceedings. Neither the Ombudsman nor any of his or her staff shall be called to give evidence before any court in respect to anything undertaken in the exercise of his or her functions (s23(1) OA).[8] Anything said or any information supplied by any person in the course of any inquiry is privileged in the same manner as if the proceedings were conducted in court (s23(2) OA).

The Ombudsman's salary is determined by the Queen's Representative and "paid out of the Government Account, without further appropriation" (s8 OA). It is not to be diminished during the continuance of the Ombudsman's appointment (s8(2) OA). Furthermore, the Ombudsman receives travelling allowances and expenses in accordance with the Civil List Act 1984 (s8(5) OA).[9]

16.2.1.3 Organisation

The office is headed by the Ombudsman, who is supported by two Assistant Ombudsmen and an office administrator. The position of the Ombudsman and that of one Assistant Ombudsman are currently occupied by women. There are no sub-offices on other Islands. Since 2009, one of the Assistant Ombudsman has primarily been working on supporting the implementation of the Freedom of Information legislation.[10]

In November 2007, Cabinet appointed the Ombudsman to "be in charge of the Cook Islands' Human Rights Office". This appointment was subsequently interpreted to mean that the Ombudsman should set up a specific human rights

[8] Except in the case of proceedings for an offence against the Official Secrets Act 1951.

[9] It is stipulated that the provisions of that Act apply as if the Ombudsman were a Minister.

[10] This work includes the preparation of agencies for the implementation of the OIA, e.g. record keeping and good records management practices, and raising public awareness.

unit within the office.[11] However, while the Ombudsman may "appoint such officers and employees as may be necessary for the efficient carrying out of his functions, powers and duties" (s10 OA), it was not possible to fund such an additional position out of the budget available in the 2008–2009 financial year. There was no additional funding available and therefore this direction was not implemented.[12] There is no up-to-date information available on whether there has been further development in the meantime. Staff are not considered public servants in terms of the Public Service Act 1975 (s10(4) OA).

Both the Ombudsman's as well as all other salaries, allowances and other expenditure payable or incurred under the OA are paid out of money to be appropriated by Parliament for the specific purpose (s28 OA). The Ombudsman shall make regular financial reports to the Government.

After the described expansions of the mandate in recent years, there are no further reform plans. Instead, the office is consolidating its structure and work flow.

16.2.2 Mandate

16.2.2.1 Object of Control

Jurisdiction of the Ombudsman under the OA covers public sector administration, including local government. There is no general clause in the OA; instead, the agencies are listed in a Schedule to the OA (Parts 1 and 2).[13] Originally, jurisdiction was limited to Central Government Departments; however, in 2007 the Ombudsman (New Schedule) Order updated the Schedule, making it very inclusive. Under the OIA, the Ombudsman investigates public sector agencies with respect to a Freedom of Information request. Jurisdiction comprises Ministers, Government Departments and agencies, including local government on requests for official information.[14]

[11] Cf www.ombudsman.gov.ck/index.php/about-us.html for details.

[12] Cf APOR Manual 2009, p. 69.

[13] Part I "Departments" stands for Ministries and Departments, including *inter alia* Corrective Services and the Police Department. Part II *inter alia* includes the Transport Licensing Authority, the Cook Islands Broadcasting & Newspaper Corporation, the Island Councils, Airport Authority and the Parole Board.

[14] In 2009, under the heading "Cook Islands Ombudsman says OIA has made workload manageable" Radio New Zealand International reported: "Inefficient record keeping in government entities is being seen as a major challenge to administering the Official Information Act in the Cook Islands. Ombudsman Janet Maki says given there are no information standards, many departments need better systems of record keeping and information management. She says since the OIA came into law in February this year, staggering its implementation across government entities by getting at least six departments up to par every three months, has made the workload manageable. 'The platform to any FOI (Freedom of Information) legislation is that you have good records that you can access quite easily and readily. And at the moment for some of the departments they would have difficulty in doing that.' Janet Maki says another challenge is a

Under the OA and OIA, the Ombudsman cannot investigate complaints against or about private individuals or privately-owned companies, the judiciary, Ministers,[15] any person acting as legal adviser to the Crown or any decision of a person in his or her capacity as a trustee under the Trustee Act 1956. Complaints are also disallowed if there is still a possibility of appeal or review to a court or tribunal on the merits unless there are special circumstances that make it unreasonable to use those appeal rights (s11(7)(a) OA). Finally, a complaint against any Police officer that may be the subject of an inquiry under the Police Act 1981 is excluded unless a complaint has already been made to the Police and the complaint has either not been investigated or, while it was investigated, the complainant is dissatisfied with the result (s11(7)(d) OA).

Under the DA, the Ombudsman has jurisdiction over both the public and the private sector in order to investigate complaints about unlawful discrimination.

16.2.2.2 Standard of Control

The Ombudsman's criteria of control are quite broad; the Ombudsman shall act if an investigation shows a matter[16] "to have been contrary to law"; "unreasonable, unjust, oppressive, or improperly discriminatory", or "in accordance with a rule of law or a provision of any act, regulation, or bylaw or a practice that is or may be unreasonable, unjust, oppressive, or improperly discriminatory; or was based wholly or partly on a mistake of law or fact; or was wrong" (s19(1) OA). The Ombudsman shall also act if a "discretionary power has been exercised" for an improper purpose or on irrelevant grounds (s19(2) OA). The Cook Islands Human Rights Office is not mentioned in the OA, and there is no specific reference to human rights as a control standard in the OA.

Procedures under the OA can be initiated by complaints of individuals or of a group of people or of a legal person with an interest in the matter (s11(1) OA), by *proprio motu* (s11(3) OA) or by referral by any committee of Parliament and the Prime Minister (s11(4) and (5) OA). All complaints to the Ombudsman shall be made in writing (s13(1) OA). However, according to information on the Institution's website, it appears as if a complaint may also be lodged orally or by letter, phone, fax, e-mail or by filling in the online form.

The Ombudsman has discretion to refuse an investigation (s14 OA) if there is an existing remedy or a right of appeal to the courts or an administrative agency, if it

---

lack of resources, but both the Ombudsman's office and Archives office in New Zealand have offered help." Source: www.rnzi.com/pages/newsphp?op=read&id=48689, posted on 26.08.2009, accessed on 17.08.2011.

[15] However, the Ombudsman can investigate complaints about advice provided to Government Ministers by Government agencies and any complaint that relates to a request for official information.

[16] To improve readability, the text only refers to "matter". However, this term includes any decision, recommendation, act, or omission.

appears to him or her that any further investigation is unnecessary, if the complainant has had knowledge of the matter for more than twelve months before complaining to the Ombudsman; if the complaint is trivial, frivolous or vexatious, vindicative or not made in good faith, or if the complainant does not have sufficient personal interest. However, it is not a formal requirement to exhaust other remedies. There may be reasons to start an investigation even when there are still alternative avenues available to the complainant for seeking redress.

Under the OIA, any qualified person (s11 OIA)[17] can request official information and the same qualified person can consequently complain to the Ombudsman (s30 OIA). Such complaint shall be made in writing (s30(3) OIA). The matters investigated under the OIA are mainly decisions (to withhold or delete information from documents released to the requester), delays or extensions to the time limits for responding to requests, charges for supplying information or the manner in which the information has been made available (s30 OIA and s14 OIA).

Under the DA, a person directly affected or a third person on behalf of another person who is directly affected may complain to the Ombudsman in case of alleged discrimination on the basis of a disability.[18]

16.2.3 Powers

16.2.3.1 Relation to the Administration

Before commencing an investigation the Ombudsman must inform the head or the principal officer of the agency affected of the intention to investigate (s15(1) OA). Every investigation must be conducted in private (s15(2) OA). Otherwise, the Ombudsman may generally regulate his or her procedure as he or she thinks fit (s15(7) OA). The Ombudsman may obtain information from any persons and make inquiries. He or she is not required to hold any hearing. However, before making a report or recommendation that may adversely affect anybody, the Ombudsman must "give to that Department or organisation or person an opportunity to be heard" (s15(3) OA). The Ombudsman may require a person to furnish certain information or documents (s16(1) OA) and he or she may enter premises (s24 OA) in the course of conducting an investigation. However, a visit without prior notice to the head of the organisation is not possible (s24(2) OA), and the Minister of Justice may exclude certain premises from being investigated by notice to the Ombudsman

[17] The term "qualified person" is defined in s2 OIA and comprises a Cook Islander, a permanent resident, or any other natural person who is resident in the Cook Island and has been so for not less than three years, and a corporate body, wherever incorporated, which has had a place of business in the Cook Islands for not less than three years.

[18] Cf APOR Manual 2009, p. 67.

(s24(3) OA).[19] The Ombudsman may further summon and examine persons under oath (s16(2) OA).

The Ombudsman may, during or after an investigation, consult a Minister respectively the chairperson of an organisation who is concerned with the matter of the investigation and must consult any Minister who so requests or to whom a recommendation has been made after investigation and before having formed a final opinion (s15(4) and (5) OA). If there is substantial evidence of any significant breach of duty or misconduct on the part of any member of any agency, the Ombudsman must refer the matter to the appropriate authority (s15(6) OA).

At the end of an investigation the Ombudsman may make recommendations to the agency and refer the matter to the appropriate authority "for further consideration" (s19(3) OA). The Ombudsman may request the agency to notify him or her, within a specified period of time, of the steps that it proposes to take to give effect to his or her recommendations. He or she must also send a copy of the recommendations to the Minister respectively the chairperson[20] concerned (s19(3) OA). If no adequate action is taken, the Ombudsman "may send a copy of the report and recommendations to the Prime Minister, and may thereafter make such report to Parliament on the matter as he thinks fit" (s19(4) OA). He or she may request an organisation listed in Schedule Part II to make a summary of his or her report available to members of the public for inspection (s20 OA).

If the Ombudsman makes a recommendation and no adequate action is taken, the Ombudsman shall inform the complainant of his or her recommendation. In any case, he or she shall inform the complainant of the result of the investigation (s21 OA). For Ombudsman investigations, the general public interest immunity against disclosure of documents is not valid, except when the Minister of Justice certifies that the giving of any information "might prejudice the security, defence or international relations" of the Cook Islands, or "prejudice the investigation or detection of offences", or disclose deliberations or confidential proceedings of Cabinet (s17 OA).

Under the OIA, the procedures are generally similar to the ones under the OA (s31–s33 OIA). At the end of an investigation, when the Ombudsman forms the opinion that information should not be withheld, he or she recommends the organisation concerned to release the information. Such recommendation becomes binding 21 working days after it was issued unless the Queen's Representative directs otherwise (s35 OIA).

The power of entry on premises (s24 OA) includes prisons. In general, before entering the Ombudsman shall notify the person in charge of his or her intention (s24(2) OA). The OA does not contain an explicit provision as to whether or not the Ombudsman can speak with persons alone.

---

[19] The Minister of Justice may exclude the right of access "to any specified premises or class of premises", if he or she is convinced that this might prejudice "the security, defence, or international relations of the Cook Islands, including the Cook Island's relations with the Government of any other country or with any international organisation" (s24(3) OA).

[20] If dealing with an organisation listed in Part II of the Schedule; in this case, a copy shall also be sent to the responsible Minister.

It is an offence to wilfully obstruct, mislead, or attempt to mislead the Ombudsman or to wilfully fail to comply with the Ombudsman's lawful requirements without justification or excuse (s27 OA). Every person committing an offence against the OA is liable to a fine not exceeding New Zealand $ 200 on summary conviction.[21]

16.2.3.2 Relation to the Judiciary

The Ombudsman cannot investigate judicial proceedings (s11(1) and (7) OA). He or she may only investigate those decisions or recommendations by the Department of Justice and the Lands (DoJL) and the Crown Law Office[22] relating purily to a matter of administration.

If there is ambiguity whether the Ombudsman has jurisdiction, he or she may apply to the High Court for a declaratory order (s11(8) OA).

Under the OIA, courts or tribunals are also not under the Ombudsman's jurisdiction (s2(6) OIA). The law foresees the possibility to seek a final decision by a court as follows: If the Ombudsman forms the opinion that information requested was correctly withheld, the requester may seek judicial review of both the initial decision to withhold the information and of the Ombudsman's determination (s40 OIA). If the Ombudsman makes a recommendation that information which was withheld should be released, the agency concerned may seek judicial review or a veto of the Ombudsman's recommendation. If the recommendation is not vetoed, the organisation holding the information is subject to the public duty to release. If the agency does not comply with this public duty, it can be enforced by a court. If an Ombudsman's recommendation is vetoed, a statutory review procedure is available to the requester (s37 OIA).

16.2.3.3 Relation to the Legislator

The Ombudsman is an Officer of Parliament (s3 OA) and as such is responsible to Parliament only. He or she reports to Parliament on the exercise of his or her functions annually (s26 OA). In addition to the usual annual reporting process the Ombudsman may report on any particular case or on general issues. There are no specific rules regarding the participation of the Ombudsman in debates in Parliament.

Parliament may make general rules for the guidance of the Ombudsman; such rules may authorise the Ombudsman "in the public interest or in the interest of any person or [D]epartment or organisation, to publish reports relating generally to the exercise of his [or her] functions under this Act or to any particular case or cases investigated by him [or her], whether or not the matters to be dealt with in any such report have been the subject of a report to Parliament under this Act" (s12 OA).

[21] The Cook Islands use New Zealand currency, New Zealand Dollar.

[22] Both the DoJL and the Crown Law Office are listed in the Schedule to the OA, Part I.

16.2.4 Other Characteristics

The Cook Islands have so far not signed or ratified the OPCAT.[23]

It is worth stressing, that under Freedom of Information legislation a recommendation of the Ombudsman becomes binding after 21 working days unless the Queen's Representative (s35(1)(2) OIA) directs otherwise, cf p. 217 above.

16.2.5 Workload

There is no current information available regarding the Ombudsman's workload.

16.2.6 Publications

The Ombudsman is required to submit an Annual Report to Parliament, covering the exercise of his or her functions under the OA (s26 OA). S26 OA grants the Ombudsman the right "to report at any other time". The Ombudsman can thus table special reports at any time, e.g. on own motion investigations. There are no specific provisions as to whether or how Parliament has to act upon submission of or on the consequences of non-submission of an Annual Report.

In September 2008, a fire destroyed the entire Ombudsman office, including the 2007 Annual Report as well as investigative material and equipment. The Ombudsman has published investigation reports prior to 2007.[24] The office has also published a brochure on the functions of the office and on the role of the Ombudsman, which is to raise awareness among the general public.

16.2.7 Annotations

There are currently no annotations.

---

[23] Cf Sect. 3.2.6.2, p. 55 for more details.

[24] Cf www.ombudsman.gov.ck/index.php/about-us.html for details.

References

Commonwealth Ombudsman (2009) Australasia and Pacific Ombudsman Region Information Manual 2009. Commonwealth Ombudsman, Canberra. www.ombudsman.gov.au/docs/APOR-Manual_20091009.pdf. Accessed 10 Nov 2011

New Zealand Law Commission (2006) Converging Currents-custom and human rights in the pacific, study paper, 1776; 17, Wellington

Further Reading

Overview of Legislation: www.ombudsman.gov.ck/index.php/legislation/ombudsmans-act.html?start=1 and www.ombudsman.gov.ck/images/stories/oi_act_2008.pdf

Constitution: www.parliament.gov.ck/Constitution.pdf

Annual reports: Currently not available online.

Chapter 17
New Zealand: Ombudsman

Michael Frahm

17.1 General Information

New Zealand was first inhabited by Polynesian Māori in about 800 AD. It was a British colony between 1840 and 1907, when it became independent and a member of the Commonwealth of Nations. New Zealand is a constitutional monarchy with a parliamentary democracy (unicameral system). The Parliament of New Zealand (Pāremata Aotearoa) consists of the Sovereign, represented by the Governor-General, and 120 Members who are directly elected for a term of three years by universal suffrage (s10 Constitution Act). Head of State is the Queen of New Zealand (Queen Elisabeth II), who is represented by the Governor-General. The day-to-day affairs of the country are managed by the Prime Minister, appointed by the Governor-General, and by the Executive Council (s6 Constitution Act).[1]

New Zealand's population today stands at approximately 4.3 million people (population density 15.6/km^2) and consists of the following ethnic groups: Europeans 56.8 %, Asians 8 %, Māori 7.4 %, Pacific islanders 4.6 %, mixed 9.7 %, and other 13.5 %.[2] Wellington, with a population of approximately 390,000, is New Zealand's capital. Below the Central Government there is a local government level with 78 local authorities all over New Zealand. There are eleven Regional Councils, twelve City Councils (which are largely urban), 54 District Councils, and the Auckland Council. Official languages are both English and Māori. New Zealand's Ombudsman Institution became a member of the IOI in 1985.

There is no single constitutional document, but rather a series of legal documents, including acts of the Westminster Parliament in England and the New Zealand House

[1] Cf BBC country profile New Zealand (http://www.bbc.co.uk/news/world-asia-pacific-15357770) and CIA World Factbook (New Zealand).

[2] According to the 2006 Census.

M. Frahm (✉)
Ludwig Boltzmann Institute of Human Rights, Vienna, Austria
e-mail: michael.frahm@univie.ac.at

International Ombudsman Institute (ed.), *Australasia and Pacific Ombudsman Institutions*, 221
DOI 10.1007/978-3-642-33896-0_17, © Springer-Verlag Berlin Heidelberg 2013

of Representatives. The Constitution Act 1986 entered into force on 1 January 1987, bringing together fragmented pieces of legislation of constitutional significance and ending the right of the Parliament of the United Kingdom to pass laws the effects of which extend to New Zealand (s15 Constitution Act). The Constitution Act 1986 is New Zealand's present-day principal formal charter. Fundamental rights are covered by the New Zealand Bill of Rights Act 1990; the Imperial Laws Application Act 1988 confirms applicability of further important statutes in the field of fundamental rights, such as the Magna Charta, the Bill of Rights and the Habeas Corpus Acts (s2 and Schedule 1 of Imperial Laws Application Act 1988).

New Zealand's legal system is based on English Common Law with special land legislation for the Māori. A separate Māori Land Court, established in 1865, maintains records of title and ownership information of Māori land and hears cases relating to Māori land. The Supreme Court of New Zealand is the final court of appeal. Below, there are a total of 66 District Courts, a High Court as first instance or appeal body, and a Court of Appeal dealing with appeals from matters heard in the High Court. Matters referred to the High Court for appeal from District Courts and certain tribunals can be taken to the Court of Appeal for a second appeal if the High Court has granted leave.

17.2 The Ombudsman Institution

Te Tari -o- Ngā Kaitaki Mana Tangata—Office of the Ombudsman - Tari o te Kaitiaki Mana Tangata
Postal address: PO Box 10152
Zipcode: 6011 City: Wellington
Phone: +64.04.473 9533
Fax: +64.04.471 2254
E-mail: office@ombudsman.parliament.nz
Website: www.ombudsman.parliament.nz

Toll free line: 0800 802 602

17.2.1 Overview

17.2.1.1 Legal Basis

After Sweden (1809), Finland (1919) and Denmark (1953), New Zealand was the fourth country in the world and the first country in the Commonwealth, to establish an Ombudsman Institution in 1962.[3] The 1962 Parliamentary Commissioner

[3] Cf Reif (2004), p. 6 and Keith (2005).

(Ombudsman) Act prescribes the office as a national Institution with a general mandate. In establishing the office, New Zealand followed the Danish model,[4] adapting it to a Common Law context as necessary.[5] The Act was modified in 1968,[6] and in 1975 the current Ombudsman Act came into force, extending jurisdiction to include local government agencies and allowing for more than one Ombudsman to be appointed (s3(1) Ombudsman Act 1975, hereinafter "OA"). Currently the office is led by two Ombudsmen, who are Officers of Parliament.[7] The OA does not grant general jurisdiction over all executive agencies. Thus, the Act's Schedule 1 (with the list of agencies under jurisdiction) needs to be amended whenever a new agency or Department is to come under the Ombudsmen's jurisdiction.

In addition to the Ombudsmen, there is a Human Rights Commission which has been accredited by the ICC as a "status A" NHRI, i.e. that it is in full compliance with the Paris Principles.[8] In addition to the Human Rights Commission, there is also the Commissioner for Children and the Health and Disability Commissioner. All three are within the Ombudsmen's jurisdiction.[9] Further, there is the Independent Police Conduct Authority (IPCA), which is not within the Ombudsmen's jurisdiction.[10]

While the OA still is the legal basis today, significant changes to the power of the Ombudsmen have taken place — mostly outside of the establishing Act. Freedom of Information legislation promulgated in the 1980s made the Ombudsmen responsible for investigating complaints about decisions concerning requests for access to official information (Official Information Act 1982, OIA and Local Government Official Information and Meeting Act 1987, LGOIMA). The Crimes of Torture Act 1989 (COTA), enabling the country to meet its international obligations under the Convention against Torture (CAT),[11] designated the Ombudsmen as a National Preventive Mechanism (NPM). In the year 2000, the Protected Disclosures Act (PDA) added powers in the field of whistle-blower protection to the Ombudsmen's tasks.

---

[4] Other than the Swedish and Finnish Ombudsmen, who have both prosecutorial powers and jurisdiction over the judiciary, the Danish Ombudsman has neither of these functions.

[5] Cf Elwood (2009).

[6] The jurisdiction of the Ombudsmen was extended to include education and hospital boards, cf Pak-Kwan (2006), p. 16.

[7] There is no statutory definition of an Officer of Parliament. The term is used to refer to certain types of independent officers who have the statutory obligation to report directly to Parliament.

[8] Cf Sect. 1.1.3, p. 6 for details.

[9] They are listed in Schedule 1 of the Ombudsmen Act, which entitles the Ombudsmen to investigate complaints filed against them.

[10] Cf Pak-Kwan (2006), p. 16.

[11] UN Convention against Torture and Other Cruel, Inhuman or Degrading Treatment or Punishment (CAT), General Assembly Resolution 39/46 of 10 December 1984, entry into force 26 June 1987.

After the founding of the office 50 years ago, numerous complaint bodies were established either overlapping or *de facto* reducing the jurisdiction of the Ombudsmen in certain fields. These bodies include not only the above-mentioned Human Rights Commission, the Commissioner for Children, the Health and Disability Commissioner and the IPCA, but also other Officers of Parliament, the Privacy Commissioner and the Inspector-General of Intelligence and Security.[12]

17.2.1.2 Legal Status and Independence

The Ombudsmen are appointed by the Governor-General on recommendation of the House of Representatives (s3 OA). An Ombudsman could be appointed on the recommendation of a simple majority of the House but, in practice, all appointments are made on unanimous recommendation of the House. Parliament can design general rules for the guidance of the Ombudsmen in the exercise of their functions (s15(2) OA). An Ombudsman is appointed for a term of five years, can be reappointed infinitely, but must retire by the age of 72 (s5 OA). There are neither any statutory qualificational requirements for an Ombudsman nor any requirements ensuring that members of the Institution reflect the composition of society. An incompatibility clause bars an Ombudsman from being a Member of Parliament or of a local authority (s4 OA). An Ombudsman shall not hold any office of trust or profit or engage in any occupation for reward outside the duties of his or her office.

As Officers of Parliament, the Ombudsmen are only responsible to Parliament and are not subject to ministerial control. They report to Parliament via the Speaker of the House at least once a year (s29 OA). The law stipulates that, if an Ombudsman believes legislative changes to be necessary after an investigation, he or she shall report this opinion to the appropriate Department (s22(3)(e) OA). In practice, the Ombudsmen also provide advice on relevant legislative, policy and administrative proposals, and the operation of official information legislation, a role provided for by the Cabinet Manual and the Guidelines of the Parliamentary Legislation Advisory Committee.

An Ombudsman can be removed or suspended from office; however, only the Governor-General, upon an address from Parliament, is competent to take such a step. According to an exhaustive list in the law, inability to perform the functions of the office, bankruptcy, neglect of duty or misconduct qualify as reasons for removal from office (s6(1) OA). If Parliament is not in session, the Governor-General may act due to the above-mentioned reasons, but can only suspend an Ombudsman until up to "two months after the beginning of the next Parliamentary session" (s6(2) OA).

Proceedings of an Ombudsman cannot be questioned or made subject to review (s25 OA). Anything said or provided in the course of a proceeding is privileged in

[12] Cf Chen (2010), p. 724.

the same manner as if they were court proceedings (s26(3) OA). Ombudsmen and their staff are immune from legal prosecution with regard to the exercise of their functions. They shall not be called to give evidence in court in relation to anything that comes to their knowledge in the exercise of their functions (s26(1) OA).[13]

Salary, allowances and other expenses are determined by the Remuneration Authority (s9 OA). As a safeguard, the law provides that the salary is not to be diminished in course of the current term of the Ombudsman's appointment. The Remuneration Authority may fix scales of salaries/allowances (or ranges of rates of remuneration), and may prescribe rules governing the application of any such scales (s12(2) Remuneration Authority Act). It does so for the Ombudsmen, the Prime Minister and other Ministers. An Ombudsman receives approximately 75 % of what the Prime Minister is entitled to.

The Chief Ombudsman may appoint such officers and employees "as may be necessary for the efficient carrying out of the functions, duties, and powers of the Ombudsmen" (s11 OA). Members of staff are not considered members of the public service in terms of the State Sector Act 1988, which underlines the independence of the office from the executive arm of government.

17.2.1.3 Organisation

If there is more than one Ombudsman, one of them is appointed Chief Ombudsman (s3(4) OA). He or she is in charge of the administration of the office, of the coordination and allocation of work between the Ombudsmen and of appointing staff (s11(1) OA). However, this position does not include the supervision of investigations conducted by the other Ombudsmen; insofar, each Ombudsman is completely independent.

While the office's headquarters are in the capital Wellington, two regional offices have been established in Auckland and Christchurch. Each Ombudsman has the responsibility for certain agencies under his or her jurisdiction. The office's Practice Leadership Team, in charge of supporting the implementation of an enhanced quality assurance regime, is led by the Ombudsman as Head of Professional Practice. It consists of the three Assistant Ombudsmen (in charge of the office Auckland, the administrative structure on Prisons, and the administrative structure on Policy and Professional Practice) and the Investigations Team Leaders. There are a total of 63 staff working in the office, including its sub-offices.[14]

The Institution is financed from funds appropriated by Parliament by a separate vote, the Vote Ombudsman (s9(1) and s31 OA). The office is accountable for its budget to the officers of the Parliament Select Committee. This Parliamentary Committee is made up of representatives from most of the political parties

[13] Exceptions exist in relation to certain offences against the state or corruption offences under the Crimes Act 1961 (s26(2) OA).

[14] As of 1 September 2011.

represented in Parliament and is chaired by the Speaker of the House. The budget for the financial year 2010–2011 was NZ$ 8,578,000 (US$ 6,848,675 as of 4 May 2012).[15]

While there are voices that point out the need for reform after 50 years of the Institution's existence,[16] no Government plans concerning this matter have been announced so far.

17.2.2 Mandate

17.2.2.1 Object of Control

There is no statutory presumption of jurisdiction over all public administrative authorities; the law rather lists all bodies falling under the Ombudsmen's jurisdiction in an enumerative way. Hence, the Ombudsmen's jurisdiction comprises any Government Department or organisation listed in Schedule 1 to the OA (s13(1) OA). These include Central Government Departments and organisations, prisons, the educational sector and hospital boards as well as local government agencies, including district, city and regional councils. The same applies to the Ombudsmen's functions under the OIA (s2 and s28 OIA) and LGOIMA (s2 and s27(1) LGOIMA); entities can also be declared subject to the Ombudsmen's jurisdiction in their own legislation. In respect to Freedom of Information complaints, jurisdiction also covers Ministers of the Crown, the Police and the New Zealand Security Intelligence Service.

In addition, state-owned enterprises (e.g. Postal Service) or statutory corporations (e.g. the Railway Services) providing public services are also under the Ombudsmen's jurisdiction. While they also provide public services, privately organised electricity and telecommunication suppliers are not under the Ombudsmen's jurisdiction. There is, however, a free and independent dispute resolution scheme available for consumers in both areas. The provision of services to asylum seekers as well as community welfare is also under the Ombudsmen's jurisdiction. Private individuals can never be the subject of an investigation by the Ombudsmen.

Complaints falling within the jurisdiction of another Officer of Parliament shall, after consultation with that office, be referred to either the Privacy Commissioner, the Health and Disability Commissioner or the Inspector-General of Intelligence

[15] Cf Annual Report 2010/2011, p. 78.

[16] Cf Chen (2010), p. 760. Chen argues that there should be *inter alia* "a single fixed term appointment for Ombudsmen of seven years" to strengthen the Ombudsmen's independence, that the law should include "a presumption that Ombudsmen have jurisdiction over all [D]epartments and organisations that exercise public power" instead of the existing enumerative list in the Schedule 1 and that the Ombudsmen should be "expressly empower[ed . . .] to undertake education about the Act [. . .]".

and Security, respectively (s17A, s17B and s17C OA). While employment-related complaints are not expressly excluded from the jurisdiction of the Ombudsmen, the Employment Relations Act 2000 confers exclusive jurisdiction to the Employment Relations Authority. Therefore, if individuals complain to an Ombudsman, such complaints will almost certainly not be investigated by an Ombudsman. Decisions made by courts, tribunals or the Parole Board[17] are also outside jurisdiction, as are Government Ministers, the Police or the New Zealand Armed Forces (s13(7) and (8) OA).

17.2.2.2 Standard of Control

The core purpose of the office is to investigate "any decision or recommendation" made or "any act done or omitted" that relates to a matter of administration[18] and affects any person or group of persons in his, her or its personal capacity (s13(1) OA). In the area of Freedom of Information, these complaints may refer to decisions on requests for access to official information (s28 OIA, s27 LGOIMA).

The Ombudsmen's criteria of control are quite broad; they shall act if, after an investigation, the matter[19] "appears to have been contrary to law"; was "unreasonable, unjust, oppressive, or improperly discriminatory, or was in accordance with a rule of law or a provision of any act, regulation or bylaw, or a practice that is or may be unreasonable, unjust, oppressive, or improperly discriminatory; or was based wholly or partly on a mistake of law or fact; or was wrong" (s22(1) OA). They are also to act if a "discretionary power has been exercised" for an improper purpose or on irrelevant grounds (s22(2) OA).

Under the OA, any person, group of people or legal entity with an interest in the subject matter can complain to an Ombudsman (s13(1) OA). Also, the OIA and LGOIMA allow anyone to request official information, the only limitation being that both natural and legal persons need to have a connection to New Zealand (in case of companies, this means that they must be incorporated in New Zealand or have a place of business in New Zealand). In addition to a complaint as catalyst for an investigation, an Ombudsman may initiate an own motion investigation at any time (s13(3) OA). Lastly, any Parliamentary Committee or the Prime Minister may refer for investigation and report any petition that is before that Committee

[17] The Parole Board's objective is to assess the risk long-term sentenced criminal offenders might pose to the safety of the community, if release prior to the end of their sentence is considered. It also sets the conditions of release for offenders with a view to their reintegration, cf www.paroleboard.govt.nz for more details.

[18] Cf Keith KJ 2005, Development of the role of the Ombudsman with reference to the Pacific. Speech held at the 22nd APOR Conference, p. 2 for more details.

[19] To improve readability, the text refers only to "matter". However, this term shall be understood as including any decision or recommendation made or any act or omission undertaken.

respectively any matter which the Prime Minister considers should be investigated by an Ombudsman that is within the office's jurisdiction to an Ombudsman with the consent of the Chief Ombudsman (s13(4) and (5) OA).[20]

Complaints can be made orally or in writing (s16 OA). They can be made anonymously, however, for reasons of practicality, the complainant's name should be given. Persons in custody have the right to lodge a petition in a closed envelope to be forwarded immediately to the Ombudsmen (s16(2) OA). Proceedings before the Ombudsmen are free of charge.

If there is an adequate alternative remedy reasonably available to the complainant or if the complainant has had knowledge of the matter for more than twelve months before he or she turned to an Ombudsman, an Ombudsman has discretion to refuse an investigation (s17(1) OA). However, it is not a requirement to exhaust other remedies, and there may be cases where an Ombudsman considers it appropriate to investigate a complaint even if there are alternative paths of redress. According to a clause barring abuse, the Ombudsman may not investigate if the complaint is "trivial, frivolous or vexatious or not made in good faith", if any further investigation is unnecessary (s17(1)(b) OA), or if the complainant does not have a sufficient personal interest (s17(2) OA).

Under the OIA and LGOIMA, an Ombudsman can investigate decisions to withhold or delete information from documents released to the requester and other acts or responses limiting or modifying the original request as well as delays for responding to a request.

17.2.3 Powers

17.2.3.1 Relation to the Administration

Before starting an investigation, mostly initiated following individual complaints (s16(1) OA), an Ombudsman is to inform the head of the Department affected and give the Department the chance to be heard (s18 OA). An Ombudsman is reasonably free in undertaking investigations, which always are to take place in private. In the course of an investigation, an Ombudsman has the right to speak with persons, including detainees, alone, if he or she so wishes (s18(2)(3) and (7) and s19 (1) and (2) OA).

He or she may autonomously regulate the investigation procedure (s18(7) OA), hear or obtain information from any person, make such inquiries as he or she thinks fit (s18(3) OA), require a person to provide certain information or documents (s19 (1) OA), and summon and examine certain persons under oath (s19(2) OA). The general public interest immunity against disclosure or production of documents is usually excluded (s20 OA). The Ombudsmen are entitled to on-site visits of any

[20] In such case, an Ombudsman shall report back to Parliament (s13(4) and (5) OA).

premises occupied by a body under their jurisdiction and may inspect them, but are required to notify the respective person in charge beforehand. In exceptional cases, the Attorney-General may exclude the right of access to certain sensitive premises (s27 OA).

If, after having finished an investigation, an Ombudsman believes that a rectification is required, he or she reports said opinion to the agency concerned and makes such recommendations as he or she thinks fit (s22(3) OA). While there is no formal time limit for investigations, the office aims to complete 90 % of its cases within six months.

An Ombudsman shall consult any Minister, respectively Mayor or chair of the organisation concerned who so requests or to whom a recommendation has been made, before he or she forms a final opinion (s18(4) and (5) OA). In addition, as a general principle an Ombudsman shall not make any comment that is adverse to any person unless the person has been given an opportunity to be heard (s22(7) OA). At the end of an investigation, an Ombudsman at first forms a preliminary opinion. Both the complainant and the organisation are given an opportunity to comment before an Ombudsman renders the final decision. A copy of the recommendation must be provided to the relevant Minister, Mayor or chairperson of the agency concerned (s22(3) OA).

While an Ombudsman has no coercive powers, the OA foresees several steps to exert some pressure in promoting the implementation of recommendations. First, an Ombudsman may request the public body concerned to notify him or her, within a specified period of time of the steps it proposes to take in order to give effect to the Ombudsman's recommendations. Second, the OA foresees the sending of a copy of the final report and recommendations to the Prime Minister and thereafter the reporting to the House of Representatives (s22(4) OA). On a local level, an Ombudsman may require a local authority to make a summary of his or her report available for inspection by members of the public (s23 OA).

Most of the above procedural steps also apply to investigations under the OIA and LGOIMA. However, when, in the course of a Freedom of Information investigation, an Ombudsman requests an agency to provide any information or document, said agency is required to comply with this request within 20 working days (s29A OIA and s29 LGOIMA).

The Ombudsmen have additional powers with regard to prisons. In case of deaths in custody,[21] the office monitors the process of the investigation of the death conducted by the Inspectors of Corrections to confirm that the investigation was properly conducted.[22] Under the Ombudsmen's own motion jurisdiction, they

[21] These additional powers are specified in a Protocol between the Chief Ombudsman and the Chief Executive of the Department of Corrections. Information provided by the Institution.

[22] According to information provided by the Institution, this means in practice that an Ombudsman investigator visits the prison, examines relevant paperwork, and attends the Inspector's interviews of significant witnesses. Ultimately, the Ombudsman is provided with a copy of the Inspector's report, and passes his or her comments on to the Chief Executive of the Department of Corrections.

also conduct investigations of selected "serious incidents"[23] in prisons and of selected systemic issues.[24]

Under Freedom of Information legislation, the requester may seek judicial review of both the initial decision and the Ombudsman's determination if an Ombudsman concurs with an agency's initial decision to withhold certain information (s29(2) and s34 OIA, s28(2) and s37 LGOIMA). In the opposite situation, the agency concerned may seek a veto of the Ombudsman's recommendation by the Governor-General (s32 OIA), respectively by the local authority (s32 LGOIMA). If a veto is not granted, the decision to release the information withheld by the respective agency can be enforced by a court. If an Ombudsman's recommendation is vetoed, a statutory review procedure is available to the requester (s32B OIA and s34 LGOIMA).

Under the PDA, the Ombudsmen are among the "appropriate authorities" to whom protected disclosures can be made. The Ombudsmen also provide information and counsel to any employee who has made, or is considering to make, a protected disclosure (s10 PDA). If the disclosure relates to an alleged serious wrongdoing of a public sector organisation, the Ombudsman has jurisdiction to investigate the subject matter of such a disclosure. In this case his or her powers are similar as under the OA (s15E (1) and (2) PDA).

The Ombudsmen are also required to advise the Secretary of Transport on applications for authorised access to personal information on the Motor Vehicle Register under the Land Transport Act 1998 (s241 Land Transport Act).

The Ombudsmen have been declared a National Mechanism designated to protect and monitor the implementation of the UN Convention on the Rights of Persons with Disabilities (CRPD); they do so within the scope of their functions under s13 OA.

It is an offence and can be sanctioned with a fine to wilfully obstruct, mislead, or attempt to mislead an Ombudsman or to wilfully fail to comply with an Ombudsman's lawful requirements without justification or excuse (s30 OA).

17.2.3.2 Relation to the Judiciary

The Ombudsmen have no jurisdiction over the judiciary (s13(1) OA). The establishing act explicitly stipulates that an Ombudsman shall not investigate any matter in which the complainant has a "right of appeal or objection, or a right to apply for a review, available to the complainant, on the merits of the case, to any [c]ourt, or to any tribunal" (s13(7)(a) OA). This exclusion is irrespective of whether

[23] There is no legally binding definition of a 'serious incident'.

[24] Following a request from the Government in 2008/2009, the Ombudsmen have agreed on taking on this enhanced role in prisons, which includes a major part in investigating deaths in custody and being the contact point for prisoners complaints. This initiative aimed at altering the public perception that the Department of Corrections was investigating itself as well as at increasing public confidence in the oversight and accountability systems in the Department.

or not the complainant has *de facto* exercised the appeal or application. Within its general powers, an Ombudsman may investigate any administrative matter, which also includes those actions by the Ministry of Justice and the Department of Corrections which are listed in Schedule 1 to the OA (s13 OA). However, courts, tribunals and other judicial proceedings and the Police are not under the Ombudsmen's jurisdiction (s13(7)(a), 7(d) OA). Likewise, Freedom of Information legislation excludes courts and tribunals, since the law's definition of the term "Department and organisation" does not include either courts or tribunals (s2(6) OIA).

If there is ambiguity as to whether an Ombudsman has jurisdiction to investigate a specific case or class of cases, an Ombudsman may address the Supreme Court by filing an application for a declaratory order to determine the question.[25]

17.2.3.3 Relation to the Legislator

Being appointed Officers of Parliament, the Ombudsmen may address Parliament for different reasons. First, they are to report to Parliament annually (s29 OA); second, if they consider it appropriate to inform the legislator on any particular case or on general issues, they may submit additional reports at any time. Third, the Ombudsmen may also, as a form of support of remedial actions proposed by them, report to Parliament on a specific case if, after the submission of recommendations to the appropriate agency, no action or no adequate action is taken (s22(4) OA).

The law does not formally foresee a broad role of the office in the field of legislative review. Only s22(3)(e) OA provides for an initiative to be taken by an Ombudsman if he or she, following an investigation, is of the opinion that a law on which a decision was based should be reconsidered.[26]

Beyond this statutory power, are the Cabinet Manual[27] and the Legislation Advisory Committee Guidelines[28] that allow for a wide involvement of the office in numerous activities related to legislation. The Ombudsmen[29] provide advice on relevant legislative, policy and administrative proposals, and the implementation of Freedom of Information legislation. To this end, Ombudsmen staff attend meetings,

[25] The determination is undertaken in accordance with the Declaratory Judgments Act 1908.

[26] However, even in such case an Ombudsman shall report his or her opinion directly to the agency concerned.

[27] The Cabinet Manual of the New Zealand Government provides that the office of the Ombudsmen should be consulted as appropriate in their areas of interest.

[28] The Legislation Advisory Committee Guidelines stipulate that the Ombudsmen should be consulted on the application of the OA and Freedom of Information legislation, when a new public body is being established.

[29] More specifically, the office's Policy and Professional Practice Advisory Group (PPPAG), led by an Assistant Ombudsman, provides this specific service.

provide verbal or formal written comments on discussion documents, options papers, and draft briefings or Cabinet papers.[30]

17.2.4 Other Characteristics

New Zealand ratified the OPCAT in March 2007.[31] Following the ratification, four institutions were designated as NPMs,[32] namely the Ombudsmen, the Children's Commissioner, the IPCA and the Inspector of Service of Penal Establishments. The Human Rights Commission was nominated as the central coordinating NPM (s16 and s26 COTA). The Ombudsmen are a designated NPM in respect to prisons, immigration detention facilities (under the Immigration Act 1987), health and disability places of detention, and youth justice residences (under the Children, Young Persons and Their Families Act 1989). In the latter area, the powers of the Ombudsmen overlap with those of the Children's Commissioner. The Ombudsmen regularly conduct own motion visits, inspect places of detention and release inspection reports.

Under Freedom of Information legislation, a recommendation of an Ombudsman becomes binding, i.e. the law imposes a public duty on the relevant agency to observe such a recommendation, from the 21st working day after the recommendation has been made unless the Governor-General (s32 OIA) or the local authority (s32 LGOIMA) directs respectively decides otherwise.

It is worth to be noted that the Ombudsmen are responsible for providing advice and counsel to (potential) whistle-blowers under the PDA. Another noteworthy feature is the fact that the name "Ombudsman" has been protected in New Zealand following an amendment of the OA in 1991. No person, other than an Ombudsman appointed under the OA, may use the name, and violation of this provision is an offence (s28A OA).

17.2.5 Workload

In the 2010–2011 reporting period, the office received 8,706 complaints and inquiries. Of these, 6,163 were made under the OA, 992 were OIA complaints and 256 were LGOIMA complaints.

---

[30] In the 2009–2010 reporting period, the office provided advice to Parliament on over 35 legislative, policy and administrative proposals. These proposals related to the provisions in the OA, Freedom of Information legislation, PDA and COTA.

[31] Cf Sect. 3.2.6.2, p. 55 for more details.

[32] Cf Sect. 4.1.3.9, p. 79 for more details.

Under the COTA, the Ombudsman inspected 23 places of detention and produced 20 inspection reports with a total of 103 recommendations for improvement. Under the UN Convention on the Rights of Persons with Disabilities, the office reviewed all complaints made and identified some 20 complaints that raised issues relevant to the Convention. Furthermore, the Ombudsman advised on 35 legislative, policy and administrative proposals.[33]

In the 2010–2011 reporting period, 62 % of the complaints came from prisoners or prisoner advocates (not all of them against the Department of Corrections).[34] The majority of complaints, namely 4,896 (79.4 %), were made against Departments of the Central Government: Department of Corrections, Ministry of Social Development, the Department of Labour (Immigration New Zealand) and the Accident Compensation Corporation (ACC).[35]

17.2.6 Publications

The Ombudsmen are required to publish an Annual Report (s29 OA). They are free to table special reports, e.g. on own motion investigations at any time. As NPM, the Ombudsmen shall prepare at least one Annual Report to Parliament and make it available to the general public (s27(c) COTA).

In addition, the office issues pamphlets, guidelines, case notes and a "Quarterly Review" aiming at informing and raising the awareness of members of the public about the office's functions.

17.2.7 Annotations

There are currently no annotations.

References

Chen M (2010) New Zealand's Ombudsmen Legislation: The need for amendments after almost 50 years. Victoria Univ Wellington Law Rev 41:723–760

Elwood B (2009) The Ombudsman travels to the Anglo-Saxon world. In: Speech held at the IOI world conference in Stockholm, June 2009, p 2

Keith KJ (2005) Development of the role of the Ombudsman with reference to the Pacific. In: Speech held at the 22nd APOR conference, p 2

[33] Cf Annual Report 2010/2011, p. 6 et seq.

[34] Cf Annual Report 2010/2011, p. 21.

[35] Cf Annual Report 2010/2011, p. 21.

Pak-Kwan C (2006) The jurisdiction of Ombudsman systems in selected places. Research and Library Services Division Legislative Council Secretariat, Hong Kong. www.legco.gov.hk/yr05-06/english/sec/library/0506rp05e.pdf. Accessed 5 Jul 2011

Reif LC (2004) The Ombudsman, good governance, and the international human rights system. Martinus Nijhoff, Leiden

Further Reading

Overview of Legislation: www.ombudsmen.parliament.nz/index.php?CID=100093

Annual Reports (2006 – 2011): www.ombudsmen.govt.nz/index.php?CID=100011

Chapter 18
Papua New Guinea: Ombudsman Commission

Michael Frahm

18.1 General Information

Papua New Guinea (PNG) consists of the eastern half of the island New Guinea and of numerous offshore islands and island groups. It gained independence from the UN trusteeship administered by Australia in 1975. It is a parliamentary democracy and Commonwealth realm. Head of State is the Queen Elizabeth II who is represented by the Governor-General. The single-chamber Parliament consists of 109 Deputies who are elected for a term of five years. The Prime Minister, appointed by the Governor-General manages the day-to-day affairs of the country together with the National Executive Council (the Cabinet).[1]

The population of Papua New Guinea is estimated at between 6 and 6.9 million, with a population density of 14.2/km^2.[2] Papua New Guinea's main ethnic groups are Melanesians, Papuans, Negritos, Micronesians and Polynesians. The country is administratively divided into 20 provinces, one autonomous region and the national capital district of the capital city, Port Moresby. Official languages are Tok Pisin, Hiri Motu and English; however, English and Hiri Motu are spoken by only 1–2 % of the population. Furthermore, there are approximately 860 indigenous languages.

The country's Constitution dates from 16 September 1975, Independence Day. It features "National Goals and Directive Principles" (art. 25(4) Const.), which include Basic and Fundamental Rights as well as Basic Social Obligations (art. 63(4) Const.). The death penalty has not been abolished in Papua New Guinea, however, the country is "abolitionist-in-practice".[3] Papua New Guinea's legal

[1] Cf BBC country profile Papua New Guinea (http://www.bbc.co.uk/news/world-asia-pacific-15436981) and CIA World Factbook (Papua New Guinea).

[2] UN estimate 2009, respectively CIA World Factbook 2010 estimate.

[3] Cf www.amnesty.org/en/death-penalty/countries-abolitionist-in-practice.

M. Frahm (✉)
Ludwig Boltzmann Institute of Human Rights, Vienna, Austria
e-mail: michael.frahm@univie.ac.at

International Ombudsman Institute (ed.), *Australasia and Pacific Ombudsman Institutions*,
DOI 10.1007/978-3-642-33896-0_18,

system is based on English Common Law. The principles and rules that formed the principles and rules of Common Law and Equity in England continue to apply as part of Papua New Guinea's underlying (i.e. Common) law (Schedule 2.2 Const.). After the country's independence, Common Law has been further developed through decisions of Papua New Guinea's own courts. The court system consists of Local Courts, District Courts, a National Court, which hears appeals from the District Courts, and the Supreme Court as the highest court, hearing appeals from decisions made by the National Court. In addition, there are Village Courts based on Customary Law, Special Tribunals dealing with land titles, and Leadership Tribunals dealing with potential misconduct in office.

18.2 The Ombudsman Institution

Ombudsman Commission of Papua New Guinea
Postal address: Deloitte Tower, Douglas Street, PO Box 1831
Zipcode: 121 City: Port Moresby
Phone: +675 308 2600 or +675 320 2555
Fax: +675 3203260
E-mail: ombudspng@ombudsman.gov.pg
Website: http://www.ombudsman.gov.pg/ or www.lawandjustice.gov.pg/www/html/118-the-ombudsman.asp

18.2.1 Overview

18.2.1.1 Legal Basis

The Ombudsman Commission has its legal foundation in the Constitution, which in art. 217–220 foresees the Commission as consisting of a Chief Ombudsman and two Ombudsmen. The Organic Law[4] on the Ombudsman Commission (OLOC) further implements the constitutional provisions, forming the frame for the Commission's work. The Commission is not based on any particular model. However, as far as the function of investigation of complaints in regard to actions of the administration is concerned, it follows the Swedish model. In addition, the Commission supervises and enforces the Leadership Code [art. 26–31 Const. and further implemented by the Organic Law on the Duties and Responsibilities of Leadership (OLDRL)] taking on anti-corruption responsibilities. The Leadership Code places state officials under explicit obligations in regard to good conduct and ethical behaviour. Furthermore, the Commission plays a role in anti-discrimination

[4] An Organic Law is a law or a system of laws that define and establish a Government, also called Fundamental Law, cf Black's Law Dictionary (2011).

activities (under the Discriminatory Practices Act 1975) and monitors the implementation of human rights.

The Commission, established after the gaining of independence in 1975, opened its office to the public the same year. In 1992, the Commission became a member of the IOI. Its jurisdiction includes all governmental bodies and their employees at federal, regional and local level. There are no other Ombudsmen with special mandates or jurisdictions. For its Leadership Code function, all public office holders as defined in the Constitution are subject to its jurisdiction (art. 26 Const). The Commission, which is not subject to direction and control by any person or authority (art. 217(5) Const.), has an oversight role over the three arms of government, acting as a check and balance. Due to this role it is increasingly referred to as the fourth arm of government.

In addition to the constitutional arrangements and the mentioned laws, the Organic Law on the Integrity of Political Parties and Candidates, the Leadership Code (Alternative Penalties) Act 1976 and the HIV/AIDS Management and Prevention Act 2003 also prescribe certain roles for the Commission.

18.2.1.2 Legal Status and Independence

The members of the Ombudsman Commission are appointed by the Head of State, who in turn acts in accordance with the advice of the Ombudsman Appointments Committee (art. 217(2) Const.). The latter consists of the Prime Minister as Chairman, the Chief Justice, the Leader of the Opposition, the Chairman of the Permanent Parliamentary Committee on Appointments, and the Chairman of the Public Services Commission (art. 217(2) Const.).

Any member of the Ombudsman Commission shall be a person of integrity, independence of mind, resolution and high standing in the community. One of the Ombudsmen must have professional accountancy qualifications and experience, and the other shall have administrative or legal qualifications and experience (s4 OLOC). There are no provisions in the law ensuring that the appointees reflect the composition of society. The term of office is six years for an Ombudsman and five years for the Chief Ombudsman. If the appointees are not citizens of Papua New Guinea, the term is three years. Members are eligible for indefinite reappointment (s5 OLOC). The upper age limit for serving as an Ombudsman is 55 years (s10 OLOC).[5]

The position of Ombudsman is incompatible with being a Member of Federal Parliament, of a provincial government body, a local government council or with being an office-holder in a registered political party. An Ombudsman further can not be "an un-discharged bankrupt or insolvent", "of unsound mind", or "under sentence of death or imprisonment" (s7 OLOC). Additionally, the law stipulates political and economic abstinence for an Ombudsman. He or she shall not actively engage in politics, engage either directly or indirectly in the management or control

[5] As an exception, a person who is between 55 and 60 years of age may be appointed for "special reasons" (s10(2) OLOC).

of a corporation or another enterprise, or acquire, by way of gift or otherwise, or use or hold in any other manner any interest in, any property of Papua New Guinea or solicit, accept or receive any other benefit in addition to his or her terms and conditions of employment (s8 OLOC). An Ombudsman may not be absent from duty for more than two weeks or more than 28 days in any period of twelve months.[6]

Commission members can be dismissed by the Prosecutor for misconduct in office under the Leadership Code. They can also be removed from office by the Appointments Committee on advice of a tribunal established under the Organic Law on the Guarantee of Rights and Independence of Constitutional Office Holders (OLGRICOH). Under this provision, the Ombudsmen may be removed only for the inability to perform their functions; misbehaviour; or breach of any Organic Law that sets out their employment conditions (s7 and s8 OLGRICOH). Ombudsmen may also resign with three months notice (s9 OLOC).

The salary and other conditions of employment of the Chief Ombudsman shall not be less than those of a judge other than the Chief Justice and the Deputy Chief Justice (art. 217(3) Const.). For the Ombudsmen, salaries are linked to that of the Prosecutor (art. 217(4) Const.). In practice, the Head of State has to determine the conditions based on advice of the National Executive Council, given after receiving a report from the Public Service Commission (s6 OLOC). S29 OLOC additionally stipulates that the Public Bodies (Financial Administration) Act 1969[7] applies to the Commission.

The Ombudsmen as well as officers and employees of the Commission are not liable for any "act or omission done or made *bona fide* and without negligence under or for the purposes [of the OLOC]" (s35 OLOC). They shall thus "not be called to give evidence in any court, or in any proceedings of a judicial nature, in respect anything coming to [their] knowledge in the exercise of [their] functions" (s35 OLOC). Any information or document in the course of proceedings of the Commission are privileged in the same manner as if the inquiry or proceedings were proceedings in a court (s35(3) OLOC).

The Constitution stipulates that the Commission is not subject to direction or control by anyone in discharging of its functions, and its proceedings are not subject to review in any way, except on the ground that the Commission has exceeded its jurisdiction (art. 217(6) Const.). All persons employed in the Commission are subject to the Commission's control and direction (s26 OLOC). Officers of the Commission are not public servants, but are employed in the service of the Commission (s25 OLOC), i.e. they are not bound by instructions from within the executive arm of government.

---

[6] Except on leave granted by the Head of State, due to illness.

[7] Now, the Public Finance (Management) Act 1995.

18.2.1.3 Organisation

The three Ombudsmen have equal power in discharging their functions, with the Chief Ombudsman as the administrative head. As *"primus inter pares"*, the Chief Ombudsman has both a casting and a deliberative vote if the vote is tied (s14 OLOC). For a quorum to conduct an inquiry, two members of the Commission are required to be present, always including the Chief Ombudsman, as he or she "shall preside at all meetings" (s14(2) OLOC). Matters are decided by the majority of votes.

The administrative structure of the Commission foresees two main divisions, the Complaints and Administrative Investigations Division, which investigates governmental bodies for wrong conduct, and, secondly, the Leadership Division, investigating misconduct of leaders. One part of the Complaints and Administrative Division is the Human Rights Unit with the task of ensuring the monitoring and implementation of international human rights obligations. There is also an Office of the Counsel and Corporate Services. In addition to the main headquarters in the capital, the Commission has three regional offices in Lae, Kokopo and Mount Hagen. In addition to the three Ombudsmen, the Commission employs 107 staff, 46 of who are female.

The Commission submits a budget proposal and determines expenditure annually. The Department of Treasury determines the budget allocation, and final approval is granted by Parliament in the annual appropriation.

The Government is in the process of establishing a Human Rights Commission (HRC). The Ombudsman Commission is involved in setting it up. While there currently is no NHRI,[8] the future HRC will be established on the basis of the Paris Principles and will aim at NHRI accreditation.[9]

18.2.2 Mandate

18.2.2.1 Object of Control

Jurisdiction extends to any state or provincial service, any governmental body, local government body, or any other body set up by statute which is either publicly funded or whose controlling authority's members are appointed by the Cabinet and any of its staff (art. 219 Const.). Jurisdiction also includes any staff of the Governor-General, Minister or leader of the opposition or any other body or person prescribed by law (art. 219(1)(v) Const.). As public service providers in the field of postal services, telecommunication, electricity supply, water supply, universities, health

---

[8] Cf Sect. 1.1.3, p. 6 for details.

[9] Information provided by the Institution.

insurance, and public hospitals are established by statute, the Commission is competent to investigate complaints against all these bodies.

Excluded from jurisdiction is the justifiability of a policy of Government,[10] a Minister or a member of the provincial executive except if it may be contrary to law or certain constitutional provisions[11] or to any act of Parliament. Further, the Commission cannot investigate the exercise of a rule-making power by a local government body or a decision of a court, except if the decision may show an apparent defect in law or administrative practice (art. 219(3)–(5) Const.).

As is mostly the case with Institutions operating according to the Ombudsmen's traditional functions, private persons cannot be subject to an investigation. However, the Commission also has the function to investigate any case of a suspected discriminatory practice in the provision of services within the Discriminatory Practice Act (DPA) and the HIV/AIDS Management and Prevention Act 2003. Discriminatory practice is defined as "discrimination either of an adverse or of a preferential kind practiced by a person or group of persons against or in favour of another person or group of persons for reasons only of colour, race or ethnic, tribal or national origin" (s1 DPA). Thus, also private individuals may be subject to an investigation if they are either holders of a licence (defined in s1 DPA) or if they are suspected of having acted, in or on premises that are subject to a licence in a discriminatory way, or if they are suspected to have incited racial hatred (s2–s4 DPA).

18.2.2.2 Standard of Control

Core function of the Commission under the OLOC is to investigate complaints in regard to any conduct of any agency or body under its jurisdiction (art. 219 Const and s13 OLOC). Also, it shall investigate alleged breaches of the Leadership Code (art. 219(1)(d) Const. and s18(1) OLDRL) and any case of an alleged discriminatory behaviour or practice (art. 219(1)(c) Const. as read with s1 DPA).

The Commission investigates whether a conduct is contrary to law, unreasonable, unjust, oppressive or improperly discriminatory,[12] based wholly or partly on improper motives, irrelevant grounds or irrelevant considerations, based wholly or partly on a mistake of law or of fact, or whether reasons should have been given for a conduct, but were not (art. 219(2) Const.). The term "conduct" only relates to a matter of administration. Therefore criminal conduct is excluded (art. 219(8) Const.). In its considerations, the Commission shall also take the Constitution's "National Goals and Directive Principles" (art. 25(4) Const.), the "Basic Rights" and the "Basic Social Obligations" (art. 63(4) Const.) into account as appropriate

[10] This includes the Federal Government as well as regional and local governments.

[11] These are the Constitution's "National Goals and Directive Principles", the "Basic Rights" or the "Basic Social Obligations".

[12] This is irrespective of whether or not it is in accordance with law or practice.

(art. 219(1)(a) Const.). Since the reference in art. 25(4) of the Constitution includes a reference to basic rights, also fundamental and human rights are included in the Commission's oversight activities.

The Commission has discretion to refuse an investigation (s16(3) OLOC) if its members are convinced that the complaint is trivial, frivolous, vexatious or not made in good faith or if the complainant has another remedy available to him or her that he or she could reasonably be expected to use. In addition, the Commission may decide that it has to focus on other matters more worthy of its attention; or that its resources are insufficient for adequate investigation. As an additional precondition, the complainant needs to show a sufficient interest in the subject of the complaint and should not delay the complaint too long. In case of alleged breaches of the Leadership Code, the Commission's discretion is more restricted and it cannot invoke the "other remedy available"- or "not-sufficient self-interest"- clause mentioned above. There is no discretion to concentrate on other cases more worthy of its attention either (s18(3) OLDRL). Any person may lodge a complaint with the Commission (s16(1) OLOC and s18(1) OLDRL), concerning any matter that is within its jurisdiction. The Commission may also investigate on its own initiative (art. 219(1) Const). Complaints may be registered by phone, fax, e-mail or in person in any of the offices. If necessary, they may need to be accompanied by documentation. Lodging a complaint is free of charge.

18.2.3 Powers

18.2.3.1 Relation to the Administration

Procedures may be initiated following individual complaints (s16(1) OLOC), by *proprio motu* (s16(4) OLOC)[13] or upon referral by any Parliamentary Committee and the Prime Minister with consent of the Chief Ombudsman (s13(4) and (5) OLOC). Practically, in case of a complaint, the Commission's assessment unit, after assessing the credibility of the information provided, makes a recommendation whether an investigation is warranted. Before the investigation begins, the Commission shall inform the person responsible of its intentions (s17(1) OLOC). In general, the Commission may decide on its own on how to regulate its procedures (s14(7) OLOC). All investigations shall be conducted in private (s17(2) OLOC) and shall give the body affected the chance to be heard (s17(3) OLOC).

The Commission may hear or obtain information from any person and make such inquiries as it thinks fit (s17(3) OLOC). It may consult a Minister who is concerned with the matter of the investigation (s17(5) OLOC) at any time during or

[13] Own motion investigations are often started in areas where trend analyses of complaints show particular areas of concern. They usually focus on systemic problems, e.g. on agencies' procedures or on defects in legislation.

after the investigation but shall consult any Minister who so requests before a final opinion is formed (s17(6) OLOC). In addition, the Commission shall not make any comment that is adverse to any person unless the person has been given an opportunity to be heard, and it shall outline the person's defence fairly in its report (s17(4)(b) OLOC). In the course of an investigation, the Commission may require a person to furnish certain information or documents (s18(1) OLOC and s21(1) OLDRL). It may summon and examine under oath any staff of any body under its jurisdiction (s18(3) and (4) OLOC and s21(3) and (4) OLDRL). The Commission may "direct that any evidence given before it, or any document, paper or thing produced to it, be not published" (s21 OLOC).

At the end of an investigation, if the Commission is of the opinion that there has been a breach of duty or wrong conduct, it shall inform the head of the body concerned in writing and make recommendations for change and shall send a copy of its report to the responsible Minister (s17(7) OLOC). In this case, the Commission can also require the relevant agency to suggest any steps it intends to take to implement the recommendations (s22(3) OLOC). If the Commission suspects a criminal offence, it may refer the matter to the Prosecutor (s22(2) OLOC). Similarly, if the Commission sees a *prima facie* case of misconduct in office under the Leadership Code, it shall refer the matter to the Prosecutor for prosecution before a Leadership Tribunal (s27(1) OLDRL).

If the Commission considers that "administrative action has produced unfair or objectionable results and that that action was caused wholly or partly by legislation", it shall forward a report on the matter to Parliament or to the respective provincial or local government body (s22(4) OLOC).[14]

Recommendations made by the Commission are legally non-binding. However, to give effect to its findings, the Commission may publish the results of any investigation by forwarding it to government officials and to constitutional office holders (s23 OLOC).[15] The Commission can also require the results of an investigation to be tabled in Parliament by providing a copy to the Speaker (s23(1)(d) OLOC). It is needless to say that, if a matter is referred to the Prosecutor, the Prosecutor is to follow the procedures established under the legislation regulating its work. As a rule, the Commission shall also forward a copy of its findings to the complainant. However, it may decide to keep a report confidential on the grounds of public security or public interest, in which case, it must inform the complainant in writing (s23(2) OLOC).

Proceedings related to the Leadership Code under the OLDRL are largely similar to the standard procedure described. However, other than the OLOC-procedure, the responsible person shall not be informed of the Commission's intention to investigate in advance; no consultation with Ministers is foreseen either. Further, there is no obligation to set out a person's defence in the statement of reasons according to

[14] Depending on whether the legislation concerned is federal, provincial or local legislation.

[15] These include the Prime Minister, Parliamentarians and other relevant bodies listed under s23 OLOC.

s20(3) OLDRL, which is required in case of OLOC-procedures by s17(4) OLOC. If the Commission determines that there is evidence for misconduct, it must refer the matter to the Prosecutor (s27(1) OLDRL). However, it must previously notify the person in question of this intention (s20(2) OLDRL). There are no rules to publish the results by forwarding them to Parliament as in s23 OLOC. Under the DPA, the procedures are similar to the procedures under the OLOC.

A Commission member may enter premises of any body over which the Commission has jurisdiction and may inspect premises and carry out investigations. Before entering, the person in charge of the premises should be notified (s36 OLOC).[16]

The Commission's human right function entitles it to visit places of detention. Under s74 Correctional Institutions Service Act, the Commission may conduct visits at any time. If possible, it should announce visits in writing in advance, usually in observation of a two weeks' advance notice.[17] Prisoners have the right to complain to the Commission without interference or influence from the institution in which they are detained (s16(2) OLOC). In practice, the Commission regularly visits prison facilities with a two-fold purpose. First, to gain a first-hand understanding of the particular correctional environment and how the prison is being managed, and secondly, to investigate complaints. Commission staff are entitled to speak to persons in detention alone.

There are criminal penalties for failing, without reasonable excuse, to attend the Commission or to produce any documents, for failure to cooperate, for refusing to be sworn or to answer any questions asked by the Commission, for giving false evidence or for contempt of the Commission (s23 and s30–s34 OLOC and s31–s35 OLDRL).

For leaders, there are also obligations sanctioned with a penalty that continue to stay in effect for three years after they cease to be a leader. If such a person without the approval of the Ombudsman Commission, accepts or holds a directorship, consultancy or any other prescribed position with a foreign enterprise within three years after ceasing to be a leader, he or she is guilty of an offence (s35 OLDRL).

A witness before the Commission has "the same privileges and is subject to the same penalties in relation to the giving of information, the answering of questions and the production of documents, papers and things as a witness before the National Court" (s18(5) OLOC).

---

[16] The Prime Minister may, after consultation with the Chief Ombudsman, exclude premises in order not to jeopardise national security, defence, or international relations of Papua New Guinea (s36(1) OLOC).

[17] According to information provided by the Institution, this allows the informing of the prisoners in advance so "they can put their name on the interview list". Also, it helps the facility's staff to "ensure that the prisoners are available for the interview". The Commission staff visiting the facility usually meets the head of the facility "for a briefing and a debriefing". The Institution added that, "[w]here possible, every attempt will be made to resolve the issues raised by prisoners and [. . .] staff during the visit while the Commission officer is present".

18.2.3.2 Relation to the Judiciary

Judicial proceedings are not under the jurisdiction of the Ombudsman Commission.[18] However, the judiciary as such is not entirely excluded from the Commission's jurisdiction, as the provisions of the Leadership Code also apply to a judge. The Commission may therefore investigate the behaviour of a judge. The Commission has the power to submit questions concerning constitutional interpretation or the application of any provision of a Constitutional Law to the Supreme Court, including any question concerning the validity of a law or proposed bill (art. 19 Const.). The Chief Ombudsman participates in judicial appointment processes, by virtue of his or her *ex officio* membership in the Judicial and Legal Services Commission (art. 183 Const. and Organic Law on the Judicial and Legal Services Commission).

The Commission regularly appears in court as a party to proceedings due to its role in enforcing the Leadership Code and its power to issue directions and special references to the Supreme Court.

While a decision of a tribunal is needed to dismiss leaders from office if they are found guilty of misconduct in office (s27(5) OLDRL), the Commission is also involved in the impeachment process, as the initial proceedings may be initiated by the Commission. This is the case if the Commission receives such a complaint or if it has formed the reasonable opinion that a leader may have breached the Leadership Code (s27(1) OLDRL). In these cases, the Commission may refer leaders to the Prosecutor, whose role it is to prosecute breaches of the Leadership Code. However, the Commission's decisions to refer leaders to the Prosecutor are regularly subject to judicial review actions, often relating to questions of procedural fairness. Furthermore, Commission directions to leaders under art. 27(4) of the Constitution also often result in judicial review actions being taken by the leaders involved.

The proceedings of the Commission are not subject to review in any way, except by the Supreme Court or the National Court on the grounds of it having exceeded its jurisdiction (art. 217(6) Const.).

18.2.3.3 Relation to the Legislator

The Ombudsman Commission reports to Parliament on its functions and workings annually through the Head of State, who presents the Commission's Report to Parliament (art. 220 Const.). The Permanent Parliamentary Committee on the Ombudsman Commission has the mandate to implement the Commission's recommendations made in its Annual Report. The Commission may also make recommendations for legislative amendments to the central or local level legislator if, following an investigation, it is of the opinion that an administrative action has produced unfair or objectionable results and that this was caused at least partly by

[18] Cf art. 219 Const. and s13 OLOC.

legislation (s22(4) and s23 OLOC). If such a recommendation is made to Parliament, discussions are held between the Ombudsman Commission and the Office of the Legislative Counsel, which has the primary responsibility to draft legislative proposals or legislative amendments.

The Commission may also report to Parliament on its functions in addition to the Annual Report (art. 220(2) Const.). After concluding investigations in an individual case, the Commission may decide to publish the results by forwarding copies *inter alia* to the Speaker of Parliament, who shall present it to Parliament within eight sitting days (s23 OLOC).

18.2.4 Other Characteristics

Papua New Guinea is not yet a state party to the Convention against Torture and other Cruel, Inhuman or Degrading Treatment or Punishment (CAT) and its Optional Protocol (OPCAT). During the presentation of the Papua New Guinea Universal Periodic Review in May 2011[19] the state parties made the recommendation for Papua New Guinea to ratify the CAT and the OPCAT. The Government has not made its position clear at this stage, although it has agreed to ratify the CAT.[20]

The Commission has a minor role regarding the monitoring of the implementation of international human rights obligations with its Human Rights Unit ensuring the monitoring or implementation of international obligations concerning human rights. All rights are described in the Constitution in art. 25 and art. 38. The Commission can examine human rights violations under its current mandate. However, the Commission's recommendations for corrective actions to administrative bodies are not legally binding, i.e. non-enforceable. Under the present legal regime there are no legal penalties for not implementing recommendations.

One special feature is the Commission's power with regard to discriminatory practice. The Commission may, either on its own initiative or following a complaint by a person affected, investigate any case of an alleged or suspected discriminatory practice (art. 219(1)(c) Constitution and DPA). The purpose of this function is to help government bodies eliminate unfair legislation or discriminatory practices against individuals.

In addition to the functions described above, the OLDRL obligates all leaders to provide a statement of income, assets and liabilities at least once a year to the Commission (s4 OLDRL). It further authorises the Commission to give directions[21] to ensure the observance of the Leadership Code (art. 27(4) Const.). Since failure to comply with a direction is itself a breach of the Leadership Code (art. 27(5) Const.),

[19] The Universal Periodic Review presentation at the United Nations Human Rights Council took place in Geneva on 11 May 2011.

[20] Cf also footnote 1.

[21] These directions may be of a general nature or aimed at a particular case.

the Commission *de facto* issues an authoritative interpretation of the Leadership Code. Similarly, any obstruction or failure to cooperate with the Commission constitutes misconduct in office (s23 OLDRL).

The Constitution furthermore grants the Commission the power to advise the Queen and Head of State and to consent to the Governor-General holding another office or position or engaging in another business outside of his or her duty as Governor-General (art. 87(3) and (4) Const.).[22]

Additionally, the Commission has the (potential) power to administer the (envisaged) Organic Laws regulating political parties, political donations and the protection of elections from outside or hidden influences (art. 129(1)(b) and (f), art. 130(1)(a) Const.).

An extra constitutional role is given to the Chief Ombudsman, who is *ex officio* member of the Judicial and Legal Services Commission, JLSC (art. 183 Const.). The JLSC appoints judges and certain other constitutional office holders like the Prosecutor.

18.2.5 Workload

The Commission reported 961 complaints in 2010, with the largest areas of complaints being entitlements in regard to different administrative areas (131 complaints), destruction of property (84) and terms and conditions of employment (71).[23] The office is working on its case management system so that in the future it will have a statistical breakdown with references to complaints from women, vulnerable and disadvantaged groups. In terms of investigations the Commission does not specifically focus on any area that falls within the ambit of its jurisdiction. Its own-initiative investigations are undertaken on an *ad hoc* basis, depending on the sensitivity of the matter, availability of relevant information and its resources.

18.2.6 Publications

The Commission is required to submit an Annual Report to the Head of State, for presentation to Parliament. The Report shall inform about the functioning and working of the Commission and shall include recommendations for improvement (art. 220(1) Const).[24] It may also include aspects of the Commission's Human

[22] This advice is given jointly with the Cabinet.

[23] In 2009, there were 1,096 complaints, mainly concerning entitlements (148 cases), unlawful exercise of office authority (73) and delays in general (68).

[24] The last Annual Report that was tabled before Parliament was the 2006 Report. Since 2007 no Annual Reports have been tabled.

Rights Unit and its objective of addressing human rights issues. The Commission may draft other reports on any aspect of its functions and workings on its own initiative or at the request of Parliament or of the Government (art. 220(2) Const.).

The Commission also publishes a monthly newsletter, which is distributed electronically and available online. It has further published two brochures as part of its community education programme: "Making a Complaint" and "Duties and Responsibilities of Leadership".

18.2.7 Annotations

An Ombudsman Commission Amendment Bill was introduced in 2010. This proposed Bill would remove certain powers of the Commission and is currently before the Courts. One of the powers in question is the power of the Commission to issue directions according to art. 27(4) Const. preventing leaders from using funds and/or from travelling overseas if it may be in breach of the Leadership Code. The court case is challenging the constitutionality of these amendments. If the court finds that the amendments are unconstitutional, they will be declared null and void, and of no effect.

Further Reading

Overview of Legislation: www.ombudsman.gov.pg/docs/relevant_laws_handbook.pdf
Annual reports: Currently not available online

Chapter 19
Samoa: Ombudsman

Michael Frahm

19.1 General Information

The Independent State of Samoa gained independence from New Zealand in 1962. Before that, it had been a German colony between 1900 and 1919, a League of Nations mandate of New Zealand from 1919 to 1945 and an UN trusteeship of New Zealand between 1945 and 1962. Samoa consists of two main islands, Savaii and Upolu, and several smaller islands (some of them uninhabited). It is a parliamentary democracy with a unicameral legislature. Parliament is elected through universal suffrage every five years. The Prime Minister and the Cabinet manage the state's day-to-day affairs.[1]

Samoa's population is estimated at about 190,000, with a population density of 63.2/km^2.[2] Ethnic groups include Samoans 92.6 %, Euronesians (i.e. persons of European and Polynesian descent) 7 % and Europeans 0.4 %. Official languages are Samoan and English. The country is administratively divided into eleven districts; the capital city is Apia.

The Constitution, dating from 1960, entered into force on Independence Day, 1 January 1962. It includes a chapter on fundamental rights. The Ombudsman is not embedded in the Constitution. The country's legal system is largely based on English Common Law, which was adapted to local customs. The court system includes two Magistrates Courts, a Supreme Court consisting of six local judges with jurisdiction in civil and criminal cases, and an Appeal Court, hearing appeals from the Supreme Court. The latter one sits once or twice a year and is overseen by

[1] Cf BBC country profile Samoa (http://www.bbc.co.uk/news/world-asia-15655855) and CIA World Factbook (Samoa).

[2] UN estimate 2008, respectively CIA World Factbook July 2011 estimate.

M. Frahm (✉)
Ludwig Boltzmann Institute of Human Rights, Vienna, Austria
e-mail: michael.frahm@univie.ac.at

International Ombudsman Institute (ed.), *Australasia and Pacific Ombudsman Institutions*, 249
DOI 10.1007/978-3-642-33896-0_19, © Springer-Verlag Berlin Heidelberg 2013

judges from overseas. In addition, there is a separate Land and Titles Court which deals with matters relating to customary land ownership and "matai" (chief) titles and which hears appeals from the Village Fono (traditional court).

19.2 The Ombudsman Institution

Komesina o Sulufaiga — Office of the Ombudsman
Postal address: Central Bank Building L5;
P. O. Box 3036, Apia
E-mail: info@ombudsman.gov.ws and ombuds@lesamoa.net
Website: www.ombudsman.gov.ws/index.html

19.2.1 Overview

19.2.1.1 Legal Basis

The Ombudsman was established in 1989 and opened its doors to the public in 1990. The Institution became a member of the IOI in 1992. The Samoan Ombudsman Act 1988 (OA) follows the New Zealand model.[3] Outside of the OA, which has not been amended since its inception, the Police Service Act 2009 gives powers to the Ombudsman in the area of auditing the work of the Police Professional Standards Unit (PSU). The office is led by the Ombudsman, who is an Officer of Parliament.[4] In Samoa there are no other Ombudsman Institutions with special mandates.

19.2.1.2 Legal Status and Independence

The Ombudsman is appointed by the Head of State on the recommendation of Parliament (s2 OA). The appointment is for three years, indefinite reappointment is possible (s4 OA). There are neither any qualificational requirements for the Ombudsman nor any requirements ensuring that the Institution reflects the composition of society. The position of the Ombudsman is incompatible with being a Member of Parliament, and the Ombudsman cannot, without approval of the Prime Minister in each particular case, "hold any office of trust or profit", or "engage in

---

[3] Ombudsman Act (New Zealand).

[4] There is no statutory definition of an Officer of Parliament. In Commonwealth jurisdictions the term is used *inter alia* to refer to certain types of independent officers who have the statutory obligation to report directly to Parliament.

any occupation for reward outside the duties of his or her office" (s3 OA). To ensure effective work of the office, the Ombudsman "may appoint such officers and employees as may be necessary for the efficient carrying out of his or her functions" (s9(1) OA). However, this competence is limited by the Prime Minister who determines the overall number of persons to be appointed (s9(2) OA).

The Ombudsman can be removed or suspended from office any time by the Head of State on the advice of Parliament. An exhaustive list in the law stipulates that removal may only be possible for "disability, bankruptcy, neglect of duty, or misconduct" (s5(1) OA). If Parliament is not in session, a suspension by the Head of State is still possible. This suspension is however limited and shall not continue in force "beyond 2 months after the beginning of the next ensuing session of Parliament" (s5(2) OA). The Ombudsman and his or her staff are immune from legal prosecution with regard to the exercise of their functions when acting in good faith. They shall not be called to give evidence in court in relation to anything that comes to their knowledge in the exercise of their functions (s22(2) OA). Anything said or provided in the course of an Ombudsman investigation is privileged in the same manner as if it were court proceedings (s22(3) OA).

Salary, allowances and other benefits of the Ombudsman are determined under the Remuneration Tribunal Act 2003 (s7 OA). Practically, the Remuneration Tribunal advises the Head of State, who, by order in writing to be published in a national newspaper, determines the salary of the Ombudsman (s6 and s9 Remuneration Tribunal Act). The salary shall be paid as "statutory expenditure out of the Treasury Fund, without further appropriation than this section" (s7 OA). Salaries of staff and terms and conditions of their appointments must be such "as are approved by Cabinet" (s9(3) OA). They are not considered members of the public service in terms of the Public Service Act and are therefore not part of the executive arm of government.

19.2.1.3 Organisation

The OA does not provide for a Deputy to the Ombudsman; however, s24 OA authorises the Ombudsman to delegate powers to other staff. The office has no additional sub-offices in the country. Structurally, in addition to the Ombudsman, the office employs one Assistant Ombudsman, one Principal Investigation Officer, one office Manager/Secretary, one Accounts Officer and one office clerk/receptionist. Two out of the six staff are female.

The office is financed out of "money to be appropriated by Parliament" for the purpose (s27 OA). In practice, the Ombudsman deals directly with the Treasury and controls its own separate budget. The office's annual budget is screened by the Parliamentary Public Accounts Committee. However, there is no parliamentary committee that examines the performance of the Ombudsman's office. The budget for the financial year 2010–2011 was Samoan Tala $ 488,071 (US$ 203,501 as of 4 May 2012).[5]

In 2011, the Ombudsman reviewed the OA and proposed to review the Schedule (referred to in s11(1) OA) which specifies to which bodies the OA applies as advised by the Parliamentary Counsel. Basis for the review is s28 OA, authorising the Head of State to amend the Schedule. The present proposal is to replace the current Schedule with a general clause in the OA itself, so that all government agencies and non-government agencies carrying out government functions are covered.

The Government has started an initiative to set up the Samoa Human Rights Commission. In 2011 a scoping exercise was undertaken with the intention to make the envisaged Commission an ICC-accredited NHRI.[6] The aim is for the Commission to be set up within the Ombudsman office, to be administrated by the Ombudsman and to equip him or her with the investigative powers for both the old and the additional functions. The Samoan Cabinet has already approved the Ombudsman to become the first Human Rights Commissioner.

19.2.2 Mandate

19.2.2.1 Object of Control

The jurisdiction of the Ombudsman is currently restricted to government bodies listed in the s11(1) Schedule annexed to the OA. According to this Schedule, Government Ministries, agencies or corporations and statutory boards (e.g. Airport Authority, Samoa Shipping Services and Public Service Commission) are subject to the scrutiny of the Ombudsman.

As far as other essential public services are concerned, the following providers are also under the Ombudsman's jurisdiction: Samoa Postal Service, Samoa Life Assurance Corporation (health insurance), Samoa Water Authority, Samoa National Provident Fund (pension insurance), Electric Power Corporation, Office of the Regulator (telecommunication), National University of Samoa, and National Health Services. Private persons, entities or other non-governmental organisations cannot be subject to an investigation. Also, decisions of the courts or of statutory tribunals are excluded, as are administrative actions that are subject to a right of appeal or objection or review on the merits by the courts and statutory tribunals (s11 (6) OA).[7]

---

[5] According to the Legislative Assembly of Samoa Approved Estimates of Receipts and Payments of the Government of Samoa for the Financial Year ending 30 June 2011, cf www.mof.gov.ws/Portals/195/SAMOA%20BUDGET/2010-2011/approved_estimates_fy2010-2011_english_version.pdf.

[6] Cf Sect. 1.1.3, p. 6 for details.

[7] The office is currently reviewing this provision.

19.2.2.2 Standard of Control

The office's main aim is to investigate "any decision or recommendation made" or "any act done or omitted" that relates "to a matter of administration and affect[s] any person or body of persons in his, her or [their] personal capacity" (s11(1) OA). The Ombudsman's criteria of control are quite broad; he or she shall act if, after any investigation, a conduct or an omission is "contrary to law", "unreasonable, unjust, oppressive, or improperly discriminatory", "based wholly or partly on a mistake of law or fact" or is "wrong" (s19(1) OA). The Ombudsman shall also act if a "discretionary power has been exercised" for an improper purpose or on irrelevant grounds (s19(2) OA). The Ombudsman may initiate an own motion investigation or investigate matters following a complaint (s11 OA). In addition, the Ombudsman shall initate investigations upon referral. Any Parliamentary Committee may refer any petition (or a matter to which the petition relates) that is before that Committee for consideration, to the Ombudsman (s11(3) OA). Also, with the consent of the Ombudsman, the Prime Minister may refer any matter which he or she considers worth investigating to the Ombudsman (s11(5) OA).

Complaints to the Ombudsman may be made by any individual, company, organisation or association with an interest in the subject matter of the complaint. Any complaint must be in writing (s13 OA) and must contain the necessary details such as the organisation complained about, how the matter complained about affects the complainant and relevant correspondence as appropriate. However, if a person has difficulties in drafting the complaint, he or she may request support by the Ombudsman's staff by telephone or in person. The issue complained about should not be older than twelve months (s14(2) OA). Additionally, if review by a court or tribunal of the merits is possible, use of this remedy should be made, as the Ombudsman has no jurisdiction to review the matter (s11(6a) OA). The Ombudsman further has discretion to refuse an investigation if the complaint is "trivial, frivolous, vexatious or is not made in good faith", if the complainant has no sufficient personal interest in the complaint or if the complaint is outside jurisdiction (s14 OA). While the OA provides for a Samoan Tala $ 10.00 fee, such a fee has never been charged from complainants.

19.2.3 Powers

19.2.3.1 Relation to the Administration

At the beginning of any investigation, the Ombudsman is obliged to inform the head of the body affected of the intention to investigate (s15(1) OA). The law stipulates that the Ombudsman shall conduct investigations in private (s15(2) OA), but is otherwise fairly free in regulating the procedure “as he or she thinks fit”, subject to the OA and any rules that may have been made by Parliament (s15(7) OA).

The Ombudsman may require a person to provide information, documents, papers or things under his or her control (s16(1) OA) and may also summon persons and question them under oath as necessary (s16(2) OA).[8] While the Ombudsman may hold a hearing, there is no obligation to do so. In cases where he or she considers to make a report that may adversely affect a Department, body or person the body affected must be given an opportunity to be heard (s15(3) OA).

During or after an investigation the Ombudsman may consult any Minister concerned (s15(4) OA). Upon request the Ombudsman must consult said Minister before forming a final opinion (s15(5) OA). If the Ombudsman is of the opinion that there is evidence for a breach of duty or for misconduct of an officer, the Ombudsman must refer the matter to the appropriate authority (s15(6) OA). Once the Ombudsman has formed his or her final opinion, he or she must report his or her opinion to the appropriate agency and must make recommendations. He or she shall also inform the Minister concerned (s19(3) OA). The OA does not foresee strong coercive powers. However, there are several steps to exert some pressure on the agency concerned to make it implement the recommendations. As a first step, the Ombudsman may request the agency to suggest which measures it proposes to take to execute the Ombudsman’s recommendations (s19(3) OA). If he or she does not receive a response or if the response received appears not appropriate, the Ombudsman may send a copy of the report and recommendations to the Prime Minister, and may thereafter report to Parliament on the matter as he or she thinks fit (s19(4) OA).

In the context of investigations, the Ombudsman has the authority to enter and inspect any premises of agencies subject to the OA and to carry out investigations (s23 OA).[9] However, before entry the Ombudsman shall notify the head of the Department occupying the premises. This includes the power to visit detention facilities, and while not explicitly stipulated in the OA, the Ombudsman is allowed to speak with detainees alone.

It is an offence and can be sanctioned with a fine of maximum 500 penalty units to wilfully obstruct, hinder, or resist the Ombudsman or to wilfully fail to comply with an Ombudsman’s lawful requirements without lawful justification (s26 OA).

19.2.3.2 Relation to the Judiciary

Decisions of the judiciary as well as acts which can be reviewed by the judiciary are excluded from the jurisdiction of the Ombudsman (s11(6a) OA). If there is

[8] Exceptions, which are to be certified by the Attorney-General, apply if the provision of information could “prejudice the security, defence, or international relations of Samoa” or might involve the disclosure of deliberations or of proceedings of Cabinet (s17 OA).

[9] Likewise, exceptions, which are to be certified by the Attorney-General, apply if the provision of information could “prejudice the security, defence, or international relations of Samoa” (s23(3) OA).

ambiguity about whether the Ombudsman has jurisdiction, an application can be made to the Supreme Court for a declaratory order (s11(7) OA). *Vice versa*, the judiciary cannot intervene regarding any decision made by the Ombudsman (s21 OA).

19.2.3.3 Relation to the Legislator

The Ombudsman is an Officer of Parliament. As such, he or she reports to Parliament on the office's work in an Annual Report (s25 OA). The law is silent about whether the Ombudsman is entitled to recommend legislative amendments. In practice, the Ombudsman recommends amendments on rare occasions, but only if appropriate and absolutely necessary.

Parliament may "make general rules for the guidance of the [Ombudsman] in the exercise of his or her functions" (s12(1) OA). These rules may authorise the Ombudsman "in the public interest or in the interests of any person or Department or organisation, to publish reports relating generally to the exercise of his or her functions" under the OA or "to any particular case" investigated by the office, whether or not the matters to deal with in such a report have been the subject of a report to Parliament (s12(2) OA).

19.2.4 Other Characteristics

Samoa has not signed or ratified the OPCAT[10] so far; currently there are no plans to this end. A potential additional new feature is the role of the Human Rights Commission for Samoa described above.

The Ombudsman has a specific role in overseeing the performance of the Police and thus fosters good administration in the public sector. The Police' Professional Standards Unit (PSU), which investigates complaints against the Police, encourages complainants and the public to turn to the Ombudsman if they are not satisfied with the handling of their concerns by the PSU. Under the Police Service Act 2009, the Ombudsman shall regularly review and report on the investigations of the PSU (s68 Police Service Act 2009).

19.2.5 Workload

In the 2009–2010 reporting period, the total number of complaints was 60. About 90 % of them referred to administrative matters; the remainder were alleged

[10] Cf Sect. 3.2.6.2, p. 55 for more details.

unreasonable actions, i.e. the failure to discharge duties. The administrative issues were often brought up by public servants who were dissatisfied with decisions or with the action respectively non-action of their agencies.

On his or her own initiative, the Ombudsman continuously monitors health services as well as the PSU.

19.2.6 Publications

The Ombudsman is required to submit an Annual Report to Parliament (s25 OA). It includes information on the exercise of the functions of the Ombudsman, on workload, statistics and case studies. Additionally, synopses of significant investigations are included. The OA does not state any consequences in case of non-compliance with this requirement. Also, the Ombudsman does not have an explicit role in parliamentary debates. Further, the Ombudsman may also table Special Reports on any issue he or she considers relevant, but has only done so if it is relevant and if it is a matter of public interest.

19.2.7 Annotations

The next challenge for the office will be the implementation of the provisions establishing the Human Rights Commission in the office of the Ombudsman and the execution of the additional tasks.

Further Reading

Overview of Legislation: www.theioi.com/downloads-ioi/2289h/Komesina%20O%20Sulufaiga%20%28Ombudsman%29%20Act%201988.doc

Annual Reports: Currently not available online

Chapter 20
Taiwan: Control Yuan

Michael Frahm

20.1 General Information

Taiwan consists of one main and several smaller islands. Following military defeat in 1895, China was forced to surrender Taiwan to Japan. China resumed control of the island after the end of World War II. When in 1949 the Communist movement prevailed on the mainland, Taiwan continued to adopt the pre-existing 1947 Constitution.[1] Due to China's "One China"-policy, Taiwan has no seat in the UN, and its application to join the UN under the name Taiwan was rejected in 2007.[2] Taiwan has become a multiparty democracy following transformations in the 1990s. Head of Government is the directly elected President. Legislator is the unicameral Legislative Yuan (the Parliament) which is elected by universal suffrage every four years. The Premier and the Cabinet (Executive Yuan) manage the daily affairs of Taiwan.

Taiwan has a total population of approximately 23.2 million people (population density 640/km^2),[3] with the Taiwanese (including the Hakka[4]) as the largest ethnic group, making up 84 % of the population, followed by 14 % mainland Chinese and 2 % indigenous people.[5] Languages spoken are Mandarin Chinese, the official language, Min Nan Chinese (or Taiwanese) and Hakka dialects. Taiwan is administratively divided into twelve counties, five municipalities and three special municipalities. The capital is Taipei.

---

[1] Cf CIA World Factbook (Taiwan).

[2] Cf news.bbc.co.uk/2/hi/asia-pacific/6913020.stm.

[3] June 2011 estimate for the end of May 2011, cf www.ris.gov.tw/web_eng/eng_index.html.

[4] Hakka are one of the ethnic groups of China and are considered a subgroup of the Han Chinese, cf www.britannica.com/EBchecked/topic/252138/Hakka.

[5] Cf CIA World Factbook (Taiwan).

M. Frahm (✉)
Ludwig Boltzmann Institute of Human Rights, Vienna, Austria
e-mail: michael.frahm@univie.ac.at

International Ombudsman Institute (ed.), *Australasia and Pacific Ombudsman Institutions*, DOI 10.1007/978-3-642-33896-0_20, © Springer-Verlag Berlin Heidelberg 2013

Taiwan's Constitution originates from 1947.[6] The Constitution envisages a five-powers-system of government with the Legislative Yuan, the Executive Yuan, the Judicial Yuan, the Examination Yuan[7] and the Control Yuan. The latter is the Taiwan Ombudsman. Taiwan's legal system is based on Civil Law. The Judicial Yuan[8] is Taiwan's highest judicial organisation. Below the Judicial Yuan, which includes the Justices of the Constitutional Court, there are 22 District Courts, a High Court (five branches), and the Supreme Court as the highest tribunal in civil and criminal cases. There is currently no ICC-accredited NHRI[9] in Taiwan.[10]

20.2 The Ombudsman Institution

Control Yuan
Postal address: No.2, Zhongxiao E. Rd., Sec.1
Zipcode: 10051 City: Taipei City
Phone: +886-2-2341 3183
Fax: +886-2-2341 0324
E-mail: cymail@cy.gov.tw
Website: www.cy.gov.tw

20.2.1 Overview

20.2.1.1 Legal Basis

The Control Yuan, foreseen in the Constitution, was established in 1948[11] and, following constitutional amendments, underwent reforms both in 1991 and in 1994.

---

[6] In addition to its 175 original articles, the Constitution contains twelve additional articles that have been added in seven rounds of revision since 1991.

[7] The Examination Yuan consists of Ministries and Commissions. Its Ministry of Examination conducts examinations for civil servants and professional and technical personnel. In addition there is a Ministry of Civil Service, which is responsible for all matters concerning employment, a Civil Service Protection and Training Commission and a Public Service Pension Fund Supervisory Board. Cf www.exam.gov.tw/cp.asp?xItem=6257&ctNode=603&mp=5 for more details.

[8] Functions of the Judicial Yuan include interpretation of the Constitution, impeachment of the President and Vice President, adjudicate civil, criminal and administrative cases and cases concerning disciplinary measures regarding public officials, see art. 77 and art. 78 Const., art. 5 of the Amended Constitution and art. 30, 43 and 75 of the Local Government Systems Act.

[9] Cf Sect. 1.1.3, p. 6 for details.

[10] According to information provided by the Control Yuan, there have been discussions in Taiwan on how to set up an NHRI which is fully in compliance with the Paris Principles. It appears, however, that, due to the unique five-powers-system of government, it may take some time to come to a consensus on this issue. The Control Yuan plays an important role in the protection of human rights.

[11] At the time of its first mandate, the Control Yuan functioned as an Upper House of Parliament with elected members.

The powers of the Control Yuan are defined in more detail in the Organic Law of the Control Yuan (also called the "Control Act") and the Organic Law of the Committees of the Control Yuan.[12] The constitutional amendments of the 1990s led *inter alia* to a new appointment process (see directly below), which was implemented for the first time in 1992.[13] In August 1994, the Control Yuan became a member of the IOI.

The Control Yuan is not based on any other Ombudsman model. Rather, it is part of the unique five-power system of government foreseen in Taiwan's Constitution. This system is based on the ideas of Sun Yat-Sen,[14] who considered the separation of powers into legislative, executive and judicial powers as inadequate. Therefore, Control and Examination powers were added to supplement the three-power system.[15] The Control Yuan has jurisdiction over all levels of government; there are no additional regional Ombudsman Institutions.

The Control Yuan draws powers not only from the Constitution and the already mentioned laws, but in addition from a range of other laws: the Act to Implement the ICESCR and the ICCPR,[16] the Act on Property-Declaration by Public Servants,[17] the Act on Recusal of Public Servants Due to Conflicts of Interest,[18] the Political Donations Act, the Lobbying Act,[19] the Law of Audit, and the Examination Invigilation Act.[20]

20.2.1.2 Legal Status and Independence

All 29 members of the Control Yuan are nominated and appointed by the President of Taiwan with the consent of the Legislative Yuan for a term of six years.[21]

---

[12] In Taiwan, an Organic Law needs to go through a three-reading procedure in the Legislative Yuan, while ordinary laws do not require such a procedure.

[13] Cf "historical background" under www.cy.gov.tw/mp21.htm for details.

[14] Sun Yat-Sen (1866–1925) is considered the father of modern China. He was the leader of the Chinese Nationalist Party (Kuomintang) and served as the first President of the Republic of China. Cf www.britannica.com/EBchecked/topic/573697/Sun-Yat-sen.

[15] Cf Chao (2010), p. 2.

[16] ICESCR stands for International Covenant on Economic, Social and Cultural Rights, ICCPR stands for International Covenant on Civil and Political Rights. By way of this Act, the provisions of both covenants become binding law in Taiwan although Taiwan is not a UN member, cf p. 257 above. In addition to the Act, the Rules Governing the Establishment of the Human Rights Protection Committee are also of relevance. Cf Liao (2001) for more details on the history of Taiwan's involvement in the international human rights regime.

[17] Including the Enforcement Rules of the Act on Property-Declaration by Public Servants as well as the Regulations Governing Examination and Browsing of Materials of Property-Declaration by Public Servants.

[18] Including the Enforcement Rules of the Act on Recusal of Public Servants Due to Conflicts of Interest.

[19] Including the Enforcement Rules of the Lobbying Act.

[20] These laws, except for the Act to Implement the ICESCR and the ICCPR, are also dubbed the "Sunshine Laws" for their function to make proceedings open to the general public.

[21] Cf Chao (2010), p. 3.

Members may be indefinitely reappointed (art. 7 Additional Articles to Const.). There are no pluralism provisions in the law to ensure that members of the Control Yuan shall reflect the composition of society. Legislation foresees the following qualificational requirements for a member of the Control Yuan: He or she must be over 35 years old and must have:

- Been elected Legislator for more than one term or provincial (municipal) councilor for more than two terms with distinguished reputation; or
- Been a senior judge for more than ten years and must have been judge or prosecutor in the High Court or Supreme Court with excellent performance; or
- Been a senior public official for more than ten years with excellent performance; or
- Been a university professor for more than 15 years with distinguished reputation; or
- Passed a Senior Qualification Examination for Professional and Technical Personnel and performed duties for more than 15 years with distinguished reputation; or
- Extensive experience in the handling of political, journalistic and cultural affairs with clean and decent reputation (art. 3.1 Organic Law of the Control Yuan).

Members of the Control Yuan may only be removed from office by other members of the Control Yuan in an impeachment process if found guilty of a violation of law or neglect of duty. The Control Yuan has established a Committee on Discipline for Control Yuan members for such cases.[22] The procedure follows the standard process as described at Sect. 20.2.3.1, below.

There are incompatibility clauses in the Constitution, according to which no member of the Control Yuan "shall concurrently hold any other public office or engage in any profession" (art. 103 Const.). Further, members shall be "beyond party affiliation and independently exercise their powers and discharge their responsibilities in accordance with the law" (art. 7 Additional Articles to the Const.). Members of the Control Yuan are immune to legal proceedings for anything done or said in pursuit of their duties and enjoy immunity to arrest or detention except when caught *in flagrante delicto* (art. 101 and 102 Const.).

The salary of the members of the Control Yuan is determined by law. The salary of the President and the Vice-President of the Control Yuan is linked to the salary of the Presidents and Vice-Presidents of the other four Yuans, and the salary of other Control Yuan members is equivalent to that of a Minister of the Executive Yuan.

[22] Art. 7(2) of the Additional Articles to Constitution stipulates that, in case of impeachment of Control Yuan personnel, also art. 95 and art. 97(2) Const. shall apply. According to these provisions, the Control Yuan may propose corrective measures or institute an impeachment.

20.2.1.3 Organisation

The Control Yuan consists of 29 members, including the President and the Vice-President (art.7 Additional Articles to the Const.).[23] Based on art. 96 Const., the Control Yuan has seven standing committees (on Domestic and Minority Nationality Affairs, Foreign and Overseas Chinese Affairs, Defence and Intelligence Affairs, Financial and Economic Affairs, Educational and Cultural Affairs, Communication and Procurement Affairs and Judicial and Prison Administration Affairs) and eight special committees (on Statutory Studies, Consultation, Administrative Appeals Review, Human Rights Protection,[24] Anti-Corruption, Discipline for Control Yuan members, Budget Planning and Administration, and International Affairs).

Two of the Control Yuan members serve the Control Yuan in the function of Secretary General and Deputy Secretary General and have the duty to oversee all Departments and offices. Administratively, the Control Yuan is structured in Departments. There is a Department on Supervisory Operations, a Department on Supervisory Investigation and a Department on Assets-Declaration by Public Functionaries as well as a Secretariat. In addition, the Control Yuan has a General Planning Office, an Information Management Office, an Accounting Office, a Statistics Office, a Personnel Office and an Ethics Office.[25] There are no sub-offices of the Control Yuan. However, members of the Control Yuan regularly visit different regions of Taiwan, as it is one of their functions to conduct "circuit supervision"[26] on a local level as well as on a central level. The Control Yuan had 465 staff in 2011.[27] Slightly less than half of all staff were women, i.e. 225 out of 465.

The Control Yuan has also set up the Ministry of Audit, including various Audit Departments and offices as subordinate agencies. While the Ministry of Audit is subordinated to the Control Yuan, its staff and budget are independent. The Auditor-General is, similarly to the process established for members of the Control Yuan, nominated and appointed by Taiwan's President with the consent of the Legislative Yuan.[28] He or she also serves a term of six years.

The Control Yuan is financed out of Taiwan's budget. All Control Yuan Departments submit their departmental budget proposals to the Control Yuan's Committee on budget planning and execution. The consolidated proposal is then sent to the Legislative Yuan for approval. The Secretary General defends the budget

---

[23] Seven out of 29 are female, as of September 2011.

[24] The Human Rights Protection Committee was established in 2000. It handles human rights cases and also collects information on human rights issues from domestic and international sources. Information provided by the Control Yuan.

[25] Cf Organic Law of the Control Yuan and Organic Law of the Committees of the Control Yuan.

[26] Cf Sect. 20.2.3.1 below, p. 264 for more information.

[27] Cf Annual Report 2010.

[28] Cf Organic Law of the Ministry of Audit and its general rules.

proposal before the Legislative Yuan on behalf of the Control Yuan. The budget for the financial year 2010–2011 was New Taiwan $ 777,123,000 (US$ 26,356,350 as of 4 May 2012).[29]

There are currently no Government plans to reform the Control Yuan. However, the Presidential Office has established a "Human Rights Consultative Committee",[30] which commenced operations on 10 December 2010, to discuss and develop human rights policies and to advise the President on human rights policies. It may well be that this Committee serves as the catalyst to set up an NHRI, which may include the Control Yuan.[31]

20.2.2 *Mandate*

20.2.2.1 Object of Control

The Control Yuan has far-reaching oversight functions. Its statutory powers include overseeing government institutions at all levels, including the judiciary, the Police and the military. These oversight powers cover public officials at both central and local level, including Head of Cabinet, Ministers, judges, prosecutors, civil servants and also employees of publicly-owned businesses.

In detail, the following bodies providing public services fall under the Control Yuan's jurisdiction: in regard to unemployment insurance, the Bureau of Labor Insurance; in regard to pension insurance, the Department of Social Affairs; regarding accommodation of asylum seekers and social living, the Social Welfare Department; regarding tertiary education, the Ministry of Education; regarding health insurance, the Bureau of Health Insurance; and regarding public hospitals, the Department of Health. Also the following non-government companies and agencies providing public services are under the Control Yuan's jurisdiction: the Taiwan Power Company (electricity supply), Chunghwa Post Co., Ltd. (postal services), Chunghwa Telecom (telecommunication), the Taiwan Railways Administration (railway) and the Taiwan Water Corporation (water supply). In general, all publicly-owned companies and entities of which Taiwan owns more than 50 % are subject to the Legislative Yuan's and Control Yuan's jurisdiction in accordance with the Law of Final Accounts.[32]

Exempted from jurisdiction are the President of Taiwan,[33] the Vice President, members of the Legislative Yuan as well as of local level legislatures. Generally, private individuals cannot be subject of an investigation.

---

[29] Information provided by the Control Yuan.

[30] The Committee is composed of both public officials and private citizens, chaired by the Vice President. Information provided by the Control Yuan.

[31] Information provided by the Control Yuan. Cf also Liao (2001), p. 104 for more details.

[32] Further, the Ministries appoint both Chair and CEO of public companies.

[33] Until 1997, impeachment of the President or Vice President was to be initiated by the Control Yuan. Since a constitutional amendment in July 2007 this power rests with the Legislative Yuan.

In accordance with the Anti-Corruption Laws, or Sunshine Laws,[34] the Control Yuan has additional control, audit, and supervisory powers with regards to senior public officials.

20.2.2.2 Standard of Control

The Control Yuan has the powers of consent, impeachment, censure, and auditing (art. 90 Const.). It investigates whether there has been any "violation of law" or "dereliction of duty" (art. 96 Const.).

Procedures can be initiated following a complaint submitted by any individual, including foreign residents. Complaints may be submitted orally in person by visiting the Control Yuan Complaints Receipt Center, in writing, by fax or by e-mail. They may also be made in person at the occasion of Control Yuan members undertaking "circuit supervision"[35] at the complainants' public body or company. Complainants are encouraged to list all facts and evidence in writing and report directly to the Control Yuan or its members. There are no fees levied for submitting a complaint.

In addition to investigations following complaints, the Control Yuan also has the power to undertake self initiated investigations. Consequently, there are a total of three categories of investigations. The Control Yuan may decide to commission another organisation to undertake an investigation (commission investigations). Moreover, the Control Yuan or one of its committees may assign investigations to a Control Yuan member (assigned investigations). Thirdly, Control Yuan members following an individual complaint or based on other information that has come to their knowledge, may initiate investigations on their own accord (self initiated investigations). The Control Yuan then assigns investigation assistants in support of the investigations.

Members of the Control Yuan also investigate whether the conduct or policy of government organisations at all levels are in accordance to the standards stipulated in the ICESCR and the ICCPR. This power is the consequence of the 2009 Act[36] which implemented both covenants. This subsequently put an obligation on all governmental institutions to avoid human rights violations (art. 4 and 5 Act to Implement the ICESCR and the ICCPR).

The Control Yuan has discretion not to investigate or to forward cases to other, more appropriate agencies for handling.[37]

---

[34] Cf Sect. 20.2.1.1, p. 259 for a list of the laws and Sect. 20.2.3.1, p. 264 for more details on the various oversight functions.

[35] Cf p. 265 below for more details.

[36] Cf footnote 16 above, p. 259.

[37] Information provided by the Control Yuan.

20.2.3 *Powers*

20.2.3.1 Relation to the Administration

Before initiating a formal investigation, any complaint is to be reviewed to determine whether it should be sent to a Control Yuan member for investigation, to a standing committee for discussion, or forwarded to a particular government agency for redress. If it falls under the statute of limitations[38] or is outside of jurisdiction, the complainant is informed of this fact by the Control Yuan's Department of Supervisory Operation.[39]

If a formal investigation is initiated, the Control Yuan first announces this intention to the organisation in question before starting investigations. In the course of an investigation, the Control Yuan may inspect Central Government Ministries, offices of local governments, and may investigate files, records and relevant documents of public or private organisations (s26(1) Control Act). The Control Yuan may also make requests to receive official documents from governmental institutions; in this context, it has the power to temporarily seize documents[40] (s27 Control Act). The Control Yuan further has the power to question government officials and to consult with other actors. If the Control Yuan investigators encounter resistance they may request support by the Police (s28(2) Control Act).

Investigations should be finalised within three months for ordinary cases or within six to twelve months for specific cases.[41] The investigation shall not be public (s26(3) Control Act). Once an investigation is completed, the Control Yuan submits a written report to the agency concerned and is authorised to "rectify the situation with the relevant institutions" by initiating an impeachment procedure, submitting a censure or proposing corrective measures.[42] The proposal of corrective measures and of impeachment are seen to be "two of the most important weapons of the Control Yuan."[43] If the conduct in question includes a criminal act or a violation of military law, the case shall be referred to the judiciary for further action. Once it is decided to refer a case to the disciplinary organisation, the Control Yuan must make the case public.[44]

If the Control Yuan proposes corrective measures in its report (s24 Control Act and art. 97 Const.), the agency concerned shall make the improvement proposed or

[38] According to art. 11 and art. 12 of „Measure of Handling People's Complaints".

[39] Cf Annual Report 2009, p. 7.

[40] The Control Yuan must seek permission of the head of the organisation in question who may refuse only for exceptional reasons (e.g. Taiwan's security interests) (s27 Control Act).

[41] The Control Yuan member(s) who investigate(s) the case decide(s) to which group a case belongs, based on the Control Yuan's "Measure of Handling People's Complaints".

[42] Cf Chao (2010), p. 5.

[43] Cf Chao (2010), p. 5.

[44] Cf Chao (2010), p. 6. To this end, the Control Yuan members hold press conferences once a case of impeachment, censure or corrective measures has been approved by the Control Yuan.

take other actions without delay and inform the Control Yuan in writing. If no response is received within two months, the Control Yuan may summon the official in charge for questioning (s25 Control Act and s20 Enforcement Rules). If there is no cooperation whatsoever and if the official in charge refuses to take appropriate action for improvement, the Control Yuan may even initiate impeachment of this person.

The initiation of an impeachment requires at least two Control Yuan members acting together. A further obstacle is the minimum of nine members[45] who shall examine the case and formally approve the impeachment procedure. Then, the case is referred to the agency in question for the superior in charge to take immediate action. If the superior in charge does not take action, the superior in charge shall be considered guilty of dereliction of duty if ultimately the offender (i.e. the person whose conduct prompted the impeachment procedure) is reprimanded (s14 Control Act). Furthermore, if an impeachment case is not settled by the disciplinary organ within three months, the Control Yuan may take action (that is, impeachment or censure) against the disciplinary organ's personnel (s19 Control Act).

If a Control Yuan member is convinced that it is necessary to suspend a public official from duty or to take other action, he or she may file a written censure against this public official. If more than three other Control Yuan members approve the censure following examination of the case, the written censure is forwarded to the superior in charge of the public official. The superior is obliged to act within one month in accordance with the Public Functionaries Discipline Act. If the superior considers no action should be taken and reports this back to the Control Yuan with appropriate explanation, this fact is considered by the Control Yuan. If more than two Control Yuan members consider it inappropriate, an impeachment shall be initiated against the censured person (s22(1) Control Act). In case this second (i.e. impeachment) proceeding is successful, the superior shall be held responsible for neglect of duty (s22(1) Control Act).

Other powers of the Control Yuan derive from the Control Act and other legislation (see above) as follows:

The Control Yuan has the power to conduct circuit supervision in various areas (s3 Control Act). At the central level, this supervision is undertaken by the respective Control Yuan committee that is most familiar with the subject matter of the central agency under supervision. Local level supervision is carried out by twelve Control Yuan teams.[46] Circuit supervision means taking a holistic view and looking at all aspects of administration. It covers the execution of a government agency's administrative agenda and its budget, the implementation of policies and the application of regulations, the performance of public servants, the implementation of cases requiring corrective measures, of how those policies and regulations affect the social conditions of the population, and the handling of complaints submitted.

---

[45] Excluding those who have initiated the case.

[46] The twelve teams are formed according to administrative areas, cf Sect. 20.2.1.3, p. 261.

According to the Examination Invigilation Act, the Examination Yuan shall invite the Control Yuan to supervise examinations carried out by the Examination Yuan or an examination organisation (s1 Examination Invigilation Act).[47] If the Control Yuan Invigilator becomes aware of any act of collusion or other acts contravening a fair, open and transparent procedure, he or she shall report back to the Control Yuan to ensure the "handling [of such case] in accordance with the law" (s4 Examination Invigilation Act).

One of the Control Yuan's powers is the power of audit (art. 90 Const. and art. 7 of the Additional Articles to the Const.). This is by and large carried out by the Ministry of Audit for the Central Government and its subordinate organisations (s3 and s4 Audit Act).[48] The Auditors' functions and obligations are entailed in the Audit Act. The Auditors generally report back to both the organisation in question and to the audit organisations responsible. They may also report to the Control Yuan and, in case of alleged criminal offences, they shall refer the matter to the judiciary and shall report to the Control Yuan (s17 Audit Act).

Taiwan's senior officials, including the President and Vice-President of Taiwan, the heads of government organisations as well as senior-ranking judges and public prosecutors shall report their assets to the Control Yuan (s2 and s4 Act on Asset-Declaration by Public Functionaries). This reporting requirement has to be complied with for the first time upon taking office, and thereafter on an annual basis. The Control Yuan shall make occasional item-by-item checks, and investigate the truthfulness of assets declarations (s11 Act on Asset-Declaration by Public Functionaries). The Control Yuan shall impose the penalties foreseen in the law for those violating these obligations or deliberately concealing assets (s12 and s14 Act on Asset-Declaration by Public Functionaries).

The role of the Control Yuan in case of the prevention of conflicts of interest is somewhat similar. According to the Act on Recusal of Public Functionaries Due to Conflicts of Interest, public officials are to prevent conflicts of interest (s10(2) Act on Recusal of Public Functionaries Due to Conflicts of Interest). If an official does not prevent conflicts of interest, the affected parties may apply for the prevention of conflicts of interest at the agency where the official serves (s12 of the same Act). If the official in question is the head of that agency, the application shall go to the agency's supervisory agency. If there is no such agency, it shall go to the Control Yuan. In such case, the Control Yuan shall investigate the matter and, if a violation of the law is confirmed, impose penalties and announce the confirmed sanctions in public.

---

[47] Except those held purely for the screening of the qualifications of the examinees (s1(1) Examination Invigilation Act).

[48] Provincial level and city Governments are audited by the Departments of Audit, and local level Governments are audited by the Offices of Audit (s4 and s5 Audit Act).

According to s4 Political Donations Act, the Control Yuan shall handle political donation disclosures.[49] The Control Yuan confirms and keeps a list of respective bank accounts for donations. The Control Yuan is to receive the accounting reports from all accounts. Eventually, the information will be published. The Control Yuan may impose fines for violation of the Act (s33 Political Donations Act).

The Lobbying Act shall "create an open and transparent procedures [*sic*] for lobbying" (s1 Lobbying Act). It outlaws lobbying by individuals in certain positions[50] and by certain entities,[51] respectively foresees certain minimum standards[52] for lobbyists and establishes a mandatory register and other disclosure requirements. Under the Lobbying Act, the Control Yuan is the authority competent to discipline the President, the Vice-President and other senior officials in case of violations of the law. In these cases the Control Yuan has the power to determine and implement punishments (s29 Lobbying Act).

Control Yuan members may also visit detention facilities without prior announcement. A Control Yuan member is allowed to speak with persons alone; he or she may be accompanied by a Control Yuan investigatory assistant.

Decisions of the Control Yuan may be challenged by the complainant or the public official concerned. They can address the Control Yuan, whose Committee on Complaint Review is authorised to review the decision.[53] If the review decision is not satisfactory, the complainant may bring the case before the courts by way of the standard legal proceedings.[54] Further, an administrative appeal may be filed at the Administrative Court.

20.2.3.2 Relation to the Judiciary

The Control Yuan oversees all government levels, including the judiciary. It cannot, however, intervene in individual court cases. Otherwise, judges, other court staff and personnel of the Judicial Yuan fall under the Control Yuan's jurisdiction. If they neglect their duties or violate laws, the Control Yuan may censure them or

[49] Political donations under the law are those made to political parties, political groups and candidates.

[50] *Inter alia*, legislators shall not lobby for a private company run by themselves or related persons (s12 Lobbying Act).

[51] *Inter alia*, other Governments, legal persons and organisations with regard to certain matters, cf s7 and s8 Lobbying Act.

[52] *Inter alia*, anyone who has committed a crime listed in s11 Lobbying Act is disqualified from being commissioned, or being assigned to serve as a lobbyist.

[53] In practice, requests for review include the issue of complaint handling, fines and punishments imposed on public officials in violation of assets report, conflict of interest or political donations. Cases that involve an application for compensation are reviewed by a different internal procedure (information provided by the Control Yuan).

[54] In accordance with either the provisions of the Code of Criminal Procedure or the Code of Civil Procedure.

initiate impeachment proceedings against them (art. 7 Additional Articles to the Const.).[55] If the defendant in an ongoing court case suspects the judge of malfeasance or of a serious violation of law requiring immediate investigation, the Control Yuan may investigate the matter. If the Control Yuan has approved an impeachment case, it is forwarded to the Judicial Yuan (Public Functionary Disciplinary Sanction Commission), which must ultimately decide on the punishment.[56]

In performing its investigatory functions, the Control Yuan may apply to a court for a court order (s28 Control Act). The Control Yuan is further obliged to refer cases that allegedly involve a criminal misconduct or a violation of a military law to the competent judicial organ for further action.

20.2.3.3 Relation to the Legislator

The Control Yuan is a "unique official government watchdog"[57] and one of the five powers of government. Consequently, the Control Yuan is not required to report to the legislator on its work. Control Yuan members are not entitled to participate in debates in Parliament either. The Control Yuan has jurisdiction over all Legislative Yuan functionaires but not over the legislator.

The Control Yuan does not have the power to propose legislative initiatives to the legislator. However, as part of its powers to propose corrective measures to the Executive Yuan (s25 Control Act), the Control Yuan could include proposals for legislative amendments when necessary.

The Control Yuan used to have the power of impeachment of the President or Vice-President of Taiwan. This function, however, has been moved on to the Legislative Yuan in 1997.

20.2.4 Other Characteristics

Taiwan is not a signatory to the OPCAT.[58] However, the Legislative Yuan has passed the Act to Implement the Convention on the Elimination of All Forms of Discrimination Against Women (CEDAW) in June 2011 and may probably pass legislation to implement OPCAT in the future.[59] In 2009, the Legislative Yuan

[55] Impeachment cases of judicial personnel must be initiated by two or more members of the Control Yuan and must be investigated and voted upon by a committee of not less than nine of its members (art.7(3) Additional Articles to the Const.).

[56] In 2010, there were 20 cases of impeachment and three cases of censure, cf Annual Report 2010, p. 44.

[57] Cf Chao (2010), p. 3.

[58] Cf Sect. 3.2.6.2, p. 55 for details.

[59] Information provided by the Control Yuan. The provisions of the CEDAW become binding law in Taiwan through this Act although Taiwan is not a UN member, cf Sect. 20.1, p. 257 above.

passed the Act to Implement the ICESCR and the ICCPR. Since then, members of the Control Yuan investigate whether conduct and policies of government organisations are in conformity with the standards as contained in both covenants.

The Control Yuan has specific duties in the field of human rights protection. Its Human Rights Protection Committee (HRPC), set up in May 2000,[60] advocates human rights and handles cases of alleged human rights violations. The Control Yuan shall advocate the abolition of deficiencies in the Government's handling of cases that may infringe human rights. The HRPC's functions are laid down in the "Rules Governing the Establishment of the Human Rights Protection Committee", based on the Organic Law of the Control Yuan. The Committee's main functions are:

- To discover cases of human rights violations and propose investigation;
- To review and study human rights cases and propose solutions;
- To provide proposals on human rights bills;
- To communicate with domestic and international human rights institutions and collect relevant information;
- To research how to promote human rights education; and
- To handle other matters related to human rights protection.

Generally, the unique system of five powers of government makes Taiwan differ substantially from other Ombudsman models. However, while the set-up is different, it must be noted that many of the functions are similar to other models assessed. The powers given to the Control Yuan are very comprehensive in comparison. The Control Yuan has far-reaching competences in the field of anti-corruption activities. The Anti-Corruption Laws (or Sunshine Laws) endow the Control Yuan with control, audit, and supervisory powers and give the Control Yuan the task of sanctioning violators and making violations public.[61]

20.2.5 Workload

In 2010, the Control Yuan handled 25,521 complaints. Of these, 484 (1.9 %) were investigated by the Control Yuan in a formal investigation procedure.[62] Most complaints referred to internal and minority nationality affairs (7,883), followed

---

[60] Cf p. 261 above.

[61] Cf Sect. 20.2.3.1 above, p. 264, for a more detailed description of these functions.

[62] Of all complaints handled, 2,845 (11.15 %) were complemented with related data by the investigated organisation; 5,557 (21.77 %) were referred to the respective administrative organisation for reference; 4,818 (18.88 %) concerned legal or administrative redress procedure; 206 (0.81 %) were out of jurisdiction; 1,764 (6.91 %) required further reference; 339 (1.33 %) lacked substantial evidence for processing; 8,714 (34.14 %) were merged with other cases; and 789 (3.09 %) were processed in other ways. Cf Annual Report 2010, p. 7 and p. 9.

by judicial and prison administration affairs (6,196) and by financial and economic affairs (5,403).[63]

Broken down into categories of investigation, in 2010 the Control Yuan saw 20 cases of impeachment and initiated three cases of censure. The Control Yuan further proposed 218 cases of corrective measures to the Executive Yuan, invigilated 22 examinations, and received assets declarations of all 11,418 officials who took office during the reporting period. The Control Yuan received 259 cases that were reported by the Ministry of Audit.[64]

The Control Yuan assessed that of the 25,521 complaints handled, a total of 22,423 (87.85 %) were related to human rights issues. They mainly referred to the right of judicial review (6,795), the right to property (6,144) and the right to work (2,474).

20.2.6 *Publications*

The Control Yuan, while not required to report to the legislature, launches three reports on its activities aimed at the general public each year. The Control Yuan Report outlines the Control Yuan's work of the preceeding year in detail; an additional bi-annual Brief Report on the Work of the Control Yuan outlines the work of the Control Yuan. In addition, an English version of the Brief Report on the Work of the Control Yuan is published annually.

Moreover, the Control Yuan issues other publications, including the weekly Control Yuan Gazette, a periodically published Control Yuan Special Gazette on the Assets Report by Public Functionaries, and a Control Yuan Special Gazette on the Accounting Report of Political donations. Furthermore, there is an e-bulletin and brochures dealing with various subject matters.[65]

20.2.7 *Annotations*

There are currently no annotations.

---

[63] Cf Annual Report 2010, p. 8.

[64] Cf Annual Report 2010, p. 14, 44, 23, 25, 35, and p. 37.

[65] Cf APOR Manual 2009, p. 112 et seq.

References

Chao LR (2010) Special powers & reports of the Control Yuan. Speech held at the 25th APOR Conference, 19 March 2010

Liao FF-T (2001) Establishing a national human rights commission in Taiwan: the role of NGOs and challenges ahead. Asia Pac J Hum Rights Law 2(2):90–109

Further Reading

Overview of Legislation:

Constitution: http://english.president.gov.tw/Default.aspx?tabid=1107

Additional Articles: http://english.president.gov.tw/Default.aspx?tabid=435

Control Law: www.cy.gov.tw/mp21.htm

Organic Law of the Committees of the Control Yuan: www.cy.gov.tw/mp21.htm (Chinese Version only)

Act to Implement the ICESCR and the ICCPR: http://law.moj.gov.tw/eng/LawClass/LawContent.aspx?PCODE=I0020028

Rules Governing the Establishement of the Human Rights Protection Committee: www.cy.gov.tw/mp21.htm (Chinese Version only)

Act on Property-Declaration by Public Servants: http://law.moj.gov.tw/eng/LawClass/LawAll.aspx?PCode=I0070005

Enforcement Rules of the Act on Property-Declaration by Public Servants: http://law.moj.gov.tw/eng/LawClass/LawAll.aspx?PCode=I0070006

Regulations Governing Examination and Browsing of Materials of Property-Declaration by Public Servants: http://law.moj.gov.tw/eng/LawClass/LawAll.aspx?PCode=I0070007

Act on Recusal of Public Servants Due to Conflicts of Interest: http://law.moj.gov.tw/Eng/LawClass/LawAll.aspx?PCode=I0070008

Enforcement Rules of the Act on Recusal of Public Servants Due to Conflicts of Interest: http://law.moj.gov.tw/eng/LawClass/LawAll.aspx?PCode=I0070009

Political Donations Act: http://law.moj.gov.tw/eng/LawClass/LawAll.aspx?PCode=D0020049

Lobbying Act: http://law.moj.gov.tw/eng/LawClass/LawAll.aspx?PCode=D0020062

Enforcement Rules of Lobbying Act: http://law.moj.gov.tw/eng/LawClass/LawAll.aspx?PCode=D0020067

Law of Audit: www.audit.gov.tw/audeng/naolaw.htm

Examination Invigilation Act: wwwc.moex.gov.tw/english/content/wfrmContent.aspx?menu_id=390

Annual Reports (2002–2010): www.cy.gov.tw/mp21.htm

Chapter 21
Tonga: Commissioner for Public Relations

Michael Frahm

21.1 General Information

The Kingdom of Tonga consists of more than 170 islands (including numerous uninhabited ones) spread over an area roughly the size of Japan. It became a Polynesian kingdom in 1845, a constitutional monarchy in 1875 and a British protectorate in 1900. In 1970 it gained full independence. Today, Tonga is a constitutional monarchy with a unicameral Legislative Assembly. Head of State is the King, whereas the Prime Minister is the Head of Government and is elected by and from the Members of Parliament and appointed by the Monarch. The Cabinet is then nominated by the Prime Minister and appointed by the Monarch. In addition, there is a Privy Council advising the Monarch.[1]

Tonga's population is estimated at approximately 105,000 people, with a population density of 159.4/km^2.[2] The only dominant ethnic group are the Polynesians. Official languages are both Tongan and English. The capital of Tonga is Nuku'alofa, and the kingdom is administratively divided into three island groups: Ha'apai, Tongatapu and Vava'u.

The Constitution, dating from 4 November 1875, was revised in January 1967 and again in July 2010. The country's legal system is based on English Common Law. The court system consists of a Magistrate's Court, a Land Court as well as a Supreme Court, whose judges are appointed by the Monarch, and a Court of Appeal with the Chief Justice and High Court justices from overseas chosen and approved by the Privy Council (art. 84 Const.).

---

[1] Cf BBC country profile Tonga (http://www.bbc.co.uk/news/world-asia-pacific-16197014) and CIA World Factbook (Tonga).

[2] UN estimate 2010, respectively CIA World Factbook July 2011 estimate.

M. Frahm (✉)
Ludwig Boltzmann Institute of Human Rights, Vienna, Austria
e-mail: michael.frahm@univie.ac.at

International Ombudsman Institute (ed.), *Australasia and Pacific Ombudsman Institutions*, 273
DOI 10.1007/978-3-642-33896-0_21, © Springer-Verlag Berlin Heidelberg 2013

21.2 The Ombudsman Institution

Office of the Commissioner for Public Relations[3]
Postal address: P.O. Box 847, Lavinia Road, Nuku 'Alofa
Phone: +676. 26 981
Fax: +676. 26 982
E-mail: primzolta@yahoo.com.au
Website: n/a

21.2.1 Overview

21.2.1.1 Legal Basis

The Office of the Commissioner for Public Relations was established and opened to the public in 2001. In 2003, the office joined the IOI. The Commissioner's role is largely similar to that of an Ombudsman, as the Commissioner for Public Relations Act 2001 (CPRA) was closely modelled after the New Zealand Ombudsman Act 1975. The Commissioner is authorised to investigate all Government Ministries and agencies except for the Cabinet and the Privy Council. There is no other Ombudsman Institution with a special mandate in Tonga.

21.2.1.2 Legal Status and Independence

The Commissioner is appointed by the King, who is under no statutory obligation to consult any other body or person (s3(1) CPRA). The appointment is for five years, but indefinite reappointment is possible (s5 CPRA). The mandatory retirement age is 72 years, and there are no statutory provisions requiring any specific qualifications or ensuring the office reflects the composition of society. All provisions of the laws and regulations relating to the Tonga Civil Service apply to the Commissioner (s3 CPRA).[4] The position of Commissioner is incompatible with being a Member of Parliament, and he or she shall not, without the approval of the Cabinet in each particular case, "hold any office for profit", other than his or her office as the Commissioner, or "engage in any occupation for reward outside the duties of his [or her] office" (s4 CPRA).

The Commissioner may at any time be removed or suspended from office by the King. An exhaustive list in the law stipulates that removal or suspension is only possible in case of disability, bankruptcy, neglect of duty, or misconduct (s6 CPRA). Proceedings of the Commissioner cannot be questioned or made

[3] About to be changed to "Ombudsman Tonga", cf p. 276 below.

[4] The Commissioner him- or herself is not a public servant, but the investigators and staff are.

subject to review (s20 CPRA). Anything said or provided in the course of a proceeding is privileged in the same manner as if they were court proceedings (s21(2) CPRA). The Commissioner and the office's staff are immune to legal prosecution with regard to the exercise of their functions. They shall not be called to give evidence in court in relation to anything that comes to their knowledge in the execution of their functions (s21(1) CPRA).

Salary and allowances are determined by the King (s8 CPRA). To strengthen the office's independence, the law provides that the salary is not to be reduced in the course of the Commissioner's appointment. All salaries shall be payable out of money to be appropriated by Parliament for the purpose (s27 CPRA). The office's staff are members of the Tongan public service.

21.2.1.3 Organisation

The office is a monocratic body headed by the Commissioner. It has no outposts in other parts respectively islands of the country. The Commissioner (the post is currently vacant)[5] is assisted by a Senior Investigations Officer,[6] an Investigations Officer, an Office Administrator, an Account Clerk/Computer Assistant and an Office Assistant.

The office is financed "out of money to be appropriated by parliament" for the purpose (s27 CPRA). The budget division of the Ministry of Finance and Planning determines the overall amount of the Commissioner's office budget based on submissions by the office setting out its planned activities. While in practical terms the budget is somewhat limited, the office perceives these restrictions in the context of the limited overall financial capabilities of the Government.

There is currently no ICC-accredited NHRI[7] in Tonga. However, the office works towards convincing the Tongan authorities to strengthen the office to become an effective integrity Institution for Tonga. To this end, the office has provided information to the Government on additional competencies believed to be a good basis for strengthening the office given the cultural context in Tonga. The views of the Government have not been made clear to date.

[5] The post of Commissioner has been vacant since November 2006. The Senior Investigations Officer, Mr Pilimisolo Tamo'ua, has acted as officer-in-charge since, and works towards convincing the Tongan authorities to strengthen the office "to become a more effective integrity Institution for Tonga." Information provided by the Institution.

[6] Currently acting as the office's officer-in-charge. According to s3(2) CPRA, the King shall appoint a person to temporarily perform the duties of the Commissioner.

[7] Cf Sect. 1.1.3, p. 6 for details.

21.2.2 Mandate

21.2.2.1 Object of Control

The Commissioner has jurisdiction over any Ministry, Department or office as well as over any of the entities listed in the annexed Schedule 2 (s2 and s11(1) CPRA). The Schedule includes relevant public service providers such as the Tonga Post, Tonga Water Board, Retirement Fund Board, Tonga Communication Corporation (telecommunications) and Tonga Power Ltd (electricity). The Cabinet and Privy Council, Parliament, the Defence Force and the judiciary are explicitly exempted from jurisdiction (s2, s11(1)(5) CPRA). Private individuals cannot be subject to an investigation. The law further exempts additional areas from the Commissioner's jurisdiction. The office has no authority to investigate any action[8] that is subject to a right of appeal or review on the merits by any court or tribunal, any action of any person in his or her capacity as a trustee, or any action of any person acting as legal adviser to the Crown or for the Crown in relation to any proceedings (s11(5) OA).

In 2008, a review of the office's establishing legislation was conducted.[9] There have been plans to introduce legislation amending the current act. The officer-in-charge was supported in developing draft legislative changes by a Commonwealth Ombudsman's officer in 2009.[10] The proposed amendments aimed at improving the capacity of the office to execute Ombudsman functions, including the publishing of additional reports (besides the Annual Report) on the outcome of investigations, improving the effectiveness of the office's work, mitigating a widespread misunderstanding or lack of awareness within the Tongan community in regard to the Commissioner's role, and clarify uncertainties in the legislation as to the Commissioner's powers in relation to awareness raising and public relations activities.

It was furthermore proposed to rename the office to "Ombudsman of Tonga", since the current title is not considered ideal, as it differs from international usage; also, it does not accurately reflect the functions of the office and is easily mistaken for other bodies such as the Public Service Commission. Lastly, the title may give rise to suspicion that the office lacks independence. Additionally, the draft amendments included a provision permitting the Commissioner to disclose information for the purpose of inquiries[11] or for any other necessary and legitimate purpose.[12] In 2009, there were also activities to establish a memorandum of understanding between the Commissioner and the Tongan Police Force, to help

---

[8] To improve readability, the text refers only to "action". However, this term shall be understood as including any decision, recommendation, act, or omission (terminology used in the law).

[9] Cf APOR Manual 2009, p. 120.

[10] Cf Annual Report (Commonwealth Ombudsman) 2008/2009, p. 121.

[11] Information considered necessary to decide whether or not a complaint should be investigated.

[12] *Inter alia*, for public awareness of the role and powers of the office.

refine the Commissioner's role in handling complaints about Police conduct.[13] The office has repeatedly pointed out to the Government the need for these reforms. Following elections in 2010 and the institution of a new Government, it appears that the situation is starting to change.[14] In 2011 a proposal for an Ombudsman and Anti-Corruption Commission was under discussion.[15]

21.2.2.2 Standard of Control

The office's main function is to investigate "any decision or recommendation" made or "any act done or omitted" that relates to a matter of administration and affects any person or group of persons in his or her or its personal capacity (s11(1) CPRA). The Commissioner's criteria of control are as follows: He or she investigates if an action "appears to have been contrary to law"; was "unreasonable, unjust, oppressive, or improperly discriminatory", or was "based wholly or partly on a mistake of law or fact; or was wrong" (s18(1) CPRA). The Commissioner shall also act if a "discretionary power has been exercised" for an improper purpose or on irrelevant grounds (s18(2) CPRA).

Any person, that is any individual, company, organisation or association, with an interest in the subject matter can lodge a complaint (s11(2) CPRA). The complaint may be made orally or in writing, yet an oral complaint shall be put in writing as soon as practicable (s12 CPRA). There are no fees connected with filing a complaint before the Commissioner. In addition to individuals addressing the office, the Commissioner may also conduct own motion investigations (s11(2) CPRA), and the Prime Minister may, with the consent of the Commissioner, refer any matter which the Prime Minister considers should be investigated to the Commissioner for investigation (s11(3) CPRA).

The Commissioner has discretion to refuse an investigation (s13 CPRA) if a complaint relates to any action of which the complainant has had knowledge for more than twelve months before the complaint is received by the Commissioner, if the complaint is "trivial, frivolous, vexatious or is not made in good faith", if the complainant does not have a sufficient personal interest in the complaint, or if it appears to the Commissioner that any further investigation is unnecessary. Generally, the Commissioner may also refuse to investigate a matter if there is another adequate remedy or right of appeal which is reasonably available to the complainant. However, it is not an absolute requirement to exhaust such remedies, and there may be cases where the office considers it appropriate to investigate a complaint.

---

[13] Cf APOR Manual 2009, p. 120.

[14] According to information provided by the Institution.

[15] Cf POA Network News Issue 26, December 2011.

21.2.3 *Powers*

21.2.3.1 Relation to the Administration

Before starting an investigation, the Commissioner is to inform the chief executive of the body affected of his or her intention to initiate an investigation (s14(1) CPRA). The Commissioner is reasonably free in undertaking investigations, which always are to take place in private (s14(2) CPRA). He or she may regulate the investigation procedure in a way he or she considers appropriate (s14(7) CPRA), may hear or obtain information from any person and may make such enquiries as he or she thinks fit (s14(3) CPRA). While the Commissioner may hold a hearing, there is no obligation to do so except in cases where he or she considers to make a report that may adversely affect a Department or organisation or person (s14(3) CPRA).

The Commissioner may require a person to provide certain information or documents (s15(1) CPRA), and may summon and examine persons under oath (s15(2) CPRA). The general public interest clause against disclosure or production of documents is normally excluded (s16 CPRA). Thus, authorities are generally required to support the Commissioner's office without restrictions. However, the Attorney-General has the authority to determine certain information as confidential even vis-à-vis a Commissioner's investigation. This applies if the Attorney-General decides that sharing the information might prejudice the security, defence or international relations of Tonga, might disclose deliberations of Cabinet or the Privy Council, or might disclose proceedings of the Cabinet or the Privy Council "relating to matters of a secret or confidential nature and [which] would be injurious to the public interest" (s16(1) CPRA).

The Commissioner is entitled to on-site visits of any premises occupied by a body under his or her jurisdiction and may inspect them, but is required to notify the respective person in charge beforehand (s22 CPRA). In exceptional cases, the Attorney-General may forbid access to certain sensitive premises (s22(3) CPRA). The right to visit includes correction centers. The law remains silent as to whether the Commissioner has the right to speak with detainees alone.

If, after having finished an investigation, the Commissioner believes that a rectification is required, he or she reports this opinion to the agency concerned, and makes such recommendations as he or she thinks fit (s18(3) CPRA). If the Commissioner considers there to be sufficient evidence of a breach of duty or misconduct of any staff, he or she must refer the matter to the appropriate authority (s14(6) CPRA).

The Commissioner shall consult any Minister, respectively chair of the organisation concerned, who so requests, or to whom a recommendation has been made, before the Commissioner forms a final opinion (s14(4) and (5) CPRA).[16]

[16] He or she may also consult any Minister respectively chair of the organisation concerned at any time during the investigation at his or her discretion.

In addition, as a general principle, the Commissioner shall not make any comment that is adverse to any person unless the person has been given an opportunity to be heard (s14(7) CPRA).

The Commissioner has no coercive powers. However, the CPRA provides for some measures aiming at persuading a body to implement recommendations. First, the Commissioner may request the public body concerned to notify him or her, within a specified time, of the steps proposed to take to give effect to the recommendations (s18(3) CPRA). Second, if the investigation relates to a Government Department, the CPRA foresees the sending of a copy of the report and recommendations to the Minister concerned and, if the investigation relates to an organisation, the sending of a copy of the report to the respective chairperson (s18(3) CPRA). If no action is taken or if the action taken is not considered appropriate by the Commissioner, he or she may send the report to the Prime Minister, who shall then table the matter before the Privy Council (s18(4) CPRA). The current law does not foresee recommendations or decisions to be made public. However, the amendments proposed by the office include the power to publicise recommendations.

It is an offence and can be sanctioned with a fine not exceeding Samoan $ 5,000 to wilfully obstruct or hinder the Commissioner, to refuse or wilfully fail to comply with a Commissioner's lawful requirements without justification or excuse, to make any false statement to, or to mislead or attempt to mislead the Commissioner. The same applies to anyone who breaches an oath made under the CPRA or who pretends (explicitly or implicitly) to hold any authority under the OA when he or she does in reality not hold that authority (s26 CPRA).

21.2.3.2 Relation to the Judiciary

Decisions of the judiciary as well as acts which can be reviewed by the judiciary are excluded from the jurisdiction of the Commissioner (s2 CPRA). *Vice versa*, the judiciary cannot intervene regarding any decision made by the Commissioner (s20 CPRA). If it is unclear whether the Commissioner has jurisdiction, an application can be made to the Supreme Court for a declaratory order (s11(7) CPRA).

21.2.3.3 Relation to the Legislator

The Commissioner is required to report directly to the Prime Minister on the exercise of his or her functions annually, with the report being tabled before Parliament by the Prime Minister. It is not explicitly foreseen in the law that the Commissioner may participate in debates in Parliament. The fact that the Prime Minister is to table the Commissioner's Annual Report may be an indication that this is not permitted, however, the Commissioner *de facto* has been summoned to Parliament at least twice in the past to answer questions of Parliamentarians.

The Commissioner has no explicit statutory duty for legislative initiatives. However, s18(3) CPRA foresees *inter alia* that the Commissioner may recommend any law on which a matter investigated was based for reconsideration. Thus, the Commissioner may recommend amendments to existing legislation, which in practice are sent to the Prime Minister, who forwards them to the Crown for policy direction and, upon return, presents them to the Cabinet for approval.

21.2.4 Other Characteristics

Tonga has neither signed nor ratified the OPCAT[17] to date. The name "Commissioner for Public Relations" is protected in Tonga. No person, other than the Commissioner appointed under the CPRA, may use the name and violation of this provision is an offence punishable with a fine not exceeding Samoan $ 1,000 (s24 CPRA).

A non-written task of the office in addition to the statutory functions specified by law is to "provid[e] constructive advice and guidance to Departments and organisations on issues relating to good administration and [handling of] complaints".[18]

21.2.5 Workload

In 2009, the office received 112 complaints and 96 complaints in 2010. Most complaints were directed against the decision-making process, delays or neglect of service by government organisations and Departments. They mainly referred to social matters.

21.2.6 Publications

The Commissioner is required to submit an Annual Report on the execution of his or her functions to the Prime Minister, who in turn shall table the report before Parliament (s25 CPRA). In addition to the work of the office, the latest report also addresses the weaknesses and limitations of the current CPRA and contains suggestions for amendments strengthening the position of the Commissioner.

[17] Cf Sect. 3.2.6.2, p. 55 for more details.

[18] APOR Manual 2009, p. 116 et seq.

21.2.7 Annotations

Current challenges relate to a structural aspect as well as to the substance of the law. First, the office has been run by the Senior Investigations Officer as the officer-in-charge since 2006. The appointment of a new Commissioner should thus be of high priority for the Sovereign. Second, after discussion of proposed amendments, these need to be finalised and, once amendments have passed the legislative process, any structural changes need to be implemented and the public needs to be informed about any new statutory tasks the Commissioner may be endowed with.

Reference

Commonwealth Ombudsman (2009a) Australasia and Pacific Ombudsman region information manual 2009. Commonwealth Ombudsman, Canberra. www.ombudsman.gov.au/docs/APOR-Manual_20091009.pdf. Accessed 10 Nov 2011

Further Reading

Overview of Legislation: http://legislation.to/Tonga/DATA/PRIN/2001-010/CommissionerforPublicRelationsAct2001.pdf
Annual Report: Currently not available online

Chapter 22
Vanuatu: Ombudsman

Michael Frahm

22.1 General Information

The Republic of Vanuatu is a small state consisting of more than 80 islands, most of them inhabited. In 1906 it came under rule as Anglo-French "New Hebrides Condominium" and gained independence from its protecting powers in 1980. It is a parliamentary democracy with a unicameral system. The 52 Members of Parliament are elected through universal suffrage every four years. The President is elected for a five-year term by an electoral college consisting of the Members of Parliament and the Presidents of the Provincial Councils.[1]

Vanuatu has approximately 235,000 inhabitants, with a population density of 19 persons/km^2.[2] The country is ethnically largely homogenous, with Ni-Vanuatus making up 98.5 % of the population. Official languages are Bislama, English and French. The capital is Port Vila (on the island Efate). Vanuatu is administratively divided into six provinces (Malampa, Penama, Sanma, Shefa, Tafea, Torba). Local parliaments, the Provincial Councils, represent the people on a provincial level. Provinces are in turn sub-divided into municipalities.

The country's Constitution dates from 30 July 1980, the Day of Independence. It contains an explicit chapter on fundamental rights (art. 5 and art. 6 Const.) and also foresees the Ombudsman (art. 61–65 Const.). The legal system is a unified system created out of the formerly dual French and British systems. With the Customary Land Tribunals it provides for special courts dealing with customary land disputes. In addition, there are Island Courts, a Magistrates Court and a Supreme Court, which is the last instance for any civil or criminal proceedings. A Court of Appeal

[1] Cf BBC country profile Vanuatu (http://www.bbc.co.uk/news/world-asia-16426193) and CIA World Factbook (Vanuatu).

[2] According to the National Census 2009.

M. Frahm (✉)
Ludwig Boltzmann Institute of Human Rights, Vienna, Austria
e-mail: michael.frahm@univie.ac.at

International Ombudsman Institute (ed.), *Australasia and Pacific Ombudsman Institutions*, 283
DOI 10.1007/978-3-642-33896-0_22, © Springer-Verlag Berlin Heidelberg 2013

for appeals from the original jurisdiction of the Supreme Court may be constituted by two or more judges of the Supreme Court sitting together.

22.2 The Ombudsman Institution

Ofis blong Ombudsman/Office of the Ombudsman/Bureau de Médiateur
Postal address: Private Mail Bag 9081, Port Vila
Street: Pilioko Building, Top Floor, Lini Highway, Port Vila
Telephone: +678.27200
Fax: +678.27140
E-mail: ombud.vt@vanuatu.com.vu
Website: n/a

22.2.1 Overview

22.2.1.1 Legal Basis

The first Ombudsman was appointed in July 1994 and just a year later, in July 1995 the office became a member of the IOI. The office, a monocratic body, is modelled after the Ombudsman Commission of Papua New Guinea. The office's legal basis are articles 61–65 of the Constitution and the Ombudsman Act 1998 (hereinafter "OA"). Art. 62 of the Constitution grants the Ombudsman jurisdiction over all public servants, public authorities and Departments and only excludes the President of the Republic and the judiciary. There are currently no other Ombudsman Institutions with special mandates and no NHRI[3] in the Republic of Vanuatu.

Like the Constitution of Papua New Guinea,[4] Vanuatu's Constitution contains a Leadership Code (art. 66–68 Const.). These provisions, implemented by the Leadership Code Act 1998 (LCA), place some special obligations for good conduct on the state's senior officials, including the President, the Prime Minister and other Ministers, Members of Parliament, and certain other public servants and officers of government agencies. The Ombudsman has been entrusted with additional functions under this law (s34-39 LCA). It is his or her duty to investigate and report on the conduct of a leader[5] following a complaint that a leader has breached this

[3] Cf Sect. 1.1.3, p. 6 for details.

[4] Also Fiji and the Solomon Islands followed this model and have promulgated a Leadership Code.

[5] The President, who must abide by the Leadership Code, is not under the Ombudsman's jurisdiction (s34(1) LCA). Art. 36 Const. foresees a procedure to remove the President from office for gross misconduct or incapacity. In such a case, the Electoral College (consisting of all Members of Parliament and the Chairmen of the Local Government Councils) is competent to act (art. 34 Const.). The threshold for introducing a motion is one third of votes of the Members of the College.

code or if the Ombudsman, based on reasonable grounds, believes that a leader may have breached this code.

22.2.1.2 Legal Status and Independence

The Ombudsman is appointed by the President after extensive consultation with senior officials. By law, the President shall consult the Speaker of Parliament, the leaders of all political parties represented in Parliament, the Chairman of the National Council of Chiefs,[6] the Chairmen of the Provincial Government Councils, the Chairmen of the Public Service Commission and the Judicial Service Commission (art. 61(1) Const. and s3(1) OA). They are similarly consulted in case of an envisaged termination of the appointment, see below (s8(1) OA). The term of office is five years (art. 61(1) Const.) and the office holder may be reappointed indefinitely (s5 OA). There is no obligatory retirement age foreseen in the law.

To be eligible for appointment, a person needs to have knowledge, understanding and appreciation of the culture, traditions and values of the Ni-Vanuatu people, be of high integrity and competence as well as politically independent, have appropriate qualifications and experience, be capable of discharging the duties without fear or favour, and be of high standing in the community (s3(3) OA). The law remains silent as to a further definition of appropriate qualifications.

The function of Ombudsman is incompatible with being a Member of Parliament, of a Local Government Council or of the National Council of Chiefs (s3(2) OA). The Ombudsman further shall not hold any other public office, or exercise a position of responsibility within a political party. The Ombudsman can be removed from office by the President after consultation with those collaborating in the appointment procedure if the Ombudsman is declared bankrupt, convicted of and sentenced for a criminal charge, incapacitated to perform his or her duties due to ill health or an accident, or if a finding of gross misconduct is made against the Ombudsman which is such as to make it inappropriate for him or her to continue to carry out the duties of the office. Similarly, his or her appointment can be terminated if a conviction is made against the Ombudsman under the LCA and he or she is dismissed from office (s8 OA).

The Ombudsman's salary is determined by the President, who shall act on and in accordance with the advice of the Council of Ministers, given after receiving a report from the Public Service Commission (s4(1) OA). The Ombudsman's salary is linked to that of a Supreme Court judge; both salary and other conditions of employment shall not be less than or inferior to those of a judge (s4(2) OA). The salary is similar to that of a Government Minister. The Government must

[6] The National Council of Chiefs is provided for by the Constitution. It consists of Custom Chiefs elected by their peers, sitting in the District Councils of Chiefs. The National Council of Chiefs has a general competence to discuss all matters relating to custom and tradition and may make recommendations for the preservation and promotion of Ni-Vanuatu culture and languages (art. 29–32 Const.).

furthermore “ensure that there is a sufficient budget allocated to the office of the Ombudsman to enable the Ombudsman to properly perform his or her functions and duties” (s42 OA).

The Constitution guarantees that no other person or body may direct or control the Ombudsman in the exercise of his or her functions (art. 65 Const.). Neither the Ombudsman nor any of the office’s employees are liable, and therefore neither criminal nor civil proceedings are to be launched against them, for any act or omission done or ordered to be done or made in good faith and without negligence under or for the purposes of the Constitution or the OA (s41 OA).

22.2.1.3 Organisation

The most senior officers after the Ombudsman are the Director of Complaints/ Investigations and the Director of the Leadership Code. The office also has a legal counsel, principal investigators and legal and administrative staff. In addition to the main office in Port Vila, there is a similarly equipped branch office in Luganville, on the island Santo. It is run by a Principal Investigator as the officer-in-charge, and has a small number of investigations and support staff. Overall the Vanuatu Ombudsman office (including the branch office) employs 13 permanent staff.

The Government is obligated to ensure that there is a sufficient budget allocated to the office to enable the Ombudsman to properly perform his or her functions and duties (s42 OA). The Ministerial Budget Committee, a committee consisting of several Government Ministers and the Heads of several government agencies, determines the budget of the Ombudsman for each financial year. Once allocated, the Ombudsman autonomously decides on the spending of the budget. The budget for the financial year 2010–2011 was Vt 52,260,931 (US$ 574,870 as of 4 May 2012).[7]

On his or her own initiative the Ombudsman has submitted a proposal for amending both, the OA and the LCA to the responsible Minister.[8] This initiative intends to furnish the Ombudsman with more power when dealing with leaders who breach the law to ensure that they are prosecuted for violations. For the LCA the main change would be the setting up of a tribunal which deals with breaches of the Leadership Code. The responsible Minister has suggested wider consultation with other non-governmental agencies and Parliamentarians in the course of which the amendments proposed may be discussed further. It appears that there is some support for this initiative; however, the Government’s stance is yet to be determined.[9]

[7] Information provided by the Institution.

[8] The Board of the Pacific Ombudsman Alliance (POA) supported the Vanuatu Ombudsman in reconvening a legislative reform discussion forum on 1 December 2010, cf POA Network News Issue 24, May 2011.

[9] Information provided by the Institution.

22.2.2 *Mandate*

22.2.2.1 Object of Control

The jurisdiction of the Ombudsman is quite comprehensive and encompasses all public servants, public authorities and Departments, except for the President and the judiciary (art. 62(2) Const.). Private persons cannot be subject to an investigation. Under the LCA the Ombudsman shall investigate and report on the conduct of all leaders (other than the President) upon complaint or by *proprio motu* (s34(1) LCA). In terms of public service providers, the Ombudsman may only investigate complaints concerning public hospitals. Postal services, tertiary education (universities), water, electricity and telecommunication services are provided by private entities, which do not fall under the Ombudsman's jurisdiction.

Once the Ombudsman has completed an investigation and forwarded his or her recommendations to the appropriate bodies, the OA explicitly restricts his or her powers in following up on the matter. The OA stipulates that a matter previously investigated cannot be investigated again. The Ombudsman must not investigate the reasons why one of his or her recommendations has not been followed or which action has been taken by the responsible person to give effect to one of his or her recommendations (s19 OA).

22.2.2.2 Standard of Control

The main criteria of control are stipulated in the Constitution, according to which the Ombudsman investigates whether a conduct was contrary to the law, based on error of law or of fact, delayed for unjustified reasons, unjust or blatantly unreasonable (art. 63(2) Const.). In addition to these criteria specified by the Constitution, the implementing legislation complements these provisions as follows: The Ombudsman shall investigate whether a conduct was "oppressive or improperly discriminatory",[10] based on "improper motives, irrelevant grounds or considerations", "contrary to natural justice", or a conduct "for which reasons should be given but were not". Regarding the Leadership Code, the Ombudsman shall investigate whether or not a leader has breached the Leadership Code (s34(1) LCA).

The Ombudsman may investigate a matter at the request of a Minister, a Member of Parliament, a member of the National Council of Chiefs or of a Local Government Council; or on his or her own initiative (art. 62 Const.). However, most investigations are initiated following an individual complaint. The Constitution allows any person or body to lodge a complaint either orally or in writing (s17 OA). A complaint made orally shall be put in writing as soon as practicable. The complainant may "claim to have been the victim of an injustice as a result of particular conduct" (art. 62(1a) Const.). Lodging complaints before the Ombudsman is free of charge.

[10] This is irrespective of whether or not it is in accordance with law or practice.

The complainant's interest must be sufficiently related to the subject matter of the complaint and he or she should not delay the complaint for too long to justify an investigation into the matter (s18(1)(c) and (d) OA). The Ombudsman may refuse an investigation if he or she is convinced that the complaint is "frivolous, vexatious or manifestly without foundation" or if an enquiry into the conduct complained of is not warranted (s18 OA). Likewise, the Ombudsman has discretion to refuse an investigation if the complaint relates to the conduct of a leader and there are other remedies available which the complainant could reasonably be expected to use (s18 OA).

In addition, if the complainant has not complained to the agency concerned prior to addressing the Ombudsman, the Ombudsman may decide not to investigate the issue. Even if the complainant has already complained to the agency, the Ombudsman may still decide not to enquire into the conduct unless and until the agency has decided against any redress (s18(2) and (3) OA). If at any stage of the enquiry the Ombudsman comes to the conclusion that adequate provision for review is made and that it is reasonable for the complainant to pursue such review, the Ombudsman may decide not to enquire into the conduct any further (s18(4) OA).

22.2.3 Powers

22.2.3.1 Relation to the Administration

Before initiating an investigation, the Ombudsman must give written notice to the person in charge of the agency concerned — or the leader, if acting under the LCA — of his or her intentions unless there are reasonable grounds for believing that this would interfere with the enquiry (s21(1) OA). The OA emphasises cooperation between the party concerned and the Ombudsman by stipulating that, if possible, the Ombudsman shall seek the cooperation of those concerned in obtaining any evidence (s22 OA).

In general, the Ombudsman may decide how to regulate the investigation procedure (s20 OA). The Ombudsman may hold enquiries (s11(1) OA, art. 62(1) Const.) and may request a person to provide him or her with information or documents needed for the enquiry (art. 62(3) Const.). If the cooperative approach fails, the Ombudsman may issue a notice in writing to any person to appear before him or her for questioning or to supply any documents needed (s22(2) OA). The Ombudsman may administer an oath to a person appearing as a witness before him or her, and may examine the witness under oath (s22(6) OA). If there is no cooperation, the Ombudsman may turn to court for a Court Order summoning said person to appear before the Ombudsman (s23 OA). In case there is no cooperation and based on a court's search warrant, the Ombudsman is also entitled to on-site visits (s24 OA).

When finalising the investigation, the Ombudsman shall draft a report but must not make a report that is adverse to an agency or a leader unless the person has been given an opportunity to be heard. The final report must include the substance of any statement that the person may have made in explanation of or opposition to the Ombudsman's conclusions (s21(4) and (5) OA). The Ombudsman may render any recommendation, including the proposal of corrective measures such as that the conduct, law or practice should be "annulled, changed, revised, cancelled, modified, more fully explained, or other specific action taken" (s29(3) OA).

The law differentiates between the bodies the Ombudsman shall forward his or her findings with the appropriate recommendations to. In case of government agencies, the Ombudsman shall forward them to the Prime Minister and the person in charge of the agency concerned (s29(2) OA). In case of the conduct of a leader, the Ombudsman shall additionally forward the findings to the President. If the leader is a member of the opposition, a copy shall also go to the leader of the oppositional party, in case of any other leader, a copy shall also go to the person or body by whom the leader was appointed or reports to (s30 OA).

Any recommendations made by the Ombudsman are legally non-binding. However, to give effect to any findings or recommendations, the Ombudsman may publicise proceedings, reports and recommendations and make reports and recommendations to the Parliament, the Prime Minister and other relevant persons and bodies (s33 OA).

The OA also foresees that those who receive the findings of the Ombudsman shall, within a reasonable period of time specified by the Ombudsman, decide upon the findings, and in case of a government agency, report back to him or her as to what action they propose to take to give effect to the recommendations (s32(1) OA). If the enquiry was made into the conduct of a leader, the Prime Minister must decide upon the findings within a reasonable period of time specified by the Ombudsman (s32(2) OA). A leader whose conduct has been enquired into must notify the Ombudsman in writing of the action planned to give effect to the recommendations and as a Member of Parliament must inform Parliament, as a member of a Local Government Council or Municipal Council inform the council, or in case of any other leader inform the person or body by whom he or she was appointed about the findings within 14 days (s32(4) OA). If a decision is made not to take any action, written notice must be given to the Ombudsman as soon as practicable (s32(5) OA).

As a rule, the Ombudsman shall publish the results of any enquiries carried out by him or her by way of a written report, including any findings, recommendations and opinions. On the grounds of public security or public interest, the Ombudsman may decide to keep a report confidential and forward it only to the Prime Minister, or to the person in charge of the agency investigated. In such a case, the Ombudsman must inform the complainant of his or her findings in writing (s34 OA).

If, as an aggravating factor, there is reasonable suspicion that criminal proceedings or disciplinary action is justified against a person, the Ombudsman shall refer the matter to the Commissioner of Police and the Public Prosecutor or to the Public Service Commission and the person in charge of the agency concerned, respectively (s31(1) OA). In case of an investigation into the conduct of a leader under the Leadership Code, the Ombudsman shall always give his or her report to the Public Prosecutor and, if the complaint may involve criminal misconduct, to the Commissioner of Police within 14 days after forwarding the findings to the Prime Minister (s34(2) LCA and art. 63(2) Const).[11]

Though not explicitly stipulated in the law, in practice the Ombudsman is entitled to visit prison facilities. He or she has to make prior arrangements directly with the correctional facilities. Once there, the Ombudsman can speak with detainees alone, may take complaints and investigate.

In order to fulfil his or her functions, the Ombudsman has privileged access rights to restricted or prohibited information. The disclosure of such information to the Ombudsman is not considered a breach of any law or duty if the requested information[12] indicates a breach of the Leadership Code. The same applies if that person has obtained any consent required by any law or duty before disclosing such information (s27 OA).

Investigations under the LCA in general follow the procedures of the OA as described above (s34(3) LCA). However, under the LCA, the Ombudsman has full access to government contracts, documents, books, accounts and any other material that relates to and is relevant to the investigation and may, by notice in writing, require any person who has possession or control of such material to deliver it to the Ombudsman.

It is an offence to improperly influence, hinder or obstruct the Ombudsman, to refuse or neglect to attend as a witness or fail to produce documents before the Ombudsman if given a notice under s22 OA, to refuse to be sworn or refuse to answer any questions relevant to the matters being enquired into and to give false or misleading evidence in any enquiry (s48–s51 OA).

22.2.3.2 Relation to the Judiciary

The Ombudsman has no authority to investigate judicial actions or any conduct of the Judicial Service Commission, the Supreme Court or other judicial bodies; only administrative practices can be investigated (s11(1) OA and art. 62(2) Const.).

The Ombudsman may utilise the judiciary in case persons fail to comply with a notice to appear for examination or to furnish certain information. In that case, the Ombudsman may apply to the Supreme Court for that person to be summoned or to furnish the information requested (s23(1) OA). If there is no cooperation of this person, the Ombudsman may receive a search warrant for premises at which

[11] It is then the Public Prosecutor's obligation to consider the report and, if he or she decides not to prosecute due to insufficient evidence, he or she shall notify the Prime Minister of the decision within seven days, giving reasons for the decision. In addition, a notice in the official gazette is to be published within 14 days, stating that the Public Prosecutor has decided not to prosecute, and setting out the reasons for the decision (s35 LCA).

[12] Either alone or in combination with other information.

relevant documents may be located from the Supreme Court, and in that case he or she has the authority to seize, retain and remove documents relevant to the investigation in question (s24 OA). If a person fails to comply with a notice by the Ombudsman under the LCA, the Supreme Court may issue an order requiring the person to comply with the notice (s34(5) LCA).

By court order a leader may be removed from office if he or she has been convicted by a court of a breach of provisions of the LCA under the Penal Code (s27 and s41 LCA). The Ombudsman has a special role in this impeachment procedure, for the initial proceedings may have been initiated based on the Ombudsman's recommendation in a public report to the Public Prosecutor after an investigation under the LCA (s34(2) LCA).

22.2.3.3 Relation to the Legislator

The Ombudsman may turn to the legislator mainly in two situations. First, following investigation in an individual case, the Ombudsman shall inform Parliament (respectively the local level legislator, i.e. Local Government Councils or Municipal Councils) if he or she is of the opinion that an administrative action has produced unfair or objectionable results and that this was caused at least partly by legislation (s35(2) OA). Second, the Ombudsman shall prepare an Annual Report to Parliament for presentation by the Prime Minster, who is the spokesperson of the Ombudsman vis-à-vis Parliament (s35(1) and s38(1) OA) and may make additional reports to Parliament as necessary (art. 63(5) Const. and s36 OA). Due to the first function in which he or she also recommends legislative amendments, the Ombudsman in practice also serves as Law Reform Commissioner. The State Law Office looks into proposed amendments, which are consequently discussed by the Council of Ministers.

The Prime Minister must report to Parliament annually on the actions that a leader or the person in charge of an agency has taken to give effect to any recommendations made by the Ombudsman following an enquiry into the conduct of that leader or agency (s39 OA).

22.2.4 Other Characteristics

To date, Vanuatu has not ratified the OPCAT,[13] and there is no information whether the Government is planning to ratify OPCAT.

An outstanding feature in the Vanuatu Ombudsman legislation is the Ombudsman's role as a mediator between the complainant, the person in charge of the government agency complained about and any other person directly affected

[13] Cf Sect. 3.2.6.2, p. 55 for more details.

by the enquiry. If the complaint relates to the conduct of a leader, the Ombudsman may also mediate between that leader and the complainant (s11(1)(f) and s13 OA). The Ombudsman may decide to initiate mediation; upon request of any party he or she must, as far as is practicable for him or her to do so, comply with such a request (s13 OA). However, if the Ombudsman considers it not possible to mediate, he or she must inform the person who requested the mediation of this in writing. The law does not contain specifications regarding the mediation process as such and regarding minimum requirement for settlement agreements between the parties.

Another special feature of the Vanuatu Ombudsman is his or her competencies in the field of disciplinary action. In cases in which the Ombudsman considers disciplinary action due to a breach of the Public Service Act, he or she shall refer the matter to the Public Service Commission and the person in charge of the agency concerned (s31(1) OA). Breaches of the Leadership Code under the LCA are to be reported and referred to the Public Prosecutor, who, within 14 days, must consider the report and, if in his or her opinion the matter requires further investigation, send it to the Commissioner of Police (s34(2) LCA). After having received the results of the Police investigations, it is then up to the Prosecutor to decide if there are sufficient grounds to prosecute the leader or any other person (s35 LCA).

The Ombudsman *de facto* also serves as the Official Language Commissioner. A citizen who considers that his or her right to obtain services in the official language that he or she uses has been violated may complain to the Ombudsman who shall conduct an enquiry (art. 64 Const.).

The law also provides for the Ombudsman to participate in any general study or enquiry if he or she believes it may enhance knowledge about or lead to the improvement of the functioning of any public authority or Department or in the quality of the leadership of Vanuatu (s37 OA).[14]

22.2.5 Workload

For 2009 the office reported 51 complaints and a total of 63 complaints for 2010. These referred mainly to breaches of laws and rules,[15] improper delays to take actions without good reasons, and unfair treatment. Of these complaints an average of five complaints per year was made by women, and only one complaint each year originated from members of disadvantaged groups. Areas mainly investigated by the Ombudsman were maladministration in Government and its agencies, discriminatory practices and breaches of the Leadership Code.

[14] According to the general jurisdiction of the Ombudsman, the President of the Republic, the Judicial Service Commission, the Supreme Court and other judicial bodies are excluded.

[15] Excluding breaches of the Leadership Code.

22.2.6 Publications

As already stated, the Ombudsman is required to submit Annual Reports to Parliament on the exercise of the functions of the Ombudsman (art. 63(5) Const. and s35 OA) and may submit additional reports on any urgent and important matter (s36 OA). Results of investigations are often published as public reports. Hard copies of these reports are available at the office in Port Vila, while electronic copies may be found online.[16] As an additional task, the Constitution foresees an Annual Report by the Ombudsman to Parliament on the observance of the three official languages (multilingualism) (art. 64(3) Const.).

22.2.7 Annotations

There are currently no annotations.

Further Reading

Overview of Legislation: www.paclii.org/vu/legis/consol_act/oa114/; www.paclii.org/vu/legis/consol_act/lca131/

Annual Reports: Currently not available online. However, public reports can be found at www.paclii.org/vu/ombudsman/

[16] These public reports can be found online at www.paclii.org/vu/ombudsman/.

Annex: Sample Questionnaire

Name of the Jurisdiction[1]

General Data

Information on the Jurisdiction

Population	
Government	
Capital	
Ethnic groups	
Languages	
Administrative division	

Legal System

Constitution	
Legal system	
Court system	
ICC accredited NHRI?	

[1] The questionnaire is based on the questionnaires developed and used by Prof. Kucsko-Stadlmayer in the book "European Ombudsman-Institutions", cf Kucsko-Stadlmayer 2008. Her questionnaires where modified and adapted to a non-European context.

International Ombudsman Institute (ed.), *Australasia and Pacific Ombudsman Institutions*, DOI 10.1007/978-3-642-33896-0, © Springer-Verlag Berlin Heidelberg 2013

The Ombudsman Institution

Name (original and in English)
Contact details
Year of establishment
Year of opening of office
IOI Membership, Entry (year)
Is the Ombudsman based on any model?
Jurisdiction (federal/regional/local level)
If federal level, are there additional regional Ombudsman Institutions?
Number of Ombudsmen (in total; how many thereof deputies?)
Number of female Ombudsmen (and deputies)
Name(s) of Ombudsman/ Ombudsmen
Are there any branchlets/outposts in other parts of the jurisdiction? If yes: where are they, are they equipped in the same way as the central office?
Internal structure of the Ombudsman Institution
Existence of other Ombudsman Institutions with special mandates
(Providing, e.g. protection for children, persons with disabilities or servicemen vis-à-vis the administration)?

Legal Basis of the Ombudsman

Name of legal basis of the Ombudsman Institution, its functioning, tasks etc (please state the source in which the law was published)
Source of legal basis (e.g. constitution, ordinary law)
Accessibility of legal basis
Availability of legal basis in English?

Mandate

Object of Control

Bodies (in the sense of e.g. public administration, public private sector, non-state legal entitities, judiciary, administration of justice, public prosecution services, legislation, others) **submitted to the control of the Ombudsman** in general

Public service providers: Which institutions deal with the below listed issues and what is their legal status? Is the Ombudsman Institution competent to investigate complaints with regard to these institutions?
unemployment insurance; pension insurance
accomodation of asylum seekers; electricity supply
post; telecommunication
railway; universities
health insurance; public hospitals
water supply; social living

Is the Ombudsman entitled to visit facilities where the freedom of movement of persons is restricted (e.g. detention facilities, hospitals)? **If yes, is he/she entitled to visit without prior announcement? Is he/she allowed to speak with persons (detainees etc.) alone? Which other rights are related to such on-site visits?**

Are there any exemptions from investigation by the Ombudsman Institution (e.g. the administration of justice, Head of State, Military/Police or Secret Services)?
May also private persons/entities be submitted to the control – if yes, under what conditions?

Standard of Control (Control Criteria)

Specification of the standard of control (e.g. legal rules, "good administration", fundamental rights, human rights) **Does the legal basis specifically stipulate the protection of fundamental and human rights as a function of the Ombudsman Institution?**

Special tasks of the Ombudsman regarding monitoring of the implementation of international obligations (in particular human rights obligations)? **If yes - which? Are also rights included which were not transformed into national law?**

Does the Government have plans to reform the Ombudsman Institution or is it currently being reformed? If so, what changes in the mandate of the Ombudsman Institution are expected in the near future?

Functions/Powers

Main Functions of the Ombudsman (and his/her Deputies)

Is the jurisdiction state party to OPCAT?

If so, does the mandate include the function of a National Preventive Mechanism (NPM) according to OPCAT?
If not, does the Government currently plan to ratify OPCAT? If so, do these plans foresee a role of the Ombudsman Institution as NPM?

Powers of the Ombudsman (and his/her Deputies)

Powers of the Ombudsman (e.g. appeal against laws or regulations or individual decisions, right to file motion for authentic interpretation of law; intervention in court proceedings; institute criminal charges against officials; coercive powers for taking evidence)

Any special powers with regard to judiciary (e.g. filing application to Constitutional Court, intervention at other courts)?

Any special powers with regard to legislator?

Any special powers with regard to initiating impeachment proceedings against public officials?

Can the Ombudsman declare the violation of human rights through an administrative body/institution in a legally binding way? If yes, what are the legal effects?

Which of the powers mentioned are coercive? Description of coercive powers.

Any *ex ante* powers – i.e. powers to **intervene in imminent violations** of law or to **prevent violations** (e.g. public relations, public awareness raising, reporting, counselling persons before violations occur, consultation day) including **violations of human rights**? **If yes, which?**

Are authorities obliged to support the Ombudsman Institution? If yes: which authorities and how are authorities obliged to support the Ombudsman Institution? (e.g. production of files, inspection of files, info, statements, other) **Does the Ombudsman Institution have any coercive powers in that regard?**

Independence Overview

Which provisions in the legal basis ensure institutional independence?

Which provisions ensure personal independence? Description of these provisions.

Which provisions ensure functional independence? Description of these provisions.

If not currently an ICC accredited NHRI, does the Government plan to have the Ombudsman Institution become an NHRI (or part of an NHRI) in the near future? If so, what modifications of the legal basis and in structure, composition and mandate are planned?

Election/Appointment and Personal Independence of Ombudsman

Election/Appointment Procedure

Election or appointment procedures of the Ombudsman

Tenure of office holder(s) (in years); reappointment/election possible, if yes - how often?

Qualifications of the Ombudsman (Including Deputies)

Any qualificational requirements laid down in the legal basis (e.g. law degree)?

What are the qualifications/backgrounds of the incumbent office holders?

Are there provisions in the legal basis to ensure that members/staff of the Ombudsman Institution reflect the composition of society ("pluralism")?

Removal/Dismissal of the Ombudsman

Can the Ombudsman be dismissed/removed? If yes - under what conditions, on which grounds, by whom?

Incompatibility

Any rules regulating the incompatibility of certain positions with the Ombudsman Institution? (e.g. membership or function in political party, union, public offices, professional activities)

Immunity

Are there any rules on immunity?

Salary

Is the Ombudsman's salary determined by law? Is it linked to the salary/ remuneration of other public officials? How high is it in comparison to a Member of Government or Parliament?

Functional Independence/Resources (Budget, Infrastructure, Staff)

Budget autonomy of the Ombudsman Institution: Who determines the amount of the budget and who decides on the spending/usage of the budget?

Annual budget of the Ombudsman Institution for the last five years available (in €)

With what infrastructure is the Ombudsman Institution equipped (e.g. premises, telephone, internet)?

Staff: Total number of employees of the Ombudsman Institution (full time equivalent)? Among them, how many female employees (full time equivalent)? Qualifications (educational background) of employees (if possible: distinction between female and male staff)?

Institutional Independence

Relationship to Legislature

Overview: Relationship between the Ombudsman and the legislature

Is the Parliament involved in appointment/election of the Ombudsman? If yes, how? (consultation; election?) **Is it involved in the dismissal/removal?**

Is the Ombudsman required to report or provide information to the Parliament? If yes, what is the content? What are the consequences - does the Parliament have to act in a specific way? What is the consequence of non-submission by the Ombudsman?

Is the Ombudsman entitled to participate in debates in Parliament and/or its committees? If yes, how often does the Ombudsman do so? Is the Ombudsman allowed to speak? Is the Parliament, the respective committee or any other state body required to discuss the Ombudsman's intervention or information submitted by him/her? Is the Ombudsman excluded from certain debates?

Is the Ombudsman entitled to legislative initiatives and to recommend legislative amendments?
If yes: How often does the Ombudsman make use of this power? In which form (submission to Parliament/part of the Annual Report)?

What is the role of such a proposal in the course of the legislative procedure (which state organ deals with such a proposal? Is the legislator or any other state body required to discuss the proposal?)?
Is there an obligation for a state organ (if so, which state organ?) to draft and table a law upon such a proposal?

Relationship to Executive

Overview: Relationship between the Ombudsman and the Executive (e.g. is there any subordination to the Executive?)

Is the Ombudsman entitled to require authorities to provide information or support?

Is the Ombudsman allowed to propose corrective measures? If yes, what is the legal value of such measures? Is the addressee obliged to react?

Is the Ombudsman entitled to on-site visits (e.g. of premises of administrative bodies) **and to inspect records, in taking evidence, in summoning witnesses? If yes - what is visited and at what intervals, is he/she allowed to visit without prior announcement? Any coercive powers in that regard?**

Relationship to Judiciary

Relationship between the Ombudsman and the judiciary

Is the Ombudsman Institution entitled to monitor the administration of justice?

Can the Ombudsman recommend to bring disciplinary charges against an official/judge or can he/she him/herself do so? If yes – how often does the Ombudsman make use of this power in practice?

Has the Ombudsman Institution powers to influence judicial decisions? If yes: how? How often does the Ombudsman make use of it in practice?

Is the Ombudsman Institution entitled to request information in pending court cases?

Is the Ombudsman entitled to file an action or present other motions to Courts (e.g. motion for an authentic interpretation by a Supreme Court) **or to bring** charges (or recommend the competent organ to bring charges) **against somebody? How often does the Ombudsman make use of such powers?**

Is the Ombudsman entitled to intervene in court proceedings?

Is the Ombudsman Institution entitled to the right of appeal?

Specify other powers

Does the judiciary see the Ombudsman Institution as part of the legislation, administration, jurisdiction or "other" (please specify)?

If the Ombudsman can declare the violation of human rights in a legally binding way (see question under "Power of the Ombudsman", above): What is the specific power of the Ombudsman? What are the (legal and factual) **differences in relation to the powers of the Constitutional Court and the Administrative Court? Does the Ombudsman have powers which both courts do not possess?**

What are the (legal and factual) **effects of such statement and who is bound by such statement? To acts of which organs can such a statement relate? Can it also relate to a final, unappealable decision?**

Investigation Procedure including Accessibility

Initiation of Investigation Procedure

How can an investigation procedure be initiatied (by individual complaints, *proprio motu*, other state bodies etc)?

In practice: how are investigations usually initiated?

The Investigation Procedure

How does the procedure of investigation look like according to the legal basis?

Is there a legally specified time limit for the duration of an investigation?

Individual Complaints

Who is entitled to lodge a complaint? (Only individuals with citizenship of the jurisdiction, everybody, also legal entities?)

What can a complaint be about (e.g. maladministration, violations of individual rights, of fundamental rights guaranteed in the Constitution…)?

Is the Ombudsman Institution obliged to carry out an investigation?

Are there any formal requirements for a complaint (e.g. time limit, in writing, minimum content such as identity, signature; exhaustion of other remedies)?

Are there any fees/expenses for the complainant?

How many complaints did the Ombudsman Institution receive in 2009 and 2010? Which areas did they mainly relate to (list three top areas and state respective percentage of the overall amount of complaints), **which of these areas were investigated?** (e.g. social affairs such as pensions, benefits, social welfare; court proceedings such as delays; administration of justice; internal security; other) **To which branch did they relate to** (executive, judiciary)?

Accessibility

Does the Ombudsman hold consultation days in other parts of the jurisdiction including in remote areas?

Is information about the investigation procedure easily available?

In which language(s) can the Ombudsman be approached? Also other than official languages? If no: who takes care of translation and bears translation costs?

Is the website barrier-free; are the premises of the Ombudsman Institution barrier-free?

Is data collected on the complainants? If yes: how many of the complaints received came from women and from vulnerable and disadvantaged groups?

Outcome of Investigation Procedures

What is the outcome of an investigation procedure (e.g. recommendation, declarative statement that a law was violated)? **What is the legal effect of the outcome? Is the administrative body obliged to react in any way? What are the consequences for addressee (i.e., what happens if he/she does not react)? Does the adminstrative body have to justify why it does not comply with a recommendation? Can the Ombudsman take steps in case of non-compliance?**

Is the outcome published (what does the legal basis say and what happens in practice)?

Is there regular monitoring whether recommendations are observed? Any statistical data as to which percentage of recommendation have been implemented by the administration?

Is it possible to review the recommendation/decision of the Ombudsman? If yes where and how?

Areas Mainly Investigated/Monitored

Which areas are mainly investigated by the Ombudsman? (e.g. social matters such as pensions, benefits, social welfare; court proceedings such as delays; administration of justice; other) **To which branch do they relate (executive, judiciary)?**

Which areas/what does the Ombudsman monitor continuously on his/her own initiative (*ex officio*)? (e.g. detention facilities, psychiatric hospitals, children's homes, refugee camps)

If the Ombudsman can declare the violation of human rights in a legally binding way (see question under "Power of the Ombudsman", above): Which human rights are mainly concerned? What is the percentage compared to the overall activities of the Ombudsman?

Publication(s)

Annual Report

Is the Ombudsman Institution legally required to publish an Annual Report? Availability online?

Who are the addressees of this Annual Report?

What kind of information is contained in this Annual Report?

Major contents of the most recent Annual Report?

Does the Annual Report contain a specific section on human rights issues?

Is the Ombudsman Institution legally required to table any other report? Does the Ombudsman have the right to table special reports (e.g. on the human rights situation)?

Is the Parliament or any other state body obliged to act upon receiving the Annual Report or a special report e.g. on the human rights situation?

Other Publications

Does the Ombudsman have the right to publish other reports or publications? Who are the addresses and what are the contents?

Relationship to Other Actors

Relationship/Networking with Other Public Bodies

Relationships between the Ombudsman and any other public institutions provided for by legal provisions

Is there any relationship/networking of the Ombudsman with international bodies or bodies from other countries (e.g. IOI; UN bodies; NHRIs)?

Civil Society

Which activities of the Ombudsman are reaching out to civil society in general?

Which of the activities aim at raising awareness for good governance, human rights issues and the tasks of the Ombudsman in that regard?

Which activities promote public relations activities of the Ombudsman (e.g. consultation days, TV/radio shows, publication of reports, website, brochures)?

In which form does the Ombudsman cooperate with civil society organisations? Names and relevance of the main organisations?

Does the Ombudsman maintain regular consultations (how often?) with the above mentioned organisations and which topics are covered by these consultations?

Bibliography

Agency FR (2010) Access to justice in Europe: an overview of challenges and opportunities. European Union, Luxembourg

Ayeni V, Hayden T, Reif LC (2000) Strengthening Ombudsman and human rights institutions in commonwealth small and island states. Commonwealth Secretariat, London

Besselink LFM (2000) Types of national institutions for the protection of human rights and Ombudsman institutions: an overview of legal and institutional issues. In: Hossain K, Besselink LFM, Selassie HSG, Völker E (eds) Human rights commissions and Ombudsman offices. National experiences throughout the world. Kluwer Law International, Dordrecht

Buck T, Kirkham R, Thompson B (2011) The Ombudsman enterprise and administrative justice. Ashgate, Farnham

Caiden GE (ed) (1983) International handbook of the Ombudsman. Evolution and present function. Greenwood Press Westport, London

Caiden GE, Valdes DA (1999) Maturation issues for the Ombudsman. In: Reif LC (ed) The International Ombudsman Anthology. Selected writings from the International Ombudsman Institute. Kluwer Law International, Dordrecht

Chen M (2010) New Zealand's Ombudsmen legislation: the need for amendments after almost 50 years. Law Rev 41:723–760

Cheng HY (1968) The emergence and spread of the Ombudsman institutions. Ann Am Acad Pol Soc Sci 377:20–30

Clark C, De Martinis M (2003) A framework for reforming the independence and accountability of statutory officers of parliament: a case study of Victoria. Aust J Public Adm 62(1):32–42

Clark D (2006) Jurisdiction and power: habeas corpus and the federal court. Monash Univ Law Rev 32(2):275–295

Commonwealth Ombudsman (2009a) Australasia and Pacific Ombudsman Region Information Manual 2009. Commonwealth Ombudsman, Canberra, Australia www.ombudsman.gov.au/docs/APOR-Manual_20091009.pdf. Accessed 10 Nov 2011

Commonwealth Ombudsman (2009b) Complaint Handling in Pacific Island Nations without an Ombudsman. Report of the 2008 Study Tour Co-ordinated by the Office of the Commonwealth Ombudsman with Members of the Pacific Ombudsman Network: www.ombudsman.gov.au/docs/international-programs/Report+on+Pacific+Island+Visitsversion+final.pdf. Accessed 13 Jan 2011

Cooray A (2000) Ombudsman in Asia. In: Gregory R, Giddings P (eds) Righting wrongs. The Ombudsman in six continents. IOS Press, Berlin

Cooray A (2009) Some reflections on the legislative context of the Hong Kong Ombudsman. Asia Pac Law Rev 17(1):53–72

Creyke R (2007) Administrative justice—towards integrity in government. Melb Univ Law Rev 31(3):705–732

International Ombudsman Institute (ed.), *Australasia and Pacific Ombudsman Institutions*, 313
DOI 10.1007/978-3-642-33896-0, © Springer-Verlag Berlin Heidelberg 2013

Fowlie F (2007) A practitioner's guide to evaluation Ombudsman Offices, Occasional Paper International Ombudsman Institute, No 83, www.theioi.org/publications/occasional-papers-archives. Accessed 5 Jul 2011

Fundamental Rights Agency (2010) National human rights institutions in the EU member states. Strengthening the fundamental rights architecture in the EU. European Union, Luxembourg

Giddings P, Sladecek V, Bueso LA (2000) The Ombudsman and human rights. In: Giddings P, Gregory R (eds) Righting wrongs. The Ombudsman in six continents. IOS Press, Berlin, pp 441–457

Gregory R, Giddings P (eds) (2000) Righting wrongs. The Ombudsman in six continents. IOS Press, Berlin

Gregory R (1999) Building an Ombudsman scheme: provisions and operating practices. In: Reif LC (ed) The international Ombudsman anthology. Selected writings from the International Ombudsman Institute. Kluwer Law International, Dordrecht

Groves M (2002) Ombudsmen's jurisdiction in prisons. Monash Univ Law Rev 28(2):181–205

Harding R, Morgan N (2008) Implementing the optional protocol to the convention against torture. Options for Australia. A report to the Australian Human Rights Commission. www.humanrights.gov.au/human_rights/publications/opcat/opcat.pdf. Accessed 17 Feb 2012

Hill ER (2001) The Ombudsman as mediator—challenges, limitations and opportunities in Vanuatu. In: Reif LC (ed) The international Ombudsman yearbook 2001, vol 5. Martinus Nijhoff, Leiden

Hossain K, Besselink LFM, Selassie HSG, Völker E (eds) (2000) Human rights commissions and Ombudsman offices. National experiences throughout the world. Kluwer Law International, Dordrecht

Jacoby D (1999) The future of the Ombudsman. In: Reif LC (ed) The International Ombudsman Anthology. Selected writings from the International Ombudsman Institute. Kluwer Law International, Dordrecht

de Jonge A (1998) Ombudsmen and leadership codes in Papua New Guinea: keeping government accountable in a rapidly changing world. Melanesian Law J 6:1–33

Koo JW, Ramirez FO (2009) National Incorporation of Global Human Rights: Worldwide Expansion of National Human Rights Institutions, 1966-2004. Soc Forces 87:1321–1354

Kofler B (2008) United Kingdom of Great Britain and Northern Ireland. In: Kucsko-Stadlmayer G (ed) European Ombudsman-Institutions. Springer, Vienna

Kucsko-Stadlmayer G (ed) (2008) European Ombudsman-Institutions. Springer, Vienna

Liao FF-T (2001) Establishing a national human rights commission in Taiwan: the role of NGOs and challenges ahead. Asia-Pac J Hum Rights Law 2(2):90–109

Maino C (1995) Ethical considerations: the leadership code of Papua New Guinea. In: Reif LC (ed) The Ombudsman concept. International Ombudsman Institute, Edmonton

McBride J (2009) Access to justice for migrants and asylum seekers in Europe. Council of Europe Publishing, Strasbourg

McLeod R (2001) Freedom of information—an Ombudsman's perspective, commentary. Fed Law Rev 29(3):359–364

Nanda VP (2006) The "Good Governance" concept revisited. Ann Am Acad Pol Soc Sci 603:269–283

New Zealand Law Commission (2006) Converging currents—custom and human rights in the pacific, study paper, 1174-1776; 17, Wellington

OHCHR (2007) Good governance practices for the protection of human rights. United Nations, New York. www.ohchr.org/Documents/Publications/GoodGovernance.pdf. Accessed 12 Oct 2011

OHCHR (2010) National human rights institutions. History, principles, roles and responsibilities, Professional training series no. 4. United Nations, New York

Oosting M (2002) Protecting the integrity and independence of the Ombudsman Institution: the global perspective. In: Reif LC (ed) The international Ombudsman yearbook, vol 5. Martinus Nijhoff, Leiden

Owen S (1999) The Ombudsman: essential elements and common challenges. In: Reif LC (ed) The International Ombudsman Anthology. Selected writings from the International Ombudsman Institute. Kluwer Law International, Dordrecht

Pak-kwan C (2006) The Jurisdiction of Ombudsman Systems in Selected Places, Research and Library Services Division Legislative Council Secretariat, Hong Kong. www.legco.gov.hk/yr05-06/english/sec/library/0506rp05e.pdf. Accessed 5 Jul 2011

Paterson M (2004) Transparency in the Modern State. Happy birthday FoI! Or commiserations? Altern Law J 29:10–14

Pearce D (1999) The Ombudsman: review and preview the importance of being different. In: Reif LC (ed) The International Ombudsman Anthology. Selected writings from the International Ombudsman Institute. Kluwer Law International, Dordrecht

Pearce D (2000) Ombudsman in Australia. In: Gregory R, Giddings P (eds) Righting wrongs. The Ombudsman in six continents. IOS Press, Berlin

Reif LC (ed) (1995) The Ombudsman concept. International Ombudsman Institute, Edmonton

Reif LC (ed) (1999) The International Ombudsman Anthology. Selected writings from the International Ombudsman Institute. Kluwer Law International, Dordrecht

Reif LC (ed) (1997) The international Ombudsman yearbook 1997, vol 1. Martinus Nijhoff, Leiden

Reif LC (ed) (2001) The international Ombudsman yearbook 2001, vol 5. Martinus Nijhoff, Leiden

Reif LC (ed) (2002) The international Ombudsman yearbook 2002, vol 6. Martinus Nijhoff, Leiden

Reif LC (ed) (2004a) The international Ombudsman yearbook 2004, vol 8. Martinus Nijhoff, Leiden

Reif LC (2004b) The Ombudsman, good governance, and the international human rights system. Martinus Nijhoff, Leiden

Reif LC (2009) The Ombudsman and the Protection of Children's Rights. Asia Pac Law Rev 17 (1):27–52

Reif LC (2011) Transplantation and adaptation: the evolution of the human rights Ombudsman. Boston Coll Third World Law J 31(2):269–310

Satyanand A (2002) Human rights in the commonwealth. The Ombudsman role. Commonw Law Bull 28:547–552

Sawer G (1968) The Ombudsman and related institutions in Australia and New Zealand. Ann Am Acad Pol Soc Sci 377:62–72

Sripati V (2005) The Ombudsman, good governance, and the international human rights system. Hum Rights Q 27:1137–1142

Stern J (2008) Sweden. In: Kucsko-Stadlmayer G (ed) European Ombudsman-Institutions. Springer, Vienna

Stuhmcke A (2003) Ombudsmen and legal practice. Where to from here? Int Leg Practicioner 28:48–51

Stuhmcke A (2008) Changing relations between government and citizen: administrative law and the work of the Australian commonwealth Ombudsman. Aust J Public Adm 67(3):321–339

Stuhmcke A (2010) 'Each for Themselves' or 'One for all'? the changing emphasis of the commonwealth Ombudsman. Fed Law Rev 38(1):143–167

Stuhmcke A, Tran A (2007) The Commonwealth Ombudsman. An integrity branch of government? Altern Law J 32(4):233–236

Taylor S (2000) Protecting the human rights of immigration detainees in Australia: an evaluation of current accountability mechanisms. Syd Law Rev 22(1):50–92

UNDP (2010) Enhancing security sector governance in the Pacific region—A strategic framework. www.undp.org/cpr/documents/jssr/ssg_pacific.pdf. Accessed 3 Aug 2011

UNDP (2005) Programming for justice: access for all. A practitioner's guide to a human rights-based approach to access to justice. United Nations, Bangkok

UNDP (2004) Access to justice. Practice note. United Nations, New York

UNDP–OHCHR (2010) Toolkit for collaboration with national human rights institutions. UNDP, OHCHR, NewYork, Geneva

del Villar K (2002) Who guards the guardians? Recent developments concerning the jurisdiction and accountability of Ombudsmen in Australia. In: Reif LC (ed) The international Ombudsman yearbook 2002, vol 6. Martinus Nijhoff, Leiden

Weiss TG (2000) Governance, good governance and global governance: conceptual and actual challenges. Third World Q 21:795–814

Wong W, Yuen R (2009) The Ombudsman in Hong Kong: role and challenges under the transformation of governance in the post-1997 Era. Asia Pac Law Rev 17(1):115–133

Yueh-chin H (1995) Role and responsibility of the control Yuan. In: Reif LC (ed) The Ombudsman concept. International Ombudsman Institute, Edmonton

MIX
Papier aus verantwortungsvollen Quellen
Paper from responsible sources
FSC® C105338

If you have any concerns about our products,
you can contact us on
ProductSafety@springernature.com

In case Publisher is established outside the EU,
the EU authorized representative is:
Springer Nature Customer Service Center GmbH
Europaplatz 3, 69115 Heidelberg, Germany

Printed by Libri Plureos GmbH
in Hamburg, Germany